THE SOCIALIST REGISTER 1992

SOCIALIST REGISTER 1992

**Edited by
RALPH MILIBAND
and LEO PANITCH**

THE MERLIN PRESS
LONDON

First published in 1992
by The Merlin Press Ltd
10 Malden Road
London NW5 3HR

British Library Cataloguing in Publication Data

The Socialist Register. — 1992
  1. Socialism — 1992
  I. Miliband, Ralph II. Panitch, Leo
355'.005

ISBN 0-85036-4272
ISBN 0-85036-4264 Pbk

Typesetting by
Computerset, Harmondsworth, Middlesex

Printed and bound in Great Britain by
Biddles Ltd, Guildford and King's Lynn

TABLE OF CONTENTS

Page

Preface   vii

The New World Order and the Socialist Agenda
Leo Panitch and Ralph Miliband   1

Global *Perestroika*
Robert W. Cox   26

Globalization – To What End?
Harry Magdoff   44

Global but Leaderless? The New Capitalist Order
Andrew Glyn and Bob Sutcliffe   76

The Collapse of Liberalism
Immanuel Wallerstein   96

Security and Intelligence in the Post-Cold War World
Reg Whitaker   111

US Military Policy in the Post-Cold War Era
Michael T. Klare   131

Europe in a Multi-Polar World
John Palmer   143

The Emerging World Order and European Change
Stephen Gill   157

Japan in a New World Order
Makoto Itoh   197

Africa: The Politics of Failure
Basil Davidson   212

The Gulf War and the New World Order
  Avishai Ehrlich   227

Ruptured Frontiers: The Transformation of the
US–Latin American System
  Roger Burbach   239

Post-Communist Anti-Communism: America's New
Ideological Frontiers
  Joel Kovel   254

Hollywood's War on the World: The New World Order as Movie
  Scott Forsyth   270

PREFACE

Like its predecessors in recent years, this twenty eighth volume of *The Socialist Register* has one theme, the so-called new world order. All the essays in the volume deal in various ways with the immense changes which have been occurring in the world since the eighties: in particular with the nature, extent and impact of the 'globalization' of capital; the fact that the United States has turned into the only 'super-power', paralleled however by its own loss of economic hegemony and its multiple internal crises; the emergence of Germany as the predominant power in Europe and of Japan in Asia; the worsening of conditions in most of the 'third world'; the shift of the ex-Communist countries towards peripheral capitalism.

In the first article, the editors examine some of these changes and the prospects which, notwithstanding neo-liberal 'triumphalism', they offer for a socialist revival. The next three essays – by Robert Cox, Harry Magdoff, Andrew Glyn and Bob Sutcliffe – present searching analyses of the political economy of the 'new world order'; and the following three essays – by Immanuel Wallerstein, Reg Whitaker and Michael Klare – discuss from different angles the role of nation states in global capitalism. The following six essays are concerned with the 'regional' aspects of global change – John Palmer and Stephen Gill with the European Community, Makoto Itoh with Japan, Basil Davidson with Africa, Avishai Ehrlich with the Gulf War and the Middle East, and Roger Burbach with the relationship between the United States and Canada and Latin America. Finally, the last two essays, by Joel Klare and Scott Forsyth discuss some ideological and cultural dimensions of the dilemmas confronting the United States in the 'new world order'.

Both Robert Cox and Stephen Gill teach international political economy at York University, Toronto; Harry Magdoff is co-editor of *Monthly Review*, New York; Andrew Glyn is a Fellow of Corpus Christi College, Oxford, and Bob Sutcliffe teaches economics at the University of Bilbao. Immanuel Wallerstein is Director of the Fernand Braudel Center at the State University of New York at Binghamton; Reg Whitaker is Professor of Political Science at York University, Toronto, and Michael Klare is

Director of the Program in Peace and World Security Studies at Hampshire College, Amhurst, Mass. John Palmer is European Correspondent of *The Guardian*; Makoto Itoh is Professor of Economics at the University of Tokyo; Basil Davidson is a distinguished writer on African affairs; Avishai Ehrlich teaches in the Sociology Department at the University of Tel-Aviv and Roger Burbach is Director of the Center for the Study of the Americas in Berkeley, California. Joel Kovel is Alger Hiss Professor of Social Studies at Bard College in New York State, and Scott Forsyth teaches Film and Video Studies in Toronto and is co-editor of *Cine Action*.

We are very grateful to our contributors for their help; and we wish to stress, as usual, that neither our contributors nor the editors necessarily agree with everything that appears in the volume. We also wish to thank Robert Albritton for his help with the editing of Professor Itoh's essay; and we also acknowledge with many thanks the help of Martin Eve, of Merlin Press, in producing this volume.

February 1992   L.P.
                                                                R.M.

THE NEW WORLD ORDER AND THE SOCIALIST AGENDA

Leo Panitch and Ralph Miliband

I

The juxtaposition of 'new world order' and 'the socialist agenda' might seem odd, at least jarring, perhaps even absurd. For is not the notion of a new world order today intended to mean, if it means anything, the establishment, finally, of capitalism's complete and definitive global sway as the twentieth century draws to a close? Socialist ideas, movements, regimes, stepped onto the world stage near the beginning of the century promising alternatives to capitalism and, indeed, presenting themselves as the historic successors to capitalism; they now take on the aspect, from the vantage point of today's *fin de siècle* 'new world order', of having been merely temporary barriers to the realization of global capitalism. The explicit reconfirmation through the 1980s that even the ambitions (let alone the deeds) of social democratic parties in the West do not extend beyond the management of capitalism seems of little moment beside the dramatic collapse of the Communist regimes in the East, given their origins, history and character as the only rival mode of economic organization that the enemies of capitalism ever were able to bring into being. 'The world', *The Economist* said in September 1991, 'used to have two seriously different ways of trying to run an economy. Today it has only one.'[1]

It is in this sense that 'the end of history' is said to be nigh. Not only have specific 20th century socialist movements and regimes run their course, but even the idea of socialism, of a future transcending capitalism, is one whose time allegedly has passed. In the conception of the new world order, humankind has no viable alternative to global capitalism. Upon this foundation and within its clearly established limits, humankind may aspire, at most, to be ruled according to the tenets of liberal democracy along the lines practised today by the leading capitalist states: this is the furthest point humanity may justly and rationally seek to reach.

Can this discourse be refuted? Can the conservative political forces which make use of it be challenged? Can the idea of a socialist future – and strategies appropriate to serious attempts at getting there – be relaunched

1

in the face of the 'new world order'? These are questions that must be addressed by socialists today.

II

The first step is to assess how much substance there is to the notion of a new world order. That notion has met with much derision, not only on the Left; for the condition of the world hardly suggests that the 'just treatment of all peoples', as invoked by George Bush as constituting international relations in the 'new order', has come into being. Yet, removed from the self-serving and cynical use of the term as a new cover for American imperialist postures, or of confused notions of a fundamental change in capitalism that goes under the appropriately vague rubric of 'new times', there is a good deal of truth in the idea that a chapter of history has come to an end in recent years, and that the chapter which is now being written has some important new features.

The most obvious of these new features is the disintegration of the Soviet Union and its elimination from the world scene as the 'other superpower'. This is of momentous importance in itself. But what gives even greater importance to the collapse of the Soviet and other Communist regimes is their embrace of the 'market economy'. What has occurred in the ex-Communist regimes is a powerful drive towards the restoration of capitalism; and this includes, as is necessarily the case with peripheral capitalisms, a process of incorporation as subordinate elements within the economic, cultural and military/strategic networks of the international capitalist system. This has gone well beyond the ambitions of the most avid proponents of market reform within the old communist regimes; and it has gone beyond the wildest dreams of the most ardent Western advocates of 'rollback'. For them, the title of Richard Nixon's recipe book on 'how to compete with Moscow' in the Gorbachev era, *1999: Victory Without War*, must have appeared naively optimistic when it was published in 1988.[2]

The transition from communism to capitalism is still full of unresolved problems: many of them will almost certainly prove to be unresolvable in terms recognizable to contemporary liberal democracy. But the will to privatize and accumulate is nevertheless there, and is strengthened by the pressure of Western governments, the International Monetary Fund and the World Bank, the international 'business community', and a host of eager academic apostles of neo-classical economics.[3] When the popular image of the American suburban shopping centre as epitomizing 'normal society' begins to fade amidst the price rises, injustices and corruptions of an actual transition to capitalism, 'Yeltsin's tutor', Harvard's Jeffrey Sachs calls a press conference in Moscow warning the political class not to flag in their enthusiasm for the free market. 'It is too easy', he tells them, 'to prey upon the confusion of the people.'[4] In other words, pay no heed to the people's cries of pain. Still, the fact that the problems may indeed be insoluble in democratic terms should not obscure the fact that it is indeed a transition to capitalism that is taking place.

Nor is the process confined to the region of the ex-Soviet Union and Eastern Europe. Unlike Gorbachev, the old Chinese Communist leadership have had no intention of loosening their monopoly of power, but they most certainly are engaged in an authoritarian transition to capitalism, and are well along that road. Other erstwhile third world 'Marxist–Leninist' regimes, like Angola or Mozambique in Africa, have renounced the label, while still others in Asia, like Vietnam, also shift towards market-oriented practices. In the Western Hemisphere, Grenada, after the murder of Bishop and the American invasion, became an offshore haven for shady banking capital; and the Sandanistas have been squeezed from office. Washington waits for Cuba finally to drop back into their imperial lap, expecting that it is not at all likely that Fidel Castro, without Soviet trade or aid, can long maintain his present course.

This liquidation of the Communist economic model is an event of historic importance. It had in recent decades produced stagnation as well as shortage, although the system of centralized planning overseeing extensive economic development had *in earlier decades* appeared impressive to a multitude of economists and others who were by no means exclusively of the Left. Indeed, urgent warnings used to be issued by many such people that the Soviet Union was launched on a course of development which would before too long bring it level with the West. Such estimates were clearly wrong, having paid insufficient attention to the qualitative differences between extensive and intensive phases of development. Still, the achievements under the extensive growth model of central planning were real enough in certain social as well as economic terms, even though it must always be stressed that the human and environmental cost they demanded was horrendous, sustainable only by highly repressive political regimes.

Such regimes were destructive of the creativity necessary to sustain socialist innovation and motivation. During the decades of stagnation, attempts at economic reform were repeatedly made in country after country, but these reforms required a degree of cooperation from workers which these regimes could not hope to achieve: either because the reforms were cast within, or ran aground against, the encrusted interests of the bureaucracy; or because they depended on price increases and increasing the level of inequality and worker insecurity. So Communist regimes entered upon a period of permanent crisis; and, in the Soviet Union, this led to Gorbachev and *perestroika*. But *perestroika* itself turned into a gigantic failure: the actual attempt to shift towards market socialism in practice threw up even more contradictions than the notion already raised in economic theory. In this context, the political opening of *glasnost* led to revolution.

In most ways, the Communist model was an appalling deformation of socialism; and there is a good argument to be made that it was not socialism at all, if one takes socialism to have as its core constituent elements not only the socialization of the predominant part of the means of economic activity, but also democracy and egalitarianism. On this ground, its disappearance in the Soviet Union and elsewhere is hardly a matter for regret. What is a matter for bitter regret, on the other hand, is something else altogether: the disappearance of the hope that existed at the beginning of *perestroika* in the Soviet Union that this might in due course produce something that would begin to resemble socialist democracy, on the basis of a loosened but predominant public sector. That hope turned out to be an illusion.

The liquidation of that possibility has large implications, not only for the ex-Communist countries themselves, but for the rest of the world as well. The fear that had haunted all conservative forces ever since 1917, namely that Communism might yet turn into an attractive alternative to capitalism, was always an element in the political chemistry that produced aid to the third world, and reform and redistribution in the advanced capitalist countries themselves. One could see, for instance, this fear in that old Cold Warrior Nixon as he tried in 1988 to work through the implications of Gorbachev for American policy: for apart from insisting on military and strategic 'preparedness' for continuing superpower conflicts in Europe and the Third World even in an era of compromise on nuclear arms control, he also contended that the United States, if it were now to defeat Communism without war, really would have to prove that it was 'not only the strongest and richest economy but also the most just society . . . Our greatest challenge in this respect is to enable all our citizens to share fully in America's success . . . We must solve the problems of the urban underclass, the homeless, the poor, the disadvantaged . . . The West will become impotent if its guiding philosophy degenerates into . . . a kind of cosmic selfishness.'[5] With the model of Communist reform gone, the spur to capitalist governments to turn such rhetoric into anything even slightly approximating reality is that much less sharp.

Moreover, even while Western socialism does – quite rightly – distance itself from the Communist experience, the fact that Communist regimes were unable to realize democratic reform and economic restructuring, and left their successors with a catastrophic legacy as well, has also been of great help to the broader anti-socialist cause, in so far as it has lent further plausibility to the notion that the only alternative to communism was indeed capitalism. Although the limitations of market freedom will not be lost on people, as they observe the suffering and perhaps even the chaos that accompanies a transition to capitalism, the notion that there is no alternative will not be effectively countered without a great effort by many people to construct a new model of socialism that appears attractive and viable. We shall return to this.

The collapse of Communist regimes also has large implications for countries in the 'third world'. For one thing, it deprives many of them of the military, economic and technical aid which they received from the Soviet Union and Eastern European regimes. This aid was a token of the fact that the Soviet Union could be reckoned on as a limited counter to the United States on the world scene, and might be counted on to extend help to revolutionary regimes and movements of national liberation. This aid was hardly costless in terms of the political, ideological and economic courses into which such regimes and movements were often channelled, but at the same time it was often a critical lifeline. The prospect of not standing alone against the massive military, political, economic and ideological power of a hostile capitalist world was an important condition of struggle against oppressions and exploitation in the 'third world'.

However much the terms of 'capitalist encirclement' and 'counter-revolution' may have been used to rationalize post-revolutionary dictatorships and incompetence, the forceful reality of such pressures must also never be forgotten. As Franz Schurmann once put it: 'In each of these countries, these leaders told their people that the new society was mortally endangered from aggressive forces abroad and subversive forces at home. In every instance, these threats were real. From the time of the October revolution, powerful foreign countries, fearing the spread of revolution or the march of red armies, did what they could do to weaken or destroy the socialist countries.'[6] The Soviet presence in the world, itself taking the shape it did in no small measure due to the ability of its leaders to appeal not only to the myth but also to the reality of 'capitalist encirclement' and 'counterrevolution', was always much the most important source of the Cold War, in so far as the Soviet Union played some role, however limited and cautious, in opposing American purposes, notably in the 'third world'. The notion that the Soviet Union constituted a major military threat to the West, indeed to the whole world, because of its insatiable craving for world domination, was always sheer myth – perhaps the greatest myth of the twentieth century. But the Soviet Union did present a permanent challenge to the United States, in so far as its potential intervention, or that of other communist regimes, might weaken American pressure against regimes and movements of which the United States disapproved.

This deterrent has now gone, and the Gulf War of 1991 was the first example of what this signifies. With Saddam Hussein's invasion of Kuwait, the issue was not whether he should be compelled to retreat, but whether this was to be achieved by military means or by diplomatic means, including concessions by the Kuwaiti ruling family to some legitimate grievances, on the one hand, and, on the other hand, the threat and, if necessary, the reality of UN sanctions against Iraq. It was clear from the early days following the invasion that the United States was intent on military action, not only as a means of repelling Iraqi aggression, but also as a way of demonstrating that governments which for one reason or another ran counter to American interests would be severely punished. In times past, the Soviet Union might have been expected to take the lead in opposing military action, whether successfully or not is not the point. Instead, Gorbachev, more and more dependent on American good will for his own survival, opted for acquiescence to the American-led military expedition against Iraq. However important Mrs Thatcher may have been in convincing George Bush that Iraq was his Falklands,' she could never have prevailed but for the sea change in the geopolitical context introduced by the liquidation of the Soviet Union as the 'other superpower'. Except for this, it is hard to believe that the United Nations could have been so easily and effectively, as Canada's former Ambassador to the UN put it, 'conscripted into the role of providing cover for US foreign policy.' As Stephen Lewis explained:

> . . . the United Nations served as an imprimatur for a policy that the United States wanted to follow and either persuaded or coerced everybody else to support. The Security Council thus played fast and loose with the provisions of the UN Charter. For instance, sanctions were invoked under Article 41, but there was never any assessment of whether those sanctions were working or might work sufficiently before the decision was made to resort to force under Article 42. Moreover, no use was made of the Military Staff Committee, which under Article 47 is supposed to direct any armed forces at the Security Council's disposal . . . In some respects . . . [this] may have been the UN's most desolate hour. It certainly unnerved a lot of developing countries, which were privately outraged by what was going on but felt utterly impotent to do anything – a demonstration of the enormous power of US influence and diplomacy when it is unleashed.[8]

All this clearly showed that there was now only one superpower in the world, whose purpose is to oversee a global capitalism. An American image of a 'new world order' was first enunciated by Woodrow Wilson at the time of the birth if Soviet Communism. It has now been repeated (with less flair, but in the face of less opposition) by George Bush at the time of the death of Soviet Communism. The promulgation of a 'new world order' is intended to herald the demolition of the barriers to global political and military, as well as economic, domination by the major capitalist powers in an international system in which the United States is preeminent.

III

But what is the nature of this global capitalism? How are we to understand its contemporary dynamics and contradictions? What weaknesses, both domestic and international, undermine the stability of this new world order in which there is now allegedly only one way to run an economy? In so far as a new chapter in history is being written, it is not only because of the collapse of Communism, but because of the features which global capitalism is revealing in our time.

At the time President Bush proclaimed his new world order, the North American economy had already entered a severe economic recession. On the first anniversary of the beginning of the Gulf War, 15 January 1992, and with no recovery in sight, George Bush conceded that the American economy was 'in free-fall'. It was a remarkable admission for a President to make, in terms of the role he must play, not only domestically but internationally, in shoring up consumer and business confidence. Unlike his carefully rehearsed outpourings scarcely a year earlier on the glory of the new order, it was a hasty response to a group of disgruntled municipal administrators and local businessmen gathered in a disused airplane hangar in a recently closed Air Force base in Portsmouth, New Hampshire. But the scene powerfully symbolized the extent to which, as the *New York Times* put it, the glory had 'frayed and faded' like the yellow ribbons: 'the sense of the war as a turning point for the nation has all but evaporated, as evidenced by President Bush's descent from triumphant commander in chief to beleaguered steward of a sagging economy.'[9]

By this time, in fact, a wide spectrum of expert opinion ranging across the ideological and theoretical divide of the economics profession had identified this North American recession as threatening to be even deeper and more stubborn than the one that inaugurated the 1980s, which was itself the most serious since the Second World War. Alan Greenspan, Chairman of the Federal Reserve Board, averred publicly that the severity of the downturn was unprecedented. W. W. Rostow, in a special article for *The Wall Street Journal*, rejected 'the assumption that we face a mild version of the Depression of the 1930s' which might be cured by another stimulus to consumption along the lines of Reagan's 1981–2 tax cuts; he called for a massive programme of public investment to restore capital stock and infrastructure. The editors of *Monthly Review* noted 'that a consensus is building up that the present recession is not a routine phase of capitalism's recurrent business cycle but rather a turning point to a new phase of capitalism's long-term trajectory . . . [inviting] comparison with the 1930s . . .'[10]

The symptoms that elicit such perspectives go well beyond new episodes in the continuing saga of decline of the 'fordist' sectors that emerged, out of the crisis of the 1930s, to form the core of the virtuous post-war circle of mass production and mass consumption. Now, alongside General Motors' $4.5 billion loss in 1991 (occasioning the impending closure of 21 plants and the loss of 74,000 jobs) needs also to be counted the $2.8 billion loss suffered by International Business Machines in 1991 (the first financial loss in IBM's history leading to a worldwide reduction in its workforce of 49,000). Similarly, just as the 'new times' computer sector as well as the 'fordist' automobile sector are affected, so are the growth poles of the North American economy: not only is the 'rust-belt' severely hit now, but also the 'sun-belt'. In the twelve months to September 1991, Los Angeles County lost 50,000 jobs and its unemployment rate suddenly moved from 6.1 to 9.3 per cent, well ahead of what was in any case a rapidly rising national rate (which by the end of 1991 had already wiped out all the employment gains during the 1980s). Metropolitan Toronto, the growth pole of the Canadian side of the continental economy, lost no less than 78,000 jobs in the same period, as its unemployment rate doubled to over 10%. A massive loss of some 400,000 manufacturing jobs in Canada since mid-1989, in the wake of the Canada–US Free Trade Agreement, an anti-inflationary programme of high interest rates and a high dollar, and the decline of the share of profits in the GDP to its lowest level since 1932, has been at the root of this. Its devastating effects have been compounded by the collapse of the real estate boom of the mid 1980s which has at the same time brought the construction industry in North America, from the building trades to architects, to a virtual standstill (by far the worst year for housing starts since 1945) with an attendant severe contraction in commercial and financial services.[11]

State and provincial governments, already overloaded by the shift of welfare expenditures from the federal level, have been caught in an unprecedented squeeze between actually declining revenues (again for the first time since 1945 in most cases) and ballooning welfare expenditures. Despite running the largest deficits in the history of subcentral governments anywhere, neither the right wing Republican administration of California nor the social democratic government in Ontario have maintained real levels of welfare, health, educational or municipal expenditure. No less than 40 states have cut or frozen benefits to families with children; as for 'able bodied' adults without children, who have never had much claim on the American welfare system in any case, some states have removed them (numbering 82,000 people in Michigan alone this past winter, for instance) from the welfare rolls entirely. Even before the onset of winter, by October 1991, the number of Americans on very low incomes who were enrolled in the federal food stamp anti-hunger programme reached 24 million, 9.6 per cent of the population, with no less than 3.2 million more people having been newly enrolled in the previous twelve months.[12] Even so, in the winter of 1991–92, a spontaneous advertising campaign for a new labour market strategy swept across the United States: people held up signs along roadways and in shopping centre parking lots, bearing the crudely-painted inscription, 'WILL WORK FOR FOOD.'

The extensive growth over the previous decade in trade, financial and investment interpenetration of the main capitalist countries also means, of course, a higher degree of coincidence of the conditions of bust as well as boom. Little noted as George Bush took industrial leaders with him to Tokyo to demand the Japanese open their market to more American car sales (about three-quarters of the $41 billion US trade deficit with Japan is in automobiles and parts) was the fact that, while the share of Japanese car sales in the American market continued to rise in 1991, the absolute number of Japanese cars sold in the US actually declined by over 5 per cent

– it was just that the American car companies sales declined even more, by over 12 per cent. Similarly, if IBM's problem was that world computer sales declined in 1991 for the first time ever, this also affected the sales and profits of Japanese (and European) firms in the industry. Huge excess capacity exists not only in the automobile sector in North America but also among the semiconductor manufacturers in Japan. With Toshiba, Hitachi and Mitsubishi (like Olivetti and Bull S.A. in Europe) experiencing significantly lower profits, they responded by cutting prices as well as production targets and reviewing investment programmes. Even while the Japanese growth rates remained over 4 per cent in 1991, domestic retail sales were at their lowest – and bankruptcies were at their highest – in decades. Despite a cut in interest rates, an actual decline in private capital investment in 1992 had been predicted by leading Japanese research institutes.[13]

Among the major European countries, the British economy had moved into recession at about the same time as the American and Canadian (and Australian) economies, more or less matching their rapid fall in annual growth rates from around 4% up to mid 1989 all the way down to an actual decline in real GDP in 1991. The Italian and French economies followed a similar trajectory, less precipitous in terms of the decline of growth rates (still holding on to about a 1 per cent rate of growth in 1991), but coming on top of rates of unemployment that were already by far the highest among the G7 countries. The German economy remained strong, and in fact registered in the fateful year of unification in 1990 the highest rate of growth (4.5%) for fifteen years. But even Germany (now including the former GDR, of course) registered virtually no growth in GDP in the last three quarters of 1991. With very broad implications for general recovery in Europe and beyond, the Bundesbank at the end of the year raised interest rates to their highest levels in postwar history to counter the attempt by German workers to recoup through wage increases the tax imposition made upon them to finance unification. The West German unions, so long held up abroad as a shining example of good sense to all others, had become the bête noire of the international financial press in the winter of 1991–92, their 'irresponsible' wage demands being blamed for preventing a general recovery.[14]

This current recession, which threatens to plunge even the advanced capitalist countries into the depression in which most the third world have already been enveloped for a decade, needs to be understood against the background and as a continuing aspect of the crisis which the post-war capitalist order entered almost a quarter of a century ago. The much vaunted 'globalization' of capitalism – a term coined to refer not to the penetration by capitalism of erstwhile Communist regions, but to the subjection of even advanced capitalist social formations to the competitive logic and exigencies of production, trade and finance undertaken on a world scale – may be seen both as cause and as consequence of this crisis of the post-war order. Indeed, if the first quarter century after the war offered the visage of a series of advanced capitalist Keynesian welfare states that had finally managed to overcome permanently capitalism's crisis tendencies, the quarter century that has followed has presented the visage of a global capitalism, transcending the managerial capacities of *any* nation state, in a permanent state of crisis.

The conditions that made possible the 'golden age' of western capitalist prosperity in the 1950s and 1960s, which coincided with the hey-day of the Cold War, were also the conditions that made plausible the claim – and the widespread belief – that capitalism had finally overcome its crisis-ridden nature. These conditions were quite special: a massive renewal of capital stock after a great depression followed immediately by a world war; large pools of cheap labour and raw materials; clusters of technological and organizational innovation bearing fruit in terms of productivity growth and consumer demand; continued military reflation through the Korean war and the Cold War. In these special conditions lay the material basis for the promise that the mass unemployment of the depression was forever a thing of the past; for the seemingly endless horizon towards which gradualist social reform could advance without fear of reversal; and even for the image held out to the 'developing' nations that they too could follow the stages of capitalist growth that would slowly but surely lead towards such a consumerist *and* welfarist nirvana. It was via the internalization of these promises, as well as in the face of the pressure of anti-communism (of course, the promise and the threat were not unrelated) that the social democratic parties and their trade union allies in the West firmly shifted the ideological rationale for their reformism towards the humane management of capitalism (which could now safely be called by another name – a 'mixed economy' would do) in place of the old rationale of a gradualist democratic path through capitalism to socialism.

This golden age era of post-war capitalism came to an end in the late 1960s and early 1970s as the special conditions that fuelled it ran their course and amidst the interrelated contradictions the great boom had generated: overaccumulation amidst declines in profitability and uneven productivity growth; increased competition amongst the advanced capitalist economies; challenges to the stability of the American dollar which by 1971 broke the Bretton Woods system of fixed exchange rates; inflationary pressures in the context of trade union militancy under conditions of near full employment; the fiscal crisis that attended a new wave of welfare state reforms; and rising commodity prices for third world resources (capped by the 1973 'oil shock').[15] The Keynesian welfare state, through its macroeconomic policy and corporatist arrangements, proved incapable of extricating national economies from 'stagflation' in these circumstances, while its vulnerability to international financial markets became increasingly manifest. For the first time in a generation, this return of crisis conditions momentarily brought back onto the agenda of a number of European unions and social democratic parties (who also inevitably felt some internal reverberations from the political and industrial radicalism of '1968') the issue of effective national control over private investment. But it was capital rather than labour that proved the more dynamic social force, less constrained by post-war institutional and ideological rigidities, and readier to try to transcend their limits.

The sheer ideological bravado which Western bourgeoisies came to display in this crisis may instructively be contrasted with the torpor and loss of confidence which the Communist *nomenklatura* exhibited in the same period, and also helps to understand the degree of emulation which motivated the Gorbachev reformers, let alone those who have followed them. The reassertion by the western bourgeoisies of their faith in competition, individualism, free trade and free markets, indeed their recoinage of the very notion of freedom in terms of the freedom to do business, was evidence of a renewed determination (in the very midst of the crisis of a post-war order in which, although they had had to compromise, they had still, after all, been the senior partner) to make the world entirely in their own image. There have been, of course, crucial material underpinnings to this ideological bourgeois renaissance. The revolution in communication introduced by the micro-chip and the spread of computer technology; the space which vastly increased flows of international trade and finance opened up for new configurations of capital mobility and accumulation; the restructuring of production in a manner that simultaneously made it more integrated internationally and more flexible locally in terms of labour and material inputs: all these were interrelated and mutually enforcing developments over the past two decades.

Combined with increasingly severe bouts of deflation between the late 1960s and the early 1980s, the labour shake out and locational shift entailed in the rationalization of the traditional mass production industries as a result of the above developments resulted in a reemergence of a structural reserve army of unemployed and underemployed in all the major capitalist countries. Meanwhile, the accompanying shift in the balance of forces between capital and *employed* labour has been unmistakable. This has been seen most graphically in the United States, where trade unions retain only 16% of the labour force, where real wages have stagnated for two whole decades, and where the ratio of the salary of a CEO for one of the hundred largest corporations to the average factory wage, which had stood at 40 to 1 in 1960 (but only 12 to 1 after taxes), stood at 93 to 1 in 1988 (and no less than 70 to 1 after taxes).[16] Even where the ballast of working class political organization in other countries laid the basis for stronger corporatist and welfare statist defences, successful bourgeois offensives to establish decentralized bargaining and/or to curtail rights to organize and to strike have been common, and through the course of the 1980s not a single welfare state remained immune from severe measures of fiscal austerity and regressive changes in taxation.[17]

As David Harvey has noted, this shift in state policy was partly a direct result, in the context of fiscal crisis and rampant inflation, of 'the growth of a new global financial system . . . which effectively checked the power of the nation-state (even the United States) to pursue any kind of independent fiscal and monetary policy that did not run afoul of the volatility of international currency markets.'[18] While the impact of this on the advanced capitalist state in terms of restraint on public welfare expenditure and public investment has been severe enough in the 1980s, for most of the third world the 1980s were literally devastating, with interest rate levels making unpayable the debt on lending so freely proferred by Western banks in the 1970s. With primary commodity prices never recovering from the severe global recession these interest rates were designed to induce, it was not in the face of too much resistance that the IMF wielded its financial whip to enforce adherence by many third world governments to the neo-liberal rules of global capitalist competition. The same fate is being visited on the ex-Communist regimes today.

The impact of the hidden hand of financial markets in putting constraints on the options of indebted states does not mean that there has been less of a role for the state in the context of globalization. The nature of state intervention has changed, but the role of the state has not necessarily been diminished. There have been important shifts in the hierarchy of state apparatuses particularly in bringing to the fore those which facilitate accumulation and articulate a competitiveness ideology, while those which fostered social welfare and articulated a class harmony orientation have lost considerable status. Perhaps most important, central bank agencies increasingly defined their role as one of making the regulation of monetary growth in their national economy consistent with their broader obligation, in terms of their international networks, to the collegial regulation of money in the world economy.[19]

The role that the annual G7 economic summits have come to play since 1975 in international coordination of this sort is instructive. It is not so much that these summits are policy-making forums, although they certainly lend legitimacy to institutions like the IMF and GATT with whose agendas they have become increasingly integrated. There are really two reasons such 'summits' are important. The first is that they work out a discourse in which all informed opinion is invited to address the problems of the day. (This is why negotiations over the wording of summit communiques is often intense: 'reducing expectations' as a way of addressing inflation, 'liberalization' as a way of talking about the global ramp of financial capital or privatization of public services and deregulation of industries or markets.) The second reason they are important is in terms of the role they play in establishing and reinforcing solidarity, often in the face of domestic democratic pressures, among the leading capitalist politicians and bureaucrats. The leaders at such summits are not only involved in a process of policing the third world's adherence to the laws of capitalism, but are also involved in cementing the adherence of each of the member countries.[20]

For the most part, this 'internationalization of the state' remains ad hoc and informal. In so far as it has become more formal, whether through GATT or the IMF at the world level or through regional treaties like the Canada–US Free Trade Agreement or the Single European Act, the role of states becomes to internalize and mediate, but ultimately to be responsible for policing adherence to the untrammelled logic of international capitalist competition within its own domain. Perhaps the process is seen most clearly in relation to 'Europe 1992', as accounted for by Streek and Schmitter:

> . . . Europe's large firms seem to have resolved at some point in the early 1980s that the increased size of production runs and investments required for world market competitiveness made it counterproductive to use their clout in national political arenas to get protection from foreign competition through subsidies, technical standards serving as nontariff barriers, or privileged access to public procurement contracts . . . The main concession governments seem to have made in return for business giving up previous claims for national protection was that the future European political economy was to be significantly less subject to institutional regulation – *national or supranational* – than it would have been in the harmonization-minded *and* social democratic 1970s when employers found themselves forced to struggle against a Community directive that would have made German-style co-determination obligatory for all large European firms. In the 1992 compromise, the project of European integration became finally and formally bound up with a deregulation project.[21]

Perhaps 'privatization' would be a better term for this project than 'deregulation' in so far as the regulatory function over market standards and entry formerly carried out by national governments is in fact taken over by regional organizations that are dominated by and primarily accountable to large corporations, even if they often include public officials who take on responsibility for international enforcement. But, whatever the most accurate term, Streek and Schmitter get at the substance of the matter when they say that while '1992 amounts to a formal devaluation of vast political resources that have come to be organized in and around the nation-state . . . they leave property rights untouched or even increase their value.' And they cogently go on to argue that for some time to come, 'whatever will occupy the place of the supranational Single European State governing the Single European Market, will likely resemble a *pre-New Deal liberal state*', with, in Marshall's terms, a high level of civil rights, a low level of political rights, '. . . and an even lower level of social rights, these being essentially limited to a set of European-wide health and safety standards. Historically intervention on health and safety matters represented the earliest stage in the history of the welfare state.'[22]

This process is not confined to Western Europe, of course, but represents what Stephen Gill has identified as a much more general shift towards a 'new constitutionalism for disciplinary neo-liberalism' involving the 'construction of legal or constitutional devices to remove or substantially insulate the new economic institutions from popular scrutiny or democratic accountability. Tendencies towards the wider adoption can be seen in the debates, for example, not only over Economic and Monetary Union of the EC . . . but also the roles of the central banks of East and Central Europe, the monetary constitution of a future Canada, as well as more general arguments made by bankers, economists and some politicians in favour of the need to constrain state autonomy over fiscal policy.'[23]

The irony of the trend towards constitutionalizing neo-liberalism is that it exacerbates rather than contains the tendencies of the new global capitalism to generate successive economic crisis (Thus, 'paving the way for more extensive and more destructive crises' and 'diminishing the means whereby crises are prevented' are not only memorable phrases: they still provide analytic as well as descriptive power.[24]) As we have seen, the neo-liberal era that has followed the Keynesian era of capitalism has had all too real effects. But what it has not created, despite all the smoke and mirrors generated by 'new times' strategists insisting that unions and the Left get on board a new 'regime of flexible accumulation' successive to the stable post-war 'fordist regime', is anything that might seriously be called 'a new productive system endowed with appropriate regulatory structures, which is capable of sustained and consistent development.'[25]

The famous 'Volker cold bath' that opened the decade entailed a unilateral decision by the American Treasury to slay the dragon of hyper-inflation via radical deflation. Although the G7 partners with whom the United States is supposed to rule the economic world resented the lack of coordination, the medicine worked, not least because it established the context for Mitterrand's strategic retreat towards austerity – with demoralizing effect on the Left around the world up to the present. The effect at home (and to a significant extent in other G7 countries) was to end inflation via deindustrialization. In the wake of this 'success', what was not permitted to others by way of fiscal stimulus was taken up unilaterally by the Americans themselves as Reagan's tax cuts and second cold war military expenditures set the grounds for the speculative boom of the mid 1980s. Streek and Schmitter appropriately recall an old Roman imperial maxim, 'quod licet Jovi non licet bovi' to describe this, but in joining with so many others in designating the Reagan deficit as 'Keynesianism in one country' they perform a travesty on Keynes not unlike that which has been so commonly visited on Marx over the past decade.[26] Just as Marx would have disavowed many of the Communisms we have known, so Keynes would have disavowed the kind of massive deficit that adds no productive infrastructure to the economy while underwriting unregulated global as well as domestic credit expansion. (By 1985 the size of the international bank credit market had increased as a proportion of world trade in goods and services from 11 per cent in 1964 to 119 per cent.[27])

While the deindustrialization of the early 1980s severely undermined the capacity of the American working class to play its part in mass consumption (Macdonald's wages just do not sustain the purchasing power that steelworkers wages used to), it momentarily appeared, during the artificial boom of the mid 1980s that the gigantic 'yuppie-style' borrowing and purchasing habits of a 'sub-bourgeois, *mass* layer of managers, professionals, new entrepreneurs and rentiers . . . [who] have been overwhelmingly successful in profiteering from both inflation and state expenditure' might sustain 'a new embryonic regime of accumulation that might be called *overconsumptionism*.'[28] But it could not last. After surviving the stock market crash of 1987 and the Savings and Loan scandal and bail-out, American capitalism entered the 1990s in a recession, which differed from the one that inaugurated the 1980s primarily in this respect: it was not one strategically induced. The G7, especially the Germans, are unwilling to accommodate continued American borrowing as they did at mid-decade. George Bush rushes off to Japan to beg for 'managed trade' and is appropriately derided there for sounding like a General Motors car salesman. And as the possibility of protectionist trade blocs looms ever larger on the horizon, the contradictions posed by neo-liberal free trade *within them* become ever clearer. The North American Free Trade Agreement with Mexico as well as Canada is directed at relocating North American production so that Mexico exports goods rather than people north of the border. But it is also necessarily directed at liberalizing trade, not least in agriculture, and the consequences of this, it is reliably estimated, will be that 'about 850,000 household heads will leave the Mexican countryside if corn subsidies fall and trade if further liberalized. Of them, more than 600,000 will head to the US.'[29]

There have been those who have argued for a long time that it was the Cold War that kept a return to depression from the West's door.[30] It is too soon to say whether we have entered one now, but this much is clear:

> . . . we live in an age of political celebration of the virtues of entrepreneurial capitalism and individualism, in an era when our technological confidence appears unbounded . . . and when spatial barriers are crumbling. Yet it is also an era . . . [which] reflects a crisis of capitalism of the deepest magnitude – a crisis that flexible accumulation has not resolved given its paltry rates of growth, the painful devaluations, the increasing class polarizations, the increasing political tensions – all in the midst of extraordinary instability, insecurity, fragmentation and change.[31]

What is the significance of this in terms of the prospects of socialist renewal in the 'new world order'? It has not been our purpose here to try to advance the case for one or another version of crisis theory. Nor do we claim to know whether the advanced capitalist world has necessarily now entered irretrievably into the depression that has afflicted most of the third world for the past decade. And we certainly do not mean to revive any such hoary myths as the old breakdown thesis, whereby the image of an ultimate capitalist crisis is made to do the hard work of socialist strategy and struggle in inaugurating a socialist future. On the contrary, we are of the view that it is through crises that capitalism historically has tended to recover its dynamism; and that where and when it is unable to do so, and where no viable revolutionary alternative or at least few means of democratic defence exist, the consequences are always appalling.

But such crises are also an opportunity for the Left to develop new forms and strategies that qualitatively enhance its capacities. Out of the long crisis of 1873 to 1896 emerged the European mass working class parties and trade unions; during the course of the Great Depression of the 1930s the models of industrial unionism in North America and of social democratic governance in Scandinavia were cast. The economic crisis that currently envelops global capitalism, even at the very moment of the ignominious collapse of its Communist nemesis, makes it possible that a different political climate entailing very different currents of thought will come to prevail against the bourgeois bravado we have grown used to over the past decade. As the shortcomings and contradictions of an unregulated market economy even in the 'affluent' societies become more and more manifest in the current crisis, the need for a comprehensive programme of radical economic change will again come to be felt more keenly in labour and socialist movements, and indeed beyond. Even in the United States, there are signs that recession and the crisis in public infrastructure, health provision, education, and collective and social services in general may be creating a space for something like a new New Deal, which would, for all its limitations, be a tremendous advance on predominant trends since World War II. In such a climate, there is an opportunity for the Left to think creatively about, and to work constructively towards, new forms and strategies that enhance its capacities to put a democratic socialism back on the agenda for the twenty-first century.

IV

All this raises the very large question of what kinds of forms and strategies, of what kind of socialism, the Left will advance in the coming years. In order to begin to answer that question, it is also necessary to take careful account of certain facts regarding current conditions and developments on a global scale.

One such fact is the movement away, not only in the Communist world, but also in Latin America and Africa, from military, single party and racial dictatorships and their replacement by at least formally democratic political regimes. 'Democracy', in relation to these regimes, means that they have adopted such democratic forms as electoral competition and the acknowledgment by the government of some elementary civic rights. On the other hand, the social order, as distinct from the political system, remains as it was, with the same social structure, with all the privileges, inequalities, exploitation, mass deprivation at one end and great luxury at the other, which this signifies. The change, from the point of view of the dominant classes, is not in the least intended to modify the social order as well as the political system. On the contrary, the introduction of democratic forms is intended to *contain* popular pressure and drive it into safe channels. Thus, for instance, was the popular upsurge which overthrew the Marcos dictatorship in the Philippines contained with the accession to power of Mrs Aquino. The same process has been at work elsewhere, and was greatly favoured by the United States and its allies in the context of the new cold war of the 1980s and the subsequent struggle for reform within the Communist states. The establishment of democratic forms, however brittle, to replace capitalist dictatorships, was structured so as to ensure that the new governments did not deviate from the path of economic, financial and social stabilization – indeed that they became more open to the blandishments of neo-liberalism with the same social groups in power, minus the generals, or with the generals under civilian control.

The limited character of the change from dictatorship to democratic forms should not, however, lead to an underestimation of its significance. For one thing, the change would almost everywhere not have occurred had it not been for the irruption of radical popular forces on the scene, which shows well enough how great is the potential for intense popular pressure against the status quo in the current appalling crisis of third world development in general. Also, the change means that the repressive methods favoured by dictatorship – imprisonment, torture, death squads – are no longer so prevalent, even if they are not altogether stopped; and democratic forms enable progressive forces, including the Left, to organize themselves more effectively than was possible under dictatorship. In some cases, the new forms and strategies adopted by the Left both were crucial to undermining the dictatorships and to mounting both grass roots and electoral challenges to the liberal bourgeoisie after the transition to democracy. Nowhere has this been more so than in Brazil, where, growing out of the popular mobilizations that made the strikes of the late 1970s effective, the Workers' Party under Luis Inacio da Silva ('Lula') was only narrowly defeated in the second round of the presidential election in December 1989. Less strategically and institutionally innovative, but nevertheless notable in a very different setting, was the challenge issued by Cardenas in Mexico – and the breadth of response – in the context of the presidential election of 1988, when the PRI (Party of Revolutionary Institutions), so long virtually unchallenged, had to resort to shadier practices than usual in order to prevail.

The pressure for change which is manifested by these and innumerable other episodes will not abate, for the simple but crucial reason that the reforms *in the social order* which its abatement would require are precisely what the people in power are most deeply committed to resist. The economic growth and development under capitalist auspices, which the dictatorships and then the liberal bourgeoisies promised would at least attenuate the dreadful conditions under which the vast majority of the population of the 'third world' is condemned to live, have proved a chimera. Given this, the chances are that the pressure for change will not only be maintained, but that it will grow.

This, clearly enough, does not mean that the inspiration behind this pressure will necessarily be left-inspired. Some of it, even much of it, if recent experience is any guide, will in some countries be reactionary, racist, xenophobic, and steeped in the worst kind of religious obscurantism. But the Left will be present on the scene, and, as experience also shows, will sometimes be the predominant force in the ranks of the opposition. It is possible, of course, that the same structural conditions of poverty and underdevelopment, of encirclement and counterrevolution as produced Communist dictatorships in the past will shape future left-wing regimes as well. But lessons can also be learned from history, with some effects on future practice. One of the effects of the collapse of Communist regimes is that it has discredited the type of political and economic system which was common to them as a model for socialist development, as well as the type of Leninist vanguard party which, in the name of quite unrealizable notions of semi-direct popular rule, ignored the difficult questions of accountability in representation, decision making and administration. If such a recent instance of new socialist party formation as Brazil's is indicative, this suggests that these questions may well be in the forefront in light of the lessons of past experience.

And what about the political conditions that will emerge from a return to capitalism in the ex-Communist countries? The market economy is today producing mass unemployment and increased deprivation, the spread of criminality, prostitution and drug trafficking, steadily rising prices, government corruption, and cuts in the social benefits which, however poorly, Communist regimes had provided and which the people had come to take for granted. Here too, the veritable anomie which has descended upon these countries has produced morbid reactions in the form of ethnic strife, inflamed nationalism, xenophobia, a recrudescence of antisemitism, etc. On the other hand, there is plenty of evidence that, however much enthusiasm the market economy may generate among the new power-holders and their advisers, the enthusiasm is not shared by the population at large. There are already signs here and there that, even whereas the old Communist regimes are most passionately rejected, ex-Communist parties with some promise of new leaders, new programmes and new forms of organization, but above all with the promise of political defence against the cruelties of the marketplace and the new primitive accumulators, are not without a good deal of support. The Polish elections of November 1991 may be symptomatic. Poland is where the free market experiment was given extreme form. In the elections, a mere 42.5% of those eligible to vote went to the polls, and voted for some twenty parties, none of which got more than 12% of the vote. Among these parties, however, the parties of the Left did remarkably well. The Democratic Left Alliance, ex-Communist, got 12.1%; the Peasants, also ex-Communist, got 8.9%; three left parties from the splintered Solidarity movement got together 12.5%. This represents a third of the electorate which bothered to vote. In addition, a centre-left party, the Democratic Union, led by the former prime minister, Tadeusz Mazowiecki, got 12% of the vote. The prime minister, Jan Krysztof Bielecki, the prime mover in the turn to the market economy, whose party obtained only 7.2% of the vote, described the result as 'a vote against the market economy'. How much encouragement socialists may draw from this election either in this or in other ex-Communist regimes is by no means yet clear. But what is clear is the imminent danger that the manifold failures of the market economy, and the resentments they will produce, may foster a creeping authoritarianism, one of whose main purposes would be to limit the political space for democratic opposition and to bring about 'political stability' at its expense, and at the expense of civic and trade union rights in general. But resistance to such a development is part of the struggle which the Left has to wage, and which, with the help of democratically-minded parties, groupings and individuals that are not part of the Left, it may hope to win.

For all the vast differences which exist between the ex-Communist countries on the one hand, and Western capitalist democracies on the other, there are also, in the perspective of the need for a socialist renewal, at least this striking similarity between them: the triumph of neo-liberal principles even over social democratic principles, let alone socialist ones. As we pointed out in the previous section, the crisis of the Keynesian welfare state brought back onto the agendas of many European unions and social democratic parties programmes which proposed to transcend the crisis by an extensive shift towards public control over private capital. By the beginning of the 1980s political forces advancing such programmes, usually accompanied by a concern to extend simultaneously the means of popular participation at work as well as in public life, figured very prominently in social democratic parties in Britain, France, Sweden and Greece. In the British case, the intra-party struggle against this was so tenacious and bitter that the public party split became an electoral liability, and those advancing the case for democratic socialist renewal were made (and this was the ultimate sign of their defeat) to bear the blame. In the other cases, social democratic governments were elected in the early 1980s with commitments to an extension of public control over capital figuring visibly on their platforms. But through the course of the decade, with more or less rapidity in the face of neo-liberal as well as older centrist and right-wing social democratic opposition, these aspects of policy were jettisoned or trivialized. Left-wing forces which had advanced these socialist options were marginalized in relation to these governments and increasingly within the parties as well.

What is perhaps most notable, however, is that it was not only democratic socialist options which were defeated, but the old social democratic model itself could not stand in the face of neo-liberalism. This was seen as the French and Greek governments swung wildly from radical socialist promise to austerity; soon they were joined by social democratic governments in New Zealand and Australia in more and more explicit neo-liberal policies. But it was most definitively demonstrated as the Swedish social democratic government (albeit from a much more extensive and secure welfare statist base) followed a similar trajectory through the course of the 1980s towards policies increasingly more attuned to the neo-liberal requirements of the 'business community' at home and abroad.

Social democracy seeks to distinguish itself today primarily by having a better recipe for competitiveness, one less dogmatically opposed to state intervention in industry than the neo-liberals in so far as it stresses the need of public support for high tech industries and for training programmes for the highly skilled labour they would employ – as if all but a few could succeed at such a game. The social democratic option at the European level offers only a minimum social policy amendment to the predominant privatization thrust, the issue of the control of capital appearing nowhere on the agenda.

Meanwhile, outside the spheres of political power, and again parallel to developments in the East, what might be called the intellectual and academic Left has also been in headlong retreat from what one of the prophets of post-modernism, Jean-François Lyotard, has contemptuously called 'mega-sagas', meaning comprehensive schemes of radical change, notably socialism.[32] It is impossible to say how long the ranks of the Left will be plagued by this fashion, but it is clear that it is an intellectual mood that was very much based on a caricature of contemporary socialist aspirations as inherently totalitarian. This ignores the extent to which the aspirations of socialists in every era, and not least of the new left of the 1960s (taken together as encompassing a new generation of radicals and an older generation of socialists and communists), entailed not a future constructed on a model of disciplined proletarian homogeneity but rather of genuine pluralist democracy in which the state would be subject to a freely associated society.

What may have unhinged so much of the Left in recent years might well have much to do with our having been thrust once again since the early 1970s into an era where the competitive dynamics of capitalism appear to have escaped any means of control. This is nothing new, as Tony Benn has recently noted, quoting an unlikely source, Harold Macmillan's *The Middle Way*, written in 1938: 'We have lived so long at the mercy of uncontrolled economic forces that we have become sceptical regarding any plan for human emancipation.'[33] What compounds this problem for the Left is that socialist aspirations have lost their traditional organizational moorings. Of two main institutional embodiments of the socialist project in the twentieth century, Communist parties have dramatically collapsed, while Social Democratic parties seem to have quite definitively divested themselves of any interest in transcending capitalist social relations, and marginalized in the 1980s even those within them who had always sought to reestablish socialist ideals and practices. But long before these developments, it had been clear that both of these institutional expressions were in socialist terms sclerotic; indeed it was this understanding that more than anything characterized the new left of the 1960s. What caused this had both to do with strategic and programmatic errors and failures, albeit of quite different kinds, and with the way in which a continually dynamic and powerful capitalism has reshaped the terrain on which these parties were founded, undermining their attachments to their traditional social bases through the cultural transformations of consumer capitalism and the socio-economic transformations entailed in the continuing deconstruction and reconstruction of industry, occupation and locale. But even if these parties were already said to be in the 1960s, and demonstrated to be in the 1980s, completely discredited as institutional expressions of a socialist project, it must also be said that nothing viable has yet arisen to replace them as such. The attempt by elements of the new left to reground the project in newer and purer marxist–leninist parties has proved, predictably even from the vantage point of the 1960s, to be utterly inappropriate and ineffective; while the various attempts at boring from within the old parties either suffered from the same faults and/or were repulsed, or, where successful, carried some Euro-Communist parties all the way to social democracy rather than to a revived socialism.

Of course the sclerosis of the old party politics has provided openings for new forms of struggle and the formation of new political identities which have enriched the left in these last decades, not least by making their presence felt in the old parties; and they have also laid the base for some new parties, albeit still mainly small ones, of socialist-feminist-ecologist orientation. But we have very far to go yet before this provides the organizational and strategic means to dispel the widespread sense that we are completely 'at the mercy of uncontrolled economic forces', to establish a sense of confidence that we may properly speak in terms of a socialist project for 'human emancipation', which amounts to more than a millennial hope, which has some real meaning, in other words, in the relevant future.

In recent years *The Socialist Register* has devoted itself to sustained and serious inquiry of what is and is not desirable and possible in terms of socialist renewal in the West.[34] We shall continue with this. Although this is not the occasion for another detailed prognosis, it may be useful to draw a few brief conclusions from our discussion here of the condition of the 'new world order'. In light of the 'globalization' tendencies of contemporary capitalism, for instance, it is a common and a welcome reaction on the Left to stress the need for a renewed internationalism, particularly in terms of strategic and organizational coordination and cohesion of parties, unions and social movements on a regional basis. It is certainly the case that such coordination of struggles and strategies is useful and necessary, in so far as this regional coordination is not premised on a beggar-my-neighbour orientation itself (as making Europe or North America competitive or protectionist as regional blocks vis-a-vis the rest of the world sometimes seems to be, for instance), but is oriented to establishing viable supranational bases for resisting the neo-liberal agenda and for establishing democratic means of controlling capital. But sometimes this internationalist focus is advanced at the expense of deriding or at least giving up on the struggles that remain so necessary at the level of the nation state, and indeed, at subnational levels. This is a false polarization of what is needed, not least because even a capitalism that is fully extended in its global reach still relies on nation states more than any other structures for its preservation and reproduction, and because progressive policy interventions in international regulatory bodies still must be made, and will continue to be made for a foreseeable future primarily via the representatives of nation states. To give up the struggle at the national level for socialist renewal in the name of a global socialism to match a global capitalism is mere romanticism.

But what strategy should guide socialist renewal even on this more realistic basis? In countries where capitalist democracy prevails, socialists have no real option but to advance their cause within the existing constitutional process, by means of a combination of electoral and extra-parliamentary activism, while attempting all the while to redefine in more substantive and extensive terms the parameters of the constitutional system itself. An approach distant both from ultra-leftism on the one hand and from the politics of accommodation of social democracy on the other will need to be elaborated and developed, given clear and relevant, short-term and longer-term policy meaning and institutional focus. This approach entails an involvement in immediate struggles over a multitude of current issues: in the current moment of economic crisis the most important must be bold programmes for economic recovery which are oriented to employing people directly in the expansion and improvement of the public infrastructure. This will, in the current balance of forces, entail capital borrowing for this purpose, but this can itself become a means of considerable popular mobilization in an emergency, along the lines of 'victory bonds' campaigns in wartime. While no such programme will allow one country to escape by itself from the economic crisis, this programme could mitigate the effects of the crisis, and lay the basis for a more ecologically sound, socially just, productive economy in the future. It would contribute, moreover, to giving people a sense that something can be done about the crisis, which is the key to further popular mobilization in even more radical directions. Socialists will have to clarify, in the latter respect, their insistence that the aims which are common to most of the Left – the creation of truly democratic and egalitarian societies – cannot be realized without the dissolution of the existing structures of power and privilege. Such dissolution still requires, as an essential but not sufficient condition, the transfer of economic power from private hands into the public domain. But it also requires finding practical means whereby to escape what Weber called the 'iron cage' of bureaucratic organization. Socialists must concern themselves not only with getting this or that policy claim represented to and recognized by the state, but with changing the administrative apparatuses of the state so that they become representative and accountable and oriented to providing the means and resources for as much decentralized and popular decision making and resource allocation in civil society as is compatible with democratic planning for common social problems. The socialist project is not about more state or less state, but a different kind of state.

Socialists can have no illusions about the speed with which they may be able to achieve a really significant advance in the fulfilment of their aims. But it is reasonable for them to believe that there is a constituency which can be won over to socialist purposes and that this constituency will grow as capitalism shows itself increasingly incapable of coping with the manifold crises which it produces. Patterns of advance will vary greatly from one country to another; and there will be setbacks as well as victories. But the gloom in which so much of the Left has been plunged in recent years is very short-sighted. For wherever one looks, there is ferment, with grievances expressed, demands made, rights affirmed. Some of it assumes profoundly unhealthy forms; but a good deal of it is progressive and speaks a language which is well in tune with socialist aspirations. In this perspective, the notion that socialism is dead says more about those who voice that notion than about future prospects.

NOTES

1. *The Economist*, 28 September 1991, p. 25.
2. Richard Nixon, *1999: Victory Without War*, New York, Simon and Schuster, 1988; see especially chapter 4, 'How To Compete With Moscow'.
3. See Peter Gowan's excellent account: 'Western Economic Diplomacy and the New Eastern Europe', *New Left Review*, 182, Jan/Feb, 1990, pp. 63–82.
4. Francis X. Clines, 'Yeltsin's Tutor Is Scrappy Defender, Too', *New York Times*, 16 January 1992.
5. *1990: Victory Without War*, pp. 318–19.

6. Franz Schurmann, 'Back to the Cold War . . . Or Worse', in *The Role of Ideas in American Foreign Policy*, University Press of New England, 1971, p. 11.

7. See Jean Smith, *George Bush's War*, New York, Henry Holt & Co., 1992.

8. 'The United Nations after the Gulf War: A Promise Betrayed', Stephen Lewis interviewed by Jim Wurst, *World Policy Journal*, Summer 1991, pp. 539–49.

9. See Peter Applebome, 'A Year After Victory, Joy Is a Ghost' and Maureen Dowd, 'Immersing Himself in Nitty Gritty, Bush Barnstorms New Hampshire', *New York Times*, 16 January 1992.

10. W. W. Rostow, 'Time to Stop Living Off Capital', *The Wall Street Journal*, 8 January 1992; 'Notes From the Editors', *Monthly Review*, Vol. 43, no. 8, January 1992. Greenspan is quoted in the *International Herald Tribune*, 18 December 1991 and 17 January 1992.

11. For general surveys, see 'When California Sneezes . . .' *Business Week*, December 30, 1991, p. 32 ff.; *Los Angeles Times*, December 29, 1991, pp. D5–6; and *The Toronto Star*, 7 January, 1992, pp. A5–6. Cf. Nate Laurie, 'Canada's in a depression – that's the bottom line', *The Toronto Star*, 16 January, p. A21.

12. See Gwen Ifill, 'Whose Welfare?' *The New York Times*, 19 January 1992, and John Saunders, 'Open Season on indigent Americans', *The Globe and Mail Report on Business*, 18 January 1992.

13. See especially the reports by Robert Thompson in the *Financial Times*, 'Forecasts differ on Japan's economy', 18 December 1991, 'Tokyo store sales in largest fall since 1965', 17 January 1992, and (with Steven Butler), 'No winners in the chip race', 12 January 1992.

14. Samuel Brittan, 'Better Frankfurt than Liverpool', *Financial Times*, 9 January 1991. For general surveys, see 'Global Chill', *Business Week*, 16 December 1991; Peter Cook, 'Recovery as elusive as ever', *The Globe and Mail Report on Business*, 2 January 1992, and Ferdinand Protzman, 'Germany's Economy Cooled in '91', *New York Times*, 16 January 1992.

15. The transition we speak of is best covered in P. Armstrong, A. Glyn and J. Harrison, *Capitalism Since 1945*, Basil Blackwell, Cambridge, 1991; and S. A. Marglin and J. B. Schor, *The Golden Age of Capitalism*, Clarendon Press, Oxford 1990.

16. See Robert Reich, *The Work of Nations*, A. A. Knopf, New York, 1991, pp. 204–5, and more generally Kevin Phillips, *The Politics of Rich and Poor*, Random House, New York, 1990; and S. Bowles et al, *After the Wasteland*, M. E. Sharpe, New York, 1990.

17. See *Capitalism since 1945*, pp. 310–311.

18. David Harvey, 'The Geographical and Geopolitical Consequences of the Transition from Fordist to Flexible Accumulation', in G. Sternlieb and J. W. Hughes, *America's New Market Geography: Nation, Region and Metropolis*, Rutgers, New Jersey 1988, p. 110.

19. This is brilliantly analyzed in a doctoral dissertation by André Drainville, *Monetarism in Canada and the World Economy*, York University, Toronto, 1991.

20. The earliest summits played an important role, for instance, in steeling the resolve of the British Labour Government to reject the alternative economic strategy upon which they had been elected and accept the IMF terms on austerity in 1975. James Callaghan describes in his autobiography how the friendship he formed with Gerald Ford at the first summits became crucial to convincing the IMF that the Labour Government was serious about cutting its public borrowing and welfare expenditures. As the Americans saw it, in the words of then Secretary of William Rodgers: 'It was a choice between Britain remaining in the liberal financial system as opposed to radical change of course, because we were concerned about Tony Benn precipitating a policy decision by Britain to turn its bank on the IMF. I think if that had happened the whole system would have begun to fall apart . . . so we tended to see it in cosmic terms.' Callaghan saw it in similar terms but, rather interestingly he personalized it: 'I never had cause to doubt Gerald Ford's word or his good faith. It may seem strange that a republican president and a Labour prime minister could work so confidently with each other. The reason was that . . . we both accepted that the interests of our two countries and of the alliance transcended political differences.' Is it surprising that in the course of providing his account of one of the greatest political crises in modern British history, he thinks it relevant to point out that he and his wife now visit Gerald Ford every year at his home 'high up in the beautiful Rocky Mountain state of Colorado'? James Callaghan, *Time and Chance*, Collins, London 1987,

pp. 430ff. The quote from Rodgers is taken from S. Fay and H. Young, *The Day the Pound Nearly Died*, London 1978, p. 30.

21. Wolfgang Streek and Philippe C. Schmitter, 'From National Corporatism to Transnational Pluralism: Organized Interests in the Single European Market', *Politics and Society*, Vol. 19, no. 2, 1991, pp. 148–9.
22. Ibid., p. 152.
23. Stephen Gill, 'The Emerging World Order and European Change', in this volume.
24. *The Communist Manifesto*, edited by F. C. Bender, Norton, New York, 1988, pp. 60–1.
25. John Grahl, 'Economies Out of Control', *New Left Review*, 185, Jan/Feb., 1991, p. 171.
26. Streek and Schmitter, *op. cit.*, p. 145.
27. N. Costello et al. *Beyond the Casino Economy*, Verso, London 1989, p. 41.
28. Mike Davis, 'The Political Economy of Late Imperial America', *New Left Review*, 143, Jan/Feb., 1984, p. 21.
29. Diana Solis, 'Corn May Be Snag in Trade Talks by Mexico, US', *The Wall Street Journal*, December 27, 1991, citing research by Raul Hinojosa Ojeda of UCLA which was funded both by the US Agriculture Department and the Mexican Foreign Relations Ministry.
30. See, most recently, 'Notes from the Editors', *Monthly Review*, January 1992.
31. Harvey, *op. cit.*, p. 110.
32. For a survey of this trend, see e.g. *The Retreat of the Intellectuals: The Socialist Register 1990*.
33. Quoted in a speech by Tony Benn, House of Commons Official Report, Wednesday, 22 January 1992.
34. See especially *Social Democracy and Beyond: The Socialist Register 1986/6*; *Socialist Renewal, East and West: The Socialist Register 1988*; and *Revolution Today; Aspirations and Realities: The Socialist Register 1989*.

GLOBAL PERESTROIKA

Robert W. Cox

Mikhail Gorbachev's *perestroika* was a revolution from above, a decision by political leadership to undertake a reform of the economic organisation of 'real socialism' which, once initiated, got out of control and spun into entropy. Underlying that decision was a vague idea that some kind of socialism could be rebuilt in the context of market forces. No one had a clear strategy based upon real social forces as to how this result could be achieved. The consequence has been a devastating destruction of the real economy, i.e. the productive capacity and the economic organisation of real (albeit ailing) socialism, and a disarticulation of social forces. Soviet *perestroika* aggravated the decay of public services, created large-scale unemployment, polarised new wealth and new poverty, generated inflation, and made a former superpower dependent upon foreign relief. Those who gained from the 'market' were preeminently well-placed members of the former nomenklatura, speculators, and gangsters. The market is the mafia.

Perestroika in the now defunct Soviet empire is perhaps the worst case of what has become a global phenomenon – worst not in an absolute sense but in the most dramatic descent from production to entropy. Global *perestroika*, more euphemistically called 'globalization', is not the consequence of a conscious decision of political leadership. It is a result of structural changes in capitalism, in the actions of many people, corporate bodies, and states, that cumulatively produce new relationships and patterns of behaviour. The project of global *perestroika* is less the conscious will of an identifiable group than the latent consequence of these structural changes. These consequences form a coherent interrelated pattern; but this pattern contains within itself contradictions that threaten the persistence of this structural whole in formation. Those of us who abhor the social and political implications of the globalisation project must study its contradictions in order to work for its eventual replacement.

26

Sources of Globalisation

It has been fashionable, especially in the Anglo-Saxon tradition, to distinguish states and markets in the analysis of economic forces and economic change. Where this distinction leads to the privileging of one to the exclusion of the other, it always departs from historical reality. States and political authorities have had a variety of relationships to economic activity, even when proclaiming non-intervention, and the market is a power relationship. (As François Perroux wrote: 'Il n'y a pas de sosie en économie'. – Economic agents are not identical twins.) Where the distinction serves to assess the relative weight of the visible hand of political authority and of the latent outcome of an infinity of private actions, it has some analytical merit.[1]

In the capitalist core of the world economy, the balance has shifted over time from the mercantilism that went hand in hand with the formation of the modern state, to the liberalism of *les bourgeois conquérants*,[2] and back again to a more state-regulated economic order, first in the age of imperialism and then, after a post-war interlude of aborted liberalism, during the Great Depression of the 1930s. The state during the 1930s had to assume the role of agent of economic revival and defender of domestic welfare and employment against disturbances coming from the outside world. Corporatism, the union of the state with productive forces at the national level, became, under various names, the model of economic regulation.

Following World War II, the Bretton Woods system attempted to strike a balance between a liberal world market and the domestic responsibilities of states. States became accountable to agencies of an international economic order – the IMF, World Bank, and GATT – as regards trade liberalisation, and exchange-rate stability and convertibility; and were granted facilities and time to make adjustments in their national economic practices so as not to have to sacrifice the welfare of domestic groups. Keynesian demand management along with varieties of corporatism sustained this international economic order through the ups and downs of the capitalist business cycle. Moderate inflation attributable to the fine tuning of national economies stimulated a long period of economic growth. War and arms production played a key role: World War II pulled the national economies out of the Depression; the Korean War and the Cold War underpinned economic growth of the 1950s and 1960s.

The crisis of this post-war order can be traced to the years 1968–75. During this period, the balanced compromise of Bretton Woods shifted toward subordination of domestic economies to the perceived exigencies of a global economy. States willy nilly became more effectively accountable to a *nébuleuse* personified as the global economy; and they were constrained to mystify this external accountability in the eyes and ears of their own publics through the new vocabulary of globalisation, interdependence, and competitiveness.

How and why did this happen? It is unlikely that any fully adequate explanation can be given now. The matter will be long debated. It is, however, possible to recognise this period as a real turning point in the structural sense of a weakening of old and the emergence of new structures. Some key elements of the transformation can be identified.

The structural power of capital: Inflation which hitherto had been a stimulus to growth, beneficial alike to business and organised labour, now, at higher rates and with declining profit margins, became perceived by business as inhibiting investment. Discussions among economists as to whether the fault lay in demand pull or in cost push were inconclusive. Business blamed unions for raising wages and governments for the cycle of excessive spending, borrowing, and taxing. Governments were made to understand that a revival of economic growth would depend upon business confidence to invest, and that this confidence would depend upon 'discipline' directed at trade unions and government fiscal management. The investment strike and capital flight are powerful weapons that no government can ignore with impunity. A typical demonstration of their effectiveness was the policy shift from the first to the second phase of the Mitterrand presidency in France.

The structuring of production: Insofar as government policies did help restore business confidence, new investment was by-and-large of a different type. The crisis of the post-war order accelerated the shift from Fordism to post-Fordism – from economies of scale to economies of flexibility. The large integrated plant employing large numbers of semi-skilled workers on mass-production of standardised goods became an obsolete model of organisation. The new model was based on a core-periphery structure of production, with a relatively small core of relatively permanent employees handling finance, research and development, technological organisation and innovation, and a periphery consisting of dependent components of the production process.

While the core is integrated with capital, the fragmented components of the periphery are much more loosely linked to the overall production process. They can be located partly within the core plant, e.g. as maintenance services, and partly spread among different geographical sites in many countries. Periphery components can be called into existence when they are needed by the core and disposed of when they are not. Restructuring into the core-periphery model has facilitated the use of a more precariously employed labour force segmented by ethnicity, gender, nationality, or religion. It has weakened the power of trade unions and strengthened that of capital within the production process. It has also made business less controllable by any single state authority. Restructuring has thereby accelerated the globalising of production.

The role of debt: Both corporations and governments have relied increasingly on debt financing rather than on equity investment or taxation. Furthermore, debt has to an increasing extent become *foreign* debt. There was a time when it could be said that the extent of public debt did not matter 'because we owed it to ourselves'. However plausible the attitude may have been, it no longer applies. Governments now have to care about their international credit ratings. They usually have to borrow in currencies other than their own and face the risk that depreciation of their own currency will raise the costs of debt service.

As the proportion of state revenue going into debt service rises, governments have become more effectively accountable to external bond markets than to their own publics. Their options in exchange rate policy, fiscal policy, and trade policy have become constrained by financial interests linked to the global economy. In Canada, among the very first acts of the heads of the *Parti québecois* government elected in Quebec in 1976 and of the New Democratic Party government elected in Ontario in 1990, both of them appearing as radical challenges to the pre-existing political order, was to go to New York to reassure the makers of the bond market. In Mexico, the government had to abandon an agricultural reform designed to expand medium-sized farming for local consumption goods, and revert to large-scale production of luxury export crops in order to earn dollars to service the country's debt.

Corporations are no more autonomous than governments. The timing of an announcement by General Motors just prior to Christmas 1991 that it was going to close 21 plants and cut 74,000 jobs[3] was hardly prompted by a particularly Scrooge-like malevolence. By informed accounts, it was intended, by appearing as a token of the corporation's intention to increase competitiveness, to deter a down-grading of its bond rating which would have increased the corporation's cost of borrowing. A large corporation, flag-ship of the US economy, is shown to be tributary to the financial manipulators of Wall Street. Finance has become decoupled from production[4] to become an independent power, an autocrat over the real economy.

And what drives the decision making of the financial manipulators? The short-range thinking of immediate financial gain, not the long-range thinking of industrial development. The market mentality functions synchronically; development requires a diachronic mode of thought. Financial markets during the 1980s were beset by a fever of borrowing, leveraged takeovers, junk bonds, and savings and loan scandals – a roller-coaster of speculative gains and losses that Susan Strange called 'casino capitalism'.[5] The result of financial power's dominance over the real economy was as often as not the destruction of jobs and productive capital. This is western capitalism's counterpart to *perestroika*'s destruction of the residual productive powers of real socialism.

The Structures of Globalisation

The crisis of the post-war order has expanded the breadth and depth of a global economy that exists alongside and incrementally supersedes the classical international economy.[6] The global economy is the system generated by globalising production and global finance. Global production is able to make use of the territorial divisions of the international economy, playing off one territorial jurisdiction against another so as to maximise reductions in costs, savings in taxes, avoidance of anti-pollution regulation, control over labour, and guarantees of political stability and favour. Global finance has achieved a virtually unregulated and electronically connected 24-hour-a-day network. The collective decision making of global finance is centred in world cities rather than states – New York, Tokyo, London, Paris, Frankfurt – and extends by computer terminals to the rest of the world.

The two components of the global economy are in potential contradiction. Global production requires a certain stability in politics and finance in order to expand. Global finance has the upper hand because its power over credit creation determines the future of production; but global finance is in a parlously fragile condition. A calamitous concatenation of accidents would bring it down – a number of failures on the Robert Maxwell scale combined with government debt defaults or a cessation of Japanese foreign lending. For now governments, even the combined governments of the G7, have not been able to devise any effectively secure scheme of regulation for global finance that could counter such a collapse.

There is, in effect, no explicit political or authority structure for the global economy. There is, nevertheless, something there that remains to be deciphered, something that could be described by the French word *nébuleuse* or by the notion of 'governance without government'.[7]

There is a transnational process of consensus formation among the official caretakers of the global economy. This process generates consensual guidelines, underpinned by an ideology of globalisation, that are transmitted into the policy-making channels of national governments and big corporations. Part of this consensus-formation process takes place through unofficial forums like the Trilateral Commission, the Bilderberg conferences, or the more esoteric Mont Pelerin Society. Part of it goes on through official bodies like the OECD, the Bank of International Settlements, the International Monetary Fund, and the G7. These shape the discourse within which policies are defined, the terms and concepts that circumscribe what can be thought and done. They also tighten the transnational networks that link policy making from country to country.[8]

The structural impact on national governments of this global centralisation of influence over policy can be called the internationalising of the state. Its common feature is to convert the state into an agency for adjusting national economic practices and policies to the perceived exigencies of the global economy. The state becomes a transmission belt from the global to the national economy, where heretofore it had acted as the bulwark defending domestic welfare from external disturbances. Power within the state becomes concentrated in those agencies in closest touch with the global economy – the offices of presidents and prime ministers, treasuries, central banks. The agencies that are more closely identified with domestic clients – ministries of industries, labour ministries, etc. – become subordinated. This phenomenon, which has become so salient since the crisis of the post-war order, needs much more study.

Different forms of state facilitate this tightening of the global/local relationship for countries occupying different positions in the global system. At one time, the military-bureaucratic form of state seemed to be optimum in countries of peripheral capitalism for the enforcement of monetary discipline. Now IMF-inspired 'structural adjustment' is pursued by elected presidential regimes (Argentina, Brazil, Mexico, Peru) that manage to retain a degree of insulation from popular pressures. India, formerly following a more autocentric or self-reliant path, has moved closer and closer towards integration into the global economy. Neo-conservative ideology has sustained the transformation of the state in Britain, the United States, Canada, and Australasia in the direction of globalisation. Socialist party governments in France and in Spain have adjusted their policies to the new orthodoxy. The states of the former Soviet empire, insofar as their present governments have any real authority, seem to have been swept up into the globalising trend.

In the European Community, the unresolved issue over the social charter indicates a present stalemate in the conflict over the future nature of the state and of the regional authority. There is a struggle between two kinds of capitalism[9]: the hyper-liberal globalising capitalism of Thatcherism, and a capitalism more rooted in social policy and territorially balanced development. The latter stems from the social democratic tradition and also from an older conservatism that thinks of society as an organic whole rather than in the contractual individualism of so-called neo-conservatism.

In Japan, the guiding and planning role of the state retains initiative in managing the country's relationship with the world outside its immediate sphere, and will likely be of increasing significance in lessening that economy's dependence upon the US market and the US military. The EC and Japan are now the only possible counterweights to total globalisation at the level of states.

Globalisation and Democracy

The issues of globalisation have an important implication for the meaning of democracy. The ideologues of globalisation are quick to identify democracy with the free market. There is, of course, very little historical justification for this identification. It derives almost exclusively from the coincidence of liberal parliamentary constitutionalism in Britain with the industrial revolution and the growth of a market economy. This obscured in a way the necessity of state force to establish and maintain the conditions for a workable market – a new kind of police force internally and sea power in the world market. It also ignored the fact that the other European states following the British lead in the nineteenth century, e.g. the French Second Empire, were not notably liberal in the political sense. In our own time, the case of Pinochet's Chile preconfigured the role of military-bureaucratic regimes in installing the bases for liberal economic policies. Ideological mystification has obscured the fact that a stronger case can probably be made for the pairing of political authoritarianism with market economics. It is perhaps worth reflecting upon this point when undertaking the task of constructing the socialist alternative for the future.

Since the crisis of the post-war order, democracy has been quietly redefined in the centres of world capitalism. The new definition is grounded in a revival of the nineteenth-century separation of economy and politics. Key aspects of economic management are therefore to be shielded from politics, that is to say, from popular pressures. This is achieved by confirmed practices, by treaty, by legislation, and by formal constitutional provisions.[10] By analogy to the constitutional limitations on royal authority called limited monarchy, the late twentieth-century redefinition of pluralist politics can be called 'limited democracy'.

One of the first indications of this development can now in retrospect be traced to the fiscal crisis of New York City in 1975. The 1960s saw the emergence of three strong popular movements in New York City: a middle-class reform movement, a black civil rights movement, and a movement to unionise city employees. Reformers captured the mayoralty with the support of blacks and subsequently had to come to terms with the unions in order to be able to govern effectively. The city could not pay through its own revenues for the new public services demanded by the coalition and for the wage and benefit settlements reached with the unions. It had to borrow from the banks. Without a subsidy that the state of New York was unwilling to provide, the city was unable to service and renew these loans. To avoid a bankruptcy that would have been detrimental to all the parties, from the bankers to the unions, the city was placed in a kind of trusteeship with members of the banking community in control of the city budget and administration. Retrenchment was directed at programmes with black clienteles and at labour costs. Blacks, who then lacked effective political organisation, were abandoned by the middle-class reformers who had mobilised them into city politics. Municipal unions were better organised, but vulnerable to their corporatist involvement with the city, and not likely to risk a bankruptcy that would threaten city employees' future incomes and pensions.[11]

This episode showed that (1) corporatism can provide a way out of a fiscal crisis provoked by the demands of new political groups, (2) this decision requires a restriction of decision power to elements acceptable to the financial market, (3) this, in turn, requires the political demobilisation or exclusion of elements likely to challenge that restriction, and (4) this solution is vulnerable to a remobilisation of the excluded elements.

During the same year 1975, three ideologues of the Trilateral Commission produced a report to the Commission that addressed the issue of the 'ungovernability' of democracies.[12] The thesis of the report was that a 'democratic surge' in the 1960s had increased demands on government for services, challenged and weakened governmental authority, and generated inflation. The Trilateral governments, and especially the United States, were suffering from an 'excess of democracy', the report argued; and this overloading of demands upon the state could only be abated by a degree of political demobilisation of those 'marginal' groups that were pressing new demands.[13]

The underlying ideology here propounded became expressed in a variety of measures intended to insulate economic policy making from popular pressures. Cynicism, depoliticisation, a sense of the inefficacy of political action, and a disdain for the political class are current in the old democracies.

Although the tendency towards limited democracy remains dominant, it has not gone unchallenged. Prime Minister Brian Mulroney of Canada sold the Free Trade Agreement with the United States in the oil-producing region of Alberta with the argument that it would forevermore prevent the introduction of a new national energy policy; but opposition to free trade, though defeated in the elections of 1988, did mobilise many social groups in Canada more effectively than ever before. In Europe, the 'democratic deficit' in the EC is at the centre of debate. Business interests are, on the whole, pleased with the existing bureaucratic framework of decision making, remote from democratic pressures – apart, of course, from the more paranoid hyper-liberals who see it as risking socialism through the back door. But advocates of the social charter and of more powers for the European parliament are sensitive to the long-term need for legitimation of a European form of capitalism.

One can question the long-term viability of the new limited or exclusionary democracies of peripheral capitalism. They must continue to administer an austerity that polarises rich and poor in the interests of external debt relationships. Very likely, they will be inclined to resort to renewed repression, or else face an explosion of popular pressures. Nowhere is this dramatic alternative more apparent than in the former Soviet empire. Whereas *glasnost* has been a resounding success, *perestroika* has been a disastrous failure. The race is between the constitution of pluralist regimes grounded in the emergence of a broadly inclusionary civil society, and new fascist-type populist authoritarianism.

The Changing Structure of World Politics

Out of the crisis of the post-war order, a new global political structure is emerging. The old Westphalian concept of a system of sovereign states is no longer an adequate way of conceptualising world politics.[14] Sovereignty is an ever looser concept. The old legal definitions conjuring visions of ultimate and fully autonomous power are no longer meaningful. Sovereignty has gained meaning as an affirmation of cultural identity and lost meaning as power over the economy. It means different things to different people.

The affirmation of a growing multitude of 'sovereignties' is accompanied by the phenomena of macro-regionalism and micro-regionalism. Three macro-regions are defining themselves respectively in a Europe centred on the EC, an east Asian sphere centred on Japan, and a North American sphere centred on the United States and looking to embrace Latin America. It is unlikely that these macro-regions will become autarkic economic blocs reminiscent of the world of the Great Depression. Firms based in each of the regions have too much involvement in the economies of the other regions for such exclusiveness to become the rule. Rather the macro-regions are political-economic frameworks for capital accumulation and for organising inter-regional competition for investment and shares of the world market. They also allow for the development through internal struggles of different forms of capitalism. Macro-regionalism is one facet of globalisation, one aspect of how a globalising world is being restructured.

These macro-regions are definable primarily in economic terms but they also have important political and cultural implications. The EC, for instance, poses a quandary for Switzerland whose business elites see their future economic welfare as linked to integration in the EC, but many of whose people, including many in the business elites, regret the loss of local control upon which Swiss democracy has been based. On the other hand, people in Catalonia, Lombardy and Scotland look to the EC as an assurance of greater future autonomy or independence in relation to the sovereign states of which they now form part. And there have been no more fervent advocates of North American free trade than the Quebec *indépendentistes*. Globalisation encourages macro-regionalism, which, in turn, encourages micro-regionalism.

For the relatively rich micro-regions, autonomy or independence means keeping more of their wealth for themselves. The *lega* in Lombardy would jealously guard northern wealth against redistribution to the south of Italy. Such motivations in other relatively wealthy regions are less overtly proclaimed. An institutionalised process of consultation (an incipient inter-micro-regional organisation) among the 'four motors' of Europe – Catalonia, Lombardy, Rhone-Alpes, and Baden-Würtemberg – has been joined by Ontario.

Micro-regionalism among the rich will have its counterpart surely among poorer micro-regions. Indeed, some of the richer micro-regions have, as a gesture of solidarity, 'adopted' poor micro-regions. Micro-regionalism in poor areas will be a means not only of affirming cultural identities but of claiming pay-offs at the macro-regional level for maintaining political stability and economic good behaviour. The issues of redistribution are thereby raised from the sovereign state level to the macro-regional level, while the manner in which redistributed wealth is used becomes decentralised to the micro-regional level.

At the base of the emerging structure of world order are social forces. The old social movements – trade unions and peasant movements – have suffered setbacks under the impact of globalisation; but the labour movement, in particular, has a background of experience in organisation and ideology that can still be a strength in shaping the future. If it were to confine itself to its traditional clientele of manual industrial workers, while production is being restructured on a world scale so as to diminish this traditional base of power, the labour movement would condemn itself to a steadily weakening influence. Its prospect for revival lies in committing its organisational and ideologically mobilising capability to the task of building a broader coalition of social forces.

New social movements, converging around specific sets of issues – environmentalism, feminism, and peace – have grown to a different extent in different parts of the world. More amorphous and vaguer movements – 'people power' and democratisation – are present wherever political structures are seen to be both repressive and fragile. These movements evoke particular identities – ethnic, nationalist, religious, gender. They exist within states but are transnational in essence. The indigenous peoples' movement affirms rights prior to the existing state system.

The newly affirmed identities have in a measure displaced class as the focus of social struggle; but like class, they derive their force from resentment against exploitation. There is a material basis for their protest, a material basis that is broader than the particular identities affirmed. Insofar as this common material basis remains obscured, the particular identities now reaffirmed can be manipulated into conflict one with another. The danger of authoritarian populism, or reborn fascism, is particularly great where political structures are crumbling and the material basis of resentment appears to be intractable. Democratisation and 'people power' can move to the right as well as to the left.

Openings for a Countertrend:
the clash of territorial and interdependence principles

The emerging world order thus appears as a multilevel structure. At the base are social forces. Whether they are self-conscious and articulated into what Gramsci called an historic bloc, or are depoliticised and manipulatable, is the key issue to the making of the future. The old state system is resolving itself into a complex of political-economic entities: micro-regions, traditional states, and macro-regions with institutions of greater or lesser functional scope and formal authority. World cities are the keyboards of the global economy. Rival transnational processes of ideological formation aim respectively at hegemony and counterhegemony. Institutions of concertation and coordination bridge the major states and macro-regions. Multilateral processes exist for conflict management, peace keeping, and regulation and service providing in a variety of functional areas (trade, communications, health, etc.). The whole picture resembles the multilevel order of medieval Europe more than the Westphalian model of a system of sovereign independent states that has heretofore been the paradigm of international relations.[15]

The multilevel image suggests the variety of levels at which intervention becomes possible, indeed necessary, for any strategy aiming at transformation into an alternative to global *perestroika*. It needs to be completed with a depiction of the inherent instability of this emerging structure. This instability arises from the dialectical relationship of two principles in the constitution of order: the principle of interdependence and the territorial principle.

The interdependence principle is non-territorial in essence, geared to competition in the world market, to global finance unconstrained by territorial boundaries, and to global production. It operates in accordance with the thought processes of what Susan Strange has called the 'business civilization'.[16] The territorial principle is state-based, grounded ultimately in military-political power.

Some authors have envisaged the rise of the interdependence principle as implying a corresponding decline of the territorial principle;[17] but the notion of a reciprocal interactive relationship of the two principles is closer to reality. The myth of the free market is that it is self-regulating. As Karl Polanyi demonstrated, it required the existence of military or police power for enforcement of market rules.[18] The fact that this force may rarely have to be applied helps to sustain the myth but does not dispense with the necessity of the force in reserve. Globalisation in the late twentieth century also depends upon the military-territorial power of an enforcer.

The counterpart today to nineteenth-century British sea power and Britain's ability through much of that century to manage the balance of power in Europe, is US ability to project military power on a world scale. The US world role in the period 1975–1991, however, contrasts markedly with its role in the period 1945–1960. In the earlier period, US hegemonic leadership provided the resources and the models to revive the economies of other non-communist industrial countries, allies and former enemies alike, and from the 1950s also to incorporate part of what came to be called the Third World into an expanding global economy. US practices in industrial organisation and productivity raising were emulated far and wide. The United States also led in the formation of international 'regimes' to regulate multilateral economic relations.[19] This post-war order was based upon a power structure in which the United States was dominant, but its dominance was expressed in universal principles of behaviour through which, though consistent with the dominant interests in US society, others also stood to gain something. In that sense the US role was hegemonic.

From the mid 1960s, the United States began to demand economic benefits from others as a quid pro quo for its military power. This mainly took the form of pressing other industrial countries to accept an unlimited flow of US dollars. General Charles de Gaulle was the first to blow the whistle, by converting French dollar reserves into gold and denouncing US practice as a ploy to have others finance an unwanted US war in Vietnam and aggressive US corporate takeovers and penetration into Europe. West Germany was initially more tractable than France, perceiving itself as more dependent upon the US military presence in Europe.[20]

By the 1980s, the rules of the Bretton Woods system, which had some potential for restraint on US policy, ceased to be operative. With Bretton Woods, one of the principal consensual 'regimes' failed. The link of the dollar to gold was severed in the summer of 1971, and from 1973 the exchange rates of the major world currencies were afloat. Management of the dollar became a matter of negotiation among the treasuries and central banks of the chief industrial powers, and in these negotiations US military power and its world role could not be a factor. Under the Reagan presidency, the build-up of US military strength contributed to growing budget deficits. A US trade deficit also appeared during the 1970s and continued to accumulate during this period. The US economy was consuming far in excess of its ability to pay and the difference was extracted from foreigners. The hegemonic system of the post-war period was becoming transformed into a tributary system. At the end of 1981, the United States was in a net world creditor position of $141 billion. By the end of 1987, the United States had become the world's biggest debtor nation to the tune of some $400 billion,[21] and the debt has continued to grow ever since. Japan became the chief financier of the US deficit.

There is a striking contrast between the US situation as the greatest debtor nation and that of other debtor nations. While the United States has been able to attract, cajole, or coerce other nations' political leaders, central bankers and corporate investors into accepting its IOUs, other countries become subject to the rigorous discipline imposed by the agencies of the world economy, notably the IMF. Under the euphemistic label of 'structural adjustment', other states are required to impose domestic austerity with the effect of raising unemployment and domestic prices which fall most heavily on the economically weaker segments of the population. Through the financial mechanism, these debtor states are constrained to play the role of instruments of the global economy, opening their national economies more fully to external pressures. By acquiescing, they contribute to undermining the territorial principle, i.e. the possibility of organising collective national self-defence against external economic forces. Any show of resistance designed to opt for an alternative developmental strategy can be countered by a series of measures beginning with a cut-off of credit, and progressing through political destabilisation, to culminate in covert and ultimately overt military attack.

The Gulf War revealed the structure and *modus operandi* of the new world order. The conflict began as a challenge from forces based on the territorial principle – Saddam Hussein's project to use regional territorial-military power to secure resources for Iraq's recovery from the Iran–Iraq war and for consolidation of a strong regional territorial power that could control resources (oil) required by the world economy, and thereby to extract from the world economy a rent that could be used to further his developmental and military ambitions. Kuwait, Saudi Arabia, and the other Gulf states are fully integrated into the interdependent world economy. Indeed, these states are more analogous to large holding companies than to territorial states. The revenues they derive from oil are invested by their rulers through transnational banks into debt and equities around the world. Within the territories of these countries, the workforce is multinational and highly vulnerable.

The United States responded to the perceived Iraqi threat in its role as guarantor and enforcer of the world economic order; and, consistent with that role, rallied support from other states concerned about the security of the global economy. The United States took on its own the decision to go to war, had it ratified by the United Nations Security Council, and demanded and obtained payment for the war from Japan, Germany, Saudi Arabia and Kuwait.

The role of enforcer is, however, beset by a contradiction. US projection of military power on the world scale has become more salient, monopolistic, and unilateral while the relative strength of US protective capacity has declined.[22] This rests upon the other contradiction already noted: that the United States consumes more than its own production can pay for because foreigners are ready to accept a flow of depreciating dollars. Part of the debt-causing US deficit is attributable to military expenditure (or military-related, i.e. payments to client states that provide military staging grounds like Egypt or the Philippines); and part is attributable to domestic payments (statutory entitlement payments, not to mention the savings and loan scandal bail-out) which by and large benefit the American middle and upper middle class.

Deficit and failing productivity result less from wilful policy than from a structural inability of the American political system to effect a change.

Domestic political resistance to cuts in the entitlement programmes is on a par with resistance to tax increases. American politicians will not confront their electors with the prospect of a necessary, even if modest, reduction in living standards to bring consumption (military and civilian) into balance with production. With no relief in the deficit, there can be no prospect of the United States undertaking the massive investment in human resources that would be needed in the long run to raise US productivity by enabling the marginalised quarter or third of the population to participate effectively in the economy. Only thus could the United States gradually move out of its dependence on foreign subsidies sustained by military power. All elements of the military/debt syndrome conspire to obstruct an American initiative to escape from it.

Structural obstacles to change exist also outside the United States, though perhaps not quite so obstinately. Those foreigners who hold US debt are increasingly locked in as the exchange rate of the dollar declines. They would suffer losses by shifting to other major currencies; and their best immediate prospect may be to exchange debt for equity by purchase of US assets. In the longer run, however, foreigners may weigh seriously the option of declining to finance the US deficit; and if this were to happen it would force the United States into a painful domestic readjustment. Indeed, it is probably the only thing that could precipitate such an adjustment.

There are, however, serious risks for the rest of the world in forcing the world's preeminent military power into such a painful course. They are the risks inherent in assessing self-restraint in the use of military power. Whether or not openly discussed, this has to be the salient issue for Japanese in thinking about their future relations with the United States and with the world.

The new world order of global *perestroika* is weak at the top. The next few years will likely make this weakness more manifest. There is a kind of utopian optimism abroad that sees the United Nations as coming to play its 'originally intended' role in the world. But the United Nations can only be the superstructure or the architectural facade of an underlying global structure of power. It could never sustain a breakdown of that structure, nor should it be asked to do so. The United Nations, for all its recent achievements in the realm of regional conflicts and in resolution of the hostage crisis, is probably today at greater risk than it was during the years of Cold War and North/South impasse when it was substantially sidelined. If the United Nations is to become strengthened as an institution of world order, it will have to be by constructing that order on surer foundations than those presently visible.

Terrains of Struggle for an Alternative World Order

Global *perestroika* penetrates the totality of structures constituting world order. It can only be effectively countered by a challenge at several levels, by a Gramscian war of position of probably long duration.

The basic level is the level of social forces. The globalising economy is polarising advantaged and disadvantaged, while it fragments the disadvantaged into distinct and often rival identities. The challenge here is to build a coherent coalition of opposition. Such a coalition must, most likely, be built at local and national levels among groups that are aware of their day to day coexistence, and are prepared to work to overcome what keeps them apart. Labour movements have an experience in organising capability and ideological work that can be used in this task, provided they are able to transcend narrow corporative thinking to comprehend the requirements of a broader based social movement.

A new discourse of global socialism that could become a persuasive alternative to the now dominant discourse of globalising capitalism remains to be created. It is the task of organic intellectuals of the countertendency not just to deconstruct the reigning concepts of competitiveness, structural adjustment, etc. but to offer alternative concepts that serve to construct a coherent alternative order. This goes beyond the strictly economic to include the political foundations of world order. An alternative future world order implies a new intersubjective understanding of the nature of world order and its basic entities and relationships.

Part of this intersubjectivity to be created will be an alternative model of consumption. Consumerism has been the driving force of capitalist *perestroika*, not only in the advanced capitalist societies but in the ex-Soviet east and in the Third World. Perhaps the greatest failure of 'real socialism' was it failure, in its fixation upon 'overtaking' capitalism, to generate alternative aspirations to those of capitalist consumerism. This paralleled real socialism's failure to envisage alternative ways of organising production to those of the hierarchical capitalist factory system. An alternative model of consumption would be one in balance with global ecology, which minimised energy and resources consumption and pollution, and maximised emancipatory and participatory opportunities for people.

The local basis for political and ideological action, while indispensible, will by itself alone be ineffective. Since the globalising tendency extends everywhere, the countertendency could be rather easily snuffed out if it were isolated in one or a few places. Many locally based social forces will have to build transnational arrangements for mutual support. The alternative to capitalist globalisation will need to build upon the productive forces created by capitalism by converting them to the service of society. The counterforce to capitalist globalisation will also be global, but it cannot be global all at once.

The macro-regional level offers a prospectively favourable terrain, most of all in Europe.[23] It is at the macro-regional level that the confrontation of rival forms of capitalism is taking place. Those who are looking beyond that phase of struggle have to be aware of the ideological space that is opened by this confrontation of hyper-liberal and state-capitalist or corporatist forms of capitalism. A similar kind of confrontation is developing between Japanese and American forms of capitalism. The long-term strategic view has to take account of opportunities in the medium-term encounter of forces.

Another major source of conflict lies in the rising power of Islamism (or what western journalists like to call Islamic fundamentalism). Islam, in this context, can be seen as a metaphor for the rejection of western capitalist penetration in many peripheral societies. Some of its aspects – the penal code, the place of women in society, the concept of *jihad* – are incomprehensible or abhorrent to western progressives. Yet Islam has superseded socialism as the force rallying the disadvantaged of much of the populations in North Africa, the Middle East, and parts of Asia. One of the more difficult challenges in building a global counterforce is for western 'progressives' to be able to come to terms on a basis of mutual comprehension with the progressive potential in contemporary Islam.[24]

The fragility of the existing global structure is felt particularly at two points: military and financial. These are the instruments of power that shape the behaviour of states today both structurally and instrumentally. They need to be more fully understood in their relationship to the goal of a future world social order.

On the military side, the struggle is bound to be asymmetrical against a concentrated monopoly of high technology military power. Strategies that rely upon a different kind of power will be required. Experience has been gained with relatively non-violent methods of opposition, e.g. the *intifada*.

Finally, rather more thought needs to be devoted to financial strategies that could be brought into play in the event of a global financial crisis. A financial crisis is the most likely way in which the existing world order could begin to collapse. A new financial mechanism would be needed to seize the initiative for transcending the liberal separation of economy from polity and for reembedding the economy in a society imbued with the principles of equity and solidarity.

NOTES

1. See e.g. Susan Strange, *States and Markets* (London: Pinter, 1988); Charles E. Lindblom, *Politics and Markets* (New York: Basic Books, 1977).
2. Charles Morazé, *Les bourgeois conquérants* (Paris: Armand Colin, 1957).
3. *Globe and Mail* (Toronto) 19 December 1991.
4. Peter Drucker, 'The changed world economy', *Foreign Affairs* 64(4) spring 1986, wrote: '[I]n the world economy of today, the 'real' economy of goods and services and the

'symbol' economy of money, credit, and capital are no longer bound tightly to each other; they are, indeed, moving further and further apart.' (p. 783)

5. Susan Strange, *Casino Capitalism* (Oxford: Basil Blackwell, 1986).

6. Bernadette Madeuf and Charles-Albert Michalet, 'A new approach to international economics', *International Social Science Journal* 30 (2) 1978.

7. The title of a forthcoming book edited by James Rosenau and E.-O. Czempiel (Cambridge University Press, 1992) which deals with many aspects of the problem of world order, although not explicitly with global finance. Susan Strange, *Casino Capitalism*, op. cit. (pp. 165–69) argues that effective regulation over finance is unlikely to be achieved through international organisation, and that only the US government, by intervening in the New York financial market, might be capable of global effectiveness. But, she adds, US governments have behaved unilaterally and irresponsibly in this matter and show no signs of modifying their behaviour.

8. There is a growing interest in the nature and processes of this *nébuleuse*. See, e.g. work of the University of Amsterdam political economy group, especially Kees van der Pijl, *The Making of an Atlantic Ruling Class* (London: Verso, 1984); Stephen Gill, *American Hegemony and the Trilateral Commission* (Cambridge: Cambridge University Press, 1990); and an unpublished dissertation at York University by André Drainville (1991).

9. See e.g. Michel Albert, *Capitalisme contre capitalisme* (Paris: Seuil, 1991).

10. Stephen Gill has referred to the 'new constitutionalism'. See his 'The emerging world order and European change: the political economy of European union' paper presented at the XVth World Congress of the International Political Science Association, Buenos Aires, Argentina, July 1991.

11. Martin Shefter, 'New York City's fiscal crisis: the politics of inflation and retrenchment' *The Public Interest* summer 1977.

12. Michel J. Crozier, Samuel P. Huntingdon, and Joji Watanuki, *The Crisis of Democracy. Report on the Governability of Democracies to the Trilateral Commission*. (New York: New York University Press, 1975.)

13. Ralf Dahrendorf, to his credit, criticised these findings in a plea 'to avoid the belief that a little more employment, a little less education, a little more deliberate discipline, and a little less freedom of expression would make the world a better place, in which it is possible to govern effectively.' (op. cit. p. 194).

14. International relations analysts use the term Westphalian to refer to an interstate system supposed to have come into existence in Europe after the Peace of Westphalia in 1648.

15. Hedley Bull, *The Anarchical Society* (New York: Columbia University Press, 1977) projected a 'new medievalism' as a likely form of future world order.

16. Susan Strange, 'The name of the game', in Nicholas X. Rizopoulos, ed. *Sea Changes: American Foreign Policy in a World Transformed* (New York: Council on Foreign Relations, 1990).

17. e.g. Richard Rosecrance, *The Rise of the Trading State* (New York: Basic Books, 1986).

18. Polanyi, *The Great Transformation* (Boston: Beacon Press, 1957).

19. 'Regime' is a word of art used by a currently fashionable school of international relations scholars, mostly American, to signify consensually agreed norms of behaviour in a particular sector of multilateral activity. See, e.g. Stephen Krasner, ed. *International Regimes*, special issue of *International Organization* 36 (2) spring 1982; and Robert O. Keohane, *After Hegemony* (Princeton: Princeton University Press, 1984).

20. David Calleo, *The Imperious Economy* (Cambridge, Mass.: Harvard University Press, 1982) pp. 51–60; and Michael Hudson, *Global Fracture. The New International Economic Order* (New York: Harper and Row, 1977) pp. 53–54.

21. Peter G. Peterson, 'The morning after' *Atlantic Monthly* October 1987.

22. It is not for me here to review the burgeoning literature debating the question of US 'decline'. Suffice to mention two contributions giving opposite views: Paul Kennedy, *The Rise and Fall of the Great Powers* (New York: Random House, 1987); and Joseph S. Nye, Jr. *Bound to Lead: The Changing Nature of American Power* (New York: Basic Books, 1990). There is very little disagreement on the basic facts: the decline of US productivity relative to European and Japanese productivity; and the extent of functional illiteracy and non-participation in economically productive work among the US population. The debate

is mainly between optimists and pessimists with respect to whether these conditions can be reversed. See Kennedy, 'Fin-de-siècle' America', *The New York Review of Books* June 28, 1990.

23. Björn Hettne, 'Europe in a world of regions', paper for the United Nations University/ Hungary Academy of Sciences conference on 'A New Europe in the Changing Global System', Velence, Hungary, September 1991.

24. An interesting work raising philosophical-ideological aspects of this problem is Yves Lacoste, *Ibn Khaldun. The Birth of History and the Past of the Third World* (London: Verso, 1984).

GLOBALISATION – TO WHAT END?*

Harry Magdoff

I

By the end of 1990, foreign direct investment – that is, investment in manufacturing, real estate, raw materials extraction, financial institutions, etc., made by capitalists of all lands outside their national borders – reached over $1.5 trillion. Actually, this official estimate grossly understates the case because it is based on book values. But even as a minimum estimate, what is significant about this number is not only its size but the unprecedented speed with which it has grown in the last two decades: the amount directly invested in foreign lands nearly tripled in the 1980s alone. Moreover, this investment went far beyond manufacturing and the extraction of raw materials. To an ever larger extent foreign capital spread to such fields as finance, real estate, insurance, advertising, and the media.

This upsurge and diversification of globalisation has been introducing new economic and political features in the countries of both the periphery and the core. In the periphery, foreign capital has penetrated more widely and deeply than ever before. In the core, the change of direction has helped produce in the world's key money markets an extraordinary spiralling of credit creation, international flows of money capital, and speculation.

This new stage of globalisation has meanwhile given rise to questions about its longer-run significance. A widely accepted theory visualises the erosion of national sovereignty at the centres of capitalism, presumably to be replaced by an 'international' of capital that will make and enforce the rules of international relations. The more thoughtful members of the ruling capitalist class are well aware how chimerical the notion of a rising international of capital is. It is true that in view of the growing complexity and the many pitfalls in the world of global finance, they seek ways to strengthen, or create new, international institutions which can help to minimise the potential chaos they face. But as much as the need is

---

* A shorter version of this essay has appeared in *Monthly Review*, February and March 1992.

understood in the abstract, and as many steps as have been taken in the hope of greater cooperation, there is no letup in the drive of nations to acquire more power and wealth. The upshot is that the speeded-up globalisation of recent years has not led to harmony. On the contrary, as we will try to show, it is itself a product of growing disharmony. Contrary to widespread expectations, sources of tension among the leading capitalist powers have increased side by side with their growing interdependence. Nor has the geographic spread of capital reduced the contradictions between the rich and poor nations. Although a handful of third-world countries, benefitting from the globalisation process, have made noteworthy progress in industrialisation and trade, the overall gap between core and periphery nations has kept on widening.

For the sake of perspective, it is worth recognising that the recent splurge in globalisation is part of an ongoing process with a long history. To begin with, capitalism was born in the process of creating a world market, and the long waves of growth in the core capitalist countries were associated with its centuries-long spread by conquest and economic penetration. In the past as in the present, competitive pressures, the incessant need for capital to keep on accumulating, and the advantages of controlling raw material sources have spurred business enterprise to reach beyond its national borders. The tempo and nature of expansion has of course varied over time, influenced by changes in political and economic conditions and the available technology for making war, transporting goods, and communicating.

While the expansion of capitalism has always presupposed and indeed required cooperation among its various national components – with respect to transportation facilities, weights and measures, monetary and credit arrangements, etc. – there never has been a time when these same national components ceased to struggle each for its own preferment and advantage. Centrifugal and centripetal forces have always coexisted at the very core of the capitalist process, with sometimes one and sometimes the other predominating. As a result, periods of peace and harmony have alternated with periods of discord and violence. Generally, the mechanism of this alternation involves both economic and military forms of struggle, with the strongest power emerging victorious and enforcing acquiescence on the losers. But uneven development soon takes over, and a period of renewed struggle for hegemony emerges.

The rise and decline of hegemonic powers

If we look back over the two centuries or so since the start of the industrial revolution, we find two periods which were clearly dominated by a hegemonic power: the British ascendancy in the middle of the nineteenth century and the US predominance in the middle of the twentieth. Interestingly enough, there were striking similarities in the rise and fall of both of these hegemonies.

Dating of historic eras is always somewhat arbitrary, but roughly speaking we can say that British hegemony lasted from the late 1840s to the early 1870s. Its rise was clearly associated with what was for that period an unprecedented boom, during which time Great Britain was by far the largest and strongest industrial and trading power. The military underpinning for its supremacy in foreign trade and colonial acquisitions was the unquestioned mastery of seapower. Lacking a sufficiently large army to control the continent, British rule was buttressed by a system of alliances designed to maintain a balance of power in Europe. The ideological backup came from the vigorous advocacy and promotion of the gold standard and the principles of free trade. The international gold standard, managed by the Bank of England, was in effect a sterling standard. As such, it was an important pillar of British economic superiority. And free trade clearly conferred an enormous advantage on the country with the most advanced manufacturing capacity.

The days of British glory, however, were numbered as the manufacturing capacity and exports of countries on the continent and the United States began to catch up. Although British predominance did not vanish overnight, its slide from the top was clearly marked as the Great Depression of 1873–1896 took its toll. Competition in foreign trade grew to the point where protectionism began to replace free trade. Intensified rivalry for additional economic and military space resulted in a mad scramble for colonies. The colonial powers acquired an average of some 240,000 square miles per year between the late 1870s and 1914, almost three times the average for the first 75 years of the nineteenth century. The German mark increasingly made inroads on the pound sterling's privileged role, threatening to unseat the London money market as regulator of the world financial system. Even Britain's naval preeminence declined in an accelerated arms race. Under these conditions, the traditional balance-of-power arrangements no longer served as a reliable guarantor of peace. And for three quarters of a century after the peak of Britain's hegemony world affairs were characterised by chaos and disharmony: two world wars, the Great Depression of the 1930s, abandonment of the gold standard, and the breakup of the international system into separate trading and currency blocs.

Eventually, however, a new international capitalist world order was once again built, this time out of the ashes of the Second World War. And again under the auspices of a hegemonic power – one with unquestionable primacy in arms, productive capacity, and finance, sufficient to whip the rest of the capitalist world into shape and run it. In place of the earlier gold standard, the US dollar was enshrined by the Bretton Woods Agreement

(1944) as the leading international currency, underpinned by Washington's undertaking to redeem dollars held by central bankers for gold. Sitting in the driver's seat, the United States promoted, as had the British, the ideology of the free market and free trade. International institutions were initiated and adapted to sustain a more or less unified imperialist network aimed at enlarging the scope of free trade, keeping reins on the former colonial world, and restraining by war or other means nations seeking to break out of the network. In military terms, American supremacy was maintained with an ever growing stockpile of nuclear bombs and military forces spread around the globe, especially surrounding the Soviet Union. Under these circumstances, the US foreign affairs agenda did not need balance-of-power diplomacy. Instead, it assumed the role of the world's policeman, expecting and when necessary insisting that allied powers and client states follow in lockstep.

US hegemony, like Britain's before it, lasted less than three decades. And similar to Britain's experience, this period was characterised by a major and unusual economic boom. Further, the hegemony withered when the boom petered out. By the late 1960s, the economic strength of other advanced capitalist nations (notably Germany and Japan) was rapidly catching up with and able to challenge US primacy in foreign trade and finance. Harmony among the leading nations was further disturbed because of the way the United States took advantage of the privileged position of the US dollar. An uncontrolled and enormous volume of dollars flowed into foreign lands to wage wars,[1] operate military bases, finance client states, and invest in foreign branches of multinational corporations, with total disregard for the promise the United States had made to back up the dollars abroad with gold. In effect, the United States in its financial as in its political and military affairs was telling the rest of the world to like it or lump it. But emerging rivals, acting either to demonstrate defiance or merely in self-defence, took up the challenge by converting masses of dollars to gold. With its gold supply rapidly shrinking, the United States eventually chose to renege unilaterally on its promise under the Bretton Woods Agreement, the linchpin of what was to have been a new era in financial harmony.

The end of dollar convertibility in 1971 was a watershed in the hegemonic role of the United States. Watersheds in history are of course rarely marked off precisely. The tension that led to Washington's closing the gold window started earlier in the 1960s. Nor was the downward slide after 1971 a precipitous one. The end of undisputed US hegemony did not mean the complete abolition of US rule, since military preeminence remained (and of course was further enhanced by the later breakup of the Soviet Union): US nuclear stockpiles, widespread military bases, and other military resources remain intact. And although American productive strength is relatively weaker than after the Second World War, it is nevertheless still very large. But things are definitely not what they used to be. The United States faces challenges from its allies, increasing limits on its financial ability, and the lessening freedom to dictate in foreign affairs. The features of the present economic and political disorder unfolded one after another in the past two decades: a spiralling inflation gripped the world economy in the 1970s; a third-world debt crisis erupted in the 1980s; foreign exchange rates fluctuated wildly; international money flows exploded to feed a growing mountain of debt and speculation.

The changing economic environment
The causal connections among these interrelated changes are not easy to sort out. But underneath it all is a common underlying phenomenon, namely, a generalised slowing down of the economies at the centre of the capitalist world. The pattern of this overall slowdown is shown in Table 1.

Table 1. Gross Domestic Product per Capita of the Industrialised Nations

Year	Dollars (at 1980 prices)	Average annual percent change	
1950	3,298	—	
1973	7,396	From 1950 to 1973	3.6%
1989	10,104	From 1973 to 1989	2.0%

Note: The dollar figures are in 1980 international dollars; that is, they are adjusted by World Bank technicians to eliminate exchange rate distortions. The countries included in the above: Australia, Austria, Belgium, Canada, Denmark, Finland, France, West Germany, Italy, Japan, Netherlands, Norway, Sweden, Switzerland, United Kingdom, and the United States. The dollar data are simple averages of GDP per capita. The percentages were calculated from the data in the World Bank Report.
Source: World Bank, *World Development Report 1991* (New York: Oxford University Press, 1991), p. 14.

As can be seen in the last column of the table, per capita Gross Domestic Product grew at an unusually high rate during the twenty-three years from 1950 to 1973. This, of course, is only an average, some countries began to slow down in the late 1960s, others later. The overall slowing down, however, was sharp and universal from 1973 to 1989. The change in average growth rate between the two periods – from 3.6 to 2.0 percent a year – amounts to a drop of 45 percent. Put another way, had the leading capitalist nations continued their earlier growth rate into the 70s and 80s, their average per capita product in 1989 would have been $13,000 (in 1980 dollars), or 30 percent higher than it actually was. We are of course talking about goods and services produced, not the income that workers and others receive. Still, the sizable decline in growth is a measure of lost potential of jobs as well as goods and services which, in addition to the .

wastage of war and armaments, are resources that under other circumstances could have been made available for socially useful purposes: homes, welfare, and environmental protection. In essence, what the significant decline in growth rates reveals is that the advanced capitalist world has been running out of steam. The special factors that stimulated a long wave of rapid growth in the 50s and 60s have lost much of their effectiveness, while new stimuli – e.g., computer and communication innovations – have proven to be insufficient to bring about full utilisation of available resources or to regain past growth rates. In the final analysis, the slowdown portrayed in Table 1 reflects a narrowing of profitable opportunities for capitalist investment.

This is demonstrated even more forcefully in Table 2, where we show the rates of change in industrial production over three decades in six leading industrialised nations. The information in Table 2 is in many ways more meaningful than the growth rates presented in Table 1. Gross domestic product is a catchall of diverse activities that is hard to measure reliably. The meaning of industrial production, on the other hand, is clear enough, its measurement has fewer pitfalls, and it is a key source of the surplus that could be available for the benefit of the rest of the economy. Here, too, we see that differences between countries can sometimes be startlingly large: note especially Japan's almost 16 percent average annual growth between 1960 and 1970 as compared with those of other countries. Nevertheless, except for the 1980s pickup in the United Kingdom after a serious drop in the 1970s, there is a marked consistency: *the growth of industrial production slows down from decade to decade* – in the relatively strong as well as in the relatively weak nations. It may be argued that the reason for this pattern is the severe recessions suffered in the early 1970s and 1980s. Actually, the direction of causation runs the other way. Deeper recessions are the product and not cause of weakness; they are indeed a distinguishing feature of stagnating economies.

Table 2. Industrial Production: Average Annual Percent Increase

	1960–70	1970–80	1980–90(a)
United States	4.9%	3.3%	2.6%
Japan	15.9	4.1	3.9
West Germany	5.2	2.3	1.8
France	6.0	3.0	1.0
Italy	7.3	3.3	1.3
United Kingdom	2.9	1.1	1.8

a) Except for the United States, the production data for 1990 are based on the first half of that year.
Source: Calculated from indexes in the *Economic Report of the President, 1986* and *Economic Report of the President, 1991*

The slowing down, which has now lasted for at least two decades, spurred capital to seek and create new profit opportunities. One consequence has been an upsurge of protectionism and the move toward bilateral agreements, such as the Canada–US and Mexico–US treaties, and long-range thinking in Washington about extending such arrangements to all of Latin America. No doubt for similar reasons, the continuing economic unification of Western Europe has met so much support in business circles there as well as concern by business elsewhere. Meanwhile, although lip service is often paid to the principle of free trade, ingenious ways are sought to create import barriers. Thus, the 1988 annual report of the Bank for International Settlements observed that 'so-called "grey-area" measures comprising voluntary export restraints, market-sharing arrangements and other non-tariff barriers designed to circumvent GATT rules continued to proliferate, bringing to an estimated 50 percent the share of world merchandise trade that is in effect "managed" in one way or another'. So much for the freedom of markets and the spirit of cooperation presumably developing among ruling classes of different nations in consonance with higher levels of globalisation.

The rising tide of foreign direct investment
As a matter of fact, it would be proper to conclude that one key measure of globalisation – the speeded-up flow of direct investment from one country to another – is itself a reaction to the stagnation described above. Capital needs no extra-special stimulus to seek out profit opportunities, and the export of capital has been a tool for growth over the ages. Still, any slowing down of economic growth intensifies the competitive drive in foreign as well as domestic markets. It should therefore come as no surprise to learn that there has been an unusually great leap in foreign investment in the 1980s. *The Economist* (December 22, 1990) highlighted what was happening: 'In the last three years of the 1980s, the flow of direct foreign investment measured in 1980 dollars was more than $100 billion a year, ten times as much as it had been in the first three years of the 1970s (again in 1980 dollars)'. The comparison made in a recent United Nations document (UN Centre on Transnational Corporations, *World Investment Report 1991*), with reference to the last seven years of the 1980s decade, illuminates the same point. Thus, between 1983 and 1989, the outflows of direct investment to other countries increased almost 29 percent a year, whereas world exports rose much more slowly at about 9 percent a year, and world domestic product even less.

Although the upsurge of foreign investment after the recession of the early 1980s was remarkably strong, its growing importance is not new. In fact, capital exports have helped shape the evolving global economy ever since the end of the Second World War. In the early postwar years the vanquished nations, of course, were not in the picture. They had too much to do on the domestic front and in any event lacked resources to send abroad. Except for such former large capital exporters as the United Kingdom and the Netherlands which could reinvest earnings from previous investments, other countries, also needing to get their postwar houses in order, were slow in getting back in the game. It was the vigorous expansion of the US multinationals in the 1950s, part and parcel of US's hegemonic role at the time, that led the way to the new stage of globalisation. By doing so, they created an environment in which giant corporations of all nations, driven by motives of self-defence as well as by their eagerness for new accumulation opportunities, had to turn multinational and widen their international base. By the end of the 1950s, foreign assets of US firms accounted for half of the world's direct foreign investment, comparable to the share held by Great Britain before the First World War. But when capital export became an important way of life for businesses of other lands, the relative status of the United States dropped. Table 3 tells the story. There we see the percentage distribution of foreign assets held by leading nations in each of the three years. Note that the data report only relative positions. The foreign holdings of each one of these countries kept on expanding throughout the period. But some increased their assets faster than others, and therefore their percentages rose. Thus, even though there was no lessening of interest by US capital in continuing to expand its

Table 3. Where Direct Foreign Investment Came From

Country of origin	1960	1973	1989
	—percent of total—		
United States	47.1	48.0	28.3
Canada	3.7	3.7	4.8
Europe	45.2	39.0	50.2
United Kingdom	18.3	13.0	16.7
Germany	1.2	5.6	9.1
Italy	1.6	1.5	3.8
France	6.1	4.2	5.3
Netherlands	10.3	7.5	6.1
Other Europe	7.7	7.2	9.3
Japan	0.7	4.9	11.5
All other	3.2	4.4	5.2
Total	100.0	100.0	100.0

Note: Here as in other tables in this article details may not add up to the totals because of rounding.

Source: International Trade Administration, US Department of Commerce. For 1960 and 1973 data, *Direct Investment Update: Trends in International Direct Investment*, Staff Report, September 1989; for 1989 data, *Trends in International Direct Investment*, Staff Paper No. 91–5, July 1991

overseas investments, the US share of the world's foreign direct assets declined from 47 percent in 1960 to 28 percent in 1989. What is especially significant is the speed with which Japan and Germany have been getting into the act. The percentage of the two combined went from 1.9 percent in 1960 to 20.6 percent in 1989 – or a rise of close to 19 percentage points.

The latest widespread and persistent rise in export of capital, it should be understood, was overwhelmingly due to an increased flow from industrialised nations to each other – between and among Western Europe, Japan and the United States. The urge to get established in Europe before the scheduled 1992 advanced unification of the European Economic Community has no doubt acted as an added spur in the last few years. But that is only part of the story, for contrary to popular impressions, a much greater share of foreign investment has always gone to industrialised rather than third-world nations.

The first wave of foreign investment after the Second World War concentrated on raw materials and other primary products. Apart from investments of this kind, capital flowed to the third world for manufacturing enterprises to profit from the exceptionally low wages and to take advantage of the demand generated by the local rich and middle classes. But the capital absorption power of many of these countries is strictly limited compared to that of the industrialised countries, where markets are far more opulent and diversified. The normal export route to these markets, however, is frequently blocked by the existence of local competitors enjoying special advantages: giant corporations with established trade structures, political and financial ties, and protective import barriers. These are among the major incentives for foreign multinationals to establish affiliates in such areas, and they have been continuously increased by pressures stemming from ongoing domestic stagnation and the speeding-up of the trend toward the creation of trade and currency blocs. The result

Table 4. Where Accumulated Foreign Direct Investment is Located

	1967	1973	1980	1989
	—percent distribution—			
Developed Countries	69.4	73.9	78.0	80.8
Underdeveloped countries	30.6	26.1	22.0	19.2
Total	100.0	100.0	100.0	100.0

Source: US Department of Commerce, International Trade Administration, *Trends in International Direct Investment*, Staff Paper No. 91–5, July 1991

of these changes shows up clearly in Table 4. Investment from abroad continues to flow to both areas, but the emphasis keeps on shifting. The accumulation of direct foreign investment located in the third world declined from 31 to 19 percent between 1967 and 1989, whereas cross investment among the advanced capitalist nations went up from 69 to 81 percent.

The changing composition of direct foreign investment

In discussions of foreign investment, attention has traditionally been focused on resource extraction and manufacturing, and this tends to obscure the fact that there has been an important shift to investment in services. New forms of economic interpenetration have occurred at various strategic levels – in finance and insurance, communications, advertising and the media, etc. Not all of this shows up on statistical summaries; sufficient details are not available as yet to get the full picture. But we have two tables – one on Japan and the other on the United States – which reveal aspects of this development.

The Japanese Ministry of Finance provides data on foreign investment, shown in Table 5. The data only start with 1951, but that has little bearing on comparability with data for other countries since Japanese foreign investment before that date was insignificant. Problems about comparability do arise because the statistics do not include assets obtained by reinvesting profits made abroad. On this ground and because of variations in industrial classification, the data for Japan and for the United States which will follow are not strictly comparable; but these differences, in our opinion, should not interfere with our present purpose, which is to get a general view of the increasing diversity of the globalisation process. Japanese firms did indeed invest beyond their borders in a wide assortment of manufacturing enterprises – mainly in electrical equipment, transportation equipment, machinery, chemicals, and steel. Nevertheless, their total assets in this area account for less than 30 percent of all overseas holdings. On the other hand, the amount invested in finance, insurance, and real estate exceeds that in manufactures. And if we add the percentage for commerce, we reach a total that is not far from half of the accumulated

Table 5. Japanese Direct Foreign Investment By Industry

	Total invested from 1951 to 1988	
	Billions of dollars	Percent of total
Manufacturing	49.8	26.7
Mining	13.9	7.5
Commerce	20.0	10.7
Finance and insurance	41.9	22.5
Real estate	20.6	11.1
All others	40.2	21.6
	186.4	100.0

Source: Japan External Trade Organisation, *Nippon 1990 Business Facts and Figures* (Tokyo, 1990)

Japanese investment overseas. This, we believe, is not an aberrational or unusual situation, but one that complements the slowdown of productive investment.

A similar picture appears when one examines the data for US foreign investment. There is an added feature to the information available for the United States, since the data in Table 6 enable us to observe a trend covering most of the post-Second World War period. What is significant is not only the changes but the timing of their occurrence. The fluctuations needed to be handled with care, for some of them are primarily statistical phenomena. Thus, the decline of investment in oil, due to the OPEC nationalisations of 1973–75, and the buying up of several countries of foreign-owned public utilities automatically affect the percentages in other areas. But this does not alter the fact that total US direct foreign investment grew at a rapid rate during the four decades covered in the chart. Hence, even when the figure for manufacturing remains at 40 percent between 1966 and 1990, the absolute amount sent abroad for such activity advanced significantly during those years. Furthermore, in many areas US firms as well as those of other countries extended their interests and profit-making in such fields as manufacturing, mining, and oil extraction without increasing their investments. This was done by licensing technology, contracting for research and development (often, as in oil, a major device for control), etc.

Table 6. US Direct Foreign Investment By Industry

	(percent distribution)		
	1950	1966	1990
Manufacturing	32	40	40
Petroleum	29	27	14
Wholesale Trade	5	7	10
Banking	(a)	(a)	5
Finance and Insurance	4	9	24
All other (b)	30	17	7
Total	100	100	100

Notes: (a) included in all other. (b) 'All other' includes mining, transportation, public utilities, retail trade, agriculture, and a variety of services. The importance of this sector decreased as US capital sold off public utility firms in Latin America.
Source: *Survey of Current Business*, February 1981 and June 1991.

Where attention needs to be focused in Table 6 is on the lines for banking and finance and insurance. There we observe an extraordinarily sharp rise after 1966, with investment in banking, finance, and insurance, reaching almost 30 percent of the total direct investment overseas in 1990. Even more striking is the fact that in 1990, as shown in Table 7, the amount invested in finance, insurance, and banking in the underdeveloped countries was $43 billion, almost one-third higher than in manufacturing. And it is equally noteworthy that US investment in the third world is more heavily weighted toward banking, finance, and insurance (40 percent) than it is in the industrialised countries (25 percent)! There are, however, two provisos that need to be considered in judging this comparison. First, the competitive struggle of the corporate giants is hottest in the developed world, which leads to a greater concentration there on manufacturing relative to finance. And second, a few third-world countries are convenient tax havens and hence are particularly attractive to financial capital. But even taking account of these factors, the emphasis on investment in financial institutions in the third world is impressive. It affords a clear indication of how far financial globalisation has in general spread and how deeply it has penetrated the daily economic life of the periphery.

Table 7. US Direct Foreign Investment in 1990

	Total	Developed countries	Under-developed countries
	—$ billions—		
All industries (a)	419.4	312.2	107.2
Manufacturing	168.2	134.7	33.6
Banking	21.4	11.0	10.4
Finance and Insurance	100.5	67.9	32.6
Petroleum	47.2	41.6	15.6
Wholesale trade	41.4	33.9	7.5
All others (b)	30.7	23.2	7.5
	—percent of total—		
All industries	100.0	100.0	100.0
Manufacturing	40.3	43.1	31.3
Banking	5.1	3.5	9.7
Finance and Insurance	23.7	21.7	30.4
Petroleum	13.7	13.3	14.6
Wholesale trade	9.9	10.9	7.0
All others (b)	7.3	7.4	7.0

(a) Does not include Netherlands Antilles and $3.6 billion of investment which cannot be properly distributed by country.
(b) Includes services, public utilities, transportation, construction, etc.
Source: *Survey of Current Business*, June 1991.

II

The globalisation of finance

The internationalisation of finance capital is a notably distinguishing attribute of the modern globalisation process. It is true that between the last quarter of the nineteenth century and the start of the First World War, European money markets, and most especially the City of London, experienced an unprecedented degree of internationalisation. But looking backward, one can see that international financial markets were then still only in their infancy. By the 1980s, under the impact of changing economic and political pressures, and assisted by new electronic and communication technology, a totally new stage of global finance had emerged – one with 'the freest-flowing and most sophisticated (that is, complicated) financial markets the world has ever known – Currencies, commodities, government and corporate bonds: all are now issued and traded around the clock and around the world'.[2]

An outstanding development of this most recent stage is the utterly new role of bank lending across national borders. In the past, such activity over and above 'normal' international business, was directed toward control and influence over other nations or to preparing for and conducting war. But taken as a whole, cross-country banking was a minor part of the world economy. For example, in the mid-1960s the volume of international banking equalled about one percent of the gross domestic product of the combined market economies of the world. But that percentage increased rapidly during the 1970s and 19870s. By the mid-1980s, the volume of international banking activity reached 20 percent of the GDP of the world's market economies. The comparison with world trade is even more striking. A normal function of international banking is to facilitate world trade, and as late as the mid-60s the volume of banking activity across national borders amounted to around 10 percent of the volume of world trade of the market economies. During the last two decades, however, the growth of cross-border banking swelled out of all proportion to the expansion of international trade: by the mid-1980s, the volume of cross-border lending by banks actually exceeded the volume of international trade of all the market economies combined.[3] Transcending its traditional role, global banking became the centre of a self-generating financial boom, spreading in ever-wider circles during the 1970s and 1980s. Not surprisingly, this ballooning of international banking was tied in with a host of new methods of financial speculation and manipulation.

At first sight it may seem paradoxical that the global financial boom coincided with a general economic slowdown and growing instability. But there is logic behind this paradox: actually the explosion of debt and speculation became an increasingly important prop for the faltering economies of the West. Government budgetary deficits, along with an upsurge of business and consumer debt shored up demand and helped sustain the production of goods and services. And as other sources of stimulus weakened, debt became an increasingly important part of the economy. Meanwhile, the financial operators, scurrying from one country to another for funds, became increasingly addicted to speculation.

Money markets grew in size and diversity to accommodate the skyrocketing demand for debt. New financial instruments were introduced which widened the base of the credit system and at the same time opened wide the gates to speculation. For example, financial futures markets (where wagers are made on what interest rates will be at a later date) emerged in the early 1970s, beginning in the United States, spreading next to London and Sydney, and then to Tokyo, Paris, and Frankfurt. Although only an infant in swaddling clothes at the start of the 1970s, the financial futures market is now one of the giants of international finance. At the start of 1990, open interest positions (the value of the contracts traded on these markets) totalled $1.2 trillion worldwide. An even faster increase took place in what are known as interest and currency swaps. This financial novelty consists of exchanges between two parties who possess interest-bearing securities or future-currency contracts, the purpose being to hedge and/or seek additional profit. Explaining the mechanics of these manipulations would take us too far afield: the reason we mention them at all is simply to illustrate how rapidly new instruments balloon in international financial markets. Swaps were almost unknown before 1980; by 1991 there were $2.5 trillion worth of such contracts outstanding in global financial markets. These data are from a Morgan Guaranty Trust Company publication, which also contains the following relevant observation:

> The [economic and financial instability of the 1970s] engendered government deficits and external imbalances that required financing on a scale unprecedented in peacetime and that exceeded the capacity or willingness of the traditionally fragmented financial markets to cover. These financing needs joined with advances in technology and communications to spawn a host of innovations, ranging from securitisation in place of intermediated bank credit to new derivative instruments, including swaps. Taken together, these financial innovations have helped overwhelm traditional and regulatory segmentation of national markets and thereby have contributed much to the effective integration of financial markets globally.[4]

In sum, on a national as well as on an international scale, the financial sectors of the advanced capitalist countries took on a life of their own. They prospered from the expansion and the accelerated circulation of the economic surplus. The expansion was achieved artificially by inflation of commodity and service prices and of asset values. And that in turn enforced a redistribution of wealth from the lower-income classes to the wealthy, in particular the elite of world finance.

For the financial boom to continue on a global scale, a sufficient supply of internationally acceptable money was of course necessary. Where did it come from? The answer is that in the beginning it came from the flood of

US dollars poured out on the world by Washington, American multinationals, and US financial institutions during the period of unchallenged US hegemony when the dollar enjoyed the good-as-gold status conferred on it by the Bretton Woods accords. It might have been thought – in fact many people did think – that when Nixon took the dollar off gold in 1971 this cosy (for the United States) arrangement would come to an end. But it didn't. By the time dollar accumulations abroad, especially in the coffers of central banks where they constituted the bulk of reserves underpinning most of the world's currencies, had grown so large that no country could afford to do anything that might threaten the dollar's value. The result was that after 1971, as before, the United States continued to pour out dollars and foreigners continued to accept them. Between 1969 and 1977 the number of dollars owned outside the United States multiplied by a factor of 4.5 and has continued to grow ever since.

The collapse of Bretton Woods thus set the core countries of the capitalist world economy on a road that soon led to an inflationary burst of liquidity and a different kind of havoc. It is true that for a short period after the end of dollar convertibility, the top-dog countries sought to find a new route to stable foreign exchange rates, which were seen as essential to the normalisation of the world economy. But a meaningful agreement was hard to come by, given the conflicting interests of the powers and a reluctance to submit to continued US domination. By March of 1973 they gave in to the inevitable and moved to floating exchange rates, thereby opening the floodgate to rampant speculation in foreign exchange markets. The blame for the disorder of the 1970s and the accompanying inflationary spiral is generally attributed to OPEC, but in reality the causal connection runs in the opposite direction: the large rise in the price of oil can more reasonably be traced to the instability in international economic relations and the inflationary pressures that emerged in the aftermath of the end of dollar convertibility. Professor Robert Triffin's comments on this period are particularly relevant:

> World import and export prices, measured in dollars, rose by less than one percent a year in the 1960s, but by more than six percent a year from 1970 through 1972, and by as much as 30 percent in the last 12 months before the explosion of oil prices in the fall of 1973. This was not unconnected, to say the least, with the enormous and mounting US deficits abroad which flooded the world monetary system, doubling world reserves from the end of 1969 to the end of 1972 . . . i.e., increasing them by as much in this short span of three years as in all previous centuries in recorded history.[5]

The disarray has continued to this day, with new twists. The price inflation of the 70s and early 80s shifted from goods and services to the value of assets (real estate, art objects, stocks, financial instruments). This was part and parcel of the growing importance of the financial superstructure throughout the advanced capitalist world:

> [World trade in goods and services] amount to around $2.5 trillion to $3 trillion a year. But the London Eurodollar market, in which the world's financial institutions borrow and lend

to each other, turns over $300 billion each working day, or $75 trillion a year, a volume at least 25 times that of world trade.

In addition, there are foreign exchange transactions in the world's main money centres, in which one currency is traded against another. These run around $150 billion a day, or about $35 trillion a year, 12 times the worldwide trade in goods and services.

Of course, many of these Eurodollars, yen, and Swiss francs are just being moved from one pocket to another and may be counted more than once. A massive discrepancy still exists, and there is only one conclusion: capital movements unconnected to trade – and indeed largely independent of it – greatly exceed trade finance.[6]

So much for the sheer magnitude of the burgeoning financial superstructure. Hardly less impressive is its instability, a concept easier to understand than to measure. Among many possible indicators, perhaps the most comprehensive is the record of exchange-rate fluctuations among the world's major currencies. The ideal of exchange-rate stability remains a subject of discussion among theorists who dream of a day when governments will cooperate voluntarily in harmonious fashion. But the reality is one of extreme and unrelenting volatility. Charts I and II are vivid illustrations of this point. From 1970 to 1978 the number of marks needed to buy one dollar fell 40 percent. As can be seen in Chart I, the roller coaster continues to this day. The mark/dollar ratio fell another 15 percent from 1978 to 1980 and then rose back to its old high by the first quarter of 1985. Between then and the first quarter of 1987 it began a major slide – this time falling by 50 percent, and has continued to move up and down since then. The rate of exchange between the yen and the dollar (Chart II) showed even more volatility between 1978 and 1985, had the same fast 50 percent fall between the first quarter of 1985 and early 1988, and has followed the yo-yo path ever since.

These charts clearly depict a financial world in disarray, surely not an orderly, let alone integrated, global system. According to the economics textbooks, reflecting today's worldwide ruling ideology, free markets are self-adjusting. Fluctuations in exchange rates and international capital flows are supposed to be caused primarily, if not exclusively, by alterations in the balance of imports and exports. When imbalances are large and more than of very short duration, they are presumably automatically brought into balance by mild self-corrective changes in exchange rates and/or capital flows. Instead, what we have these days are enormous capital movements that receive little guidance from Adam Smith's invisible hand. Speculation on a grand scale (trading in currencies are a major source of profits for many of the world's largest banks); government interventions in currency markets in an (often vain) attempt to put a lid on extreme fluctuations; and changing domestic interest rates in competition for money capital – these are among the leading factors that contribute to the substantial swings in capital movements between countries and the volatility of exchange rates.

Chart I. German Marks per US Dollar   Marks per dollar

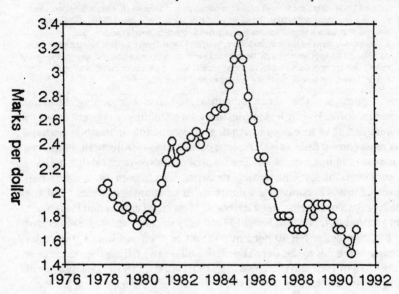

Chart II. Japanese Yen per US Dollar   Japanese Yen

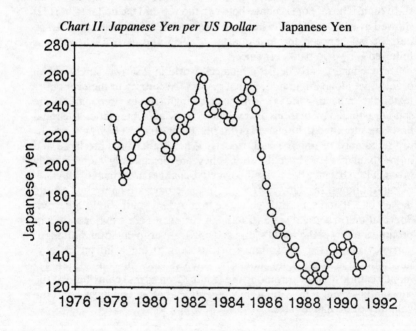

The disorder that developed in step with the decline of US hegemony is also reflected in the rising role of the German mark and Japanese yen as international currencies. As discussed earlier, a critical aspect of America's rule in the first couple of decades after the Second World War was the role of the dollar as the key international currency. What has been happening on that score shows up in the changes of official holdings of foreign exchange, as shown in Table 8. Each country needs to keep reserves either in gold or internationally accepted foreign currencies in order to settle imbalances generated by trade and other international transactions. In essence, the data in this table reveal a drift of the world economy to a multicurrency monetary system. Although the US dollar so far remains the major reserve currency for international transactions, its prominence has been dropping rather sharply. As late as 1975, the member countries of the IMF still kept almost 80 percent of their foreign exchange reserves in US dollars. By 1989, that percent had dropped to 60 percent. As was shown above with respect to the shifts in foreign direct investment, the decline in the dollar as a reserve currency was matched by the growing importance of Germany and Japan.

Table 8. Share of National Currencies in Holdings of Foreign Exchange by Central Banks or Treasury Departments

	1975	1983	1989
	—percent distribution—		
US Dollar	79.4	71.4	60.2
Pound sterling	3.9	2.5	2.7
German mark	6.3	11.8	19.3
Japanese yen	0.5	5.1	7.9
All other	9.9	9.3	9.9
Total	100.0	100.0	100.0

Source: International Monetary Fund, *Annual Report*, various issues.

The volume of Germany's merchandise exports is now roughly equal to that of the United States. In addition, Germany has been assuming a leading role in the European Monetary System. An important measure of a currency's international role is its use in exchange-market intervention by central banks. In this respect, the mark has been rapidly growing in influence. Thus, in 1979–82, US dollars accounted for approximately 72 percent of the money used by central banks to intervene in the European Monetary System, while 24 percent of the interventions were then made with German marks. In 1986–87, on the other hand, the dollar role fell to 26 percent, while that of the mark rose to 59 percent.[7]

The information in Table 8 also reflects the internationalisation of the yen, its use as a reserve currency rising from one-half of one percent in 1975 to 8 percent in 1989. The rise is noteworthy, but hardly reflects Japan's growth as a world banker. Japan is in fact still playing a modest role compared to the United States and Germany. Germany's relative importance, as noted, has been enhanced by the lead it has taken in the European Community.

In Asia no formal alignment of countries comparable to the European Community has as yet emerged, but it is significant that the yen's role as a reserve currency is much higher there than on the world scale (18 percent of official holdings of reserve currencies by selected Asian countries). 'The yen's emergence as an essential component of the international monetary system,' states a recent study, 'is directly related to its role as a key currency within Asia'.[8]

The drift toward the polarisation of three key currencies coincides with tendencies toward the emergence of clusters of nations in which each one of the three major capitalist powers is especially prominent. But before entering on that topic we need to examine where and how the third world fits into the global system.

III

The third world in the global system
Despite the striking transformations in the world capitalist system since the end of the Second World War, two major distinguishing features of the third world did not change in general, and in a fundamental sense, the chains of dependency binding the periphery to the centre remain. Secondly, the gap between the periphery and the centre, as throughout the history of capitalism, keeps on widening. The evidence for the most recent period is presented in Table 9, where the gross domestic product (GDP) per capita of the third world is compared with that of the advanced capitalist countries. What stands out clearly is that with only one exception the gap between the two keeps on getting wider – in prosperous as well as in stagnating periods. As shown in the first line of the table, in 1960 the per capita GDP of the underdeveloped countries combined was only 8.7 percent of that of the industrialised nations. But even that abysmally small percentage fell during the prosperous 1960s (to 7.4 percent), and then still further (to 6.1 percent) during the stagnating years from 1970 to 1987 (the latest year for which complete data are available at the time of writing).

This trend was true not only for the third world as a whole, but for practically every region, in the better-off as well as the poorer areas. Although the trend is clearly pronounced for the whole period shown in the table, there were some departures from the trend in interim years for particular countries, brought about by short-term changes in terms of trade and most dramatically by the OPEC price boosts in the 1970s. But, except for the Middle East, the improvement in the relative standing of other oil producers was of brief duration. Before long they were back in the widening-gap rut along with the non-oil producers. The one exception, as noted above, was the Middle Eastern oil producers whose relative position improved significantly between 1970 and 1987.

Table 9. Gap Between Developed and Underdeveloped Market Economies

	Gross Domestic Product Per Capita: Underdeveloped Countries as a Percent of Developed Countries		
	1960	1970	1987
All Underdeveloped Market Economies	8.7%	7.4%	6.1%
Africa (a)	6.9	5.6	3.5
Latin America (b)	22.2	17.9	12.5
Oil Producers	31.3	26.3	12.0
Others	20.0	15.3	12.7
Asia-Middle East	16.7	14.9	19.6
Oil Producers	18.9	16.7	27.8
Others	15.2	13.5	11.8
Asia-East and Southeast	5.3	4.5	3.8

(a) South Africa not included.
(b) Includes Caribbean region.
Source: Calculated from (a) 1960 data-United Nations, *Yearbook of National Account Statistics, 1974*, Vol. III, and (b) United Nations, *National Accounts Statistics: Analysis of Main Aggregates*, 1987.

The story for the rest of the third world is clear enough. During the decades of intensified globalisation and the increasing dominance of market economies, the per capita GDP of Africa (other than South Africa) as a percent of the per capita GDP of the core countries was half of what it had been in 1960, and the relative standing in 1987 of even the more favoured countries of Latin America was only three-fifths of what it had been in 1960.

An examination of the table shows that the gap did not widen as much in east and southeast Asia as in the other major third-world regions. And the reason for this is the progress made in China. According to the World Bank's *World Development Report 1991*, China, with 40 percent of the region's population, had a per capita growth rate of 5.7 percent between 1965 and 1989, which compares with much lower rates for other large countries in the region, for example, India's 1.8 percent and Pakistan's 2.5 percent. The 'four tigers' (South Korea, Taiwan, Singapore, and Hong Kong) experienced higher annual rates than did China (6 to 7 percent during the same period). But their impact on the last line in Table 9 is minor, because their combined population is less than 3 percent of the entire region.

As the foregoing makes clear, there can be no doubt about the reality of the widening gap between the living standards of the core capitalist countries and those of the underdeveloped countries of the periphery. At first sight, however, this may seem strange. After all, the post-Second World War period was, by historical standards, one of rapid and sustained capitalist expansion, and it was characterised by a new worldwide awareness of the deeply rooted disparities which existed between the rich countries and what came, precisely in this period, to be called the third world. The colonial peoples had been awakened by the Russian and Chinese revolutions and were struggling for their own freedom and a chance to develop their economies. The Communist countries and their supporters elsewhere were singing siren songs, and the imperialists were responding with their own promises based on the supposedly scientific discoveries of a new discipline called 'development economics'. The governments of the industrialised countries set ambitious targets for foreign aid and joined with their less fortunate third-world 'partners' to push through the United Nations resolutions and programmes looking to the elimination of evils inherited from an unenlightened past. While all this was going on, was it really possible that the gap between the rich and poor countries was widening? And if that was indeed so, how could it be explained?

Well, it was so, and the explanation, while not simple, is certainly no mystery. The truth is that a system built on inequality in the command of human and natural resources works in many ways not only to reproduce itself but to increase the extent of the in-built inequality. The mechanisms of this process vary in different communities ranging from the local through the national to the global. At a global level, the most important can be encompassed under three headings: foreign investment, money lending, and international trade. These are matters of urgent concern to governments, central banks, and various international agencies (IMF, World Bank, UN), with the result that comprehensive statistics are gathered and published which enable us to observe and quantify some of the critically important aspects of the relationship that exists between the core and the periphery. In what follows, we focus on the first two. To use a favourite expression of the late Paul Baran, that is where the dog is buried in this age of burgeoning globalisation.

A bare outline of the main facts to which we want to call attention is presented in Table 10. Balance-of-payment statistics, on which this table is based, summarise a country's foreign transactions. They are generally constructed in two parts. The first is called the balance on current accounts. This covers the day-to-day economic transactions between nations – primarily imports and exports of goods and services, transfer of money between individuals (for example workers with jobs in foreign lands sending money back to the family), and payments connected with investments (such as profits, royalties, and interest on borrowed money). The second part of the balance of payments deals with capital transactions – investments and loans.

Now in the normal course of events, when a country is faced with a deficit in its current account (when what it owes for goods and services bought abroad exceeds money earned there), it has to come up with funds to settle the balance. Few can do what the United States is able to do, which is to pay with their own currency. (Eventually, a persistent current-account deficit can create serious trouble even for a country as rich as the United States. If the rest of the world resists the acceptance of more US dollars, the likelihood is that the international value of the dollar will fall precipitously and create havoc in financial markets.) If those in the periphery do not have enough gold or foreign currency in reserve, they have to get hold of 'hard' money – in other words, universally accepted currency. For that reason, a deficit country can only cope with its deficit by borrowing abroad or attracting foreign capital.

Let us now look at Table 10, which presents a combined current-account balance of payments for third world countries other than South Korea, Taiwan, Singapore, Hong Kong, and major oil producers. The first line of the table summarises the balance of all day-to-day payments to and receipts from abroad – except for payments to foreign corporations and banks (including the World Bank and IMF). Note that in each one of the last five years, the balance was positive, more was received than was paid

Table 10. Selected Underdeveloped Countries: Current-Account Balance of Payments (a)

	1986	1987	1988	1989	1990
	\-billions of dollars\-				
Balance of payments on all current transactions except net payments abroad of interest, dividends, and fees to foreigners	+5.8	+14.9	+16.8	+12.4	+18.9
Net payments of interest, dividends and fees to foreigners	−41.0	−41.8	−46.1	−49.5	−50.3
Current-account balance of payments	−35.2	−26.9	−29.3	−37.1	−31.4

(a) Total of all underdeveloped countries except South Korea, Taiwan, Hong Kong, Singapore and countries whose exports of fuel are more than 50 percent of all their exports.

Source: Calculated from data in Bank for International Settlements, *61st Annual Report* (Basle, 10 June 1991)

out. Now let us move to line 2, which records the profits, royalties, and fees sent to the home offices of multinational corporations, interest on debt to foreign bankers, bondholders, the IMF, and the World Bank. There we find not just negative numbers (money flowing out) but ones that far exceed the surpluses shown in line 1.

If there aren't enough foreign-exchange reserves in the treasury to cover shortfalls, the affected nations must borrow still more or attract additional foreign investment. This in turn will make the negative numbers in line 2 still larger in subsequent years. If this continues, a critical point is eventually reached when the deficit burdens become unmanageable, as occurred in the 1980s debt crisis. The IMF and the World Bank then come forward as rescuers – rescuers not only of the borrowing countries but also of the lending banks whose profits and stability depend on their loans continuing to be serviced. As the crisis evolves, international lenders become more restrictive in their lending and more heavy-handed in the restraints imposed on the borrowers. Loans are made on condition that borrowers adopt policies aimed at forcing larger positive balances between exports and imports (line 1). What these policies mean in practice is usually fewer social benefits, a squeeze on wages, and a drastic reduction of imports. But since a large proportion of imports is needed for domestic production, the import cutback affects largely goods needed to meet the people's basic needs. The result of these restraints, compounded by sharp declines in prices of many primary products exported by the third world, is a severe decline of income during the 1980s in Latin America and Africa, where some of the heaviest borrowing from abroad took place. In the case of Latin American countries, the *physical* volume of exports increased substantially but the *money* received did not because of the drop in prices. At the same time, the cost of imports increased – the terms of trade (ratio of export prices to import prices) went against them just when they desperately needed improvement. For the third world as a whole the terms of trade fell 16 percent between 1980 and 1988.

To cope with the crisis, private and public lenders continue lending to indebted countries just to make it possible for the latter to continue servicing past debt. But the infernal logic of debt servitude has its way, as shown in Table 11. The data, as reported in the 1990 *Annual Report of the World Bank*, summarise the debt situation in the 111 countries that report to the World Bank. The first column shows the actual amounts of long-term debt disbursed each year in the 1980s by private and public lenders. Although lending continued, in order to prevent a wholesale collapse of banks in the main capital markets, the emphasis turned more and more to disciplining the borrowers, chiefly through the agency of the IMF. As the amount of new money lent declined from year to year (column 1), any benefits of the new funds to the borrowers kept on diminishing. The reason is the fast growth of the funds needed each year to pay principal and interest on the accumulated debt (column 2). The key column is, of course, the fifth. As the new debt issued went down and the debt servicing went up, by 1984 and thereafter more money went out of the periphery every year than came in.

Table 11. Long Term Debt: Amount Issued to Borrowers vs. Amount Repaid ($ billions)

Year	New Debt issued	Repayments for Debt Service			Net Received by Borrowers [col. 1–col. 2]
		Total	Principal	Interest	
	(1)	(2)	(3)	(4)	(5)
1980	106.4	75.8	43.7	32.1	30.6
1981	123.4	86.9	46.2	40.7	36.5
1982	116.4	96.2	48.3	57.9	20.2
1983	95.3	90.8	44.0	46.8	4.5
1984	90.8	100.7	47.8	52.9	−9.9
1985	87.6	107.3	53.1	54.2	−19.7
1986	88.4	112.1	59.7	52.4	−23.7
1987	88.3	122.5	68.9	53.6	−34.2
1988	95.7	133.3	72.9	60.4	−37.6
1989	86.9	129.8	70.3	59.5	−42.9

Note: The data are for 111 indebted countries in the World Bank's reporting system. Column 1 represents the loans made each year by public and private lenders to the reporting countries. Column 2 presents the total payments by these borrowers for interest and repayment of principal on their total debt accumulation.

Source: *The World Bank Annual Report 1990*, p. 32.

With debt as with foreign investment by the multinationals, while the foreign funds might be used for developing productive resources, the net result, in the short as in the long run, is (1) a transfer of economic surplus from the underdeveloped countries to the centres of capital, and (2) an entrenchment of dependent ties from the weaker to the stronger nations. Thus the third world as a whole remains what it has been throughout the history of capitalism, the locus for capital accumulation and profit-making by giant corporations and financial institutions of the advanced capitalist nations.

The export solution
According to the conventional wisdom, there is a way out for the third world if only its economies were further oriented to exports – in other words, become further tied to the global economy. But in reality, as noted above, international trade is one of the main mechanisms for perpetuating

the gap between the core and periphery. Moreover, the globalisation process has resulted in even greater dominance of foreign trade by the giant multinationals. The dominance takes various forms, ranging from the crudest type of exploitation to the 'normal' operations of the free market's invisible hand.

An instructive illustration of the former was recently provided in a World Bank research report, which contained a study of the prices paid by former colonies in Africa for imports of iron and steel products between 1962 and 1987. It turned out that 'for the full 26-year period, the [prices they paid for standard products] *always* exceeded those of developed market economy countries'. It is estimated that the consequent losses by ex-French colonies in Africa during the period studied 'exceeds the long-term debt of 12 of the former colonies in 1987 and approximately equals the combined debt ($2.2 billion) of Burkina Faso, the Central African Republic, Chad, and Mauritius'. Sales by Britain, Belgium, and Portugal to former African colonies exhibited similar patterns of overpricing.[9]

This and other types of unequal exchange have not been alleviated by increased globalisation. Nor has the growth of the multinationals improved traditional areas of third world exports of raw materials. It is true that in the early decades after the Second World War, both the demand for and prices of many raw materials grew substantially. But it has been the other way around since the onset of stagnation in the world economy. A weighted index of commodity prices (other than energy) records a drop of more than 50 percent between the early 1970s and 1990. At the same time the demand for many commodities has also been declining, because of improved efficiency in the manufacturing process as well as increased use of substitutes (plastics, ceramics, optical fibre). These changes, on top of the customary wide fluctuations in demand and prices, demonstrate once again the unreliability of primary products as a trustworthy source of growth, let alone stability.

The popular answer to this dead end has been to follow in the footsteps of the four 'tigers'. They provide the inspiration and the romance of what might be possible. Usually South Korea is picked as the ideal model for escape from underdevelopment. Echoes of this theme are heard with greater frequency these days also in Beijing, Warsaw, and Moscow. The engine of growth and escape from the debt trap, according to this line of reasoning, is to be found in a major expansion of exports of manufactured goods.

Leaving aside what the Korean model has meant for the health and welfare of the Korean people, it is clear that its achievement of an impressively high growth rate was tied in with the ability to produce and find export markets for steel, machinery, autos, and other manufactured products. And, indeed, South Korea's exports of manufactured goods per capita has started to resemble that of the industrialised countries. Even though its $1,364 manufactured exports per capita in 1989 is well below that of Germany, France, England, and Japan, it belongs in that league, far removed from the typical third world country. Thus Korea's per capita level of manufactured exports is 100 times larger than India's; 50 times Pakistan's; and over ten times Mexico's and Brazil's, two countries who have looked to export of manufactures as their engine of growth. The question therefore arises, if South Korea did it, why not every other underdeveloped country?

Table 12. Third World Exports as a Percent of World Exports of Manufactured Goods

	1966	1982	1986
All underdeveloped countries	11.2%	13.3%	13.8%
Latin America	3.7	3.0	2.9
Brazil	0.9	1.3	1.2
Mexico	0.4	0.3	0.6
Other L.A. countries	2.4	1.3	1.1
Africa	2.4	0.9	0.7
Asia–Middle East	0.3	0.8	0.7
Asia–East and Southeast	4.1	8.4	9.3
Hong Kong	0.7	1.2	1.3
Korea, Republic of	0.1	1.9	2.2
Singapore	0.4	1.1	1.0
Taiwan	0.3	1.9	2.6
Other	0.7	0.2	0.2
Underdeveloped countries, excluding the 4 Asian countries or territories	9.6	7.3	6.8

Source: Magnus Blomström, *Transnational Corporations and Manufacturing Exports from Developing Countries* (New York: United Nations, 1990), p. 11.

An examination of Table 12 will help to get some perspective for an answer to this question. The data show the share of world exports of manufactured goods sold by the third world. Asia (other than the Middle East) clearly had phenomenal success along these lines – more than doubling its share from 4.1 percent in 1966 to 9.3 in 1986. That obviously was entirely due to the performance by the four 'tigers'. Apart from these four, Mexico and Brazil showed a degree of improvement. But when you look at the picture as a whole, the result is far from impressive. In the twenty years covered by Table 12, the underdeveloped countries' share of the world's exports of manufactured products rose by 2.6 percentage points, from 11.2 percent in 1966 to 13.8 percent in 1986. Why then so little, in fact insignificant, change in face of the great leap in Asia? The answer shows up in the bottom line. Other than the four countries or territories in Asia, the periphery's share of world trade in manufactures *fell by almost a third between 1966 and 1986*. We would have to go too far afield at this time if we were to examine all the aspects of both the very slow growth of the third world's share of manufactured goods exports and, within the third world, the shift to the Pacific. The overall picture is nonetheless significant in bringing down to earth the idle illusions about the windows of opportunity for the third world in the process of globalisation, especially in view of the experience revealed in the above table and considering the extent to which the giant multinational corporations narrow the trade channels for independent rivals. Moreover, competition is bound to intensify, and government-imposed trade barriers to spread, in times of general economic slowdown. Clearly, obstacles do not mean that all doors are tightly shut. There is no reason why here and there some export markets will not be penetrable by some countries. What facts and history show, however, are that degrees of freedom are very much restricted.

The issue of limits to the third world becoming a more or less independent participant in the globalisation process arises in full force in considering the question raised above, why can't all other third world countries do what Korea did? For that we propose a simple numbers exercise. Let us assume that the rest of the underdeveloped countries were able to carry out the Korean model – that is, attain South Korea's level of $1,365 exports of manufactured goods per capita. (Korea's ratio is by far the lowest of all four tigers.) The population of the rest of the third world is over 4 billion. Hence, if we can let our imagination go, and assume that the 4 billion could successfully export at the same ratio as South Korea, they would need to sell abroad $5.5 trillion of manufactures. But the entire world trade in manufactures these days is less than half that amount, about $2.1 trillion. To whom would the extra $5.5 trillion be sold? Where are there markets for such an enormous leap in business, or anything conceivably near that number? Let us consider once more the data in Table 12. With all the energetic expansion of manufactured exports from 1966 to 1986 by the four 'tigers' and other newly industrialising countries like Brazil and Mexico, all that the underdeveloped nations were able to latch on to was below 15 percent of the world total. In 1989, the most recent year for which such data are available, the third world's share of the $2.1 trillion foreign trade of manufactured goods was no more than 13 percent.

There is an instructive paradox in Korea's and Taiwan's ability to industrialise and penetrate the privileged trade preserves of the industrial countries. (We are omitting the city-states of Hong Kong and Singapore from this discussion because their history and structure make them especially exceptional.) For their start was made during a hiatus in direct foreign investment and other economic ties – in other words when their ties to the imperialist network of investment and trade were at a minimum:

For the twenty years between the end of World War II and the mid-1960s, transnational corporations were virtually absent from the scene. Japanese investments were confiscated at the end of World War II and did not reappear as an important factor until the mid-sixties. Nor were US companies important actors during this period. North American transnationals were busy taking over the fledgling consumer durables industries of Brazil and Mexico, dominating them through tightly concentrated sets of oligopolistic, wholly owned subsidiaries; but they showed little comparable interest in East Asia. Not only were Taiwan and South Korea small and poor, they had no history as previous markets for US markets and little familiarity with the consumer durables on which import-substituting industrialisation was based in Latin America. Even more important, previously successful Communist armies sitting just north of the thirty-eighth parallel and just the other side of the Formosa straits made Taiwan and South Korea very unattractive investment sites to political risk analysts.

In the early 1960s, their colonial trade patterns disrupted by the Japanese defeat, South Korea and Taiwan embarked on what Bruce Cummings calls 'remarkably similar import-substitutions programs' in which key industries were 'protected by and nurtured behind a wall of tariffs, overvalued exchange rates, and other obstacles to foreign entry'. This early period of withdrawal from international markets was critical to the construction of an industrial base in both countries. Nor was the tendency to ignore the apparent logic of the international market simply a passing phase.[10]

There are undoubtedly other factors that distinguish the experience of Korea and Taiwan. But it would be hard to underestimate the importance of the loose links to the imperialist centre in the early days of their industrialisation, and the later offsetting pressures of the two powers in the Pacific, the United States and Japan. The situation today is obviously very different from the early postwar years. Accelerated globalisation in the midst of stagnation stimulates the industrial powers to seek even closer ties with third world countries, which serve as assets in the search for a higher rung in the hierarchical ladder.

IV

The road to trade, investment, and currency blocs

The competition for privileged positions leads to the formation of blocs and clusters of weaker nations centred on one or more of the major powers. These formations are still in an early stage of development, but the tendencies in that direction are becoming increasingly clearer. It is therefore not surprising that several recent UN publications have called attention to these developments. Reports by UNCTAD and GATT discussed the development of tripolar trade blocks and trade centres. The UN Centre on Transnational Corporations added to the title of its most recent report (*World Investment Report 1991*): 'The Triad in Foreign Direct Investment'. The Triad refers to the three main economic poles in international economic and financial relations – the European Community, Japan, and the United States. The European Community as a whole is treated as a pole in view of the vast amount of cross investment that has taken place within the community. The question of the European Community having its own internal pole in Germany is not discussed.

The Transnational Centre study concentrates on the clusters connected with global flows of foreign direct investment, but also takes note of the connections between the latter and trade and currency groupings. We discussed earlier the growing international role of the German mark and the Japanese yen. With respect to currency blocs, this report focuses on the dollar bloc:

> Over the past two decades, developing countries appear to be moving towards a system in which their currencies appear to be linked, more or less closely, with currencies of major home regions, depending upon the strength of their trade, investment and financial relationships. Thus, a dollar bloc appears to exist, composed largely of countries in Latin America and the Caribbean, along with a few other countries, such as some oil-exporting countries whose ties to the dollar are undoubtedly due to the fact that the world price of oil is quoted in dollars. In most cases, those countries operate a managed float versus the dollar, or a float tied to economic indicators which are themselves linked to the dollar.[11]

The Latin American dollar bloc is of course a product of the history of US penetration of Latin America. Although European and Japanese business firms are also active here, the United States remains the dominant foreign investor and trader in a number of Central and South American countries. At present, Mexico is the magnet for US investment in Latin America, and is likely to become even more so if the US/Mexico free trade is put into effect. Establishment long-term planners visualise the formation of a US–Canada–Mexico free-trade bloc that will evolve into one for all the Americas, while some already speculate about the dollar becoming the currency of the entire area.

As is well known, relations among the powers are shifting in the Asian Pacific. Although the US military machine is firmly planted in the Asian Pacific, accompanied by an extensive presence in the political and economic affairs of that area, America's status is not what it once was. It remains the major investor and economic influence in its former colony, the Philippines, and is a prominent influence in the political and economic affairs of other countries in that region as well. Its role, however, is being eroded by the active rise of Japanese influence in the region. Japan is now the top trading partner with South Korea, Singapore Malaysia, and Indonesia. It is the dominant foreign investor in South Korea and Indonesia and since the mid 80s appears to be fast approaching that status in Thailand and Hong Kong. Moreover, as pointed out in a study for the US Congress (Congressional Research Service, *Japan's Expanding Role and Influence in the Asia-Pacific Region*, September 7, 1990):

> Although Japan's role as an exporter of manufactured goods and an importer of primary products from Asia-Pacific countries is long-standing, its post-1985 emergence as the leading source of capital and technology, and as a growing market for manufactured goods, has made Japan the 'core economy' and financial nerve centre of the region.

A seemingly coordinated policy is discernible behind these changes, one that includes foreign aid, firm trade ties, foreign loans and investments, and the shifting of manufacturing operations to low-wage countries. According to *The Economist* (July 15, 1989), the underlying strategy is aimed at integrating the 'four tigers' and those aiming to join the ranks of the 'tigers' (Thailand and Malaysia) 'into something that would look a lot like a greater Japan Inc.' The same article describes The New Asian Industries Development Plan, sponsored by the Japanese Ministry of International Trade and Industry (MITI) and a related ASEAN-Japan Development Fund as 'at the cutting edge of Japan's initiative to organise the industrial integration of East and Southeast Asia'.

The third cluster of currency, trade, and investment is of course centred on the European Community. For the most part these are ties that were generated in former European colonial possessions in Africa and Asia. But new windows of opportunity have arisen for the EC in Central and Eastern Europe. Since 1985, EC members are the dominant foreign investors in Yugoslavia, Czechoslovakia, Hungary, and Russia. The strategic outlook for the European Community – an outlook that has deep historical roots, especially in the case of Germany – is the creation of a periphery in Central and Eastern Europe, resembling the regional networks of investment, finance, and trade being built by Japan in Asia and the United States in the American continents.

None of this should be interpreted to mean that the major powers have any intention of withdrawing from the world scene. Quite the contrary. The United States, to be sure, wants to see the entire globe as its domain. And while Germany and Japan do not have the military might to stalk the world, they are major players in the global arena of trade, finance, and investment. Things may change if and when firm trade and investment walls are erected around the several regions. But in the absence of such sharp separation, competitive economic struggles will no doubt continue on a global scale. In the absence of the kind of breakdown as occurred in the 1930s, it is reasonable to expect a continuation of the tension between globalisation, on the one hand, and furtherance of blocs, on the other. The latter serve both offensive and defensive strategies. They can be assets in the struggle for a position at the top of the hierarchy of nations. Apart from that, ties with peripheral dependencies can be especially useful to core countries in times of stagnation, financial turbulence, and potential major crises. It should come as no surprise that when domestic economies lose steam and internal problems accumulate, the stronger nations turn more energetically to external expansion for relief.

The pressure toward expansion necessarily produces political as well as economic strains among nations, as is evident in the thrust by major powers for greater independence from the United States. Note, for example, the following dispatch in the *Wall Street Journal*:

Across a wide range of issues, from trade to foreign aid to interest rates, the US and Europe increasingly find themselves at odds. And the Europeans, confident in the strength of a unified European economy and freed from the Soviet threat, are less willing than ever to bend to US pressure.

Listen, for instance, to German Chancellor Helmut Kohl speaking to a group of business students in Switzerland. 'Europe's return to its original unity means that the 90s will be the decade of Europe, not Japan', he said in a recent 45-minute speech, which made only one brief reference to the US. 'This is what we've all dreamed about. This is Europe's hour'. (July 15, 1991).

This is of course largely bravado. The unified Europe Kohl anticipates is still in a process of formation. There are stumbling blocks along the way which may prevent its realization. Nevertheless, what is interesting here is that these remarks are not out of harmony with the aspirations and long-run strategies of the German ruling class, which, judging from history, are firmly rooted. In recent times, that strategy shows up in Germany's assumption of the leadership role in Western Europe, its thrust towards Central and Eastern Europe, as well as a widening of the distance from the United States. Its regional economic predominance can be seen in the central role of the mark in the European currency unit and in the nature of the negotiations for further unification of Western Europe's currency system. As for the moves towards growing assertiveness, the most recent example at the time of writing was the way Germany pressured the European Community to recognise the independence of Croatia and Slovenia, to which the United States and the UN acceded in order to avoid a clash with Bonn.

Japan too has been moving decisively in the direction of greater independence. During the first decades after the Second World War, Japan operated under the US umbrella. Beginning in the 1970s, Japan has been increasingly moving away from its earlier subservience to the United States in diplomatic matters, advancing its own political as well as economic interests in the region, even when they conflict with those of the United States.

Although history does not repeat itself in precise fashion, it is worth noting that these centrifugal tendencies echo similar developments that emerged (a) between the Great Depression of the nineteenth century and the First World War, and (b) between the Great Depression of the 1930s and the Second World War. Carrying such analogies too far and in mechanical fashion can be misleading. Nevertheless, they merit attention, because the resemblances are not mere accidents. Rather, they arise from similar economic and political forces.

The process of globalisation has produced much that is new in the world's economy and politics, but it has not changed the basic ways capitalism operates. Nor has it aided the cause of either peace or prosperity.

NOTES

1. It is little recognised how significant the wars were to Japan and Germany in jump-starting their economies during the Korean War and strengthening their upswings during the Vietnam War. The influence of the Korean War on the Japanese takeoff was especially noteworthy, as summarised in an interesting recent book: 'Just two months after . . . the Korean tinderbox burst into flames . . . as the only nearby industrialised nation with adequate manufacturing capacity, Japan's underemployed factories and work force benefited enormously from Korea's misfortune between 1950 and 1955, first as suppliers of war materials and services for United Nations and after the July 1953 armistice, as suppliers of materials needed for the reconstruction of South Korea. Former Economic Planning Agency official Tatsuro Uchino estimates that special procurement, broadly defined, during the period pumped between $2.4 and $3.6 billion into the capital-starved Japanese economy and accounted for an amazing 60 to 70 percent of all of Japan's exports. Also significant for Japan's postwar economic development, this unanticipated expansion of demand was strongest in industries such as textiles, steel products, and automotive equipment, the very sectors that would lead Japan's export drive during the 1950s and the 1960s.' (Robert C. Angel, *Explaining Economic Policy Failure, Japan in the 1969–1971 International Monetary Crisis*, New York: Columbia University Press, 1991.)
2. *The Economist*, April 27, 1991.
3. Ralph C. Bryant, *International Financial Intermediation*, Washington D.C., The Brookings Institution, 1987, p. 22.
4. Morgan Guaranty Trust Company, *World Financial Markets*, April 1991.
5. 'The International Role and Fate of the Dollar', *Foreign Affairs*, Winter 1978/79, pp. 270–1.
6. Peter F. Drucker, 'The Changed World Economy', *Foreign Affairs*, Spring 1986.
7. George S. Tavlas, *On the International Use of Currencies: The Case of the Deutsche Mark*, Princeton University Essays in International Finance, March 1991.
8. George S. Tavlas and Yuzuru Dzeki, 'The Internationalization of the Yen', *Finance and Development*, IMF, June 1991.
9. Alexander J. Yeats, 'African Countries Pay More For Imports', *Finance and Development*, IMF, June 1990.
10. Peter Evans, 'Class, State, and Dependence in East Asia: Lessons for Latin Americanists'. This significant essay appears along with other informative and thoughtful essays in Frederic C. Deyo, ed., *The Political Economy of the New Asian Industrialism* (Ithaca: Cornell University Press, 1987).
11. United Nations Centre on Transnational Corporations, *World Investment Report 1991*, p. 79.

GLOBAL BUT LEADERLESS?
THE NEW CAPITALIST ORDER[1]

Andrew Glyn and Bob Sutcliffe

Globalization and hegemony

It has become very common in the history of socialist political economy to see capitalism as a system in the process of becoming progressively more internationalized or, in a more trendy term, globalized. Marx, in particular, saw capitalism as having a constant tendency to expand without limit and become the world's first worldwide economic system. And this was an aspect of capitalism which to many socialists at the start of the century indicated the ripeness of the system for revolution since in theory socialism was conceived of in almost exclusively international terms. Today there is again a very widespread belief that capitalism has recently and rather suddenly become much more globalized. In an age, however, where socialism, if it is conceived at all, is conceived in much more national terms, this is often seen less as a precursor of the system's demise and more as a source of difficulty in controlling or transforming it.

The globalization of capitalism could mean one of two things. In the first place it can refer to the spread of capitalist relations of production. In this sense the last 40 years period has seen the continuation and probably the acceleration of a very long term trend towards the extension of capitalism. There have been a number of sharp changes. The postwar incorporation of women into the paid labour force on a large scale in some industrialized countries has meant a partial transfer of labour from non-capitalist household relations to capitalist relations. There has since the start of the 1980s been a wave of denationalizations which represent a shift from state capitalism to a more pure market-regulated capitalism. And finally since 1989 there has been the overthrow of 'actually existing socialism' and its replacement with capitalist relations.

The disruptions caused by this latter process bear some relationship to the process described by Marx as primary accumulation which ushered in the industrial capitalist system. In that case a 'free' labour force was created by the destruction of the feudal rights of peasants on the land and thus to a means of livelihood which was not dependent on market forces. Workers in Eastern Europe and the USSR had similarly 'feudal' rights to

76

employment relatively independently of the market value of what they produced. They are now losing those rights in a new large scale creation of a 'free' labour force in the formerly socialist countries.

In the Third World more people have been separated from pre-capitalist rights than have been absorbed into new employment under capitalist relations. In fact the failure of that employment to appear has led to the emergence on a large scale of petty commodity production (the so-called informal sector). Nonetheless, all in all as far as this first meaning of globalization is concerned, capitalism has become more globalized, in some respects in a quite dramatic sense, in recent years. Not only in absolute numbers but also relative to the population, more people today than at any time in history work under classically capitalist relations (i.e. they live off profits or interest or they sell their labour power to a capitalist institution which produces a marketed commodity).

The second possible meaning of globalization refers to an increase in the international interdependence of the world economic system. Some major form of interdependence has clearly existed for centuries. The origins of modern capitalist accumulation in the 18th century, as has often been analysed, were based on a world economy in which industrial production in Western Europe, the slave trade from Africa and slave plantations in the Americas were interdependent. And thereafter successful accumulation in the industrial countries was closely related to economic transformation, and often deterioration, in the Third World. Nowadays when the Third World, as we shall see, plays a diminished role in the world economy, interdependence is more often interpreted as referring to the different advanced capitalist countries.

The implicit definition of globalization defined as interdependence is composed of various elements, including the following:

–national economies are increasingly interlinked, the health of one being considered to be conditional on the health of the others. Consequently economic fluctuations have become more coordinated among the major economic powers. This might be called macroeconomic unification since it represents the idea that the world is now really a single economy in the macroeconomic sense. That means that the main determinants of income and employment can now only be understood at a global and no longer a national level. A corollary of this idea is that the national state retains very little power of macroeconomic management because the major economic variables are strongly influenced by macroeconomic trends and policies elsewhere.

–the patterns of production and consumption in the world are increasingly interdependent. The international division of labour has changed in a way that each nation or region now depends more and more on others for its supplies of goods and for markets for its own products.

–markets are more integrated in a more general sense: the market for goods and services, the market for capital and financial instruments and the market for labour are characterized by high levels of exchange and few obstacles.

–a more microeconomic definition based not on the national economy but on the firm. In this sense the world economy is regarded as dramatically more global because corporations are dramatically more global. There are two aspects to this: one is that corporations are more global in the location of their assets or their markets or in their personnel and management and so are less rooted in any one nation state; the other is that they operate a more global division of labour within the firm by locating different parts of their manufacturing processes in different countries.

Globalization is one of the criteria by which the condition of the world economy can be characterized at a particular historical moment. There are, of course, others. And of these one of the most important is the extent to which any nation exercises hegemony over the rest. Hegemony here means the domination of the system by one country resulting from its inordinate economic weight or the ability to impose certain rules of economic behaviour on the rest of the world which produces for the hegemonic nation exceptional international power or exceptional advantages or both.

During the last two hundred years the fundamental nature of the world economy has changed on several occasions in respect both of its degree of globalization and also of the extent to which one nation is hegemonic. Just as there is a widespread belief that it has recently become unprecedently global, so there is also a matching belief that it is undergoing a major shift of hegemony, concretely that the period of US hegemony is coming to an end.

The purpose of this article is to evaluate these two beliefs. In order to do so it is useful to characterize the state of the system at any moment along these two dimensions: globalization and hegemony. First, how 'open' is the system, in terms of the importance of trade and capital flows, and thus how closely are individual countries tied to one another and disciplined by forces operating at the international level? Second, to what extent is there a hegemonic power which can enforce certain rules of the international economic game?

Such a dual characterization generates in principle four polar cases. Hegemonic systems, with relatively open or closed economies; leaderless ones with relatively open or closed economies. Very schematically, the gold standard represented a hegemonic system (UK dominance) but with market forces imposing discipline on relatively open economies, the centre of gravity being represented by the policies and performance of the UK. The 1920s and 1930s represented a non-hegemonic system with relatively closed economies pursuing independent policies.[2] In the 1950s and 1960s the USA was the hegemonic power presiding over relatively closed economies and with discipline exerted through IMF and other non-market channels of US power as well as through markets. Finally the decline of US domination left the world economy leaderless in the 1970s and 1980s with increasingly open economies disciplined by market forces, but without a unique centre of gravity.

The world economy has now experienced all of the four possible options under this schema. Now, therefore, the alternatives are for the present pattern to continue or for the system to revert to a previous one, or at least a variant of a previous one. This would involve either the evolution of a new leader (or conceivably a coherent leadership group) or a reversal of the trend towards openness or both.

Degrees of openness

(a) *Trade*

It is a commonplace of analyses of the long-boom of the 1950s and 1960s that trade was an engine of growth, and indeed the volume of trade grew one and a half times as fast as production. Since 1973 the discrepancy has been less, but trade growth has still been one third faster than output growth.[3] The result has been to increase export shares of GDP, implying that an increasing proportion of production is for international markets. This in turn increases the roles played by the expansion of those markets and individual countries' competitiveness within them. Since one country's exports are another's imports, increased penetration of domestic markets is implied (in the four big European economies imports of manufactures took around 30% of domestic markets by the mid-1980s). Such competition within the domestic market reinforces the impact through exports of the country's *relative* competitiveness on its *absolute* performance.

It is important to keep this rise in export shares in historical perspective. Figure 1 presents figures for export shares of the OECD countries taken as a whole, of Latin America, of Asia and of the USSR. The increase in the share of exports in GDP for the OECD countries during the 1950s and 1960s conforms to expectations. The rise was slower after 1973 and, most strikingly, even by the late 1980s exports had not regained the share of GDP achieved before World War I. For Latin America the export share was far lower throughout the whole post-war period; in both Asia and the USSR the post-war increases left the shares at low levels, hardly exceeding those of 1913. The second part of the figure shows the evolution of export shares for the main blocs of OECD countries. Even within Europe, where the thrust towards trade liberalization was strongest, export shares by the end of the 1980s were only a little above those of 1913. So the relatively rapid expansion of OECD trade after 1950 represented a reversal of the

Export Shares 1913–87
Merchandise Exports % of GDP

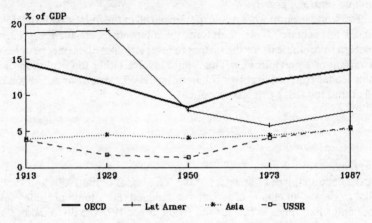

Export Shares: ACCs 1913–87
Exports as % GDP, current prices

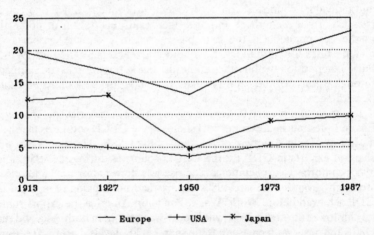

Source: calculated from Maddison, A. *Dynamic Forces in Capitalist Development,* op cit table F7. Maddison, A. *The World Economy in the Twentieth Century,* op cit tables A2, D4.
Note: for Latin America, Asia (excludes Japan) and USSR data is at constant prices, all averages are weighted by GDP.

introversion of the world of the previous 40 years, rather than a move towards a qualitatively new level of internationalization.[4]

This data excludes trade in services, but since exports of services amounted to a little less than 4% of GDP in 1989 (as compared to 14.5% for goods), they do not greatly affect trends. Indeed the rising importance of services, which are traded only to a very limited extent, is a major reason for the rather slow growth of export shares since the 1970s. Within manufacturing an increasing proportion of market shares are met by imports. But the impact of this on trade shares was muted by the decline in the importance of manufacturing in GDP – for the OECD as a whole this fell by one fifth during the period 1960–67 to 1980–89 (29.3% to 23.1%). During the same period the services sector, which only accounted for one sixth of world trade, increased its share of GDP from 53.8% to 62.6%.[5] Another factor limiting further increases in trade shares has been that the process of tariff reduction which helped boost trade has been practically exhausted. By 1980 industrial countries tariffs averaged less than 10% (down from some 25% in 1950), and by 1990 were around 5%. Moreover 'non-tariff barriers' such as the Voluntary Export Restraints which limit Japanese car exports into Europe and USA have risen in importance (by 1986 covering 18% of industrial country trade).[6] The OECD noted that only Australia, Japan, New Zealand and Turkey amongst its 24 members 'ended the 1980s with trade regimes that were more liberal than at the beginning'.[7] And one market is characterized by high and universal protectionism – that for agricultural goods. The rise in agricultural trade is not the result of opening markets but of managed trade, especially from North America to the USSR and China.

The basic conclusions are that, whilst the post-war period has seen a rapid increase in trade shares for the ACCs (advanced capitalist countries), (a) the increase has broadly returned these economies back to the position before the First World War; (b) it does not apply outside the ACCs; (c) if intra-European trade is excluded and Europe is regarded as one unit, then trade shares for the main blocs of ACCs, let alone Asia and the ex-USSR, are extremely small (Europe's total commodity trade was 22.9% of GDP, but extra-European trade only 6.5%); and (d) further increases are limited by the rising importance of services (even in the absence of more intense protectionism).

An evaluation of the interrelation between the various trading blocks depends on the direction of trade as well as its overall amount. The importance of various trading areas in 1989 for each other is shown in Table 1 below. Japan is the most important trading partner for no other trading area and second most important only for the Asian bloc. Intra-bloc trade is overwhelmingly important for Western Europe and very important for N. America (if Mexico were included to reflect its role in the Free Trade Area intra-trade would be even more dominant). For the less developed areas N. America is overwhelmingly important for Latin America, and most important for Asia;[8] Europe is overwhelmingly important for Africa, the Middle East and Eastern Europe. Japan's exports to developing areas are concentrated in Asia, N. America's in Asia and Latin America whilst Europe has a much broader spread. Comparison with 1979 suggests the increasing importance of the N. American market for Japan and for the rest of Asia; elsewhere both Latin America and Africa seem to have been increasing their concentration of trade (with N. America and Europe respectively). Intra-trade (eg trade within Europe), as a percentage of trade with all advanced countries, has become a little less important for both Europe and N. America.[9] All the blocs of advanced countries show strongly increased proportions of trade with each other (Japan being the most spectacular case with its share of trade with ACCs rising from 41% to 57%, one important influence being the fall in oil prices). The Middle East and to a lesser extent Africa and the Eastern block have declined in importance amongst less developed markets, whilst Asia has increased vastly in significance.

(b)*Capital flows*
Even if the story of openness to trade is more complex than might be imagined, surely capital flows show unprecedently increased internationalization. A valuable paper by Robert Zevin demonstrates that in fact the position is rather similar to that in trade. There have of course been major increases since the 1960s in international flows and thus the integration of national financial markets. But the starting point was the very closed post-1945 economy, with strong controls on movements of capital; and it is difficult to support the claim that the financial markets now are qualitatively more internationalized than before World War I. Zevin's discussion of co-movement between interest rates and share prices in different national financial markets before World War I 'confirm the high degree of international capital market integration . . . for the gold standard era . . . data on international assets and liabilities relative to domestic assets and income tell a similar story: higher in the nineteenth century than today, highest by far in the gold standard era . . . measures [proportions of foreign securities traded on national markets] of transnational securities trading and ownership are substantially greater in the years before the First World War than they are at present. More generally, every available descriptor of financial markets in the late nineteenth and early twentieth centuries suggests that they were more fully integrated than they were before or have been since'.[10]

The one aspect of capital flows not discussed in the above account is possibly the most important for overall integration of the world economy. Gross flows of financial investment (eg UK purchases of US equities and US banks lending to UK firms) make owners of financial assets less

Table 1: Patterns of trade, 1989

% of area's trade with	Trading Area							
	N. America	W. Europe	Japan	Lat. America	SE Asia	Mid. East	Africa	East Bloc
Advanced capitalist countries	**69**	**84**	**57**	**71**	**63**	**63**	**74**	**32**
of which:								
North America	45	10	58	62	40	21	17	13
Western Europe	31	85	32	30	27	53	76	70
Japan	21	4	-	7	30	23	5	15
Developing countries plus east bloc	**31**	**16**	**43**	**29**	**37**	**27**	**26**	**68**
of which:								
Latin America	34	13	7					
South East Asia	50	27	63					
Middle East	8	16	15					
Africa	5	17	2					
Eastern Bloc	6	27	13					

Source: Calculated from GATT, *International Trade*, 1989/90 table A3, Geneva 1991.
Note: Trade is commodity imports and exports.
ACCs include Australasia.

dependent on economic developments in their own countries as their portfolios are 'diversified'. The abolition of exchange controls, pioneered by the Thatcher government in 1979, has undoubtedly generated much greater integration of financial markets. But internationalization of production takes place only through 'direct' foreign investment overseas in production facilities. From low rates in the 1950s, even from the USA, it grew to reach 10–15% of home investment firstly in the USA in the 1960s, then in Germany in the 1970s and finally in Japan in the 1980s (see Table 2). These are substantial figures, but with the exception of the UK (and one or two smaller countries like Switzerland and the Netherlands), domestic investment by domestic capital easily dominates both direct investment overseas and foreign investment at home.

Nonetheless, an important new feature of contemporary globalization has been the growth of the multinational or transnational corporation, still only in its infancy by the time of World War I. Most large industrial and financial corporations are in some sense multinational. In the mid-1980s nearly one third of the sales and more than one third of the employment by the world's 68 largest manufacturing corporations (those with annual sales greater than $10 billion) was accounted for by their foreign subsidiaries.[11]

Much of what is counted as direct investment, however is not of archetypal multinational kind – invasion of a domestic market, for instance Nissan setting up near Sunderland. Rather it represents what is really a 'portfolio' investment by a holding company with very little implication for the industrial structure of the host country, as when Hanson Trust purchases a US industrial company or a Japanese financial institution buys an office block in Manhattan. This is not so far removed from the investment in foreign bonds which was typical of foreign investment in the nineteenth century.

Foreign investment and trade are both alternative and complementary forms of globalization. They are alternatives because firms may try to conquer foreign markets either through exporting from a home base like most Japanese companies until recently or through setting up foreign subsidiaries like many European and US companies. They are complements when the international division of labour within companies (a long established characteristic of multinationals with raw material production activities abroad and a growing feature of other manufacturing multinationals) leads to the movement of goods across national borders as part of the same integrated production process. The GATT has roughly estimated that around one third of what appears in the figures as world trade consists in fact of movement of goods between different branches of the same multinational corporation.[12]

Trade for the major ACC blocks of 5–10% of GDP combined with foreign ownership of domestic capital and domestic ownership of foreign capital of order 5–10% of domestic capital stock presents a picture of

Table 2. Direct foreign investment (% of net domestic business investment)

Outward	1960s	1970s	1980s
USA	13.3	15.2	7.7
Japan	1.1	4.7	10.3
Germany	3.7	10.6	16.1
UK	9.3	37.2	65.6
Inward			
USA	1.8	6.3	13.6
Japan	0.5	0.4	0.3
Germany	5.7	6.4	2.9
UK	5.4	27.3	29.4

Source: OECD *Industrial Policy*, Paris 1989; Armstrong, P., Glyn A. & Harrison, J. *Capitalism Since 1945*, Blackwell, Oxford, 1991. Table A5.

important, but hardly overwhelming internationalization of production. Overwhelmingly production is nationally (or in the case of Europe, regionally) owned and oriented.

A recent UN report has highlighted the pattern of foreign investment, which in many respects parallels that of trade described above. Of the European Community's overseas investment, the proportion located in other EC countries rose from one quarter to one third during the 1980s; even excluding this intra-investment, the stock of EC investment reached the same level as that of the US. The stock of Japanese investment was growing much more rapidly, but had only reached about one third of the US or EC level by the end of the 1980s. The great bulk of this direct investment from ACCs was to other advanced countries, with inflows into both US and UK being especially strong (see Table 2). During the 1980s the developing countries share of foreign investment declined from around one quarter during 1980–84 to one sixth during 1988–89.[13] Different parts of the developing world were primarily associated with the same particular ACC blocs as is the case for trade (US with Latin America, Japan with Asia, W. Europe with East Europe), but the USA was also the dominant investor in some Asian countries. There is some indication that US domination of foreign investment in some parts of Latin America is being ceded to Europe (eg Brazil) and in some parts of Asia to Japan (Taiwan and Singapore).

(c)Labour

If goods and capital markets have become more but not unprecedently open the same is not at all true of the labour market. On the contrary, the

1970s and 1980s have seen in most of the ACC countries a strong tendency to tighten immigration controls and to restrict in particular the immigration of unskilled workers from the Third World.

There have been three large waves of such immigration during the postwar period. The first was from North Africa, the Caribbean, Turkey and Yugoslavia to Western Europe during the height of the postwar boom. This came to an end with the crisis which opened in 1973 and today there are increasing demands in Europe to limit immigration even further and even to repatriate earlier immigrants. Immigrants now compose a significant proportion of the population in a number of Western European countries (7 percent in France, 5 percent in Germany and around 3 percent in the UK, Belgium and the Netherlands; in all cases the percentage of the labour force is higher).

The second wave was from the Middle East, South and South East Asia to the oil producing countries of the Gulf. This began in 1973 with the rise in the oil price and rapidly tapered off after the fall in oil prices in the mid 1980s. It was also dealt a major blow by the war against Iraq in 1991. By the mid 1980s, however, immigrant workers composed the majority of the workforce in some of the Gulf states (over 60% in Saudi Arabia, over 70% in Kuwait and over 80% in the United Arab Emirates).

The third wave of immigration has been from Central America and East Asia to the United States. This is the only one which continues even though there too there is some tendency to tighten controls. The balance of forces for and against immigration is very different from that in Europe; in the USA it is politically more difficult to implement draconian immigration controls due in part to the strength of established immigrant communities and to the greater power of anti-racist forces compared to Western Europe. During the 1980s it is estimated that there were around 1 million immigrants a year, representing an addition of about 4 percent to the existing population per decade.

The world labour market is not homogeneous. The market for some skills is very global. It is relatively easy for a highly skilled worker such as an atomic physicist or an airline pilot or a surgeon to migrate where they want. But the market for unskilled labour is hardly at all globalized and shows every sign of becoming even less so. This is a very important limitation to the globalization of the world economy. The monstrous bureaucracy which controls unskilled immigration in the world (passports, visas, work permits, immigration services) is a construction which has grown almost continuously since 1913. In the late nineteenth century the world was in principle more open from this point of view than today. There were less restrictions on moving across national borders, many of which had not yet been fully defined. And in countries such as Italy and Ireland emigration led to a bigger relative outflow of population than any country of emigration today; while in countries like the United States and Australia the number of immigrants was a much higher proportion of the existing population than today.

US leadership

Figure 2 presents the most basic data indicating the relative strength of the USA in relation to Europe and Japan. Whether we look at production, exports or, even more crucially, average labour productivity in the economy as a whole, and in the manufacturing sector which is so central to trade, the process of 'catch-up' with the USA is evident for the period up to 1973. Japan, starting from by far the lowest level, is clearly the more spectacular case; but Europe overtook the USA in total production and caught up substantially in terms of productivity. If the pre-1973 trends had continued Europe would have overtaken the US in manufacturing productivity by 1988 and Japan by 1983.

But compared to its rivals, US performance was less weak after 1973. Just as the golden age was less spectacular in the USA, so the extent of tarnishing after 1973 was less extreme. Indeed in terms of both total production, and of manufacturing productivity, the USA has actually grown a little faster than Europe. Moreover whilst growth in Japan has continued to exceed that in the USA, the differential is far smaller than in the 1960s. If the trends in the US and Japan continued as in the period 1973–87 it would not be until 2003 that Japan overhauls the US in manufacturing productivity and not until 2065 that Japan would exceed the USA in terms of total production.[14]

So why has the 1980s been a period of such perceived US weakness, reflected in humiliating lectures on fiscal orthodoxy being delivered to the US by European and Japanese leaders at G7 meetings? The weakness of the trade balance, with the current account in deficit to the tune of 1.7% of GDP on average has been seen as the crucial problem. Whilst a number of OECD countries experienced deficits twice as large or more in relation to their GDPs (New Zealand, Ireland, Portugal, Australia, Greece and Denmark), the very size of the USA, and the centrality of the dollar in the international monetary system, guaranteed that prominence would be accorded to its deficit.

The position of the USA in world trade is further clarified by Table 3. The USA ended the 1980s still more or less level with Germany as top merchandise exporter; and between 1973 and 1989 lost much less of its share of manufacturing exports (down from 12.9% to 12.4%) than did Germany (down from 16.8% to 14.0%). But the USA was no longer leading exporter in any one of the major manufacturing categories; moreover its imports of manufactures rose hugely (from 11.8% of total world imports in 1973 to 16.4% in 1989). Indeed chemicals was the only manufacturing category in which US exports exceeded imports in 1989.

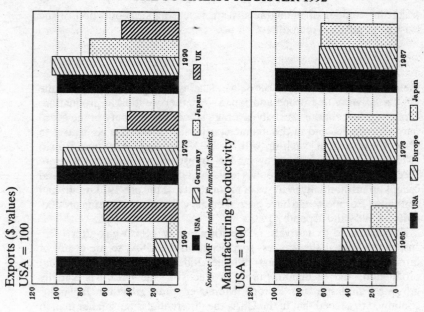

Exports ($ values)
USA = 100

Source: IMF *International Financial Statistics*

Manufacturing Productivity
USA = 100

Source: Hooper, P. and Larrin, K. 'International comparisons of labour costs in manufacturing' *Review of Income and Wealth*, December 1989

figure 2 here

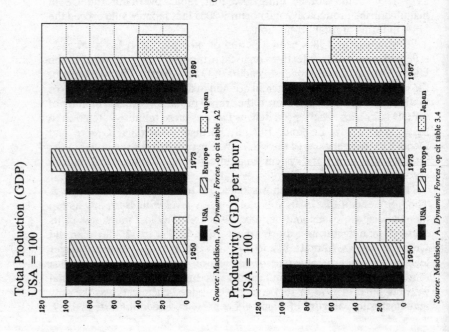

Total Production (GDP)
USA = 100

Source: Maddison, A. *Dynamic Forces*, op cit table A2

Productivity (GDP per hour)
USA = 100

Source: Maddison, A. *Dynamic Forces*, op cit table 3.4

The huge US deficits in machinery and transport equipment accounted for much of the overall deficit and was taken as the key symbol of US industrial decline. Of the USA's chief rivals, the continued breadth of German manufacturing export success (including textiles and clothing) stands out despite its loss of world trade share. Such breadth is in strong contrast to Japan's narrower focus on machinery and transport equipment (with an astounding surplus of $165 billion).

Table 3. Export Rankings 1989

Leading exporters by categories	USA	Germany	Japan	Net US Exports ($bn)
Total Merchandise	1	2	3	−128.9
Services	1	4	5	24.5
Food	1	4	–	14.6
Materials	1	8	–	5.7
Metals	1	3	14	−5.1
Fuels	11	–	–	−46.1
Manufactures	2	1	3	−99.7
Iron & Steel	11	=1	=1	−7.7
Chemicals	2	1	6	16.1
Machinery & Trans. Equip.	=2	=2	1	−54.8
Office Eq.	2	3	1	−15.8
Automobiles	3	2	1	−47.9
Textiles	10	1	5	−2.0
Clothing	12	5	–	−23.8

Source: calculated from GATT *International Trade* 1989–90 Geneva 1991 tables IV.3–IV.55; – means that the country is not in the first 15 exporters.

The disastrous trade performance of the US reflected a number of factors. In the early 1980s the soaring dollar dealt a drastic blow to manufacturing industries. The subsequent decline in the dollar did help to close the trade gap, but studies suggest[15] that even when the dollar falls sufficiently to ensure that US costs rise no faster than in its competitors, there is still a trend to deterioration in the trade balance; so that it requires progressive real devaluation of the dollar of perhaps 1% per year to overcome the underlying weakness of US industry as compared to its rivals.

The trade deficit has had a serious impact. The stock of US net assets held overseas has been run down so that the US became a large net debtor (nearly $300 billion by the end of 1989, when calculated at current market values,[16] obliterating the net receipts of investment income from abroad which during the 1980s had paid for about one seventh of merchandise exports. The dollar's status as *the* reserve currency weakened. Its share in official reserves of foreign exchange fell from 78.4% at the beginning of 1973 to 56.4% at the end of 1990 (whilst the share of D Marks rose from 5.5% to 19.7% and the share of Yen from zero to 9.1%).[17] The decline in the share of the dollar may seem rather modest in the light of its embattled position in the later 1980s. In fact, however, it partly reflects that embattled position since the central banks of surplus countries were forced to acquire vast holdings of US dollars when they sold their domestic currencies to prevent their values rising against the dollar. Such a greater depreciation of the dollar would have increased its competitiveness and restored the US trade balance, but at the expense of reduced competitiveness, and thus reduced profits from exports, of the surplus countries (Japan, Germany, Taiwan, Korea).

The Third World

If the present degree of globalization of capitalism in the world as a whole can partly be seen as regaining the levels of globalization attained before 1913, this conclusion does not apply to the position of the Third World. The share of Africa, Asia and Latin America in world trade is now substantially lower than before 1913. This reflects a major decline in the relative importance of tropical raw materials in world trade which has become increasingly the exchange of manufactured goods for manufactured goods.

This long-term structural reason for the decline of the trading importance of the Third World has been joined in the period since 1973 by a major short-term crisis in many poorer countries which has led to a new sharp collapse in their relative participation in the world trading system. Latin America's share of world exports fell from 12.4 percent in 1950 to 5.5 percent in 1980 and only 3.9 percent in 1990; Asia's was 13.1 percent in 1950, rose to 17.8 percent in 1980 and fell back again to 14 percent in 1990. And Africa's share all but disappeared: in 1950 it was 5.2 percent, in 1980 4.7 percent and in 1990 only 1.9 percent. In 1955 exports from Africa were three times those of Japan; by 1986 the exports of Japan were four times the exports from Africa.

How does this square with the often-trumpeted fact that the share in world trade of the Third World as a whole has risen? The answer is that while the advanced capitalist countries have become more homogeneous during the last 50 years the countries of the Third World have experienced a sharp polarization. Only a few have entered in an important way into the expansion of world trade and most of these are in Asia (especially the so-called Newly Industrializing Countries). Four Asian countries (South

Korea, Taiwan, Hong Kong and Singapore) produce between them about one half of the total manufactured exports of the Third World.

The picture for international investment is rather similar. Between 1950 and 1980 the share of all foreign investment going to the Third World held roughly constant at about 25 percent. But after 1984 the share fell sharply to well under 20 percent. As with the case of trade, investment in Third World countries is very unequally distributed. It goes in significant quantities to only a few resource-rich countries and the newly industrializing countries (including China) while the so-called 'least developed countries' are increasingly excluded. In the second half of the 1980s this group received only 0.1 percent of all foreign investment, down from 0.4 percent in the first half of the decade. Once again Africa and most of Latin America as well as some Asian countries are failing to participate in the growing globalization of the rest of the world. And this is not because they have an alternative economic system but because they are increasingly marginalized within the system of which they form a part.

Conclusions

During the period since World War II the nature of the world economy has changed very considerably. There has been a vast extension of capitalism to areas and activities not previously organized in a capitalist way. And there has been a vast growth of capitalist production. Neither of these processes has been smooth and continuous. Growth has been punctuated by crises and is now much slower than 20 years ago. And capitalism has expanded very suddenly by the reincorporation of the formerly socialist countries.

The system has also become more integrated or globalized in many respects. Both international trade and international investment have expanded faster in nearly all years than production. There have been many new projects of economic integration and cooperation and many barriers to international economic relations have fallen. Nonetheless what has resulted is still very far from a globally integrated economy. Protectionism is widespread and in some of its forms is growing. Agriculture is universally protected and controlled. The labour market is hardly at all global. In short the world economy is considerably more globalized than 50 years ago; but much less so than is theoretically possible. In many ways it is less globalized than 100 years ago. The widespread view that the present degree of globalization is in some way new and unprecedented is, therefore, false. One reason perhaps why this false view has gained credence on the left is that it seems to explain a loss of national economic independence which in turn has contributed to the decline of socialism. It is interesting to contrast this with the attitude of the left towards the internationalization of the world economy before World War I when it was almost universally welcomed as a natural prelude to the arrival of socialism.

The 20th century is sometimes known as the American century. At the economic level the United States has been a hegemonic power for possibly 30 years of the century. But it is evident that in many ways US hegemony has been eroded during the last 20 years. US hegemony, like British hegemony in the century before, was in part the consequence of its military victories and the way those were achieved. If it is true, as Wallerstein has rather convincingly argued,[18] that hegemony requires major military victories by the hegemonic power, it does not look as if any newly hegemonic power will challenge the USA in the medium term. The USA has lost its unchallenged economic superiority but retains its military dominance; this probably allows it to retain more of the prerogatives of hegemony than its purely economic position would warrant.

The Gulf War raised in a sharp way the possibility that the USA would attempt again to use its military muscle to reassert its dominant position. But as Arthur MacEwan persuasively argues[19], it will be increasingly difficult for the USA to play this card given the end of the Cold War. And securing massive contributions from Germany and Japan towards the cost of the war will not restore the USA's economic dominance; it will simply spread the costs of policing the world.

In any case, it seems inconceivable that either Japan or Europe could secure the necessary degree of economic dominance over the USA and Japan by the end of the century.[20] Differences in growth rates are too small at present to change the relative weights of the major blocs decisively in anything other than the very long term, short of a major catastrophe befalling one or more of them.[21]

The fundamental issue, then, seems to be whether the organization of the world economy will become increasingly polarized and conflictual or whether the trend will be towards increasing co-operation between the USA, Europe and Japan. One important trend noted already is towards the relations of each major blocs with the LDCs becoming increasingly polarized (Europe with Africa and E. Europe, Japan with E. Asia, North America with Latin America). In Asia a whole range of co-operative patterns are being canvassed with Japan (see Itoh this volume); enlargement of the EC to include E. European countries is also in prospect. This does not seem necessarily to indicate either conflict or co-operation. The crucial point here is the interpenetration, by trade and investment, among the major blocs. Whilst this interpenetration is limited it must be a factor increasing the likelihood of co-operation. Co-operation has been evident in the area of stabilization of exchange rates (with $150 billion reputedly being spent by central banks to stabilize the dollar after the Louvre Accord in 1987). The Uruguay Round hangs in the balance whilst some success is still possible. But we should be warned against assuming that, just because co-operation seems rational in the self-interest of nations, it will actually take place. Only a few months before the guns opened fire in 1914, Norman Angell, a famous contemporary economic pundit had predicted in his book *The Age of Illusion* that the degree of interdependence of the major European economies had made war no longer conceivable.

There are forces making for the new emergence of confrontation between the major capitalist powers after a long period of relative peace and co-operation. One is the collapse of the common enemy, the USSR, with China still a not very plausible successor. The second is the existence of economic competition between the major powers, exacerbated by the international slump of the beginning of the 1990s, which is already producing a rising level of verbal and economic conflict between the three major capitalist power centres. But things are a long way from a military trial of strength let alone the emergence of a new hegemonic power.

At a minimum it seems safe to predict that the world economy will continue without a clear leader and that this situation will result in a higher level of conflict between the major powers than in the previous 50 years. Whether these conflicts will remain at the level of bickering or whether they will lead to major structural changes, in particular to the consolidation of economic blocs which already to some extent exist in practice, is impossible to predict. The world shows almost no signs of moving from a high level of economic globalization towards the formation of a serious global state.

NOTES

1. Our thanks to Bob Rowthorn and the editors for comments.
2. Charles Kindleberger is responsible for one of the most influential analyses in these terms: '. . . the international economic and monetary system needs leadership, a country which is prepared, consciously or unconsciously, under some set of rules that it has internationalized, to set standards of conduct for other countries; and to seek to get others to follow them, to take an undue share of the burdens of the system, and in particular to take on its support in adversity . . . Britain performed this role in the century up to 1913; the United States in the period after the end of the Second World War . . .' (Kindleberger, C. *The World in Depression 1929–39* Allen Lane, London, 1973, p. 28).
3. For 1950–73 the figures are 7.7% pa for exports as compared to 5.1% pa for GDP, for 1973–87 4.5% pa for exports, 3.4% pa for GDP. The source is Maddison, A. *The World Economy in the 20th Century*, OECD, Paris, 1989 tables 3.3, D.5; these data refer to 32 countries of which half belong to OECD.
4. Figure 1 shows OECD exports as a share of GDP at *current* rather than constant prices. This makes a significant difference because exports are concentrated in manufactures, whose prices have risen systematically slower than those of production as a whole because of faster productivity growth in manufacturing. For Germany between 1950 and 1973 the share of exports in current prices slightly more than doubled, whilst in constant prices the rise was fourfold. The share of exports in current prices is the best indicator of the share of the country's resources which are devoted to production of exports (since the same increase in productivity which reduces relative prices also implies relatively less labour is employed per unit of output). For other countries/blocs only the constant price figures are given by Maddison.

5. OECD *Historical Statistics 1960–89*, OECD, Paris, 1991 tables 5.2–5.4.

6. *Economist*, 20 September, 1990.

7. *Financial Times*, July 15, 1991.

8. For what is described as 'East Asia', including Japan, Australia and New Zealand and the NICs, but excluding China and India, trade with North America is as important as intra-bloc trade (Schott, J. 'Trading Blocs and the World Trading System' *World Economy*, March 1991 table 1A).

9. European intra-trade has increased as a proportion of its total trade, but this reflects declining importance of trade with developing areas. As a measure of integration, intra-trade as a proportion of trade with advanced countries is the best measure.

10. Zevin, R. 'Are World Financial Markets More Open? If So, Why and With What Effects?' in T. Banuri & J. Schor (eds) *Financial Openness*, Oxford University Press, 1992, pp. 51–2.

11. Calculated from Appendix Table B1, United Nations Centre on Transnational Corporations, *Transnational Corporations in World Development*, United Nations, New York, 1988.

12. See David Gordon, 'The global economy: new edifice or crumbling foundations', *New Left Review*, March/April 1988.

13. United Nations Centre on Transnational Corporations, *World Investment Report 1991: The Triad in Foreign Direct Investment*, United Nations, New York, 1991.

14. International comparisons of output and productivity are notoriously tricky and the figures used in the chart, showing Japanese productivity only 63% of the US level in 1987 may seem rather low. In particular the EC Commission has produced figures showing that Japanese manufacturing productivity reached the US level in 1985. But the EC figures are per worker rather than per hour and Japanese workers are estimated by Maddison, A. *Dynamic Forces in Capitalist Development*, Oxford University Press 1991 table C9 to work about 25% longer hours per year than US; so the EC figures suggest hourly productivity around 80% of the US level. Moreover the series used in the chart do not seem far out of line with other estimates for earlier periods. It seems unlikely, therefore, that by the mid-1980s Japanese manufacturing productivity was much above 70% of the US level, which would imply a level of about 75% in 1992. The EC figures are valuable in underscoring big differences within manufacturing; they show output per worker in electrical and electronic goods more than twice as high in Japan than in the USA, whilst in food, beverages and tobacco and in construction materials it was around 40% of the US level in 1985 (Emerson, M. *The Economics of 1992*, Oxford University Press 1988 table 1.1.3).

15. Lawrence, R. 'Current Account Adjustment – An Appraisal', *Brookings Papers on Economic Activity*, 1990, II pp. 343–382.

16. *Financial Times*, June 10, 1991.

17. IMF *Annual Report*, Washington 1991 table 1.12.

18. Immanuel Wallerstein, *The Politics of the World Economy*, Cambridge, 1984, pp. 37–46.

19. MacEwan, A. 'Why the Emperor can't afford new clothes', *Monthly Review*, July/August 1991.

20. Writing in 1973 Kindleberger considered only the rise of Europe relatively to the USA, raised the possibility of one or another assuming a dominant position and then pondered on co-operative versus conflictual solutions if there continued to be no dominant power (op. cit, p. 308). Aglietta (Aglietta, M. 'Capitalism in the Eighties', *New Left Review*, November/December 1982) also discounts the ability of Japan to continue its rapid growth, and raises the possibilities that either the USA will recover its economic dynamism and thus its leadership role, or else a fracturing into regions will occur with the potential both for Europe to recover its dynamism and for destructive inter-capitalist rivalry, especially in the context of an international credit crisis. Bob Rowthorn (Rowthorn, B. 'Imperialism in the Seventies – Unity or Rivalry', *New Left Review*, September–October 1971) raised the likelihood of economic conflict between Japan, a more unified Europe and the USA.

21. Projections of post 1973 differences of productivity growth rates on to 2020 show Japan about 50% above that of the USA and most Western European countries around the US level (Rowthorn, R.E. 'Productivity and American Leadership' review of Baumol et al,

forthcoming in *Review of Income and Wealth*, table 8). In the very long term, therefore, *if existing trends continue*, Japan will acquire a decisive productivity advantage (see also the broadly similar conclusions in Baumol, W., Batey Blackburn, S. & Woolf, E. *Productivity and American Leadership*, MIT Press, 1989 chapter 12 which occasioned Rowthorn's alternative, perhaps more plausible estimates).

THE COLLAPSE OF LIBERALISM

Immanuel Wallerstein

The years 1989–1991 mark a decisive turning-point in contemporary history. On that almost everyone seems to agree. But turning from what to what? 1989 is the year of the end of the so-called Communisms in Eastern Europe, and 1991 marks it for the erstwhile USSR. The years 1990–91 are the immediate time boundaries as well of the so-called Persian Gulf war.

The two events, intimately linked, are nonetheless entirely distinct in character. The end of the Communisms marks the end of an era. The Persian Gulf war marks the beginning of an era. The one closes out; the other opens out. The one calls for reevaluation; the other for evaluation. The one is the story of hopes deceived; the other of fears still unfulfilled.

Yet, as Braudel reminds us, 'events are dust', even big events. Events make no sense unless we can insert them in the rhythms of the *conjonctures* and the trends of the *longue durée*. But that is less easy to do than it sounds, since we must then decide which *conjonctures* and which structures are most relevant.

Let us start with the end of the Communisms. I have called it the end of an era, but which era? Shall we analyse it as the end of the postwar epoch 1945–1989, or as the end of the Communist epoch 1917–1989, or as the end of the French Revolutionary epoch 1789–1989, or as the end of the ascension of the modern-world system, 1450–1989? It can be interpreted as all of these.

Let me put aside, however, the last possible interpretation for a while, and start by analysing it as the end of the epoch 1789–1989, via 1848 and 1968. Note well, not for the moment via 1917. How may we characterise this period: that of the industrial revolution? that of the bourgeois revolution(s)? that of the democratisation of political life? that of modernity? All of these interpretations are commonplace, and all have some (even much) plausibility.

A variation on these themes, one that would perhaps be more precise, might be to call the era 1789–1989 the era of the triumph and domination of liberal ideology, in which case 1989, the year of the end of the so-called Communisms, would in fact really mark the downfall of liberalism as an ideology. Outrageous and implausible, amidst the revival of the faith in the free market and the importance of human rights, you say? Not all that much. But, in order to appreciate the argument, we must begin at the beginning.

In 1789, in France, a political upheaval occurred to which we have given the name, the French Revolution. As a political event it passed through many phases, from the initial phase of uncertainty and confusion to the Jacobin phase, and then, via the interim of the Directory, to a Napoleonic phase. In a sense we can argue it was continued subsequently in 1830, in 1848, in 1870, and even in the Resistance during the Second World War. Through it all, it had as its slogan 'liberty, equality, fraternity' – a clarion call of the modern world that has proved to be superbly ambiguous.

The balance-sheet of the French Revolution in terms of France itself is very uneven. There were irreversible changes that were real changes, and there were many seeming changes that changed nothing. There were continuities from the *Ancien Régime* via the revolutionary process, as Tocqueville showed long ago, and there were decisive ruptures. This balance-sheet for France is not, however, our concern here. The bicentennial and its platitudes are over.

It is rather the impact of the French Revolution (interpreted widely) on the world-system as a whole that is the theme I wish to explore. The French Revolution transformed mentalities and established 'modernity' as the *Weltanschauung* of the modern world. What we mean by modernity is the sense that the new is good and that it is desirable, because we live in a world of Progress at every level of our existence. Specifically, in the political arena, modernity meant the acceptance of the 'normality' of change, as opposed to its 'abnormality', its transitory character. At last, an ethos consonant with the structures of the capitalist world-economy had become so widely diffused that even those who were uncomfortable with this ethos had to take it into account in public discourse.

The question became what to do about the 'normality' of change in the political arena, since those who have power are always reluctant to cede it. The differing views about how to handle the 'normality' of change are located in what we have come to call the 'ideologies' of the modern world. The first ideology on the scene was 'conservatism', the view that change would be retarded as long as possible, and its extent kept as minimal as possible. But note, no serious conservative ideologue has ever suggested total immobility, a position that it had been possible to assert in previous eras.

The response to 'conservatism' was 'liberalism', which saw the break with the *Ancien Régime* as a definitive political rupture and as the end of an era of 'illegitimate' privilege. The political programme incarnated by liberal ideology was the perfection of the modern world by means of the further 'reform' of its institutions.

The last of the ideologies to make its appearance was 'socialism', which rejected the individualistic presumptions of liberal ideology, and insisted that social harmony would not come about automatically by unleashing individuals from all the constraints of custom. Rather, social harmony had to be socially constructed, and for some socialists it could only be constructed after a further historical development and a great social battle, a 'revolution'.

All three ideologies were in place by 1848 and have conducted noisy battles with each other ever since, throughout the nineteenth and twentieth centuries. Political parties have been created everywhere, ostensibly reflecting these ideological positions. There has to be sure never been an uncontested definitive version of any of these ideologies, and there has also been very much confusion about the dividing lines between them. But in both learned and popular political discourse it has been generally accepted that these ideologies exist and represent three different 'tonalities', three different styles of politics with respect to the normality of change: the politics of caution and prudence; the politics of constant rational reform; and the politics of accelerated transformation. Sometimes we call this the politics of the right, the centre, and the left.

There are three things to note about the ideologies in the period following 1848. I say, following 1848, because the world revolution of 1848 – which combined the first appearance of a conscious workers' movement as a political actor with the 'springtime of the peoples' – set the political agenda for the next century and a half. On the one hand, the 'failed' revolution(s) of 1848 had established clearly that political change was not likely to be as rapid as the accelerators wanted, but neither would it be as slow as the cautious hoped. The most plausible prediction (not wish) was constant rational reform. Thus triumphed in the core zones of the world-economy the liberal centre.

But who was to effectuate these reforms? This is the first anomaly to notice. In the first blossoming of the ideologies, between 1789 and 1848, all three ideologies had situated themselves in positions that were firmly anti-State in the antinomy State-Society, whose centrality in political thought was equally a consequence of the French Revolution. Conservatives had denounced the French Revolution as an attempt to use the State to undermine and negate the institutions thought to be basic to Society – the family, the Community, the Church, the monarchy, the feudal orders. Liberals however had also denounced the State as the structure which prevented each individual – the actor considered to be basic to the constitution of Society – from pursuing his interests as he/she saw fit in what Bentham called the 'calculus of pleasure and pain'. And socialists had denounced the State as well on the grounds that it reflected the will of the privileged, rather than the general will of Society. For all three ideologies then, the 'withering away of the State' seemed an ideal devoutly to be wished.

Yet, and this is the anomaly we are noting, despite this unanimously negative view of the State in theory, in practice, especially after 1848, the exponents of all three ideologies moved in multiple ways to strengthen state structures. Conservatives came to see the State as a substitute mechanism to constrain what they considered to be the disintegration of morality, given that the traditional institutions could no longer do it, or could no longer do it unaided by the State police institutions. Liberals came to see the State as the only efficient, only rational mechanism by which the pace of reform could be kept steady, and oriented in the right direction. And socialists after 1848, came to feel that, without obtaining state power, they would never be able to overcome the obstacles to fundamental transformation of the Society.

The second great anomaly was that, although everyone said there were three distinct ideologies, in political practice, each ideological party tried to reduce the political scene to a duality, claiming that the other two ideologies were basically alike. For conservatives, both liberals and social-ists were believers in Progress, who wished to utilise the State to manip-ulate the organic structures of Society. For socialists, conservatives and liberals represented mere variations on a politics of the defence of the status quo and of the privileges of the upper strata (old aristocracy and new bourgeoisie combined). And for liberals, both conservatives and socialists were authoritarian opponents of the liberal ideal, the flourishing of individuals in all their potentialities. This reduction of three ideologies to a duality (but in three different versions) was in part no doubt mere passing political rhetoric, but more fundamentally it reflected the constant recon-struction of political alliances. In any case, over the course of 150 years, this repeated reduction of the trinity to dualities created a great deal of political confusion, not least of all in the meaning of these labels.

But the greatest anomaly of all was that in the 120 years after 1848, that is, at least until 1968, under the guise of three ideologies in conflict with each other, we really had only one, the overwhelmingly dominant ideology of liberalism. To understand this, we have to look at what was the concrete issue under debate during the entire period, the fundamental social problem that required a solution.

The great 'reform' that was called for, if the capitalist world-system were to remain politically stable, was the integration of the working classes into the political system, thereby transforming a domination based merely on power and wealth into a domination of consent. This reform process had two main pillars. The first was the according of suffrage, but in such a way that, although everyone would vote, relatively little institutional change would occur as a result. The second was transferring a part of the global surplus-value to the working classes, but in such a way that the largest part remained in the hands of the dominant strata and the system of accumula-tion remained in place.

The geographical zone in which such social 'integration' was required most urgently was that of the core states of the capitalist world-economy – Great Britain and France above all, but the United States, other states in Western Europe, and the White settler states as well. We know that this transformation was steadily implemented in the period 1848–1914, and that by the time of the First World War, the patterns of universal suffrage (albeit still only manhood suffrage in most places) and the welfare state were in place, even if not yet fully realised in all these states.

We could say simply that the liberal ideology had realised its objective and leave it at that, but that would be insufficient. We must notice as well what happened in the process to both conservatives and socialists. The leading conservative politicians turned themselves into 'enlightened conservatives', that is, virtual competitors with official liberals in the process of the integration of the working classes. Disraeli, Bismarck, and even Napoleon III stand as good examples of this new version of conservatism, what might be termed 'liberal conservatism'.

At the same time, the socialist movement in the industrialised countries, even its most militant exemplars such as the German Social-Democratic Party, became the leading parliamentary voices for the achievement of the liberal reforms. Through their parties and their trade-unions, they exerted 'popular' pressure for achieving what the liberals wanted, the taming of the working classes. Not only Bernstein but Kautsky, Jaurès, and Guesde as well, not to speak of the Fabians, became what we might call 'liberal socialists'.

By 1914, the political work of the industrialised countries was largely divided between 'liberal conservatives' and 'liberal socialists'. In the process, purely liberal parties began to disappear, but this was only because all significant parties were de facto liberal parties. Behind the mask of ideological conflict stood the reality of ideological consensus.

The First World War did not break this consensus. Rather, it confirmed it and extended it. The year 1917 was the symbol of this extension of the liberal consensus. The war had started by an assassination in a peripheral zone of the world-economy, Bosnia-Herzogovina. The moment had come for the core states to go beyond the narrower objective of integrating their own working classes and think about the integration of that larger segment of the world's working classes, those that lived in the peripheral and semiperipheral zones of the world-system. In the language of today, the issue had now become the taming of the South in ways parallel to the taming of the working classes internal to core zones.

There were two versions of how to resolve North–South issues. The one was put forward by that herald of the renewal of liberalism on a world scale, Woodrow Wilson. Wilson asked the United States to enter the First World War 'to make the world safe for democracy'. After the war, he called for the 'self-determination of nations'.

To which nations was Wilson referring? Obviously not to those of states in the core zone. The process of the construction of effective and legitimate state machineries in France and Great Britain, even Belgium and Italy, had long since been completed. Wilson was talking of course of the nations or 'peoples' of the three great empires in process of dissolution: Russia, Austria–Hungary, and the Ottomans – all three comprising peripheral and semiperipheral zones of the world-economy. In short, he was talking of what we today call the South. After the Second World War, the principle of the self-determination of nations was to be extended to all the remaining colonial zones – in Africa, Asia, Oceania, and the Caribbean.

The principle of the self-determination of nations was the structural analogy at the world level of the principle of universal suffrage at the national level. Just as each individual was to be considered politically equal and have one vote, so each nation was to be sovereign and thus politically equal and therefore have one vote (a principle today incarnated in the General Assembly of the United Nations).

Nor did Wilsonian liberalism stop there. The next step after suffrage at the national level had been the institution of the welfare state, that is, a redistribution of a part of the surplus-value via governmental income transfers. The next step at the world level after self-determination was to be 'national (economic) development', the programme put forth by Roosevelt, Truman, and their successors after the Second World War.

Needless to say, conservative forces reacted with their usual prudence and distaste to the clarion call of the Wilsonians for global reform. Needless to say as well, after the disruptions caused by the Second World War, conservatives began to see the merits in this liberal programme, and Wilsonian liberalism in practice became after 1945 a liberal-conservative thesis.

But 1917 had of course a second significance. It was the year of the Russian Revolution. Wilsonianism was hardly born when it was faced with a great ideological opponent, Leninism. Lenin and the Bolsheviks appeared on the political arena in protest primarily against the previous transformation of socialist ideology into what I have called liberal socialism (the same thing as Bernstein's revisionism, to which Lenin attached the Kautsky position as well). Leninism therefore was proposing a militant alternative, initially by its opposition to workers' participation in the First World War, and then by the seizure of state power in Russia by the Bolshevik Party.

We know that socialists everywhere in 1917, including in Russia, had expected the first socialist revolution to occur in Germany, and that for several years the Bolsheviks awaited the fulfilment of their own revolution by one in Germany. We know the German revolution never came and that the Bolsheviks had to decide what to do.

The decision they took was twofold. On the one hand, they decided to build 'socialism in one country'. They thus entered into a path in which the primary demand of the Soviet state vis-à-vis the world-system became its political integration as a great power in the world-system and its economic development via rapid industrialisation. This was Stalin's programme but it was that of Khrushchev, Brezhnev, and Gorbachev as well. Thus the programme in practice was one of the Soviet state demanding its 'equal rights' on the world scene.

What then of world revolution? Lenin initially founded the Third International in theory to pursue in militant ways the tasks that the Second International had in effect renounced. The Third International soon turned however into a mere foreign policy adjunct of the USSR. The one thing it never did was stimulate real insurrections of the working classes. Instead, the focus of activity shifted, beginning with the Baku Congress of the Peoples of the East in 1921, to which Lenin invited not merely Communist parties but all sorts of nationalist and national liberation movements.

The programme that emerged from Baku, and that became in reality the programme of the world Communist movement, was the programme of anti-imperialism. But what was anti-imperialism? It was a translation into more aggressive and impatient language of the Wilsonian programme, of the self-determination of nations. And in the period after the Second World War, as one after the other of these national liberation movements came to power, what programme did they put forward? It was the programme of national (economic) development, usually relabelled socialist development. Leninism, the great opponent of liberal-socialism at the national level, was beginning to look suspiciously like liberal-socialism at the world level.

Thus, just as in the period 1848–1914, the liberal programme of the taming of the working classes in core zones via universal suffrage and the welfare state was implemented by a combination of socialist militancy and sophisticated conservative astuteness, so in the period 1917–1989, the liberal programme at a world scale, the taming of the South, was being implemented by a combination of socialist militancy and sophisticated conservative astuteness.

The second world revolution of 1968, just like the first world revolution of 1848, transformed the ideological strategies of the capitalist world-economy. Whereas the revolution of 1848, via its successes and its failures, ensured the triumph of liberalism as an ideology and the eventual transformation of its two rivals – conservatism and socialism – into mere adjuncts, the revolution of 1968, via its successes and its failures, undid the liberal consensus. The revolutionaries of 1968 launched a protest from the left against this consensus, and above all against the historic transformation of socialism, even Leninist socialism, into liberal-socialism. This took the form of a resurgence of various anarchist themes, but also, perhaps above all, of Maoism.

In the wake of the breaching of the worldwide liberal consensus by the so-called New Left, conservative ideology was also renewed for the first time since 1848 and became once again politically aggressive rather than defensive. Sometimes this was given the name of neo-conservatism but sometimes it was called neo-liberalism, which reflected the fact that its programme was primarily to remove constraints on the market and thereby to regress on welfare state reallocations, the first such significant regression in a century.

How can we account for the world revolution of 1968, and its consequences for ideological strategies? In terms of their structure of the world-system as a whole, we can say that the politics of liberalism – the taming of the world's working classes via suffrage/sovereignty and welfare state/national development – had reached its limits. Further increases of political rights and economic reallocation would threaten the system of accumulation itself. But it had reached its limits before all sectors of the world's working classes had in fact been tamed by being included into a small but significant part of the benefits.

The majority of the population of the peripheral and semiperipheral zones were still excluded from the operations of the system. But so were a very significant minority of the populations of the core zones, the so-called 'Third World within'. And in addition, the world's women became conscious of their profound permanent exclusion, at all class levels, from true political rights, as well as, for the most part, from equal economic rewards.

What 1968 represented therefore was the beginning of the reversal of the cultural hegemony the world's dominant strata had, with great assiduity, been creating and strengthening since 1848. The period from 1968 to 1989 has seen the steady crumbling of what remained of the liberal consensus. On the right, conservatives increasingly sought to destroy the liberal centre. Compare the statement of Richard Nixon – 'we are all Keynesians now' – with the campaign of George Bush in 1988 against the 'L-word', L for liberalism. Witness the virtual coup d'état in the British Conservative Party where Margaret Thatcher ended the tradition of enlightened conservatism that had gone back beyond Disraeli to Sir Robert Peel in the 1840's.

But the erosion was even greater on the left. It took the form most tellingly of the disintegration of the liberal-socialist regimes. In response to the patent inability of almost all of these regimes, in peripheral and semiperipheral zones, even the most 'progressive' and rhetorically militant among them, to achieve national development to any significant degree, one after the other of regimes with a glorious past of national liberation struggle lost their popular legitimacy. The culmination of this process was the so-called 'Collapse of the Communisms' – from the advent of Gorbachevism in the USSR and of 'special economic zones' in the People's Republic of China to the fall of the one-party Communist systems in all the countries of eastern Europe.

In 1968, those who were frustrated with the liberal consensus turned against the liberal-socialist ideology in the name of anarchism and/or Maoism. In 1989, those frustrated with the liberal consensus turned against the quintessential exponents of liberal-socialist ideology, the Soviet-style regimes, in the name of the free market. In neither case was the alternative proposed one to be taken seriously. The alternative of 1968 quickly proved meaningless, and the alternative of 1989 is in the process of doing the same. But, between 1968 and 1989, the liberal consensus and the hope it offered for gradual improvement in the lot of the world's working classes was fatally undermined. But if it is undermined, there can then be no taming of the working classes.

The true meaning of the collapse of the Communisms is the final collapse of liberalism as a hegemonic ideology. Without some belief in its promise, there can be no durable legitimacy to the capitalist world-system. The last serious believers in the promise of liberalism were the old-style Communist parties in the former Communist bloc. Without them to continue to perform this function, the world's dominant strata have lost any possibility to control the world's working classes other than by force. Consent is gone, and consent has gone because bribery had gone. But force alone, we have known since at least Machiavelli, is insufficient to permit political structures to survive very long.

II

Thus we come to the meaning of the Persian Gulf crisis, the beginning of the new era. In this era, the only effective weapon of the dominant forces is becoming force. The Persian Gulf war, unlike all other North–South confrontations in the twentieth century, was an exercise in pure *Realpolitik*. Saddam Hussein started it in this fashion, and the United States and the coalition it put together responded to it in the same way.

Realpolitik was never absent of course from previous conflicts. It informed the Congress of Baku in 1921 as well as the arrival of the Chinese Communist Party into Shanghai in 1949. It was part and parcel of the Bandung declaration of 1955, of the Vietnam war, and of the Cuban confrontation of 1962. It was always an integral part of the strategy of the antisystemic movements – witness Mao's maxim, 'political power comes out of the barrel of a gun' – but force was always an adjunct to the central organising motifs of antisystemic ideology. The South, the peripheral zones, the world's working classes had fought their battles under the banner of an ideology of transformation and hope, in which there was a clear ideological appeal to popular power.

We have been arguing that the forms this ideological struggle of the world's antisystemic movements took were less militant than they seemed or than they claimed. We have said that the world's antisystemic forces had in fact been pursuing, in large part unwittingly, the liberal ideological objectives of homogenising integration into the system. But, in so doing, they at least offered hope, even exaggerated hope, and invited adherence to their cause on the basis of these hopes and promises. When the promises were finally seen to be unfulfilled, first there was fundamental uprising (1968) and then there was the anger of disillusionment (1989). The uprising and the disillusionment were directed more against the presumably anti-systemic liberal socialists than against the pure vintage liberals. But no matter, since liberalism had achieved its objectives via these liberal-socialists (and to be sure the liberal-conservatives as well), and had always been able to be effective alone.

Saddam Hussein drew the lesson of this collapse of the liberal ideological carapace. He concluded that 'national development' was a lure and an impossibility even for oil-rich states like Iraq. He decided that the only way to change the world's hierarchy of power was via the construction of large military powers in the South. He saw himself as the Bismarck of an eventual pan-Arab state. This was not the Bismarck of enlightened conservatism, but the Bismarck who was the leader of a state fighting an uphill battle in the interstate system. The invasion of Kuwait was to be the first step for Saddam Hussein in such a process, and would have as a side benefit the immediate solution to Iraq's debt crisis (elimination of a main creditor plus a windfall of looted capital).

If this was an exercise in pure *Realpolitik*, then we must look at the calculations. How must Saddam Hussein have evaluated his risks and therefore his chances of success? I do not believe he miscalculated. Rather I believe he reasoned in the following manner: Iraq had a 50–50 chance of winning in the short run (if the US hesitated to respond), but if Iraq moved, the US would find itself in a no-win situation where the US had a 100% chance of losing in the middle run. For a player of *Realpolitik*, these are good odds.

Saddam Hussein lost his short-run 50–50 gamble. The US reacted with the use of its maximal military strength, and of course was unbeatable. Iraq, as a country, has emerged much weakened from the war, albeit less totally knocked out than the US seemed to think it would accomplish. But the political situation in the Middle East is fundamentally unchanged from that of 1989, except that the political responsibility of the US has increased considerably without any significant increase in its political ability to defuse the tensions. Whatever the short-run developments, the continued erosion of the US middle-run political role in the world-system will continue unabated, given the continuing erosion of the US competitive position in the world-market vis-à-vis Japan and the European Community.

The long-run question that is open is not what developments will occur in the North, which are fairly easy to predict. When the next long upturn of the world-economy occurs, the likely poles of strength will be two: a Japan–US axis, to which China will be attached, and a pan-European axis, to which Russia will be attached. In the new expansion and new rivalry among core powers, each pole concentrating on developing its principal semiperipheral zone (in the one case China, in the other case Russia), the South will in general be further marginalised, with the exception of enclaves here and there.

The political consequence of this new economic expansion will be intense North–South conflict. But if the North has lost its weapon of ideological control of the situation, can the antisystemic forces, in the South and those elsewhere supporting the South, that is (in older language), the world's working classes, reinvent an ideological dimension to their struggle?

As the ideological themes of yesteryear, those incarnated in socialist and anti-imperialist doctrines, have used themselves up, we have seen three principal modes of struggle emerge. Each has created enormous immediate difficulties for the dominant strata of the world-system. None of the three seems to pose a fundamental ideological challenge. One is what I would call the neo-Bismarckian challenge, of which Saddam Hussein's thrust has been an example. The second is the fundamental rejection of the Enlightenment *Weltanschauung*, whose strength we have seen in the forces led by the Ayatollah Khomeini. The third is the path of individual attempts at socio-geographical mobility, whose major expression is the massive unauthorised ongoing migration from South to North.

Two things stand out about these three forms of struggle. First, each is likely to increase manyfold in the 50 years to come, and will consume our collective political attention. Secondly, the world's left intellectuals have reacted in extremely ambiguous fashion to each of these three forms of the struggle. Insofar as they seem to be directed against the dominant strata of the world-system and to cause the latter discomfort, left intellectuals have wanted to support them. Insofar as each is void of ideological content, and hence politically reactionary rather than progressive in middle-run political consequence, left intellectuals have taken their distance, even considerable distance, from these struggles.

The question is what choice left forces have. If 1989 represents the end of a cultural era that ran from 1789 to 1989, what will be, what can be, the new ideological themes of the present era? Let me suggest one possible line of analysis. The theme of the era just past, that of modernity, was the virtue of newness and, in the political arena, the normality of change. This theme led, as we have tried to argue, steadily and logically to the triumph of liberalism as an ideology, that is, to the triumph of the political strategy of conscious, rational reform in the expectation of the inevitable perfecting of the body politic. Since, within the framework of a capitalist world-economy, there were (unrecognised) inbuilt limits to the 'perfecting' of the body politic, this ideology reached its limits (in 1968 and 1989), and has now lost its efficacity.

We are now into a new era, an era I would describe as the era of disintegration of the capitalist world-economy. All the talk about creating 'a new world order' is mere shouting in the wind, believed by almost no one, and in any case most improbable of realisation. But what ideologies can exist if we are faced with the prospect of disintegration (as opposed to the prospect of normal progressive change)? The hero of liberalism, the individual, has no significant role to play amidst a disintegrating structure, since no individual can survive very long in such a structure acting alone. Our choice as subjects can only be that of groups large enough to carve out corners of strength and refuge. It is therefore no accident that the theme of 'group identity' has come to the fore to a degree unknown before in the modern world-system.

If the subjects are groups, these groups are in practice multiple in number and overlapping in very intricate ways. We are all members (even very active members) of numerous groups. But it is not enough to identify the theme of the group as subject. In the 1789–1989 era, both conservatives and socialists sought, albeit unsuccessfully, to establish the social primacy of groups, in the one case of certain traditional groupings, in the other case of the collectivity (the people) as a singular group. We must in addition put forward an ideology (that is, a political programme) based on the primacy of groups as actors.

There seems to be only two ideologies one can conceivably construct, although at this point neither has been fully constructed in fact. One can put forth the virtue and legitimacy of the 'survival of the fittest' groups. We hear this theme announced in the new aggressivity of proponents of neo-racist themes, which are often clothed in meritocratic garb rather than in the garb of racial purity. The new claims are no longer necessarily based on old narrow groupings (such as nations or even skin-colour groups), but rather on the right of the strong (however *ad hoc* their grouping) to hold on to their loot and protect it within their fortress localities.

The problem with the neo-Bismarckian and the anti-Enlightenment thrusts in the South is that they are inclined eventually to come to terms with their compeers in the North, thereby becoming merely one more fortress locality of the strong. We see this clearly in the politics of the Middle East of the last 15 years. Faced with the threats represented by Khomeini, Saddam Hussein was supported and strengthened by all sectors of the world's dominant strata. When Saddam Hussein moved to grab too large a share of the loot, these forces turned against him, and Khomeini's successors were happy to rejoin the dominant pack. This easy switching of alliances says something about the politics of the dominant strata (and the hypocrisy of their cant about concern with human rights), but it says something as well about Khomeini and his group and about the Baathist party under Saddam Hussein as well.

There is an alternative ideology to the 'survival of the fittest' groups that can be constructed around the primacy of groups in an era of disintegration. It is one that recognises the equal rights of all groups to a share in a reconstructed world-system while simultaneously recognising the non-exclusivity of groups. The network of groups is intricately cross-hatched. Some Blacks, but not all Blacks, are women; some Moslems, but not all Moslems, are Black; some intellectuals are Moslem; and so on ad infinitum. Creating real space for groups in the social system necessarily implies creating space within groups. All groups represent partial identities. Defensive frontiers between groups tend to have the consequence of creating hierarchies within groups. And yet, of course, without some defensive frontiers, groups can have no existence.

This then is our challenge, the creation of a new left ideology in a time of disintegration of the historical system within which we live. It is no easy task nor one that can be accomplished overnight. It took many, many decades to construct the ideologies of the post-1789 era. The stakes are high. For when systems disintegrate, something eventually replaces them. What we now know of systemic bifurcations is that the transformation can go in radically divergent directions because small input at that point can have great consequences (unlike in eras of relative stability such as that which the modern world-system enjoyed from circa 1500 to recently, when big inputs had limited consequence). We may emerge from the transition from historical capitalism to something else, say circa 2050, with a new system (or multiple systems) that is (are) highly inegalitarian and hierarchical, or into one that is largely democratic and egalitarian. It depends on whether or not those who prefer the latter outcome are capable of putting together a meaningful strategy of political change.

In the capitalist world-economy, the system works to exclude the majority (from benefits) by including in the work-system in a layered hierarchy all the world's potential work force. This system of exclusion via inclusion was infinitely strengthened by the diffusion in the nineteenth century of a dominant liberal ideology which justified this exclusion via inclusion, and managed to harness even the world's antisystemic forces to this task. That era, happily, is over. Now we must see if we can create a very different world-system that will include all in its benefits via the exclusions involved in the construction of self-conscious groups that nonetheless recognise their interlacing.

The definitive formulation of a clear antisystemic strategy for an era of disintegration will take at least two decades to develop. All one can do now is put forward some elements that might enter into such a strategy without being sure how all the pieces fit together, and without asserting that such a list is complete.

One element must surely be a definitive disjuncture with the past strategy of achieving social transformation via the acquisition of state power. It is not that assuming governmental authority is never useful, but that it is almost never transformatory. The assumption of state power should be regarded as a necessary defensive tactic under specific circumstances in order to keep out ultra-right repressive forces. But state power should be recognised as a *pis aller*, which always risks a relegitimation of the existing world order. This break with liberal ideology will undoubtedly be the hardest step to take for antisystemic forces, despite the collapse of liberal ideology I have been analysing.

What goes with such a rupture with past practice would be a total unwillingness to manage the difficulties of the system. It is not the function of antisystemic forces to solve the political dilemmas that the increasingly strong contradictions of the system impose upon the dominant strata. The self-help of popular forces should be seen as quite distinct from negotiating reforms in the structure. This has been precisely the trap into which all antisystemic forces, even the most militant ones, were led during the liberal ideological era.

Instead, what antisystemic forces should be concentrating upon is the expansion of real social groups at community levels of every kind and variety, and their grouping (and constant regrouping) at higher levels in a non-unified form. The fundamental error of antisystemic forces in the previous era was the belief that the more unified the structure the more efficacious. To be sure, given a strategy of the priority of conquering state power, this policy was logical and seemingly fruitful. It is also what transformed socialist ideology into liberal-socialist ideology. Democratic centralism is the exact opposite of what is needed. The basis of solidarity of the multiple real groups at higher levels (state, region, world) has to be subtler, more flexible, and more organic. The family of antisystemic forces must move at many speeds in constant reformulation of the tactical priorities.

Such a coherent non-unified family of forces can only be plausible if each constituent group is itself a complex, internally democratic, structure. And this in turn is only possible if, at the collective level, we recognise that there are no strategic priorities in the struggle. One set of rights for one group is no more important than another set for another group. The debate about priorities is debilitating and deviating and leads back to the garden path of unified groups ultimately merged into a single unified movement. The battle for transformation can only be fought on all fronts at once.

A multi-front strategy by a multiplicity of groups, each complex and internally democratic, will have one tactical weapon at its disposal which may be overwhelming for the defenders of the status quo. It is the weapon of taking the old liberal ideology literally and demanding its universal fulfilment. For example, is not the appropriate tactic faced with the situation of mass unauthorised migration from South to North to demand the principle of the unlimited free market – open frontiers for all who wish to come? Faced with such a demand, liberal ideologues can only shed their cant about human rights and acknowledge that they do not really mean freedom of emigration since they do not mean freedom of immigration.

Similarly, one can push on every front for the increased democratisation of decision-making, as well as the elimination of all the pockets of informal and unacknowledged privilege. What I am talking about here is the tactic of overloading the system by taking its pretensions and its claims more seriously than the dominant forces wish them to be taken. This is exactly the opposite of the tactic of managing the difficulties of the system.

Will all of this be enough? It is hard to know, and probably not, by itself. But it will force the dominant forces into more and more of a political corner and therefore into more desperate countertactics. The outcome would still be uncertain, unless the antisystemic forces can develop their utopistics – the reflection and the debate on the real dilemmas of the democratic, egalitarian order they wish to build. In the last period, utopistics was frowned upon as political diversion from the priority tasks first of gaining state power and then of national development. The net result has been a movement based on romantic illusion and hence subject to angry disillusionment. Utopistics are not utopian reveries, but the sober anticipation of difficulties and the open imagining of alternative institutional structures. Utopistics have been thought to be divisive. But if the antisystemic forces are to be non-unified and complex, then alternative visions of possible futures are part of the process.

The year 1989 represented the agonising end of an era. The so-called defeat of antisystemic forces was in fact a great liberation. It removed the liberal-socialist justification of the capitalist world-economy and thus represented the collapse of the dominant liberal ideology.

The new era into which we have entered is nonetheless even more treacherous. We are sailing on uncharted seas. We know more about the errors of the past than about the dangers of the near future. It will take an immense collective effort to develop a lucid strategy of transformation. Meanwhile, the disintegration of the system goes on apace, and the defenders of hierarchy and privilege are wasting no time to find solutions and outcomes that will change everything in order that nothing change. (Remember that di Lampedusa said this as a judgment of Garibaldian revolution.)

There is reason neither for optimism nor for pessimism. All remains possible, but all remains uncertain. We must unthink our old strategies. We must unthink our old analyses. They were all too marked with the dominant ideology of the capitalist world-economy. We must do this no doubt as organic intellectuals, but as organic intellectuals of a non-unified worldwide family of multiple groups, each complex in its own structure.

SECURITY AND INTELLIGENCE IN THE POST-COLD WAR WORLD

Reg Whitaker

'The end of the world's ideological division has not signified an era of peace and prosperity but has led to the emergence of a great empire, the Empire of the North, absolutely rich, which controls the most advanced forces of knowledge.'

Fernando Collor de Mello, president of Brazil, July 1991

'THE CIA: OUR BUSINESS IS KNOWING THE WORLD'S BUSINESS.'

CIA recruiting slogan aimed at attracting Hispanic, Asian and native Americans.

The end of the Cold War raised a number of expectations, among them the prospect of a net reduction in the world's stock of armament overkill, whether nuclear or conventional. It quickly became apparent that these expectations were naive. To be sure, the Red Army may self-destruct or more or less disintegrate, as a by-product of the disappearance of the Soviet Union as a state. The United States, on the other hand, has shown no inclination to reduce significantly its military might. President Bush's declaration of a New World Order and the killing frenzy of Desert Storm in the Gulf showed that the end of the Cold War is a distinctly asymmetrical process.

The Imaginary War

The Cold War was, in Mary Kaldor's inspired phrase, an 'Imaginary War'.[1] The superpowers threatened each other with nuclear holocaust, but despite this – or rather, because of this – they never actually confronted one another directly in battle. The surreal quality of this 'war' (as Hobbes wrote, 'War consists not in battle only, or the act of fighting; but in a tract of time, wherein the will to contend by battle is sufficiently known')[2] lay in its juxtaposition of the apocalyptic threat of the more dire violence on the one hand and the mundane reality of accepted spheres of influence on the other. Politically, diplomatically and ideologically the two blocs were apparently ranged against each other in a death struggle, yet each politely refrained from placing its hands directly on the other's throat.

The effect of Cold War rhetoric on Cold War practice was like that of drink on lechery, as reported by the porter in Macbeth: 'it provokes the

111

desire but it takes away the performance'.[3] Although the 'Wizards of Armageddon', sheltered in their thinktank-sponsored armchairs, dreamed the deaths of millions in counter-strikes and kill-ratios,[4] the real fighters were handcuffed. The US Army fought against surrogates to a bloody stalemate in Korea and to a convulsive and debilitating defeat in Vietnam. The Red Army crushed the citizens of its own 'socialist' bloc in Hungary and Czechoslovakia, and eventually gave up in despair in Afghanistan. Only once, during the Cuban missile crisis, did the USSR and the USA ever come to the brink of direct military confrontation – and that moment was so terrifying that both drew back chastened.

There was another side to the Cold War, a decades-long campaign in which assaults were made behind enemy lines, casualties sustained, battles won and lost. This was the shadow war of espionage, counter-espionage and covert actions. The armies were the security and intelligence agencies of West and East, the CIA and the KGB, and the multitude of other forces lined up on one or the other side. In the war that could never become a real war, espionage became a kind of prophylactic outlet for frustrated aggression. As an entire generation of spy novelists and film-makers understood very well, intelligence was the pornography of the Cold War.

The end of the Cold War raised surprisingly few expectations of multilateral disarmament of the security and intelligence establishments. Like the case of the military, the process has been decidedly asymmetrical. The former East Bloc agencies have dissolved along with their Communist-ruled states. The KGB was divided into three agencies following the disastrous role of the KGB head in the ill-fated coup of the hard-liners. Then with the dissolution of the Soviet Union, even these three new forces would appear to have further divided and devolved into smaller national security and intelligence forces along republican lines, of uncertain provenance and function.

In the West, however, there has been little rethinking. Despite a somewhat surprising call from Senator Daniel Moynihan to put the CIA to bed under the supervision of the State Department, few public figures have apparently given much thought to the problem, let alone suggested any major changes. Some spy writers have flailed about with public ruminations about the future visibility (and profitability) of their genre, but the real spymasters have carried on, business pretty much as usual.

As with the 'peace dividend' which was never paid, the failure to demobilise the security and intelligence apparatuses represents more than a simple case of bureaucratic inertia – although the latter ought not to be discounted as a factor. It is true that bureaucratic empires are congelations of vested interests which do not disappear simply because the reality on which they have been premised has disappeared. But there is a deeper reason why things are unlikely to change much. And this suggests that the Cold War was less a unique world order, than a phase, a 'tract of time', in which persistent interests among capitalist states took on, for a prolonged historical moment, a particular pattern. With the collapse and disappearance of Soviet Communism, those persistent interests are reasserting themselves, unmediated by the Red spectre. Security and intelligence will continue to play an important role in the capitalist state system. Specifically, it is a powerful tool most readily available to the United States in its attempted reassertion of hegemony in the New World Order.

What Is Intelligence?

The simplest definition of intelligence is the systematic and purposeful gathering of information by states about other states. It is assumed that states harbour potentially hostile intentions toward other states, along with the capabilities of inflicting actual damage – and that they wish, for obvious reasons, to conceal these intentions and capabilities. It is in the national interest of states to penetrate the secrets of their rivals (intelligence), while at the same time protecting their own secrets (counter-intelligence). In short, intelligence is a structural element of the modern state-system in which a Hobbesian state of nature is the fundamental international condition, limited only by balances of power – or in the recent Cold War era, by a balance of terror.

Intelligence is thus intimately connected to war, or to preparation or anticipation of war, and indeed is often seen by practitioners as war by other means. Modern espionage as an art developed first in the era of great power rivalry preceding the first world war and achieved its greatest technical advances in the hothouse atmosphere of scientific innovation during World War II. The unprecedented hyperdevelopment of lavishly-funded and technologically-oriented intelligence establishments which has characterised the past four decades has been, of course, intimately connected to the Cold War. Military intelligence in the narrow sense has always been associated with national armies and has even been institutionalised in the form of the 'military attachés' posted to foreign missions who are always, to some degree or another, spies (often tacitly, sometimes cheerfully accepted as such by all concerned). But characteristic of the modern era in intelligence rivalry is the much broader base of knowledge deemed ultimately relevant to the coercive capacities of states: science and technology; industrial potential and resource bases; the political strength and autonomy of the state elites and their relations with the dominant social forces; real foreign policy intentions and motives; the strength and durability of alliances with other states; domestic counter-intelligence and security capabilities.

In the century of total war and of permanent national security states maintained even in peacetime, *everything* is potentially relevant to national security. At least since World War II there has been a persistent connection between intelligence and academia, both in terms of individuals crossing between the two worlds[5] and of parallel styles of work. Both industries are, after all, in the information business: how knowledge is gathered, processed and interpreted. The differences are that intelligence is targeted on information which is deliberately concealed or protected by other states, and that it is a product consumed exclusively in the first instance by the governments that sponsor it.

There are broadly speaking two kinds of sources of intelligence data: human and technical – or HUMINT and TECHINT in the jargon of the trade. HUMINT encompasses information gathered by or from people, ranging from traditional spies running networks of agents, to highly-placed dedicated 'moles' within targeted governments, all the way to occasional sources who may even be unwitting, or half-witting elements of an operation. TECHINT encompasses all means of gathering information through technology: this ranges from traditional signals intelligence involving the interception and decryption of encoded communications to recording and mapping of electromagnetic impulses and satellite-based imaging. Highly sophisticated surveillance of land, oceans and space is now possible through a wide variety of technical means, from electronic listening-posts to spy satellites.

Typically, HUMINT-based intelligence agencies (the CIA and MI6) tend to be larger and more labour-intensive than TECHINT agencies (the National Security Agency [NSA] or the Government Communications Headquarters [GCHQ]), but with smaller budgets than their capital-intensive TECHINT counterparts. Of course, even TECHINT must be directed by people, for purposes set by people. Perhaps for this reason, it is also typical that HUMINT agencies tend to be at the top of the bureaucratic intelligence hierarchy. For instance, the head of the CIA is officially designated as the Director of Central Intelligence to whom the Director of the NSA is subordinate.

For many years there was considerable controversy within intelligence communities about the relative merits of HUMINT and TECHINT. The Israelis, proud of their alleged prowess in traditional HUMINT, were once scornful of American reliance on technology, but in recent years they have apparently joined in the TECHINT game with the launch of their own spy satellites. While it remains true that certain kinds of information can only be gained from human sources – particularly questions of motive and intent[6] – it is also increasingly obvious that espionage at the close of the twentieth century has become pre-eminently a matter of technological reach and capacity. The resultant huge capital investments and the advanced research and development infrastructure required for high-tech innovation entail serious political implications, to which I shall return.

The Use and Misuse of Intelligence

The immediate impact of the ascendancy of TECHINT has been the exponential increase in the sheer volume of information available. To take one example: the dense electronic eavesdropping coverage of the former Soviet bloc carried out under the UKUSA agreements of 1947 directed by the NSA and the GCHQ was regularly scooping a vast amount of everyday communications out of the sky for over forty years. To take another example: the access of the NSA and thus the CIA to the computer networks of international airlines means that close monitoring of all movements of persons across borders by air is possible. The question is what sensible use can possibly be made of all this mind-boggling scope for accumulating bits of information, the vast majority of which is obviously 'noise'? While it is true that electronic data processing makes possible the storage and retrieval of a volume of information unimaginable in the pre-computer age, the most sophisticated and complex programmes cannot indicate what kind of information is worth looking for, nor can they decide what the accumulated information means, or what use should be made of it. In other words, *interpretation* is still a human prerogative. It is, however, unclear how much this prerogative is being exercised in practice, or to what extent the technology is blindly driving the intelligence machinery. The metaphor of the sorcerer's apprentice no doubt remains pertinent.

Intelligence is a product to be consumed by governments. The tasks of intelligence are in theory set by governments, and the intelligence machinery exists to fulfill the political agenda. In practice there are at least two limitations on this theory: first, governments rarely know what it is they want from intelligence; second, the bureaucratisation of the intelligence process creates significant inertia and rigidities which may prove resistant to even the occasional burst of activism on the part of the political leadership.

Ironically, the opposite effect sometimes has pernicious consequences: a government driven by an ideological demon may demand a particular intelligence product. The Reagan White House did not want to hear about the military and economic weakness of the Evil Empire since this would undermine its remilitarisation agenda. The 1991 confirmation hearings of Robert Gates as Director of Central Intelligence elicited copious testimony from former agency analysts detailing how Gates had perverted the interpretation of intelligence on the Soviets to 'fit' the Cold War preconceptions of Reagan's Director, William Casey. One consequence of this cooking of intelligence was that the Americans were caught ludicrously unprepared for the collapse of the Soviet state.

Covert Action

Discussion has so far been confined to intelligence as information gathering. The notoriety of intelligence tends to attach much more to what the Americans call 'covert action', or what the former KGB termed 'active measures'. Covert action refers to attempts to actually influence events in targeted countries by surreptitious means. This could include a range of activities from concealed support for particular political forces, covert propaganda and disinformation, and indirectly instigated economic destabilisation, to covert support for paramilitary attempts to overthrow a regime, or even political assassination. In this way US intelligence helped overthrow governments in Iraq and Guatemala in the 1950s, Chile in the 1970s and Nicaragua in the 1980s, and sponsored or assisted untold mischief and suffering in other parts of the world on behalf of American policy goals (southern Africa and Indonesia being two grisly examples). Although outright bloodshed has been confined to the Third World, the CIA covertly intervened from time to time in Italy against the Communist party and has, of course, offered hidden subsidies and other forms of assistance to right-wing trade unions, anti-Communist publications and cultural organisations throughout the world.[7] The KGB, despite a luridly exaggerated reputation thanks to anti-Communist extremists and Western intelligence, never came close to emulating the global reach of American covert activity. But it did try. French and British agencies have been active in their traditional spheres of influence abroad, and the Israelis have certainly not shrunk from covert activities within Arab states, and against Palestinian 'terrorists' (loosely defined) on the international stage.

It seems inevitable that intelligence as information-gathering will spill over into intelligence as covert intervention. Only small countries with relatively limited security stakes and no real external clout appear capable of confining themselves to simply gathering and interpreting information. To great powers, or to smaller powers with critical regional security concerns, the temptation to transform intelligence capacity from passive to active is overwhelming. It is not hard to see why. Intelligence even in the more passive sense involves the development of 'assets' in targeted countries. Why not convert these assets when the occasion demands from sources of information to active agents of influence, or at least elements of operations designed to influence rather than simply track events? The temptation has rarely been avoided, despite a questionable record of long-term political benefit to the intervening power. The overthrow of the Mossadegh government in Iran by the CIA in 1953 was for years accepted within the agency as a textbook example of 'how to', but the return of the Shah scarcely turned out to be in the long term interests of the United States. Much of the impetus in the 1970s and again during the Iran-Contra affair for greater Congressional oversight of US intelligence activities abroad arose from the perceived damaged to US prestige and interests caused by the cowboys of covert action. None of this scepticism can realistically be expected to do more than confine future covert actions within certain guidelines for the prior advice and consent of Congress behind firmly closed doors.[8] The existence of networks of intelligence assets at the disposal of big powers is similar to the maintenance of large standing armies: if they exist, they will likely be used.

The Domestic Face of Intelligence

None of these various faces of 'external' intelligence are without domestic consequences, often of the most serious nature. The emergence of the national security state as a state form in the late twentieth century inherently blurs, if not obliterates, the distinction between external and internal surveillance. Eisenhower warned of the military–industrial complex which had arisen as a result of the Cold War. Of course, no state could practise militarism abroad and remain immune from the effects of militarism at home. The same is true for the kinds of permanent interventionism abroad represented by an intelligence establishment. Intelligence entails counter-intelligence. Counter-intelligence requires an intensive regime of internal security: censorship, propaganda, security screening, loyalty tests, surveillance and active discouragement of domestic political dissent, even the occasional political trial *pour encourager les autres*.

The more aggressive and intrusive a state's external intelligence activity, the more lurid its imagination about the covert threat posed by its enemies. The rise of McCarthyism in the United States in the late 1940s and early 1950s coincided with the high point of Western-sponsored disruptions, destabilisations and even armed banditry behind the Iron Curtain. By the time America had come to terms with the existence of an effective Soviet sphere of influence in Eastern Europe, McCarthyism was largely banished from the American public realm as an excessive and dangerous response to the Soviet threat. A more routinised and institutionalised form of the domestic security regime followed, in keeping with the institutionalisation of the Cold War as a relatively stable system. But even safely within the 'legitimate' sphere of state action, the domestic security regime remains one primarily of repression.[9]

Above all, the identification and isolation of security 'risks' rests on the naming of certain personal or group attributes – ideological certainty, but sometimes ethnic or religious – as inherently 'risky' by association with external enemies. During the Cold War era, 'Communist' beliefs, sympathies or associations (often defined pretty elastically) were in effect proscribed in countries like the United States and the Federal Republic of Germany, or severely circumscribed within ineffectual ghettoes in countries like Italy and France. The shrunken horizons of the universe of political discourse under such regimes are obvious: we will live with the effects for generations.

More recently, with the end of the Cold War, there appears to be general agreement that the Reds-under-the-bed, for whom there had been a furious hunt for four decades, either never existed or long since expired unnoticed while under deep cover. With the threat of terrorism and the Gulf War, however, different kinds of 'risks' have risen to the notice of Western security establishments. As a series of judicial scandals has embarrassingly enfolded in Britain, it has become obvious that being an Irish Catholic in England can be potentially dangerous to one's health. Complaints have similarly been raised by people of Arabic origin or Moslem faith about being targeted as security risks. During the Gulf War a number of British residents of Arabic origin were rounded up for deportation, even though some of them were actually anti-Saddam Hussein in their politics. In the era of intelligence wars, there are always potential enemy agents within and thus always a need for political policing.

The implications of permanent political policing for the practice of liberal democracy need little elaboration – although large sections of the British parliament and press apparently see no problem in domestic spying. In the United States, Congress and the media have fitfully, but not without occasional effect, cast baleful eyes on domestic surveillance by the state. Other Western countries such as Canada and Australia have developed mechanisms for accountability of security agencies.[10] Freedom of information laws are also of some significance in focusing public attention through investigative journalism and scholarship. The British government remains obdurately against reform, despite evidence of MI5 involvement in attempts to destabilise or discredit the Wilson Labour government, and perhaps even the Heath Conservatives.[11] Legitimate criticism of British disregard for civil liberties aside,[12] there is probably not in practice a great deal of difference between the security regimes in any of the Western states. Where a persistent threat to public order and safety exists (as is the case in Britain with the IRA), the repressive potential will be extended. But the point about the domestic implications of intelligence establishments is that even in the absence of genuine threats, the machinery remains in place, to be activated when required.

C'est La Guerre

The dramatic collapse of the Soviet Bloc is an epochal event in the history of modern intelligence. Intelligence on a global scale was organised around the central fact of the Cold War since the late 1940s. While there were regional conflicts which importantly shaped the goals of smaller players (most notably the Middle East), even these were tied inexorably to the bipolarities of the Cold War, given the insistence of the superpowers on imposing Cold War alliances and antagonisms. The Third World was an extended battlefield over which the two blocs waged indirect intelligence wars over regional and local issues redefined in globally strategic terms. And the Third World was also a kind of Cold War Monopoly board over which the major players fought to directly control especially valuable properties upon which could be erected intelligence counters: strategic listening posts, staging bases for agents, points for disseminating propaganda and disinformation.

Within the two blocs, the superpowers imposed their hegemony over their smaller partners under a rigorous system of dominance and subordination in intelligence sharing. The UKUSA agreements of 1947 were the foundation for a global network of sophisticated electronic eavesdropping technology, but the subtext, as it were, of these agreements was the institutionalised hegemony of American TECHINT with its nervecentre at the Fort Meade, Maryland, headquarters of the NSA. The British were established as 'senior', but in practice subordinate, partners, while smaller countries like Canada, Australia and New Zealand are *de jure*, as well as *de facto*, junior partners. Other countries have been added later to the network but as 'third parties'.[13] There are a number of points to make about this arrangement. First, the entire world-wide network was always targeted at the Soviet Bloc: the intelligence objectives of all the partners have thus been congealed in a Cold War pattern. Second, American leadership has always meant that to a considerable extent, allies feed raw, or semi-finished, intelligence to the US. In exchange they receive back intelligence interpreted by Washington. This has always seemed like a good deal to junior partners since it allows them access to a finished product which they could never develop on their own, but needless to say it allows the United States to diffuse its own interpretation of the world. Finally, the sharing of intelligence brings with it an additional American lever of influence over its allies: American security standards and methods are imposed upon other countries as necessary protection for American secrets.

The connection is made all the more effective by the fact that it typically works at the interbureaucratic liaison level rather than at the politically sensitive level of elected governments. An embarrassing by-product of the murky and suspicious affair of KAL 007, the Korean airliner shot down over Soviet airspace in 1983, was the public disclosure of intelligence gathered from a US listening post on Japanese territory, which co-operating Japanese signals intelligence officers had agreed to keep secret from their own military superiors as well as government officials.[14] International intelligence 'communities' thus form a curious kind of bureaucratic Internationale operating under the noses of and sometimes even against the wishes of national governments. MI5's Charlie McCarthy, Chapman Pincher, once wrote that from the point of view of the British intelligence establishment, dependence on the international connection is 'so great and cooperation so close that I am convinced security chiefs would go to any length to protect the link-up'.[15] Including, as Pincher has enthusiastically endorsed, actively destabilising a government elected by the British people.

Of course there have been tensions within the Western intelligence community. The Americans were enraged at the alleged laxity of the British following the series of spy scandals in the 1950s and 1960s involving Burgess, Maclean, Philby, Blake and others. For their part, the British have harboured feelings of resentment at American presumption.[16] The French have typically played their own game from time to time, within the limits of their resources, on occasion reportedly bugging and spying on American officials.[17] And the Israeli–American intelligence connection is one which has drawn much curious attention, especially since the conviction of the American civil servant Jonathan Pollard for espionage on behalf of Israel.[18] Yet so long as the Cold War endured as the overarching framework for intelligence activity, these tensions were kept marginal. For instance, it has recently been revealed that 'for a decade and a half the United States has provided substantial covert assistance to the nuclear forces of France' – in violation of US law and in contradiction to France's public protestations of an autonomous military stance.[19] Even so egregiously bloody-minded an act of independence as the deliberate destruction by the Israeli air force, with the loss of 34 American lives, of the American surveillance ship the *USS Liberty*, which had been monitoring Israeli operations during the 1967 Arab–Israeli war, was quickly swept under the carpet by both governments so as not to endanger the anti-Soviet alliance in the Middle East.[20]

What To Do When The Enemy Vanishes

And then the global antagonist of the past half century simply vanished. There had been warnings of this strange disappearance, but the hardliners in Western intelligence agencies were quick to dismiss reports of imminent Soviet demise as clever KGB disinformation designed, in one of the favourite clichés of the Cold Warriors, to 'lull us into a false sense of security'. Reaching again into the old cliché bag, these same 'experts' declared that unlike squishy liberal appeasers, they harboured no 'illusions' about the Soviet beast. In fact it was precisely the hardline orthodoxy that turned out to be the greatest illusion of all. The intelligence community by and large believed the smoke and mirrors show put on by the Wizard of Oz and could scarcely credit their own eyes when a shrunken, unprepossessing and pathetic little figure finally crept out from behind the facade.

This reluctance is understandable when we consider how much is at stake. It is nothing less than the entire institutional and ideological underpinning of intelligence in the postwar world. And in particular it is American hegemony over the Western intelligence community. Alliances, after all, work when there is a common enemy. There is moreover a huge capital and labour investment in Cold War-driven intelligence. TECHINT is like a gun; however sophisticated the technology, it must be pointed at a target. Reconnaissance satellites, for instance, have fixed orbits and cannot be simply and cheaply redeployed to new targets. But HUMINT too has its own 'inertial thrust' (to steal a phrase from E. P. Thompson). Years of painstaking work in building up networks of agents and sources will not be easily cast aside. Counter-intelligence targeted almost exclusively on the KGB has produced a substantial investment in personnel. Of course bureaucrats will be reluctant to start over again.[21] But the point of no return has finally been reached. After the breakup of the Soviet Union, the 'Soviet threat' to the West no longer frightens even small children and impressionable generals.

A new intelligence paradigm is required to replace the old. One outcome which can be ruled out of court at the outset is that intelligence will be phased out, having outlived its usefulness. Apart from the usual motives of bureaucratic survival, and the ingenious ways in which intelligence agencies with their privileged control over information can manipulate their own job descriptions, the disappearance of the old antagonist should not prove fatal. The preconditions for intelligence as a permanent government function lie in the modern state system. The Cold War was simply a particular configuration of this system. In gauging the effect of the end of the Cold War, it is imperative not to mistake the rhetoric of the Cold War for the reality. Ideological polemics and nuclear sabre-rattling aside, the Cold War had settled into a balance of power system by the early 1950s which fostered a great deal of stability and predictability in international relations. Part of this stability was based somewhat ironically on the 'war by other means' which was intelligence. Specifically, TECHINT in the form of a satellite reconnaissance regime became an important element of trust between the superpowers. As John Lewis Gaddis puts it, 'the fact that the Americans and Russians have actually *cooperated* in spying on one another was in itself, for many years, one of the better kept secrets of the Cold War'.[22] The ability of spy satellites to detect and thus prevent surprise attacks was tacitly recognised by both sides as useful; as a consequence, both sides cooperated to ban anti-satellite weaponry which could have threatened this element of stability. More recently, high-tech surveillance capabilities provided the basis for reductions in arms. The sticky point of on-site inspections was in reality just the icing on the cake. Now that the former Soviet Union has become an unprecedented international phenomenon, a decomposing nuclear power, American surveillance capabilities allow for relatively effective management of the reduction and perhaps even elimination of the ex-Soviet atomic arsenal. Things could still go wrong, with horrific consequences, but American intelligence can at least track the movements of weapons and missiles with great accuracy. It is unlikely that any of the Soviet successor states can hide a nuclear capacity from the eyes in the sky.

The same, of course, goes for smaller states with pretensions to become nuclear powers (viz., Iraq and Pakistan). Here too American intelligence will play a key role in policing the spread of nuclear arms. Politically, the American role might well be criticised as selective and hypocritical (the scandal of the Israeli bomb is one which will stick in many Third World, especially Arab, throats), but the extremely uncomfortable fact remains that with the end of the Soviet counterbalance, a jittery world can have little recourse but to rely on American self-interest to prevent further nuclear proliferation – and thus to rely on a continued American global surveillance regime.

Satellite reconnaissance was not the only area where Soviet–American cooperation in intelligence predated the end of the Cold War. Although the Reagan CIA had tried unsuccessfully in the early 1980s to force the phenomenon of international terrorism into a Cold War mould (the ludicrous 'Bulgarian plot' to kill the Pope being the most egregious item),[23] by the late 1980s, the tone had shifted significantly, with various American intelligence officials noting that both states had a common cause in working against international 'anarchy' perpetuated by unruly non-state actors. In October 1989, a group of retired top-level CIA and KGB officials met under the auspices of the RAND Corporation in Santa Monica, California to explore a 'dialogue' on co-operation against terrorism.[24] This was public, but it appears that more serious secret contacts may have been made between the two old antagonists.[25] It may be assumed, although there has been no official confirmation, that the Soviets shared intelligence on Iraq and on forces allied to Saddam Hussein with the Americans during the Gulf War.

All these cooperative glimmerings have, of course, been rudely superceded by the rush of events. There is perhaps little left in Moscow now for the Americans to cooperate with. The remnants of the KGB are now being gobbled up by the successor states. The hope of the professionals in the organisation in the aftermath of the failed coup against Gorbachev was that they could give up their odious role in internal repression and become a more 'legitimate' external intelligence agency like the CIA. The dismemberment of the Soviet state leaves such a prospect without a base. Yeltsin has already shown an appetite for incorporating an internal security force, and other republics may well follow suit – especially when power struggles like that in Georgia ensue, as they certainly will. Some of the least admirable elements of the old KGB may thus be recreated in a series of smaller internally-directed forces. But what is less and less likely is that any external intelligence capacity with global reach will survive, certainly nothing remotely comparable to the KGB of old.

Even this development may have less significance than might appear on the surface. There is growing evidence that the once-vaunted reputation of the KGB (fattened long ago on the defections of ideologically-motivated spies like Kim Philby) was about as grotesquely overdrawn as the persistently alarmist reports of alleged Soviet military might. From at least the 1970s, Western intelligence was actually gaining far more high-level moles than they were losing in the other direction. One of the most important of these double agents, Oleg Gordievsky, has recently published, with Christopher Andrew, a documentary record of KGB instructions to its foreign operations in the late 1970s and early 1980s – the picture painted is of incompetence and stupidity on a scale almost derisory.[26] The decline and collapse of the USSR was actually foreshadowed in the decline into senility of its intelligence establishment.

American intelligence was already preeminent on a global scale long before the end of the Cold War. The collapse of the Soviet state does not mean an unexpected victory for the US; it does mean that US intelligence is now free to turn its power on targets of its own choosing without having to anticipate the moves of an antagonist who had long since lost his touch but lingered on in the game as a nuisance.

Fighting the Next War

What will intelligence agencies do in the post-Cold War world? I have already suggested an important, indeed necessary, role for (US) TECH-INT: monitoring nuclear disarmament and policing nuclear proliferation. More controversial is the continued role of the US and other Western states in the Third World. There is little reason to anticipate any diminution of intelligence activity here. The imposition of Cold War definitions on regional Third World conflicts was always an artificial operation which masked the real material interests which the US was advancing.[27] These interests remain and, if anything, can now be pursued more nakedly than in the past, without having to pander to rhetorical contests with the Soviet about anti-imperialism and national liberation. This may mean that covert activity, as such, may give way to more overt use of force, as already in Grenada, Libya, Panama and Iraq. In this sense the intelligence arm may be relied upon less than the military arm when there is little fear of local interventions escalating into world war. Yet it remains true that military interventions are costly, risky, and require considerable priming of domestic public opinion. Covert activity is always tempting as an apparently cheaper and 'cleaner' means of getting something done; the political risks, although considerable, are more easily concealed in the short run – always a tempting prospect to governments. Thus we might anticipate continued covert action in the Third World as an adjunct or accompaniment to greater reliance on the overt threat of military intervention.

The Future of the Counter-Terrorism Industry

Another intelligence requirement, to which I alluded earlier, is counter-terrorism. The threat posed by non-state actors to international order has been greatly magnified by those with a stake in puffing up a post-Soviet threat which can mobilise public support for increased security expenditures. Notorious atrocities like airliners blown out of the sky have raised understandable fears on the part of ordinary citizens for their own safety. The actual incidence of terrorist assaults on innocent third parties is extremely low (more Americans die annually from dog bites than from terrorist attacks), but as acts designed for maximum publicity they elicit a public *frisson* out of all proportion to their incidence. A counter-terrorism industry (partly in government but also located in the private sector) has done very well by exploiting these fears.[28] Characteristically, the 'experts' insist that the political causes of terrorist actions are irrelevant but that resources should be spent on maximum force, especially of a technological kind, to prevent the effects of terrorism.[29] This operational principle allows the US to attack progressive movements in the Third World as 'terrorist' and even to claim the moral support of the 'international community'. The invention of 'narco-terrorism' (Noriega) and 'techno-terrorism' (Saddam Hussein) as made-in-Washington constructs allow considerable scope for intrusive American penetration of the national sovereignty of Third World states, just as 'state-sponsored terrorism' justified the air attack on Libya.

The Americans, however, have a problem with counter-terrorism. The weapons and methods available to violent non-state actors tend to be peculiarly resistant to surveillance by the favoured means of TECHINT. Reconnaissance satellites can yield astonishingly detailed information about many things, but they cannot indicate much about movements of small numbers of terrorists planning, say, to assemble and detonate a bomb at a location known only to them. And technology will go only so far in permitting detection of bombs and other terrorist devices. Only human agents are likely to yield the kind of specific intelligence which can actually prevent actions by infiltrating and countering terrorist cells. There does not seem to be strong evidence of Western success in this regard. One shortcut which has tempted American counter-terrorism has been to strike alliances with elements already operating in the shadowy world of terrorist activity – with dangerous consequences, as evident from American disasters in Lebanon. Worse yet is American sponsorship of right-wing forces eager to employ terrorist methods against left-wing movements. The Frankenstein monster of Renamo in Mozambique is a case so egregarious that the State Department has actually felt compelled to denounce that group's barbarities.

The search for effective counter-terrorist methods has very much strengthened the ties between United States intelligence and the hard right in Israel, centred in the military and intelligence establishment and the Likud party. This in turn creates dissonance and conflict within the American state in the making of Middle Eastern policy. Although the State Department would obviously like to see an Arab–Israeli settlement that would protect oil supplies while allowing the Americans to turn their attention to other parts of the world, the influence of the Israeli hardliners not only on US public opinion but on those elements of the national security apparatus with which they have formed tactical alliances, forms significant blockages. Other, less dramatic, rigidities are similarly imposed in other regions by parallel alliances.

Although terrorist activity seems to have gone into some abeyance since the late 1980s, it may well return to prominence in the decade ahead. American military hegemony, and American willingness to use its power directly and nakedly in the new unipolar post-Cold War world, may displace frustrated national movements onto the desperate plane of international terrorism. This will force the US to expand its human as well as its technical intelligence capacities, and will inevitably entangle US policy in the complex snares of tactical alliances with dubious forces, both state and non-state. In short, the counter-terrorism industry has a future which it certainly does not deserve on its own merits. And we can anticipate the maintenance, even the enhancement of many elements of the repressive domestic security regime that came as part of the Cold War package.

Intelligence in a World of Shared Hegemony

If the demise of the Soviet bloc means the end of bipolarity in the old sense, it does not mean the end of divisions over hegemony within the capitalist world. One of the functions of Western intelligence cooperation during the Cold War, as I tried to make clear earlier, was integrating the Western bloc under American hegemony through inter-bureaucratic linkages. Relatively effective as this was, it cannot survive the end of the Cold War unscathed. The distrust between states that underlines the very existence of intelligence was only partially repressed within the Western alliance by a common anticommunist ideology. Without this glue, divisions of interest will widen. Whether or not NATO remains intact in one form or another, the NATO allies will increasingly spy on one another, especially when economic and commercial secrets are at stake. And in the context of global capitalist competition, America will find increasing reason to spy upon Japan, and vice versa, while Europe will remain suspicious and watchful in regard to both the North American and Far Eastern economic blocs.

This scenario might seem to indicate an end to American intelligence hegemony, but this is not necessarily the case. As Stansfield Turner, former Director of Central Intelligence under President Carter, has written in a recent piece on 'Intelligence for a New World Order': '. . . we live in an information age . . . Information always has been power, but today there is more opportunity to obtain good information, *and the United States has more capability to do that than any other nation*'.[30] Turner is right. Just as America remains the dominant military power in the world, overshadowing Europe and Japan in sheer might, so too the US has by far the greatest espionage capacity. In HUMINT, decades of global CIA involvement has left the US with by far the most extensive networks of human assets. This is also the case in the capital-intensive area of TECH-INT. Other countries have gone into the satellite reconnaissance business, but the cost of matching the US capability is prohibitive.[31] Moreover the US has a big technological lead derived from its years of specialisation and the high priority granted research and development of imaging technology by the American state. Americans may not be able to produce automobiles and home entertainment equipment to compete commercially with the Japanese, but they can take on any comers in high-tech espionage.

At the outset of the Cold War, America held combined military and economic hegemony over the capitalist world. At the outset of the New World Order, America has lost much economic ground to its Japanese and European competitors, but retains its military hegemony. A key question for American policy-makers is how to use this military superiority to maintain its broader leadership. The kind of costly adventure represented by the Gulf War in which American arms were bankrolled by Japanese and German money seems a dubious means of maintaining hegemony: playing global rent-a-cops only confirms America in its addiction to a Pentagon capitalism which further erodes its commercial competitiveness. Is *fin de siècle* America then locked into a vicious cycle of decline? This is too large a question to be addressed here, but I would like to point to some implications of the role of intelligence.

Stansfield Turner makes an interesting point in this regard when he asserts that in the New World Order

> the preeminent threat to US national security now lies in the economic sphere. The United States has turned from being a major creditor nation to the world's largest debtor, and there are countless industries where US companies are no longer competitive. That means we will need better economic intelligence. The United States does not want to be surprised by such worldwide developments as technological breakthroughs, new mercantilist strategies, sudden shortages of raw materials or unfair or illegal economic practices that disadvantage the country.

There needs to be, Turner adds, a 'more symbiotic relationship between the worlds of intelligence and business'.[32] The retired CIA director may have put his finger on the most important new development for the immediate future.

Each of the three capitalist economic blocs will have traditional political security concerns. Europe will be particularly concerned about the politically and economically unstable transitions to market systems in Eastern Europe and the former Soviet Union. Japan will have a strong interest in political developments in China, Korea and southeast Asia. And America will maintain a keen interest in the stability of pro-American regimes in Latin America and the Caribbean. Effective intelligence will be an obvious requirement in each case. But beyond these concerns are the direct economic rivalries among the blocs. Intelligence is already employed extensively in the private sector: industrial espionage is a specialised corporate function.[33] There are at least two broad areas where economic intelligence can be of utility in the new era of capitalist competition. States can offer intelligence assistance to their own nationally-based corporations in spying on foreign competitors, stealing technology, offering sophisticated 'risk analysis' to corporations operating abroad, and so on. On the other side, governments will find it expedient to privatise or contract out to the private sector elements of their intelligence operations which they wish to keep at arm's length (viz. the Iran-Contra affair). This is Turner's 'symbiotic relationship' between intelligence and business. It presents the prospect of a new and enhanced role for the national capitalist state in the era of global competition as well as a further blurring of the lines between the public and private sectors. It also raises interesting questions about the nationality or home base of multinational corporations. American policy-makers, for instance, will have a delicate problem when dealing with American-based business taken over by Japanese capital. These are new and unprecedented problems for the intelligence world which were rarely glimpsed in the old Cold War days.

The second area of economic intelligence is the production of what might be called macro, as opposed to micro, economic information. International competitiveness can be enhanced by the availability of detailed world resource inventories, long-range forecasting of shifting weather patterns, the impact of new technologies, global migration movements, demographic transformations, impending environmental problems and their implications, and so on. The awesome capacities of TECHINT allied to electronic data processing might actually be put to better use when applied to these kinds of problems than to the massing of vast amounts of trivial bits of information about the Cold War 'enemy'.

In relation to both macro and micro economic intelligence, the Americans are much better placed than their European and Japanese competitors. Both the latter start from weaker technological bases and lack the existing global reach of American intelligence. The Europeans have particular problems of diseconomies of scale. Despite the growing economic integration of the European Community, intelligence remains fragmented into national services, divided by traditional jealousies, with little immediate prospect of pooling their resources on a community-wide basis. Yet without such pooling, they cannot hope to offer the kind of assistance to European corporations that the US intelligence community can offer its corporations. Japan also suffers from an underdeveloped intelligence arm, which it is currently trying to beef up. Japanese corporations are good sources' of economic intelligence but they apparently do not always share this with the state and Japan thus lacks an effective coordinated public-private intelligence capacity. One Japanese official recently described Japanese intelligence as 'half a century' behind its competitors.[34] Efforts to catch up run into resistance both at home and abroad, given Japan's past history of militarism and expansion.

Intelligence does offer America an advantage in the economic competition between the three blocs. Whether it can use this advantage over the long run is another matter. After all, it must still produce the goods that will sell on world markets. But beyond the competitive advantage of blocs, there is a broader and grimmer perspective in which to place the role of intelligence in the service of wealth. The capital-intensive, high-technology control of information at the end of the twentieth century is yet one more formidable power of the capitalist blocs over the Third World, as well as over the former Communist states.

As the gulf between the rich and poor nations widens and the helplessness and despair of the wretched of the earth deepens, we can appreciate the prescience of the Brazilian president in discerning a post-Cold War 'Empire of the North', 'which controls the most advanced forces of knowledge'. Intelligence is one more weapon in the hands of the strong.

NOTES

1. Mary Kaldor, *The Imaginary War: Understanding the East-West Conflict* (Oxford 1990).
2. Hobbes, *Leviathan*, Part I, Chapter 13.
3. *Macbeth*, Act 2, Scene 4.
4. Fred Kaplan, *The Wizards of Armageddon* (NY 1983); Thomas Powers, *Thinking About the Next War* (NY 1983); Gregg Herken, *Counsels of War* (NY 1985).
5. For American examples: Robin Winks, *Cloak & Gown: Scholars in the Secret War, 1939–1961* (NY 1987) and Barry M. Katz, *Foreign Intelligence: Research and Analysis in the Office of Strategic Services, 1942–1945* (Cambridge, Mass. 1989). In Britain, the code-breaking triumphs of Bletchley Park were only made possible by the active recruitment of academics.
6. One of the best examples of the irreplaceable value of HUMINT was a colonel attached to the Polish General Staff in the early 1980s who was working for US intelligence. Although satellite and other TECHINT intelligence pointed to a large Soviet military buildup near the Polish border during the intensification of the Solidarity-inspired legitimation crisis of the regime, this informant was able to tell the Americans that the Polish generals intended to pre-empt a Czech-style Soviet intervention by their own military coup, which was of course carried out with the declaration of martial law in 1981.
7. John Prados, *Presidents' Secret Wars: CIA and Pentagon covert operations since World War II* (NY 1986); William Blum, *The CIA: a Forgotten History. US Global Interventions Since*

World War II (London 1986); Gregory Treverton, *Covert Action: the Limits of Intervention in the Postwar World* (NY 1987).

8. Loch K. Johnson, *A Season of Inquiry: Congress and Intelligence* (Chicago 1988); Frank J. Smirst, Jr., *Congress Oversees the United States Intelligence Community 1947–1989* (Tennessee 1990).

9. See an earlier article of mine in *The Socialist Register* (1984), 'Fighting the Cold War on the home front: America, Britain, Australia and Canada', 23–67.

10. Reg Whitaker, 'The politics of security-intelligence policy making in Canada 1, 1970–1984', *Intelligence and National Security* 6:4 (October 1991); 'The politics of security-intelligence making in Canada 2, 1984–1991', *Intelligence and National Security* 7:2 (April 1992).

11. Steve Dorrill and Robin Ramsay, *Smear!: Wilson and the Secret State* (London 1991); David Leigh, *The Wilson Plot* (London 1988); Paul Foot, *Who Framed Colin Wallace?* (London 1989).

12. Paddy Hillyard & Janie Percy-Smith, *The Coercive State: the Decline of Democracy in Britain* (London 1988); K. D. Ewing & G. A. Gearty, *Freedom Under Thatcher: Civil Liberties in Modern Britain* (Oxford 1990); Clive Ponting, *Secrecy in Britain* (London 1990); Patrick Birkinshaw, *Reforming the Secret State* (Bristol 1990).

13. Jeffrey T. Richelson & Desmond Ball, *The Ties That Bind: Intelligence Cooperation between the UKUSA Countries* (Boston 1985); James Bamford, *The Puzzle Palace* (NY 1983).

14. Seymour Hersh, *The Target is Destroyed* (NY 1986) 57–62; 139–49.

15. *Inside Story* (NY 1979) 38.

16. Perhaps the most subtle rendering of the tensions between British intelligence and the American 'cousins' can be found in the novels of John LeCarré.

17. Roger Faligot and Pascal Krop, *La Piscine: the French Secret Service Since 1944* (NY 1989); Jeffrey T. Richelson, *Foreign Intelligence Organizations* (Cambridge, Mass. 1988) 151–90.

18. Two recent books query aspects of this relationship: Andrew and Leslie Cockburn, *Dangerous Liaison: the Inside Story of the US–Israeli Covert Relationship* (Toronto 1991) and the controversial *The Samson Option: Israel's Nuclear Arsenal and American Foreign Policy* by Seymour Hersh (NY 1991).

19. Richard H. Ullman, 'The covert French connection', *Foreign Policy* 75 (Summer 1989) 3–33.

20. For details of this little known but chilling incident – an astonishing example of biting the hand that feeds – see James M. Ennes, Jr., *Assault on the Liberty* (NY 1979). The attack was implausibly passed off by the Israelis as an 'accident'.

21. As late as November 28, 1991 the Director of the Canadian Security Intelligence Service told puzzled parliamentarians that Soviet espionage remained the leading counter-intelligence preoccupation of the agency (Geoffrey York, 'No reduction yet in Soviet spying, CSIS head reports', *The Globe & Mail*, 29 Nov. 1991). Within a couple of weeks, the Soviet Union had disappeared.

22. 'Learning to live with transparency: the evolution of a reconnaissance satellite regime', in Gaddis, *The Long Peace: Inquiries into the History of the Cold War* (NY 1987) 196.

23. The appearance of the preposterous *Terror Network* by Claire Sterling in 1981 occasioned one of the more amusing examples of self-destructing intelligence. Not known for his wide-ranging reading, Ronald Reagan did peruse this piece of anti-Soviet hysteria, and told CIA director William Casey he should too. Casey was impressed enough to order the agency to get on the tail of the Soviet connection as elucidated by Sterling. Appalled professionals in the agency had to point out that Sterling was merely regurgitating disinformation carefully spread by the CIA itself. This became known in the trade as a case of 'product blowback'.

24. This meeting has been reported in a volume edited by John Marks and Igor Beliaev, *Common Ground on Terrorism: Soviet–American Cooperation Against the Politics of Terror* (NY 1991).

10. LeCarré, always a sensitive barometer of such matters, has George Smiley sitting on a joint committee on terrorism with the KGB in his most recent novel (*The Secret Pilgrim*) published at the end of 1990.

26. *Instructions from the Centre: Top Secret Files on KGB Foreign Operations, 1975–1985* (London 1991). At one point Gordievsky was required to leave a giant artificial brick – large enough to accommodate 400 £20 notes in a cavity – on a path in Coram's Fields in Bloomsbury, to be picked up by an illegal newly landed in Britain. It was lucky for the KGB that this Keystone Cops operation did not end with a passer-by tripping and injuring themselves on this object.

27. 'The irony of US policy in the Third World is that while it has always justified its larger objectives and efforts in the name of anticommunism, its own goals have made it unable to tolerate change from *any* quarter that impinged significantly on its interests.': Gabriel Kolko, *Confronting the Third World: United States Foreign Policy, 1945–1980* (NY 1988) 292.

28. See Edward Herman and Gerry O'Sullivan, *The 'Terrorism' Industry: the Experts and Institutions that Shape Our View of Terror* (NY 1989).

29. For a sensitive and discriminating discussion of the causes of terrorism, see Richard Rubenstein, *Alchemists of Revolution: Terrorism in the Modern World* (NY 1987), a book either ignored or rejected by the counter-terrorist industry.

30. Stansfield Turner, 'Intelligence for a New World Order', *Foreign Affairs* (Fall 1991) 151 [emphasis added].

31. Michael Krepon, 'Spying from space', *Foreign Policy* 75 (Summer 1989) 92–108; Jeffrey T. Richelson, 'The future of space reconnaissance', *Scientific American* 264:1 (January 1991), 38–44. The British *Zircon* spy satellite project had to be shelved when journalists revealed its existence – and its cost. The clumsy attempt to ban a television exposé demonstrated that the real reason for secrecy was to conceal the project from the British taxpayers, not the Soviets, who would certainly have noticed when it went into orbit.

32. Turner, 'Intelligence', 151–2.

33. Richard Eells & Peter Nehemkis, *Corporate Intelligence and Espionage: A Blueprint for Executive Decision Making* (NY 1984); Herbert Meyer, *Real World Intelligence: Organized Information for Executives* (NY 1987).

34. David Sanger, 'Japanese expanding intelligence services', *The Globe & Mail*, 2 January 1992.

US MILITARY POLICY IN THE POST-COLD WAR ERA

Michael T. Klare

The Persian Gulf War of January-February 1991 was the first major crisis of the Post-Cold War Era, and for many analysts represents a watershed in the evolution of US military strategy. 'The Second of August 1990 will be remembered for generations to come as a turning point for the United States in its conduct of foreign affairs,' General Carl E. Vuono of the Army observed in 1991 – 'the day America announced the end of Containment and embarked upon the strategy of power projection.'[1] But while it is certainly true that the Gulf War will have a substantial and long-lasting impact on US military thinking, it is important to recognise that the process of reshaping US grand strategy for the Post-Cold War era began well before the onset of the Persian Gulf crisis, and arose as much for domestic considerations – in particular, from a need to articulate a viable rationale for maintaining a large military establishment in the absence of a credible Soviet threat – as it did from international developments. In evaluating this process, two key developments require particular attention:

First, the Gulf War institutionalised *a new paradigm of combat* that will in all likelihood govern US military planning for a generation to come. To describe this new paradigm, we can use the term 'mid-intensity conflict,' meaning conflict that falls below the level of 'high-intensity conflict' (or all-out global war between the United States and the Soviet Union), and above the level of 'low-intensity conflict' (or counter-insurgency and small-scale military operations such as those conducted in Grenada and Panama).

Second, the Persian Gulf war legitimised *a new assertion of Pax Americana*, or the discretionary use of US military power by the President to protect and enforce certain rules of international behaviour that have been dictated by Washington. This posture is often confused – sometimes intentionally – with the concept of a 'New World Order', but, as I will argue, these are two very different concepts.

Having introduced these two basic propositions, let me examine each in greater detail.

The new military paradigm:

Until 1990, the United States military had only two clear paradigms to guide its strategic thinking – the paradigm of high-intensity conflict (HIC), or all-out war with the Warsaw Pact on the plains of Europe, and the paradigm of low-intensity conflict (LIC), or counter-insurgency and police-type operations in underdeveloped Third World areas. The first, HIC, was developed in response to the threat posed by massive Soviet forces in Eastern Europe. This paradigm envisioned the use of heavy tank forces backed by artillery and airpower in sustained, massive battles stretching across Germany, Czechoslovakia, Poland, and adjacent countries. Although the United States was prepared to fight such a war with non-nuclear weapons, it also reserved the right to employ nuclear weapons on a first-use basis to avert defeat in such a conflict.

The second paradigm was developed in the late 1950s and early 1960s in response to an upsurge of guerilla warfare (or 'wars of national liberation', as they were known at the time) in the colonial and ex-colonial areas of Africa, Asia, and Latin America. The LIC or 'counter-insurgency' paradigm involved US military and economic aid to threatened Third World regimes and, *in extremis*, direct US military intervention (as in Vietnam and the Dominican Republic). The strategy of counter-insurgency was discredited by the US defeat in Vietnam, but was revived again in the Reagan era under the banner of low-intensity conflict. In line with current US military doctrine, LIC also includes counter-terrorism, narcotics interdiction, pro-insurgency (or support for anti-communist insurgencies in the Third World), and small-scale 'contingency' operations like those conducted in Grenada and Panama.[2]

These two paradigms effectively governed the organisation and 'armamentation' of US military forces (what the military calls *force structure*), as well as the strategies and doctrine governing the actual use of US forces, for most of the Cold War era. Thus, in response to the HIC threat, the United States maintained 'heavy' forces equipped with large numbers of tanks, rockets, artillery pieces, and support aircraft; for LIC, it established 'light' forces that could be rapidly deployed to distant locations. Each of these sets of forces, moreover, had their own sets of strategies, tactics, and doctrines.

This was where things stood in December 1989 when, for all practical purposes, the Cold War came to an end. For many people, the end of the Cold War was viewed as a great blessing, allowing for the reallocation of resources from the military to the civilian sector; for the US military establishment, however, it was seen as an unmitigated disaster. Why is this so? The answer lies in the fact that the two paradigms described above provided no rationale for the continued maintenance of large military forces in the post-Cold War era, and thus the Pentagon faced massive cutbacks in military appropriations. There was no such rationale because the end of the Cold War swept away the likelihood of a high-intensity conflict in Europe, and with it, the sole justification for maintenance of heavy, well-equipped forces. All that was left, it appeared, was the LIC paradigm – and this mission can easily be performed by a force one-tenth the size of the existing US military establishment. And it doesn't take much imagination to realise that the reduction of the US military to a force one-tenth its present size would produce enormous pain and hardship for the professional military class, for US defence contractors, for the legions of think-tank analysts, and for all the other groups and institutions that depend for their livelihood on high levels of military spending.

Needless to say, this powerful collection of constituencies did not respond passively to this impending disaster. Rather, they sought to invent a new enemy and a new paradigm that would justify retention of large military units in the post-Cold War era. And, not surprisingly, they *did* discover a new enemy: emerging Third World powers equipped with large, modern conventional forces and the rudiments of a nuclear/chemical/ missile capability. To combat these powers, they argued, we would need a new military paradigm – what they called 'mid-intensity conflict'.[3]

The selection of emerging Third World powers as America's new adversary was influenced to some degree by a number of studies conducted in the late 1980s on US strategy options in the 1990s. Most prominent of these was *Discriminate Deterrence*, the 1988 report of the US Commission on Integrated Long-Term Strategy. Although focused largely on the alleged threat from the USSR, the Commission warned against over-emphasis on the Soviet threat and called for greater attention to Third World threats. 'An emphasis on massive Soviet attacks lead to tunnel vision among defence planners,' the report noted. 'Apocalyptic show-downs between the United States and the Soviet Union are certainly conceivable . . . but they are much less probable than other forms of conflict.' Most worrisome of these other forms of conflict, the report argues, are regional conflicts in the Third World. Because future advers-aries in such conflicts are likely to be armed with increasingly potent weapons, any American efforts to prevail in such encounters 'will call for use of our most sophisticated weaponry.'[4]

This image of US forces engaged in intense combat with regional Third World powers was explored in much greater detail by a task force as-sembled in 1989 by the Center for Strategic and International Studies (CSIS) of Washington, D.C. In their final report, *Conventional Combat Priorities*, the task force identified such encounters as the most significant contingency facing US forces in the 1990s and beyond. 'With the decline of the Soviet military threat to Europe, conflicts that might be termed "mid-intensity" will dominate US planning concerns,' the report noted. The growing likelihood of such encounters 'will provide a key justification for military budgets during the 1990s and will establish most of the threats against which US forces are sized, trained, and equipped.'[5]

The identification of emerging Third World powers as the new adversary had many attractions for the US military in 1990. These countries possess large forces with modern weapons, including ballistic missiles and high-performance aircraft, and thus any war against them would require the use of large, well-equipped American forces. Also, because they possess (or are thought to possess) weapons of mass destruction, they could be portrayed as a genuine threat to regional and international stability – and thus Washington could argue that military action is needed to crush their nuclear and/or chemical capabilities.

This perception of the new adversary was already fully entrenched in Washington prior to the Iraqi invasion of Kuwait in August 1990. Indeed, we can trace the emergence of the new paradigm to President Bush's first major speech on national security affairs, at the US Coast Guard Academy in May 1989: 'The security challenges we face today do not come from the East alone,' he noted. 'The emergence of regional powers is rapidly changing the strategic landscape. In the Middle East, in South Asia, in our own hemisphere, a growing number of nations are acquiring advanced and highly destructive capabilities – in some cases, weapons of mass destruction, and the means to deliver them.' In response to this threat, he argued, the United States must adopt new anti-proliferation measures and, if necessary, 'must check the aggressive ambitions of renegade regimes.'[6]

This notion of combat against 'renegade regimes' armed with modern conventional weapons and nuclear or chemical capabilities became the new planning model for the US military. Thus, in January 1990, Secretary of Defense Dick Cheney told Congress that the United States must 'recognise the challenges beyond Europe that may place significant demands on our defense capabilities.' In face of these challenges, he argued, the Pentagon must adopt strategies 'that rely more heavily on mobile, highly ready, well-equipped forces and solid, power-projection capabilities.'[7]

This perspective was developed even more fully in an April 1990 article by General Vuono, the Army Chief of Staff:

> Because the United States is a global power with vital interests that must be protected throughout an increasingly turbulent world, we must look beyond the European continent and consider other threats to our national security. The proliferation of military power in what is often called the 'Third World' presents a troubling picture. Many Third World nations now possess mounting arsenals of tanks, heavy artillery, ballistic missiles, and chemical weapons . . . The proliferation of advanced military capabilities has given an increasing number of countries in the developing world the ability to wage sustained, mechanised land warfare. The United States cannot ignore the expanding military power of these countries, and the Army must retain the capability to defeat potential threats wherever they occur. *This could mean confronting a well-equipped army in the Third World.*[8] (Emphasis added.)

This prophetic statement is just one of many such remarks made by high-ranking US military officers in the spring of 1990, suggesting that senior officials had reached consensus on a new, MIC-oriented military posture months before the Iraqi invasion of Kuwait. Consistent with this posture, the Department of Defense and the individual military services began to reconfigure US capabilities from an HIS-oriented force to an MIC-oriented force. Moreover, in the spring of 1990, the Pentagon conducted an elaborate, computerised war game, 'Operation Internal Look '90,' featuring Iraq as the hypothetical enemy.[9] Now, in reporting these developments, I do not mean to suggest that the United States was actively looking for a fight with Iraq, but I do believe that the adoption of this paradigm by US military officials led the Pentagon leadership to welcome a war with Iraq once the prospect of such an engagement presented itself. In the words of General Colin Powell, 'It was nice to have Desert Storm come along now,' before Iraq had fully developed its military capabilities. 'Not that it's nice to have a war, but if it was going to come, this was a good time for it.'[10]

Once the war began, US forces employed the strategies and doctrines that had already been developed for such a contingency – i.e., the use of superior firepower and technology to crush a numerically superior but technologically inferior opponent. This approach had originally been developed to ensure a NATO victory in any major conventional conflict with the Soviet Union. As spelled out in NATO's 'Follow-on Force Attack' (FOFA) strategy and the US Army's 'Airland Battle Doctrine' (ABD), the new approach called for simultaneous allied attack on the enemy's first, second, and third echelons of troops, along with the prodigious use of 'smart' weapons to destroy enemy communications systems, radars, air bases, road systems, and other vital facilities.[11]

With the end of the Persian Gulf War, this strategic approach is now being standardised as the new US military posture for the 1990s. To quote Secretary Cheney from his testimony before the House Foreign Affairs Committee on March 19, 1991:

> The Gulf War presaged very much the type of conflict we are most likely to confront again in this new era – major regional contingencies against foes well-armed with advanced conventional and non-conventional weaponry. In addition to Southwest Asia, we have important interests in Europe, Asia, the Pacific and Central and Latin America. In each of these regions there are opportunities and potential future threats to our interests. We must configure our policies and our forces to effectively deter, or quickly defeat, such regional threats.[12]

In accordance with this outlook, Cheney urged Congress to support the maintenance of large, well-equipped US forces capable of overwhelming any future adversaries in the Third World. To satisfy this requirement, he testified, 'We must be able to deploy to regions of US interest sufficient forces with the capabilities needed to counter a wide variety of contingencies.' In particular, this will entail 'a high airlift and sealift capacity, substantial and highly effective maritime and amphibious forces, a full and sophisticated array of combat aircraft, both heavy and light Army divisions, and appropriate special operations forces.'[13]

In line with this outlook, senior US strategists have begun to hammer out a blueprint for the combination of weapons and forces that would best serve US needs for the mid-intensity conflicts of the future. Based on the record of Operation Desert Storm, and what is known of the Pentagon's evolving plans for MIC, we can identify some of the weapons and forces that are likely to dominate the Pentagon's 'wish list' for US military capabilities in the mid- to late 1990s:

★ *Strategic mobility*: If US forces are to prevail in future regional conflicts, they will have to arrive quickly and in sufficient strength to overcome formidable local forces – and this, in turn, means possessing adequate numbers of long-range ships and aircraft to transport and sustain a substantial US force in distant areas. 'The Army must be deployable,' General Vuono observed in April 1990. 'Even the most combat-ready land force cannot protect our national interests if it cannot deploy sufficient combat power to the fight in time to make a difference.'[14] Arguing that existing US mobility assets are inadequate, Vuono and other senior officers have called for increased investment in air- and sealift capabilities. A likely beneficiary of this stance is the C-17 long-range transport plane, which has heretofore been a frequent target for Congressional budget-cutting.

★ *Mobile firepower*: Once US troops arrive at distant battlefields, they must be capable of fighting and defeating well-equipped, professional armies. To prevail in such confrontations, US forces must come equipped with large numbers of potent weapons – weapons that pack a mighty punch, but that can be moved quickly to distant battlefields. The highest priority, in the view of many military experts, is for a light, air-transportable tank-killing vehicle. This can be a wheeled gun system like the Marine Corps' Light Armoured Vehicle (LAV), or some equivalent system. Given the difficulty experienced by the Pentagon in moving heavy M-1 and M-60 tanks to Saudi Arabia during the early weeks of Operation Desert Shield, it is likely that the armed services will accelerate the development and procurement of light armoured vehicles in the years to come.

★ *Advanced tactical aircraft*: To back up American ground forces in future MIC engagements, the Pentagon will continue to rely – as it did in the Persian Gulf – on tactical airpower to ensure control of the skies above the battlefield and for strikes against enemy ground forces. Because many Third World countries possess modern fighters and air-defence systems of Soviet or Western European manufacture, US combat planes must be capable of overcoming enemy defences and delivering their ordnance when and where needed. Thus, while the existing US inventory includes many late-model fighters along with the newly-introduced F-117A 'stealth' aircraft, pentagon officials insist that the United States must acquire a host of newer and more capable aircraft in the decade ahead. To perform the 'tac-air' mission in the twenty-first century, the Air Force is proceeding with developing of a new combat plane, the F-22 Advanced Tactical Fighter (ATF).

★ *Advanced 'standoff' missiles*: Given the growing sophistication of Third World artillery and air defence systems, it is considered essential that American forces be able to fire highly accurate missiles at critical enemy targets (air bases, command centres, military factories, tank formations, and so on) from distant, out-of-sight locations. To accomplish this, the Pentagon is rushing development and production of an assortment of advanced 'standoff' missiles – so-called because the launch platform (whether aircraft, helicopter, or ship) can stand back and fire its munitions from well beyond the range of enemy defences. These weapons – many of which witnessed their first combat use in the Persian Gulf conflict – employ sophisticated sensors and onboard microcomputers to locate, track, and strike their intended target. Examples of such systems include the *Tomahawk* sea-launched cruise missile (SLCM), a Navy weapon used for precision attacks on heavily-defended targets; the GBU-24, a laser-guided bomb used in precision strikes against Iraqi military installations; and SLAM (Standoff Land-Attack Missile), a derivative of the Harpoon anti-ship missile used by carrier-based aircraft to attack Iraqi port facilities and military targets.[15]

★ *'Middleweight' combat formations*: Ultimately, the successful conduct of MIC operations will require the introduction of new combat formations (brigades, divisions, and so on) that can be sufficiently powerful to defend themselves against well-armed Third World adversaries. At present, the US Army has both 'heavy' divisions designed for massive tank battles in Europe and 'light' divisions intended for police operations in the Third World. As became apparent during the early weeks of Operation Desert Shield, neither of these two formations is ideally suited for MIC – the heavy divisions because they cannot be moved quickly to distant theatres of operations, and the light divisions because they are essentially defence-less against enemy armour and artillery. What is therefore needed, in the view of many strategists, is a class of 'middleweight' forces configured specifically for MIC. Such forces, according to military analysts at CSIS, should possess 'the firepower, mobility, and survivability of heavy divisions, but [be] as rapidly deployable as light infantry divisions.'[16]

These, and other such systems, are likely to dominate Pentagon spending programmes in the 1990s. And while *total* US military spending is likely to decline, spending on MIC-oriented programmes can be expected to increase.

The Reassertion of Pax Americana

The second major outcome of the Persian Gulf conflict that merits our attention is the renewed assertion of *Pax Americana*, which I would define as the unbridled use of military force in the protection of strategic US assets abroad and in enforcing certain rules of international behaviour deemed beneficial to America's continued political and economic paramountcy.

Here, too, one can see the emergence of this outlook in US military thought before the outbreak of the Persian Gulf conflict. In essence, this outlook holds that the United States is a global power with vital economic interests in many parts of the world – interests that are shared in many cases by the Western industrial powers with which the United States is closely aligned. This outlook further holds that these interests are threatened by social, economic, and political disorder in the Third World, and that, for lack of any suitable alternative, the United States must shoulder responsibility for the protection of such interests and for the maintenance of global law and order.

This outlook is clearly articulated in President Bush's important address on national security policy of February 7, 1990. America's post-Cold War strategy, he noted, assumes that 'new threats are emerging beyond the traditional East-West antagonism of the last 45 years.' These threats must now receive the same attention once accorded to the Soviet threat. 'Clearly, in the future we will need to be able to thwart aggression, repel a missile, or protect a seaplane, or stop a drug lord.' To do so, moreover, 'we will need forces adaptable to conditions everywhere. And we will need agility, readiness, sustainability. We will need speed and stealth.'[17]

Essential to this mode of thinking is the conviction that the United States must be prepared to use force when necessary to carry out the missions described by President Bush. As suggested by General A.M. Gray, the Commandant of the Marine Corps,

> The international security environment is in the midst of changing from a bipolar balance to a multipolar one with polycentric dimensions. The restructuring of the international environment has the potential to create regional power vacuums that could result in instability and conflict. We cannot permit these voids to develop through disinterest, benign neglect, or lack of capability if we are to maintain our position as a world leader and protect our global interests. This requires that we maintain our capability to respond to likely regions of conflict.[18]

For students of history, this will read a great deal like the concept of 'world policeman' espoused by President Teddy Roosevelt and other American policymakers at the turn of the century. And while current US leaders are reluctant to employ this particular term, it is clear that they were beginning to think this way in 1989 and early 1990, months before the outbreak of the Persian Gulf crisis. Thus, in a January 1990 article on US Strategy in 'The New Postwar Era', Senator John McCain of Arizona wrote that:

> If anything, the global conditions that led us to make these uses of force [in Korea, Vietnam, Grenada, and Libya] are likely to be even more important in the future. 'Glasnost' does not change the fact that there has been an average of more than 25 civil and

international conflicts in the developing world every year since the end of World War II [and that] the US economy is critically dependent on the smooth flow of world trade. . . .

Our strategy and force mix must reflect the fact that our friends and allies are even more dependent on global stability and the free flow of trade than we are. At the same time, it must reflect the fact that no other allied or friendly nation will suddenly develop power projection forces, and that it would not be in our interest to encourage other nations to assume this role. *The US may not be the 'world's policeman', but its power projection forces will remain the free world's insurance policy.*[19] (Emphasis added.)

Essential to this outlook is the belief that the United States – and *only* the United States – has the capacity to employ military force on a global basis in the protection of vital Western interests. This, in fact, has become the central premise of America's post-Cold War military posture. As noted by Dick Cheney in a remarkable speech before the National Press Club on March 22, 1990, what distinguishes the United States from other Western powers, 'is that we're willing to put US troops on the ground. The message to friends and enemies alike is that *Americans are willing to risk their lives to insure the security of our friends and allies.*'[20] (Emphasis added)

Again, this perspective was well developed in Washington prior to the outbreak of the Persian Gulf conflict, but there is no doubt that the Kuwait crisis gave it much greater legitimacy. Thus, in a statement typical of the language used by many in Washington in the autumn of 1990, former Assistant Secretary of Defense Richard Armitage observed that the US decision to send troops to the Gulf demonstrates that 'There is absolutely no substitute for decisive, clearheaded American leadership.' Those pundits who until recently were predicting the decline of American power, he noted, 'must now acknowledge that the United States alone possesses sufficient moral, economic, political and military horsepower to jump-start and drive international efforts to curb international lawlessness.'[21]

With the successful outcome (at least in military terms) of Operation Desert Storm, this principle has become fully enmeshed in US strategic thinking. Thus, in a speech before the House Foreign Affairs Committee on February 6, 1991, Secretary of State James Baker affirmed that 'more clearly than we could have ever imagined a year or even six months ago, the world emerging from the end of the postwar era will be shaped by the United States of America and by its international allies.'[22] General Colin Powell put this in more vivid terms: 'I like to say that we're not the superpower or super-policeman of the world, but when there is trouble somewhere in the world that we least expect, it's the United States that gets called on to perform the role of being the cop on the beat.'[23]

When and where will the United States next serve as 'the cop on the beat'? That is, of course, very hard to predict in advance. When questioned on this point in April 1991, General Powell replied, 'Think hard about it. I'm running out of demons. I'm running out of villains. I'm down to Castro and Kim Il Sung.'[24] The fact is, however, that the United States is not likely to 'run out of villains' at any time soon. Given the likelihood of political and social disorder in a world of grossly uneven economic development *and* resurgent ethnic and religious loyalties, there is no end to possible threats to US interests around the world. As suggested by General Vuono in the Spring 1991 issue of *Foreign Affairs*:

> The United States clearly need not, and indeed should not, insert itself into every regional squabble. But it does not have the luxury of treating warfare in the developing world with indifference. The archaic concept of 'fortress America' simply retains no strategic relevance for the United States in the 1990s. Military strategists and military leaders must anticipate that US forces will be called on to advance and protect American interests in regional conflicts ranging from insurgencies to full-scale conventional wars against powerful land armies.

This view is clearly shared by Secretary of Defense Cheney and other senior Pentagon officials, and is certain to govern the organisation and deployment of US military forces in the post-Cold War era. There are, however, a number of potential impediments to the full implementation of this strategy.

The first of these impediments is largely economic in nature: the costs of fighting high-tech wars keep going up, while the ability of the United States to sustain such costly endeavours appears to be going down. President Bush was able to sidestep this contradiction in the Persian Gulf crisis by arm-twisting US allies into paying most of the costs of the war. It is unlikely, however, that the allies will always be willing to do this in the future – Iraq was an unusual adversary in that Saddam Hussein's designs on Kuwait and the Gulf threatened the interests of so many countries, and it is unlikely that future Third World adversaries will arouse such universal fear and loathing. When contemplating military action against an enemy considered less threatening by the world community, therefore, the United States may find that its allies will balk at providing the necessary cash, and thus, faced with the prospects of going it alone, may conclude that the financial costs (if not the costs in human lives) are just too high.

The second major impediment is more of a conceptual – or if you will, of a moral nature. To appreciate this, it is necessary to recall that the reassertion of *Pax Americana* is occurring at the same time that President Bush and Secretary Baker are attempting to articulate the concept of a 'New World Order' based on international peace and cooperation. Although admittedly vague, the concept does entail certain idealistic goals and themes that are probably shared by a large proportion of the world's population. In a belated effort to define this concept, Mr Bush noted on April 14, 1991 that the New World Order 'refers to new ways of working with other nations to deter aggression, and to achieve peace. It springs from hopes for a world based on a shared commitment among nations large and small to a set of principles that undergird our relations – peaceful settlement of disputes, solidarity against aggression, reduced and controlled arsenals, and just treatment of all peoples.'[26]

Clearly, this articulation of a 'New World Order' overlaps to a degree with the concept of *Pax Americana* as I have described it, and, indeed, many in Washington are trying to squeeze the two concepts into the same conceptual box. I would argue, however, that the two concepts are *not* interchangeable, and that the pursuit of one automatically precludes the pursuit of the other. The concept of a New World Order, however trivialised by Mr Bush, does imply important changes in the way the United States will conduct its international relations; *Pax Americana*, on the other hand, entails a return to the imperial behaviour of the early twentieth century.

Consider the President's words: The New World Order, he says, implies 'the peaceful settlement of disputes, solidarity against aggression, reduced and controlled arsenals, and the just treatment of all peoples.' As I understand these words, this would mean the use of sanctions and diplomacy to end the Persian Gulf crisis, not the use of force as implied by *Pax Americana*; it would mean solidarity against all aggressions, including those by America's friends (e.g., Morocco in the Western Sahara, Indonesia in East Timor, Israel in southern Lebanon), and not just those by its long-term adversaries; it would mean a moratorium on US arms transfers to the Middle East, not the current US rush to sell billions of dollars' worth of new high-tech weapons to America's allies in the region; and it would mean respect for the human rights of all oppressed peoples, not just those in countries ruled by America's adversaries.

These are important distinctions, and they are increasingly evident as such to significant segments of the American population. True, there is a large reservoir of jingoism in the population that can be tapped by the President to mobilise support for adventuristic military operations abroad, as demonstrated by the Panama invasion and Operation Desert Storm. But the US public also expects Washington to behave in an ethical and even *noble* fashion abroad, and increasingly the dictates of morality seem to imply the superiority of negotiations over combat and of collective action (via the United nations) over unilateralism. While US behaviour in the Persian Gulf can be seen as a triumph of unilateralism, it is also true that Bush worked very hard to cloak US action through a barrage of UN resolutions. And, having established this precedent, it will be very hard for Washington to intervene abroad – even in the manner of the Panama operation - without first gaining international support. The need to act in accordance with the presumptions of a New World Order (or to give the *appearance* of doing so) could, therefore, act as an inhibition on the adventuristic use of force by the US government.

At this point, it is still too early to predict how these contrary trends – the reassertion of *Pax Americana* on one hand and the inhibitionary pressures of economics and morality on the other – will play themselves out in the years ahead. Nevertheless, it appears that the paradigm of mid-intensity conflict is firmly entrenched in official thinking, and that the principle of presidential war-making has received a significant boost. It is also apparent

142   THE SOCIALIST REGISTER 1992

that these precepts enjoy considerable support in the US Congress and among those Americans who take comfort in America's status as a military superpower at a time of declining economic vigour. In the absence of any substantial challenges to these two precepts, therefore, it is likely that they will dominate US foreign and military policy for the indefinite future.

NOTES

1. Carl E. Vuono, 'National Strategy and the Army of the 1990s,' *Parameters*, Summer 1991, p. 12.
2. For discussion of US doctrine of counter-insurgency and LIC, see: Michael Klare and Peter Kornbluh, eds., *Low-Intensity Warfare* (New York: Pantheon, 1988), esp. chaps. 1-4.
3. The author first discussed the concept of MIC in 'The New Military Paradigm,' *Technology Review*, May/June 1991, pp. 28-36.
4. US Commission on Integrated Long-Term Strategy, *Discriminate Deterrence* (Washington: Government Printing Office, 1988), pp. 10, 13, 33-34.
5. *Conventional Combat Priorities: An Approach for the New Strategic Era*, Report of the CSIS Conventional Combat 2002 Project (Washington: Center for Strategic and International Studies, May 1990), p. 23.
6. Presidential address at US Coast Guard Academy, New London, Conn., May 24, 1989 (White House transcript).
7. *Department of Defense Annual Report*, January 1990. p. v.
8. Carl E. Vuono, 'Versatile, Deployable, and Lethal,' *Sea Power*, April 1990, pp. 57-63.
9. See *Atlanta Constitution*, Oct. 25, 1991.
10. Quoted in *Air Force Times*, April 15, 1991.
11. For discussion of the new NATO strategy and the weapons technologies involved, see Klare, 'NATO's Improved Conventional Weapons,' *Technology Review*, May-June 1985, pp. 34-40, 73.
12. Statement of Dick Cheney before the House Foreign Affairs Committee, March 19, 1991 (Dept. of Defense transcript).
13. *Ibid.*
14. Vuono, 'Versatile, Deployable, and Lethal,' p. 63.
15. For further discussion of the high-tech bombs and missiles used by Coalition forces in the Persian Gulf War, see: Klare, 'High-Death Weapons of the Gulf War,' *The Nation*, June 3, 1991, pp. 722, 38-42; and Dave Walker and Eric Stambler, '. . . And the Dirty Little Weapons,' *Bulletin of the Atomic Scientists*, May 1991, pp. 20-24
16. *Conventional Combat Priorities*, p. xx.
17. Speech before the Commonwealth Club of San Francisco, Feb. 7, 1991 (White House transcript).
18. Gen. A.M. Gray, 'Defense Policy for the 1990s,' *Marine Corps Gazette*, May 1990, p. 18.
19. John McCain, 'The Need for Strategy in the New Postwar Era,' *Armed Forces Journal* (January 1990), p. 44.
20. Statement of Dick Cheney before the National Press Club, Washington, D.C, March 22, 1990 (Dept. of Defense transcript).
21. Richard Armitage, 'To Lead and Pay,' *Washington Times*, Aug. 16, 1990.
22. Statement of James Baker before the House Foreign Affairs Committee, Feb. 6, 1991.
23. Quoted in *Dallas Morning News*, March 3, 1991.
24. Interview in *Air Force Times*, April 15, 1991.
25. Carl E. Vuono, 'Desert Storm and the Future of Conventional Forces,' *Foreign Affairs*, pp. 54-55.
26. Statement at the Air University, Maxwell Air Force Base, Ala., April 13, 1991 (White House transcript).

EUROPE IN A MULTI-POLAR WORLD

John Palmer

I

The seismic changes which have transformed Europe as a whole in the past few years cannot be understood purely in terms of developments within Europe. The fact that political union is even on the European agenda reflects deep-seated global economic and political trends as well as internal factors. At the heart of these changes has been the decline of the bi-polar system dominated by the two super-powers – the United States and the former Soviet Union. This has been accompanied by the gradual and uneven emergence of a multi-polar system based on a number of regional economic and (I will argue) increasingly political blocs. Global trends towards economic and political regionalisation are a factor in the thinking of EC political leaders. It is too soon to say definitively whether the attempt through GATT to negotiate a world-wide trade liberalisation will not succeed, but it is clear that the price of failure is likely to be an accelerated drift towards regional trade protectionism ('Fortress Europe', 'Fortress America') with all the implications this has for political and security arrangements.

As well as an emerging European bloc – structured around the European Community but likely to draw in the rest of Western Europe and many of the countries of Central and Eastern Europe – there is also an embryonic North American bloc being formed on the basis of the US/Canada/Mexico Free Trade Agreement. But efforts are also being made in Washington to secure the integration – on terms that are far from being agreed – of a series of Central American countries which are likely to revolve, as minor satellites, around the North American regional economy.

An East Asian or Pacific Rim region is also emerging around the economic power of Japan, and to a lesser extent the so-called Newly Industrialised Countries of East Asia including the Association of South East Asian Nations (ASEAN). However, some fundamental political issues affecting Japan's political and security role in the region have still to be resolved before a credible and cohesive grouping similar to the EC or even the NAFTA can develop.

There are other, aspirant, regional groupings which are being formed by other semi-developed capitalist economies – sometimes (as in the case of Turkey and the Turkic speaking central Asian countries) including re-publics of the former Soviet Union. Similar developments are underway in Latin America (the Andean Pact and the proposed Central and Latin American common markets) and Africa (through the OAU). These, however, are essentially defensive responses to the regionalisation of the advanced capitalist economies.

A key and – as yet unresolved – question is whether the development of this new system of regional blocs during the 1990s will prove to be merely an interim stage in an evolution towards an integrated global economic and political system or whether the regional blocs will prove more durable. Moreover their emergence may be associated – at least initially – with a period of global depression, trade protectionism, and international in-stability which could set back rather than advance the goal of 'a new global economic order'.

In such a perspective, the international economic and trading system might come to resemble some of the features of intra-imperialist conflict which were characteristic of the pre-1914 world. There is no guarantee that such conflicts will not spill over from the economic to the political and even the military domain, although the inhibitions on unilateral or aggressive action imposed by the mere existence of international bodies such as the UN, the IMF, etc., are considerable.

This is also why the leading capitalist states are keen to establish a new International Order with international structures designed to contain conflicts and minimise instability. This may involve some strengthening of the United Nations as well as, at a regional level, the Conference on Security and Cooperation in Europe as instruments for resolving conflicts. Either way, the present international system, which has been based on the hegemony of the United States, as mediated through bodies such as GATT and the International Monetary Fund, is now being eclipsed. There are distinct signs that the GATT itself, which is desperately seeking agreement on a new round of international trade liberalisation may lose authority as a result of a series of inter-regional bloc trade deals which retain elements of protectionism.

Renewed economic expansion and the undoubted opportunities repres-ented by the opening up to western market-style capitalism of the former 'Communist' states would clearly be propitious for the evolution of these new global regions. In these circumstances, the global regions may play a key role in the restructuring of the world economic system so as to contain the frictions generated by 'intra-imperialist' competition. But the initial costs to the advanced capitalist countries arising from the transformation of the former Soviet Union and Eastern Europe – coming at a time of conjunctural global recession and possibly even depression – may simply be judged too great. It seems increasingly unlikely that 'the West' will mount the Marshall Aid scale of assistance needed by the countries of Eastern European and Commonwealth of Independent States if they are to manage a switch to parliamentary-democratic (as opposed to Pinochet-style) capitalism.

In the latter event political chaos, civil wars and the rise of nationalist authoritarianism in these states may fatally weaken any tendency to global economic expansion. But even in the relatively benign scenario of sustained expansion, global regionalisation will tend to marginalise further and deepen the subordination of 'Third World' poor countries particularly in Africa and very likely of large areas of Latin America.

II

In spite of the 'triumph' of the United States in the Cold War, its economic decline has now come to the point where the Bush Administration is being forced to question its 'globalist' political and military pretensions. A major reexamination is already underway in Washington of America's capacity to sustain a world-wide military system of military bases and alliances. The decline of US economic power – as measured in part by its balance of trade and payments deficits but also by the huge and continuing federal government budget deficits – suggests that the United States will be forced to abandon much of its post-war neo-imperial role. The growing inadequacy of the domestic American wealth-producing industrial base to service the international investment, military and other commitments of the United States means that the system is now precariously dependent on the inward flow of short term financing from outside the US, most obviously from Japan.

The decline has necessarily underlined the scale of the change in power relations with some of America's major allies – notably Japan and western Europe. Having at first sought to challenge and contain that shift of power (notably by seeking to counter the growth of European demands for joint leadership with the US of the Atlantic alliance), the Bush Administration appears readier to accept and adapt to the new realities. Nowhere has this foreign policy adjustment been more brusque than in the clear switch by the Bush Administration from any lingering 'special relationship' with Britain. This has now been replaced with at least the attempt at a closer and less patronising relationship with a united Germany.

It would be quite wrong to suggest that the US has voluntarily 'given up' its leadership positions in the global agencies of its former economic hegemony – such as the International Monetary Fund, the World Bank, the General Agreement on Tariffs and Trade or the Organisation for

Economic Cooperation and Development. It is trying to hold on to its dominant position vis-à-vis its European and Japanese allies and rivals, but increasingly fears it will fail. But the signing of the Canadian/US free trade agreement and the efforts in Washington to restructure a closer relationship with Mexico betoken new priorities associated with a narrower and more limited regionalism in some ways reminiscent of pre-war isolationism.

A new 'regionalist' defence doctrine now underpins the Bush Administration's commitment to the Strategic Defence Initiative. SDI and the 'magic pebbles' theory of a North American shield against nuclear attack is in the longer run incompatible with a meaningful commitment to America's global alliances, as the European member states of NATO realised with alarm when Reagan unveiled the first versions of SDI in the early 1980s. United States opinion-formers are actively debating the extent to which the US can sustain anything like its traditional commitment to NATO. This in turn is fuelling the debate about the 'transformation' of NATO in the light of the new security situation in Europe following the disintegration of the Warsaw Pact and the Soviet Union.

There is a widespread acceptance on both sides of the Atlantic that if NATO is to continue as an active political, let along military alliance, it must primarily be under European rather than American leadership. However, there are divisions among the Europeans about whether this should be institutionalised within the EC or within the Western European Union, which is a half way house body between NATO and the EC. The collapse of the Soviet Union and the haemorrhaging of the economic (and ultimately political and military) power of the United States have stimulated this debate about future European security policy, more than that, the new security environment in Europe has directly led to discussions about the institutional character on a pan-European association – based on the Conference on Security and Cooperation in Europe – which would directly link the countries of the European Union (including almost all the states now in the European Free Trade Association (EFTA)).

There are even suggestions that, with the end of the Cold War and the emergence of new nationalist conflicts of the Yugoslav type in the former 'Communist' east, NATO may have to become a servicing agency for a collective (CSCE based) European security order. There is a parallel logic behind the creation of the North Atlantic Cooperation Council linking NATO and the former members of the Warsaw Pact. Significantly, while the active denuclearisation of the other former Soviet republics now uneasily grouped in the Commonwealth of Independent States is being pursued, the NATO states appear content to let Russia act as its nuclear Cossacks on its frontiers with Asia and the Islamic world.

Some argue that this will allow a new 'division of labour' between the United States and its west European allies in running a military/political alliance which may be expected to reorient its 'threat assessment' focus from the Soviet bloc to the alleged 'threats' outside NATO's traditional European arena – notably in the Middle East and Africa. Others believe that the United Nations should be given the political authority and the military capacity to act in crises outside Europe rather than NATO or the European Community as such. In any event, the US military presence in western Europe will in the near future be a fraction of what it was during the Cold War years. The German perspective is that the new European security order should be non-nuclear but this could be reversed if the CIS breaks up into warring nationalist, and nuclear, mini states.

Working out a new partnership between the United States and the emerging European Union will not be easy. Quite apart from the issue of how the costs of such an alliance would be shared, the realities of conflicting interests in key regions of the Third World cannot be ignored. A case in point is the Middle East where the traditionally close relationship between the United States and Israel has pointed up the different priorities it has followed in the region compared with western Europe which places a higher value on its links with the conservative Arab regimes. There are, moreover, potentially serious trade and other commercial conflicts between US and West European interests in there regions which are bound to become increasingly important for foreign and security policy strategists if the early 1990s are years of recession and trade protectionism. There are also a number of political contradictions evident in the unfolding relationship between the European Community and its new client states in Eastern Europe. For although their incorporation in the European free market system is designed to be more or less total, the European Community governments are reluctant to offer the East Europeans a clear promise of eventual political membership of the EC.

III

This reluctance is all the more striking since the European Community is embarked on a number of ambitious projects which – if they are successful – will bring it much closer to becoming a supra-national quasi-federal European state. This will not only involve the completion in 1993 of the barrier- and frontier-free internal EC market but also the parallel realisation of economic and monetary union including – towards the end of the decade – a single currency with all that this implies for control of monetary and even fiscal policy.

Moreover the majority of EC states – whatever the reservations of the British – want to go even further and lay the basis for a political union. In plain language this will lay the basis for a supra-national federal European state which would assume responsibility from national states for a growing range of key political issues including aspects of foreign policy and defence. This was the overridicling – if unfulfilled – objective of many EC leaders at Maastricht.

It should not be thought that the advocates of federalism are bent on the creation of a 'nightmare of a centralist Euro-super state', as Thatcher has alleged. The process envisaged is rather more complex and would involve not only the retention of national states for a range of functions but also encouragement to disperse governmental functions 'down' to regional and other bodies with which the EC institutions would have greater direct contact.

Due for the most part to obdurate opposition from the British Tory government to anything smacking of supra-nationalism and particularly to proposals to extend the role of the European Parliament, the EC remains a clumsy instrument of mainly inter-governmental power. By no stretch of the imagination can it be described as a federal state.

Power – it is true – is being centralised in key areas – including foreign, security and (implicitly) defence policy as well as control of frontiers, and police and legal 'cooperation'. But the increased decision-making authority of the Twelve is, for the most part, to take place outside of the institutions and jurisdiction of the Rome Treaty. To that extent the new centralising powers of the Twelve will not be subject to any effective democratic European, let along national, parliamentary control.

This said, however, the longer term direction now being taken by European integration is unmistakably towards some form of supra-national federalism. The rearguard action fought by John Major at Maastricht is likely to do no more than delay the emergence of something resembling a United States of Europe by the end of the decade.

Already the signposts are being erected for the next moves to a more federal-style European Union. The process seems certain to embrace not only the existing twelve EC member states but a growing number of other western and even some eastern European countries as well. By the end of the 1990s, there may well be an embryo federal European government (developed probably out of a hybrid mixture of the present EC Commission and the Council of Ministers which legislates for the member states.)

The new executive will in some (as yet very uncertain) way become more fully accountable to the directly elected European Parliament. The emerging European Union could, by the end of the century, expand to include as many as thirty countries.

A majority of EC governments – led by Germany – favours a relatively decentralised form of federation. In part, this no more than reflects the specific historical experience of Germany (whose own decentralised, power-checking constitution was largely imposed on it by the victorious allies after the war against Hitler) but it also reflects the growing political influence of regional power structures in Belgium, Italy, Spain and elsewhere.

Its advocates insist that such a federal-style constitution would not only set a limit to the eventual transfer of sovereignty and political authority to the European Community institutions but would also tend to shift political decision-making below the level of the 'nation state'. The trend throughout the EC states – with a few exceptions – is already towards regionalisation.

In some cases, such as the 'United Kingdom', the phrase 'nation state' is in any case a misnomer since the state – reflecting its imperial formation – is itself multi-national. That is one reason why defeat of a Tory government, the creation of a Scottish assembly and new regional bodies elsewhere in the UK and moves to deeper European political union could interact explosively during the 1990s.

There is nothing inevitable about any of this and it is conceivable that the trend to a European federal union could be reversed and that there could even be a creeping economic and political re-Balkanisation of western Europe. The recent advance of the extreme right wing, above all in France, but to a lesser extent in Germany and Belgium, does also pose a potential threat to the pro-European integrationist centre-right christian democrat/ social democrat establishment in western Europe.

European capital, however, appears overwhelmingly in favour of the key provisions of European economic and political union. This is hardly surprising since the agenda of economic and monetary union is in large measure the consequence of the European internal market and the Single European Act of 1986.

The European frontier and barrier-free market represents the key strategic objectives of the major formations of capital in Western Europe which have long been convinced that only with a home market of several hundred million consumers can they hope to withstand the global challenge of American and – in particular – of Japanese capital. Equally important, most sectors of European capital want to see the development of some embryo European state. This is in part to act as protector and advocate of its interests in an unstable international environment and in a world economy where commercial conflicts are on the increase. There is a near universal view that even the larger national states lack the power and resources to play this role effectively in future.

However neither the European Union nor even the single market represents the unalloyed interests and priorities of capital. There are deep divisions between different sectors of capital about the balance which should be struck between global trade liberalisation and a greater or less degree of industrial protection. The motor and electronics industries are – for instance – increasingly advocates of European protectionism while the chemical and financial sectors are resolutely in favour of global free trade. It is far from clear where the balance between free trade and advocates of a protected 'Fortress Europe' will lie if the 1990s are years of stagnation or even depression.

The European Union process has also had to take into account the corporatist and social policy commitments of the dominant political formations of both Social and Christian Democracy. These parties are insistent – for example – that the emerging European political union must have appeal to working people (in large measure their electorates) through a mix of policies to appeal to consumers, workers and 'citizens'. Some of these proposals are contained in the controversial EC Social Charter of Workers' Rights which has aroused so much bitter opposition from the British Tory government.

This reflects no more than the existing balance of class and political forces between the right and organised labour (whether social democrat, christian democrat or Communist-led trade unions) in the majority of the EC countries. The great exception is of course Britain where the defeats imposed on organised labour and the left under twelve years of Thatcherism have had the result that the Christian/Social Democrat consensus on minimal social rights for organised workers and the EC Social Charter as a whole can appear in some way 'radical' or – in the words of Margaret Thatcher herself 'socialism by the back-Delors'.

The federalist case gives major emphasis to the need to extend the role and political authority of the directly elected European Parliament. Under the European Union treaty agreed in Maastricht, the European Parliament has secured only minimal and largely negative powers over EC legislation. But there is growing pressure particularly in Germany for the further extension of law-making powers to the European Parliament in an early 'review' of the Maastricht treaty. Ultimately the Commission and the Council of Ministers would be subject to greater control and the European Parliament would be given a greater degree of joint legislative powers with the Council.

The majority of EC governments believe the future Presidents of the Commission – which is the day to day EC executive – should be appointed by the European Parliament rather than national states and that the President should select the other Commission members in consultation with national governments. More important, the majority also believe that unlike the situation today, no law should be passed by the Council of Ministers (which is the de facto legislative power at present) in the face of a majority vote by members of the Parliament.

The British government argues that in the interests of democratic accountability and national 'sovereignty', control over EC decision makers should be exercised by national Parliaments. But under the treaties of accession which all countries signed on acceding to the Community, national Parliaments long ago lost the right to amend or reject decisions of the Council of Ministers. It is therefore the merest demagogy to claim that Westminster (or other national Parliaments) are threatened by the move to give more power to the European Parliament. It is the Council, especially now that it takes more and more decisions by majority vote, which is truly unaccountable to anyone and which is most threatened by moves to strengthen the European Parliament.

IV

With this highly delicate process underway, some EC states appear fearful that any enlargement of the Community would risk complicating or even blocking the whole process of European Community economic and political union. But with the collapse first of the Berlin Wall and then of the Soviet Union, the view has gained ground that both enlargement and moves to federal union are not only compatible but necessary. Some governments, hitherto sceptical of political union, now see it as the best framework for the longer term containment of the economic and political might of a united Germany.

The (now virtually impossible) exclusion of EFTA countries from political membership of the EC to say nothing of the East Europeans would not prevent their being drawn ever closer into the all-enveloping dynamic of the EC single European market. But it would mean that even the relatively privileged 'EFTANS' would be little more than politically neutered client states of the EC powers while the struggling east European economies could end up as the de facto economic satrapies of the European community.

In Eastern Europe, the Czechoslovak government in particular has made it quite plain that it will not be satisfied with mere economic association with the EC and will want to be guaranteed full membership – albeit after an undetermined period of transition. And several EFTA states may soon follow Austria and Sweden's lead and make an all-out bid for full EC membership. The Hungarians and the Poles will not want to be left behind by the Czechs – although the government in Warsaw is under no illusion about the desperate state of its economy and the possible social and political upheavals which may be triggered by its Chicago school style transition to fully market systems. In the civil war ruins of the former Yugoslav state, the Slovenes and Croats are already flirting with the idea of direct links with the EC.

The odds are, therefore, that by the middle of this decade the pressure for an enlargement of the EC to fifteen or even twenty or more member states may become irresistible and this could grow to thirty or more by the end of the decade. The consequences of such a radical shift in the economic and political gravity of the EC could be significant. It would, for instance, increase the relative weight of social democratic and left of centre governments within the Community political institutions and would also involve the integration of avowedly neutral states at a time when the fundamental direction of Europe's future foreign and security policies will be under debate.

For the left in the European Community, this perspective raises problems and opportunities, while it is not the job of the left to advocate EC membership to the East Europeans (or anyone else), it is the job of the left to defend their right to be members of the Community whether or not their foreign and security policies conflict with the NATO ideologues and whether or not they are paragons of free market virtue in the eyes of the West European establishments.

But quite apart from some concern that an enlarged Community might imperil the existing strategy of the present EC states for closer economic and political integration, other political factors are also in play. A significant section of the Eurocracy – and more importantly of EC national governments – are apprehensive that the accession of countries such as Sweden (even after the defeat of the Social Democrats), Austria and Norway with their traditional commitments to a strong welfare state and ambitious environment protection policies would push the EC as a whole away from free market economic priorities. The emergence of the CSCE as a pan-European security agency would also make the accession of 'neutrals' into the EC less problematic.

We are then facing the likelihood (though not the certainty) of a 'United States of Europe' emerging from the process of European union within the EC and linking a growing number of other East and West European states. These states will be economically bound by the 'single' European capitalist market but they will also have to cede to the European Union a wide range of powers over policies hitherto the prerogative of the national states and of broader alliances such as NATO.

This emerging European state is lending urgency to the demands for some greater system of democratic political accountability by the EC institutions. This demand takes two forms. In countries such as Britain (though very little elsewhere) it focuses on the need for the British state and/or the Parliament at Westminster to exercise greater surveillance and control over decision-making in Brussels.

The trouble with this is that first the treaties of accession, under which the EC member states signed the Rome Treaty as the Community's constitutional doctrine, and then with the Single European Act of 1987, have enormously reduced the scope of national governments and national Parliaments. Only within a perspective of breaking from the EC and – therefore – challenging the economic integration which has driven the Community – does it make sense to seek to restore some role to purely national Parliaments since the accountability of individual governments to such assemblies is undermined by the fact that the Council, collectively, takes more and more decisions on a majority vote basis.

The only alternative – supported with greater or lesser enthusiasm in most other EC countries – is to make the directly elected European

Parliament the main law-making body in the Community. This would also involve the existing executives (both the Commission and the Council of Ministers) being fully and directly accountable to the European Parliament.

However important it is to fight for the extension and radicalisation of democracy within the actual EC institutions, the left must also confront the need for a Europeanisation of the politics and organisations of labour and of the new social 'green' and other allied movements. To date, labour movements have been slow to recognise, let alone respond to, the new realities of integrated EC economies, trans-national companies, the Europeanisation of hours, working conditions, collective bargaining and increasingly of elements of social and labour laws.

The new social movements – notably women, the green movement and the peace movement – have been significantly quicker to see what is happening and to begin to respond on a transnational, European basis. However, until very recently the political left has also been reluctant to come to terms with the enormous implications for both theory and strategy of what is happening in Europe. In a number of countries, modest but significant space has begun to open up for independent 'green/left' socialist movements, both as a consequence of the implosion of Stalinism and the de facto shift to the right by orthodox social democratic labour parties. This is true of Denmark and Holland and in different ways of Belgium, Italy and for a period of Germany.

The construction of a programme (or series of programmes) for the European green/left and – more generally for the labour movement – in alliance with the new social movements in both western and eastern Europe is an urgent priority. Ironically, socialists bring to this task a wealth of initiatives and innovatory ideas which can help construct a 'prefigurative' socialist project with real imagination and mass appeal even during the past decade and more of reaction and defeats.

The issue of democracy will have to be at its heart – democracy at the level of the regional, national and European state but also democracy in the workplace and in the community. It should go without saying that the demand for popular control over the process of European integration should encompass but in no way be restricted by the European Community institutions. On the one hand the left cannot afford to adopt an abstentionist position on the issues raised by the European Parliament's demands for far greater control over the Commission (and even more important) the Council of Ministers. At present the Twelve are involved in building a bourgeois state without bourgeois democracy and many areas of decision-making are deliberately kept secret.

Nowhere is this more blatant than in the proliferating intergovernmental bodies – legally not a formal part of the EC institutions or the Rome Treaty – involved with drawing up arrangements for the free movement of peoples within the 1992 single market. Not only is this freedom likely to be restricted in the name of state action against trans-national crime and terrorism but there are grave dangers that the already illiberal rules applying to immigrants and those seeking political asylum from outside the Community will face a de facto white, ethno-centric Fortress Europe regime.

Security and defence policy also escapes direct democratic scrutiny at present and must be brought within the scope of the European Parliament. But the Commissioners individually as well as collectively should be elected by MEPs and not appointed by an indirect and unaccountable process of political office-jobbing.

But the question of democratic accountability is also posed in relation to any new institutions created out of the CSCE, or the Council of Europe, for the putative pan-European confederation. Notably, just before its demise, the Soviet Union, among others, went so far as to propose eventually giving such a body some limited supra-national decision-making powers – for instance in setting higher mandatory trans-national standards of environment protection.

It is against this background of accelerating European integration that the left will also have to review its wider strategy for the labour movement and for socialist politics. In the past 'national' strategies occupied the centre ground of socialist politics with international, including European objectives, at best a side issue. This will have to change fundamentally. Over this decade, the struggle for power will – increasingly – have a European rather than a national focus. In the immediate future, it will be vital for the left to think through its programme of demands and strategic objectives which will – in growing measure – be aimed at the institutions of the emerging European state.

Quite apart from the issues posed by European unification and integra-tion, the single market process makes the development not merely of trans-national collective bargaining long overdue but also the emergence of trans-national unions. This question has been posed most sharply by those trade unionists – notably in the engineering and metal working industries – who have had most practical involvement in a coordinated European strategy to reduce working hours. Even some of the more conservative sections of the trade union bureaucracy – such as the Engi-neering Union leadership in Britain – now appear to accept the need to move to de facto European trade union and European wide bargaining. The underdevelopment of rank and file (including combine committee) organisation is a pressing problem for the trade union left.

Alongside this there is a need to develop prefigurative policies covering such questions as environmentally and socially sustainable forms of eco-nomic growth, transnational democratic planning, new forms of European public ownership, conversion from arms production, the encouragement of worker cooperatives, the development of the economy of social caring and innovative applications of human centred technologies. As a reaction sets in against the prevailing free market economic liberalism of the 1980s, and as the pressures from protracted recession intensify, it will be essential for the left to begin to articulate a supra-national socialist economic strategy which can both inform specific transitional demands on social democratic and reformist governments and provide the foundations for a European socialist economic alternative.

Such a programme will run completely counter to the rigidly free market and deflationary bias of the present proposals for economic and monetary union. The left must also champion the demand to make the proposed European Central Bank and the Council of Ministers fully accountable to the European Parliament. The alternative economic strategy advanced by the left can have no truck with specious nationalist options such as devaluation or national economic protectionism. the only effective opposition to a reactionary EMU will be the emergence of an effective trans-frontier and supra-national campaign for growth, jobs and higher living standards. This must also include some concept of protected economic zones where the economically less advanced national and regional economies can be safeguarded against distorted developments imposed by the unrestricted impact through the international market of the more advanced capitalist economies. This will be of particular relevance to the countries of Central and Eastern Europe and the republics of the CIS.

The left has a wealth of experience, ideas and analyses developed and even tested in the hard laboratory of real life during the past decade and more of reaction. There is political space opening up for a credible European left which combined the best of the socialist – including the marxist tradition – with the radical impulses from the green and nationalist/regionalist movements as well as feminism and the other new social movements.

The past few years has seen the emergence of such a new green/left. It received much inspiration from the establishment and subsequent development of the West German Green party, notwithstanding that party's bitter internal divisions over the relationship of socialist politics to environmental priorities. The recent general election in Holland brought modest but significant gains for the Green Socialist Left party (although not 'orthodox greens'). And parallel movements, with rather different origins, notably the Norwegian Left Socialists and the Danish Peoples' Socialists have also made impressive advances in the past few years to the left of the social democratic parties.

This embryo West European left, with which the Socialist Society and the Socialist Movement in Britain seek closer relations, has also established links with new left parties and groups in Eastern Europe. These include the Polish Socialist Party (Democratic Revolution) and those

Russian socialists organised around the ideas of Boris Yagarlitsky. Discussions between green/socialists and independent left organisations are taking place in more than a dozen West and East European countries about the political basis for cooperation and joint action.

The failed models of Stalinism and Thatcherite free market capitalism and the superficial platitudes of much social democratic politics creates openings and also dangers. If the left does not organise to respond to the challenges of capitalism at the hour of European union, then the resulting vacuum may be filled by the re-emerging forces of right wing – even fascist – populism of the kind being developed by Le Pen in France and by even more openly neo-nazi tendencies elsewhere.

This is one reason why the left must resist incorporation in a new 'Europeanist' project which merely provides a progressive sounding rhetoric for a protectionist, white, ethnocentric and objectively intolerant, racist and repressive European Union. A more immediate danger for the left particularly in countries such as Britain remains incorporation into nationalist currents opposing European integration in the name of 'sovereignty' or even 'parliamentary democracy'.

Unless the new Europe is part of the world-wide movement for human liberation, it will remain part of the problem and not part of the solution of the crisis of modern society. The contribution which a socialist Europe could make to global emancipation is enormous. This should be the source of our inspiration and hope for the challenges ahead.

THE EMERGING WORLD ORDER AND EUROPEAN CHANGE: THE POLITICAL ECONOMY OF EUROPEAN UNION

Stephen Gill

I. The Global Political Economy and the Emerging World Order

The dialectic of integration-disintegration and world order
Transformations in the global political economy of the 1970s and the 1980s, including the momentous events in Eastern Europe and the former Soviet Union, have created a set of conditions now linked to a renewed impetus towards the economic and political unification of the EEC. Beyond this immediate horizon, discussions are under way concerning the prospects of a future enlargement and deepening of the EEC's geographical, social, economic and political potential.

This might, in the long-term, lead to the possibility of Europe, understood as a collection of states, coordinated through the institutions and processes of the EEC, becoming a more coherent politico-economic entity and actor in the emerging world order, with sufficient capability and resources to offset American and Japanese power in the global political economy, a proposition that I would wish to challenge here. However, looking at the question of Europe in this way abstracts from many of the key social forces which are simultaneously integrating and disintegrating sets of socio-economic structures and institutions, not just in Europe, but world wide. Thus what seems to be emerging is a recomposition of dominant socio-economic forces and associated political forms within the global political economy, and a corresponding fragmentation and division of many other social forces, reflecting an intensification of global inequality, and a restructuring of global power relations.

As we approach the twenty-first century what we may be witnessing, therefore, is a kind of 'patterned disorder': movement towards the attempt to consolidate a new form of hegemony within the core of the system, although one which has a quite different social basis to the one which preceded it, that is from 1945 to around 1970. In this light, the discussions at the July 1991 Group of Seven (G7) summit are of considerable interest,

157

not only because of the scope and nature of the agenda (which included the restructuring of the USSR, the reconstituting of the United Nations, an abortive attempt at a major ecological initiative, involving a massive debt-for-nature swap to save the Brazilian rainforests, and the usual questions relating to trade protectionism and macroeconomic relations between the G7 and the rest of the world). It is important because it helps to highlight the vanguard forces within the emerging world order, and how they serve to configure what might be called 'the pyramids of privilege' in the world order structures that the G7 seeks to bestride. The G7 has now supplanted the former US–USSR summits as the major focus of world attention and highlights the conditions for entry into the 'core' institutions in the global power structure.

G7 attempts to mobilize a new consensus around President Bush's concept of a 'new world order' reflects the complex interplay between ideas, institutions, and material capacities (production and military power), and the way, under certain conditions, these might be synergized into a coherent concept of action. However, the divisions within the ranks of the G7 on a number of questions (e.g. on how to respond to first Gorbachev's then Yeltsin's pleas for assistance, with France, Germany and Italy, plus the EEC ranged against Canada, Japan, the USA and the UK on the nature and scope of assistance; the USA and the EEC disagreements on GATT negotiations) show that struggles continue even within the ranks of the privileged. Whilst, therefore, there appears to be a movement towards the reconsolidation of the core of the system, we simultaneously see the break up of previous forms of state, economic and political crisis, war, famine and ecological disaster.

This dialectic of integration-disintegration is associated with what I call a triple crisis of world order, operating at the economic, political and more broadly socio-cultural 'levels', in the 'First', 'Second' and 'Third Worlds'. The purpose of this paper is to probe the nature of this world order, in so far as it can be understood by focusing on the abstract entity which we call 'Europe'. Thus with regard to questions of the unification of (western) Europe, I attempt to situate selectively, from a political economy perspective, some of these social forces and processes of change. I will endeavour to place these within a discussion of the deeper dialectics and dynamics of global change, especially in the period since 1971. Moreover, since order is a political concept, we need to ask 'order for whom, and for what purposes?'

In this light, the G7/EC debates concerning the changing policies of the World Bank and the IMF with regard to the control of arms proliferation reflect a reconsideration of the question of how the 'North' is to incorporate the 'South' in a reconstituted hegemony, that is how to spread hegemony beyond the 'core'. Here it is worth noting that Gramsci's concept of hegemony involved both coercive and consensual aspects of power: that is to say power relations which were perceived as legitimate or acceptable were necessarily underpinned by material power and a coercive apparatus. Thus the initiatives concerning the Third World discussed here should also be related to the development of new concepts of military mobilization and intervention on the part of the USA and its NATO allies: the US Rapid Deployment Force, a centrepiece of US mobilization for the 1991 Gulf War (the RDF was created after the Iranian Revolution) is now to have a European counterpart.

That the post-war schemes for incorporating Third World countries have been flawed is now more recognized, as, perhaps, are the limits and contradictions involved in supporting (cynically) any right-wing dictatorship for Cold War reasons, or else for reasons of access to strategic resources. In this light, the strengthening of state structures in the South (and not simply the privatization of state structures and the pressure to liberalize markets) will be crucial, for example, in providing more effective environmental management and better control over weapons proliferation: issues which directly or indirectly affect G7 interests. Less weapons in the Third World would, moreover, add to the effectiveness of Rapid Deployment Forces. These developments, in so far as they reflect any coherent response on the part of international organization, can be related to the wider aspects of the 'new constitutionalism' which I discuss with reference to Europe in the second half of this essay, that is the political project of attempting to make liberal democratic capitalism the sole model for future development, with the military forces of the major, 'core' countries reconfigured in ways which, in conjunction with the deepening and spread of commoditization and market forces, add a further disciplinary aspect to the emerging order.[1]

Global restructuring and transnational capital

Here I focus on selected aspects of the global restructuring of socio-economic and political relations. An assessment of the recomposition of social structures and political arrangements during the 1960s, 1970s and 1980s is crucial to understanding the complexities of the 'new' Europe and for the redevelopment of a social ontology of the world order. In particular, I highlight the importance of the growing (structural) power of internationally-mobile capital. This is a development with enormous implications, not only for the European Community (and more specifically the operation of the EMS and its possible development into fully-fledged monetary union), but for the world order *in toto*.

The recessionary conditions of the 1970s and 1980s gave rise to greater demands for social protection and mercantilism, as uncompetitive 'smoke-stack' industries were either eliminated or placed under considerable competitive pressure, often from more efficient foreign firms. The advanced countries moved towards more information-based, high-technology, 'post-Fordist', and more 'flexible' forms of production. Traditional forms of organized labour were placed largely on the defensive. Sensing they were gaining the upper hand, right-wing forces pressed for policies which would begin to reverse the tendencies towards the growth in the size and resources of the state, partly to eliminate the tendency towards fiscal crisis. Their arguments were strengthened by many of those on the left, which criticized the corporatism and Keynesianism of the welfare-nationalist capitalist states, showing how its development was contradictory, and beset by tendencies towards not only fiscal (and economic), but also, in Habermasian terms, rationality and legitimation crises.

In this vein, the utility of the welfare state was increasingly questioned as stagflation and recession, with growing unemployment, began to place financial constraints on state budgets, as well as growing strains on the post-war political consensus built around, in Charles Maier's phrase, the 'politics of productivity', that is a series of corporatist bargains between labour and capital.[2] These bargains took different forms in the metropolitan capitalist countries but involved similar industrial structures and forms of conflict resolution. Moreover, each set of arrangements presupposed consistent economic growth and an international division of labour organized primarily between countries, understood as 'national economies', or national producers, interacting and competing internationally, with the US pump-priming the system's liquidity through the international use of the dollar.

By the 1970s the era of cheap energy seemed to be over, the rise of transnational companies and the rise of the newly-industrializing countries heralded the onset of dramatic changes in the international division of labour as well as the collapse (or erosion) of corporatist bargains, and the possibility of Keynesian policies on a national level was increasingly undermined by these changes and the growing scale, power and mobility of financial capital, in particular, the movement of speculative capital as a force to destabilize domestic economic activity and to exacerbate balance of payments and exchange crises. This was the fundamental lesson learned by the British Labour government in 1976 when it had to go to the IMF for a loan to meet its financing needs. In accepting IMF conditions, the Labour party was split and Denis Healey became Britain's first monetarist chancellor, a step which split the Labour party and heralded the era of Thatcherism and the end of corporatism in Britain.[3]

This political change in 1970s Britain proved to be significant for the conjunctural restructuring of Europe in the 1980s. Whereas corporatism varied throughout Europe – with West German corporatism less statist than that in France, in many major west European countries, banks and financial capital were highly integrated with industrial capital, and financial services and banking were closely regulated (as was the case in the USA following the Glass-Steagall provisions). When the Conservative government under Thatcher came to power in 1979 with its neo-liberal mandate, it moved quickly to eliminate exchange controls and towards financial deregulation in response to US deregulatory initiatives in the mid-1970s. Moreover, the role of London as a cosmopolitan world-city, the axis of the pax britannica is important here, and needs to be understood in Braudellian terms: London markets and their financial centrality were central to the spread and extension of world capitalism, at least since the late eighteenth century. Given the current place of the City as the centre for the Euromarkets, and the key financial centre in Europe more generally, in the 1980s, at least in the European context, Britain's deregulatory moves can be seen as akin to a 'Trojan horse' for transnational capital to penetrate the national corporatist structures of continental Europe. This argument is consistent with the policies of the Thatcher government relative to the EEC, for example, with regard to the Social Charter, which is discussed in part two of this essay.

How do we understand the nature of some of the forces of integration/ disintegration noted above, and their effects in terms of transformations occurring in the post-war world order? My starting point is to examine the new dynamics of the capitalist global economy. Here the forces of transnationalization and globalization (for example, transnational companies favouring and embodying international production and exchange and capital mobility) have steadily expanded, and have been engaged increasingly in a struggle *vis à vis* more nationalist and protectionist blocs of forces, that is those seeking to assert or maintain some form of social control over key aspects of economic and political life at the national level. The latter are associated with what might be called national capitalism, that is systems premised on the protection (or promotion) of domestic social interests from (or relative to) international competitors, both through the development of systems of military and social security, and through control over production and finance through state capitalism and nationalized banks. These forces serve to restrict capital mobility, and tend to focus international economic activity on export-led growth.

The struggle between internationally-mobile and more nationalist (or parochial) political, economic and social forces intensified on a world-wide basis following the global recession of 1979–82, the most severe since the 1930s: a specific conjuncture which served to crystallize and intensify trends set in motion during the 1950s and 1960s. The recession catalyzed widespread restructuring of capital (massive bankruptcies and mergers) and a decline in the power of organized labour in the metropolitan states, particularly that associated with declining sectors of production. Partly because of Reaganomics and the unleashing of a process of supply-side, competitive deregulation, the 1980s saw the beginnings of a period of tax-cutting, very high real rates of interest and a scarcity of internationally-available capital (mainly because the vast majority of this was sucked into the US). The sum of these very complex changes was a period in which the profile of the major capitalist states began to shift politically away from the politico-economic consensus between labour and capital, and away from the former balance between the domestic and international economy. The regime of high rates of interest, allied to inflation (which was lower after the purgative effects of the 1979–82 recession) and the intensification of competition was linked to a growth of indebtedness of various kinds (personal, corporate, sovereign). The growth of indebtedness reflected, in part, a loss of control by the authorities over credit creation, partly because of the existence of Euromarkets and financial innovation. Loss of control over credit expansion implies that the control of inflation is more difficult.[4]

Apart from the rise and fall of the 'Second' Cold War, and war in the Middle East, the decade was characterized by international financial fragility, an international monetary system in crisis, and more generally, macroeconomic instability and economic crisis in most parts of the world. Some commentators, such as Susan Strange, in her book *Casino Capitalism*, suggested that finance and money were becoming decoupled from the system of production and trade, causing major contradictions for economic development. According to Strange, the world economy was being destabilized in part because of short-term time horizons and speculative flows of capital in a financial system which increasingly resembled a game of (Russian) roulette. State action, led by the USA, was needed to redress this central problem in global macroeconomics.[5]

In this context, then, the deregulatory and macroeconomic policies of the US were generally identified as bearing heavy responsibility for global instability, along with the gyrations and generally economically perverse behaviour of the international financial markets (which the US government had refused to regulate). However, it was also market forces which had driven the dollar through the roof in the first half of the 1980s, raising the political costs of 'malign neglect' of the dollar in US domestic politics, by stoking the fires of protectionism. The rest of the world seemed powerless to influence substantially the policies of the US administration until 1985, when for example, the US responded with the so-called Baker initiatives at the Plaza meeting, attempting to co-ordinate policies with its Group of Seven allies on exchange rates and Third World debts. Even here, there was evidence that the dollar had already begun to fall in February (the Plaza meeting was in September 1985), and the Baker moves were probably primarily motivated by domestic politics, and by strategic considerations, since many of the key debtor states were in the Americas. In sum, for the US case, market pressures seem to have forced the Administration into increased political management of the exchange rate: the US case shows how increased capital mobility can sometimes lead to a 'disciplining' of state policy via an overvaluation of the exchange rate. This G7 macroeconomic coordination process has continued, but with very mixed results so far. For example it is not clear whether under G7 pressure, Japan expanded its money supply and lowered interest rates after the crash, resulting in the asset inflation in the stock and property markets thereafter.[6]

At the heart of this issue, however, is a substantial growth in the structural power of internationally mobile capital (partly reflected in its relative scarcity: this was by contrast with the 1970s, when, because of petro-dollar recycling and low real rates of interest, there was a glut of such capital). Competition to attract such capital, by both governments and producers intensified, in the form of attempting to provide a regulatory and general politico-economic environment which would be attractive to international investors and internationally-mobile capital. This development occurred at the moment when there was an apparent decline in the ability of most governments in the system to control economic activity within their own borders. Although this is an over-simplification, it seems largely the case that the traditional mercantilist and statist forms of capitalist development (associated with the Bretton Woods order, which placed some restrictions, for example, on the mobility of financial capital) were placed on the defensive by the growth in the power of the most mobile, knowledge-intensive and competitive firms. The result has been a new, more outward-looking form of mercantilism, with states competing to provide macro- and micro-economic, regulatory and broader political frameworks to induce long-term direct investments, as well as short-term portfolio capital (with some long-term portfolio capital, such as 20-year bonds) to finance government operations.

Taken together, these developments are symptomatic of a deep structural crisis or transformation in the emerging global political economy. This is linked, directly or indirectly, to domestic socio-political crises in all categories of state within the system: the Third World, the (former) Communist States and, in a somewhat different way, the heartland of metropolitan capitalism.

II. European Economic and Political Union: Limits and Possibilities

The transformations occurring in Western Europe can be understood in terms of the imperatives of a more globalized, competitive, dynamic and mobile capitalist system, as well as the relatively poor performance of west European economies (including West Germany) in 1979–85. Some commentators wondered if western Europe was too social democratic and welfarist, when compared to the US, especially in the context of the US economy's ability to create new jobs. Given the trends of the 1970s, this prompted a concerted political response to re-establish the competitive position and coherence of European social and economic forces in a period of global restructuring. The slogan for this programme is, of course, '1992'.

Indeed, this has become more than a slogan, since it has taken on the form of a social myth suggesting a more dynamic, forward-looking pan-European political and economic identity in the next millennium, implying that the twenty-first century will be the European century, rather than the 'Pacific century'.

To grasp the total nature of the monumental transformations occurring in the European political, strategic, economic and social landscape, we need to think dialectically. Crucial to the explanation of the changes in Europe during the 1980s and 1990s is an examination of the forces operating both globally and within and across the two systems and logics of socio-economic development of East and West (although perforce my discussion focuses on the EC and Germany). Similarly fundamental is the change in the strategic relations between the Soviet bloc and NATO, a change which is also bound up with the inception of economic entropy and a corresponding socio-political *impasse* in the successors to the USSR. By reviewing these changes we can evaluate the likely potential for an integrated Europe to emerge as a global superpower in the twenty-first century.

Western Europe: political union and the 'new constitutionalism'
Although uneven in its impact and trajectory across Western Europe, the unfolding economic crisis of the 1970s and 1980s largely explains the 1992 programme. West European growth rates in the 1970s and early 1980s were much lower than the world average, and the EEC as a whole seemed to be faced with a future of continuing relative decline. Thus the 1992 initiative needs to be understood as a concerted response to the neo-Spenglerian 'Europessimism' of the 1970s and early 1980s. It can be understood as an attempt to revitalize Jean Monnet's goal of a United States of Europe, at least for its most enthusiastic proponents, although in a quite different form, and under new conditions in the global political economy.

The key to this aim was the creation of an integrated economic space with its own central banking institutions and to move politically towards increased economic convergence and co-ordination among the 12 member states. This space would be premised on two things: first a regional set of political institutions which could consolidate and protect this region *vis à vis* European and East Asian challenges. Second, the increased salience of market forces and the spread of micro-economic rationality: in this sense '1992' equals 'marketization'. This implied, then, a further move away from the era of Keynesianism and the social contract which, together with the Cold War structures, had constituted the basis for the post-war political order in Western Europe, in order to create the pre-conditions for renewed European competitiveness.

Although it took the form of a transnational political initiative, a key catalyst for the 1992 initiative was the formation of the European Round-table, a coalition of big European transnational companies (TNCs) led by Phillips. Along with the European Commission, the Roundtable pro-moted the Single European Act (the main legal statute mandating the 1992 programme), as well as, in concert with private and central bankers, the Delors Plan for Economic and Monetary Union (EMU). Wayne Sandholz and John Zysman show how the 1992 process has been shaped and promoted by a transnational alliance or historic bloc involving the Euro-pean Commission, pan-European TNCs and neo-liberal governments within the 12. This process contrasts with the earlier phases of EC integration, which were shaped in the era of 'national champions', state capitalism, national corporatism, and social and economic protection, co-ordinated through the processes of intergovernmentalism.[7]

So far, considerable progress has been achieved at both the level of the single market (with the deregulation of financial services probably the most significant element in the context of this discussion) and the develop-ment of the economic-institutional superstructures which will supervise and regulate the new enlarged economic space. German unification ap-pears to have generally accelerated this process. Common to these EEC initiatives, then, was economic necessity, or the growing perception and reality of international economic challenges. Thus a massive effort was made to synergize European forces to meet the competitive challenge from high-technology US and Japanese firms, and to unify public eco-nomic institutions so as to countervail better the effects of US and Japanese power and policies, as well as incipient challenges from their firms and those from the newly-industrializing countries (NICs). A situa-tion of divide and rule was of benefit, not only to the US and Japan, but also to internationally-mobile capital, relative to the less competitive European companies and their governments.

Reflecting a kind of synthesis (or series of bargains and trade-offs) between, on the one hand, German social market ideas and French statism and instutitionalism, and on the other, Anglo-Saxon free market ide-ologies, the debates over the monetary and macro-economic and other aspects of the EC has been premised, in so far as they have a single focus, on what can be called the discourse of the 'new constitutionalism'. By this I mean the move towards construction of legal or constitutional devices to remove or insulate substantially the new economic institutions from popular scrutiny or democratic accountability. Tendencies towards the wider adoption of this position can be seen in the debates, for example, not only over Economic and Monetary Union of the EC (with most of the critical comment in this regard aimed at the European Commission, rather than the principles associated with EMU), but also the roles of central banks in East and Central Europe, the monetary constitution of a future

Canada, as well as in more general arguments made by bankers, economists and some politicians in favour of the need to constrain state autonomy over fiscal policy, etc. This discourse can also be seen as serving to constitute the debate over the role of international organizations, such as GATT and the IMF/World Bank, and the new European Bank for Reconstruction and Development (EBRD).

Nonetheless, a key problem for the future of West European integration (apart from the German Question to which we return below) is the general lack of political legitimacy and democratic accountability across the whole panoply of European institutions (with the possible exception of the European Court): what is generally termed the 'democratic deficit'. This is mainly because each member state (especially Britain) is reluctant to cede more control to the supra-national institutions of the European Community, and there has been little support until recently to increase the weight and representativeness of the European Parliament. Not surprisingly, given its increased population since unification (as well as a concern for issues of legitimacy and the support for deeper political unification of Europe), the German government has begun to press for greater political weight to be assigned to the European Parliament. However, the problem of popular legitimacy is still a long way from being solved, especially in Britain, where suspicion and parody of all things European, and of Brussels in particular, runs high despite the fact that a wider range of economic and political interests have come to the conclusion, to use Mrs Thatcher's favourite phrase, 'there is no alternative' to closer union with Europe. The British government dislikes the word 'federalism' which, it argues implies *dirigisme*, by French *énarques* and *polytechniciens* led by the likes of Jacques Delors, and centralization of powers in the Brussels bureaucracy and unwelcome judicial review by the European Court.

Part of the reason for this is the way in which the institutional development of the EEC proceeds through the incrementalism of the Intergovernmental Conferences, with political union the key agenda item at Maastricht 9–10 December 1991. In this sense, when I speak of the 'new constitutionalism' I do not mean the construction of a Federal Constitution for the EEC from something akin to first principles, like the Founding Fathers of the American Constitution, although there has been much pressure for this type of approach in the press, such as the *Economist* and the *Financial Times*, newspapers which reflect the vantage point of liberal, transnational capital. Their position may find a wider resonance, since few citizens in Europe are able to distinguish clearly between the European Council (summit meetings of Heads of State), the Council of Ministers, the European Union (nine of the 12 coordinating military policies) and the European Parliament. Thus there is popular confusion over the division of powers and responsibilities in the EEC, their possible reordering between institutions and across different levels of government: European, 'national' or local.

Nevertheless, the debates over political union have sharpened the questions concerning the future of the EEC, and the outcome of the negotiations will determine the outcome of EMU, since Chancellor Kohl has made it clear that he has made political union the price for surrendering the autonomy of the Bundesbank. The questions raised by EMU are difficult ones, and any timetable for EMU (now targeted for completion by 1999) must clarify the degree of economic convergence needed prior to monetary union, and the degree of economic discipline it can impose on the 12, especially with regard to fiscal deficits, as well as institutional questions. The Maastricht summit appears then to have agreed to increase moderately the importance of the Parliament (giving it co-decision powers with the Council of Ministers on limited questions and the right to approve the Commission President and the rest of the EEC executive every four years, but little say on EMU and foreign policy); to extend the principle of majority voting to cover the environment and other issues (with social policy a key exception), and it encourages, though does not mandate, common foreign and defence policies. This reflects the fact that it is very difficult to bridge the divisions over many of the key issues, for example over foreign and defence policy cooperation and the relationship to NATO and the US.

I will now discuss the two key 'economic elements' in European union, and then address the issues related to the development of a common foreign and defence policy.

Economic and monetary union: discipline and policy convergence
It is perhaps no accident that many transnational companies are at the vanguard for EMU, as it will reduce or even abolish certain exchange risks (and will generate some gains in lower transactions costs). These risks are associated, on the one hand, with the uncertainty involved in floating exchange rate systems in the context of very high levels of international capital mobility, and the way in which speculative movements of capital tend to exaggerate exchange rate movements. On the other hand, since the deregulation of financial markets has radiated from US initiatives, and because of the links between US and European rates of interest and exchange rates, the second aspect of uncertainty concerns the consistency of US macroeconomic policies, and the propensity of the USA (e.g. in the early 1980s) to engage in unilateral, as opposed to coordinated international economic policy. The USA has had frequent recourse to the dollar weapon (its own currency is the key currency for international transactions, giving the US the ability to impose seigniorage gains and an inflation tax on the rest of the world, that is to transfer real resources into the USA),

both to improve the competitiveness of the US economy and to force the burden of adjustment onto other countries.

Thus the international rationale for EMU, as was the case at the outset of the European Monetary System (EMS), is partly defensive (the offsetting of risk) and partly to synergize European political potential to offset (and thus to discipline) US unilaterlism in matters of money and finance. It is significant, therefore, that many European bankers are less wedded to the pure market philosophy associated with many of their fraternity in the USA, and have been concerned at the impact of US policies for much of the period since the late 1960s. Seen in a slightly different way, then, as early as 1979, at the instigation of first Roy Jenkins, the President of the EEC, and, more importantly Chancellor Schmidt of West Germany and President Giscard of France, the inauguration of EMS was meant to reduce the vulnerability of European economies to the whims of short-term mobile capital. Underlying the EMU idea is the notion that increased capital mobility implies larger optimum currency areas. In effect the US policies of benign or 'malign' neglect of the exchange rate question during periods of the 1970s and 1980s reflects the relative size and self-sufficiency of the US economy when compared with even the largest EEC countries, or the EEC as a whole. An EMU can also be seen as a political insurance policy relative to the rise of Japanese financial and money power, as the yen becomes increasingly used as a reserve currency and as Tokyo financial markets become deeper, more flexible and more international.[8]

At the heart of these developments is, as I have called it, the 'new constitutionalist' discourse. More specifically, it is crucial to see how many of the debates have been framed around the growing hegemony of a reformulation of concepts of sovereignty and discipline, in matters of political economy. The discourse concerns institutional arrangements designed to insulate key economic agencies, especially central banks, from the interference of elected politicians, who, it is argued, have a tendency in liberal democracies to inflate the economy for electoral purposes or to use the 'inflation tax' to indirectly improve the government's financial position. For example, the former UK Chancellor of the Exchequer, Nigel Lawson, who engineered an inflationary boom to win the 1987 General Election for the Conservatives in Britain, is now in favour of independent banks and a strengthening of the GATT and IMF surveillance.

Key elements in the new hegemonic discourse concerning desirable macroeconomic policies are the concepts of market efficiency, discipline and confidence, and policy credibility and consistency, viewed from the standpoint of both the ideology of sound money as well as new theories in neo-classical economics, such as rational expectations theory.[9] At the heart of the debates over EMS and EMU is a concern at the implications of the massive growth of capital mobility (e.g. the offshore markets), and the implications of destabilizing speculative movements of capital for balance of payments discipline in individual European countries. In the 1970s these effects were somewhat contradictory from the viewpoint of financial discipline, since borrowing on the Euromarkets was an option that many governments could turn to for financing deficits, and thus avoid painful adjustments to 'shocks' such as the rises in oil prices. This was possible because of a glut of internationally-available capital caused by the rise in oil prices and the need to recycle petrodollars, in large part through the Euromarkets. The latter grew massively in size during the next two decades.[10]

By the 1980s, however, with higher real rates of interest and a tightening of credit conditions for most countries (the USA being a notable, albeit partial exception), nearly all deficit governments came under increased pressure to adopt anti-inflationary, tight money policies, in order to avoid sustained outflows of capital and a substantial loss of foreign exchange reserves. This has also put pressure on the taxation regimes in different countries, especially with regard to (not increasing) withholding taxes and more generally those affecting the rate of return on capital: this partly explains EEC initiatives to harmonize value-added taxes. In the European context, the configuration of the EMS around the deutschmark (the anchor currency) and the hard money anti-inflation stance of the Bundesbank served to reinforce this discipline, with the result that it is generally accepted that the EMS has had a deflationary bias. However, German positions appear to be unchallengeable, although the idea of a more fully-fledged monetary union is seen by other member governments (notably the French), as a means of offsetting this economic power in political institutions.

Thus the Delors Report of 1989 stressed the need to adopt '*binding procedures*' to constrain national authorities, and the need to reinforce commitments to price stability, and advocated the setting up of a European Reserve Fund with its key objective 'to be the symbol of the political will of the European countries and thus reinforce the *credibility* of the process towards economic and monetary union'; with a system of European Central Banks, '*committed to the objective of price stability*', and '*independent of instructions* from national governments and Community authorities'; in macroeconomic policy it meant that countries would have to submit to imposed policy *constraints*.[11] This is understood to mean the commitment of monetary (and fiscal) policy to a particular substantive direction, irrespective of the desires of elected policy makers to inflate the economy for electoral reasons or else to impose seigniorage gains and/or an inflation tax as a means to ease public financing problems and/or devalue existing government debt. A binding exchange-rate constraint, would, of course, also simultaneously eliminate the option of devaluation of the currency for reasons of international competitiveness. In practice this is likely to mean Bundesbank standards, always assuming that political support for these arrangements is sustained in EC member countries (a severe exchange crisis for a member country might swiftly lead to a reimposition of exchange and credit controls and an abandonment of EMS membership). So far EMS rules have been non-binding, although in practice, member countries have behaved *as if* they were, with the changes in French policy between 1981–3 as dramatic evidence of French commitment to both the EMS and its foreign policy goal of greater European integration.

A good example of the impact of such constraints is Sweden, which has shifted away from the famous 'Swedish model' towards neo-liberalism. Thus, in anticipation of EC entry in the mid-1990s, Sweden pegged the krona to the deutschmark, and thus subordinated its monetary policy to that of the Bundesbank. There was a sudden flight of capital out of the krona in early 1992. This followed the failed coup and final demise of the USSR, which had provoked a massive Finnish devaluation (given the dependence of the Finnish economy on trade with the USSR) amid fears of a collapse in the Nordic banking systems. Sweden was then forced to increase its nominal rate of interest by six per cent and impose a draconian financial squeeze to defend the parity of the krona and stem the capital outflow.

The real challenge to EMS cohesion is likely to emerge in the aftermath of 1992, that is after complete financial liberalization in the EEC, given that both France and Italy – two of the countries with traditionally weak currencies in the EMS – have abolished capital and exchange controls, and in many countries there are still substantial fiscal problems (and it is worth emphasizing, the EMU process mandates tight constraints on budget deficits), with high levels of government indebtedness. Moreover, full EMU would mean that some countries would have to forego substantial seigniorage gains: the main cases here are Greece, Italy, Portugal and Spain, where it accounted for 6–12 per cent of government revenues in the late 1980s.[12] The other main challenge will come from the behaviour – or misbehaviour – of the dollar relative to the deutschmark, which (apart from sterling, which is declining in international importance) is the only world-class currency in the EMS. In the case of Italy, a lot will depend on the government's ability to reduce government budget deficits.

In this light it is significant that Italy has dismantled the system of wage indexation, *scala mobile*, has 'divorced' the Treasury and the Central Bank (relieving the latter from the obligation to buy unsold T-bills, although not of its obligation to finance up to 14% of public expenditure through an overdraft facility). In 1987 the Italian government served notice that it intended to make liberalization of capital flows irreversible so as to tie the hands of any future parliaments.[13] In effect, the liberalization of capital markets means that it becomes impossible to impose different regulations on financial intermediaries, lowering regulations to their lowest common denominator, leading to a decline in reserve holdings and a fall in seigniorage. Only through capital controls can a single country sustain its use of the inflation tax and maintain higher reserve requirements for banks. There is some debate as to the results of these policies. Some argue that the long term gains to tax revenue for the state will be higher in a liberal regime, because they will tend to maximize government revenue in the long run, in so far as they are associated with higher rates of capital accumulation and economic growth, and thus a widening tax base.

Stage One of EMU has begun, and it has been agreed that Stage Two will begin by 1994, partly because the Germans wish to sustain the deutschmark as the anchor for monetary stability and discipline in Europe. The IGC on political union is paralleled by a Monetary IGC, which also met in Maastricht. The monetary questions cannot, of course, be separated from the fiscal questions, and much discussion has taken place during 1991 concerning the limits on budget deficits and the structure of taxation, issues of profound importance to the management of the macro- and micro-economic policy alternatives open to future governments. German unification has given a breathing space to other EEC countries on this question, given the high budget deficits associated with the costs of transition. The conditions surrounding phasing in of Stage Two of EMU will in practice probably include the following: fiscal sanctions by the Commission could be applied to member states, but in all likelihood this would require unanimity in the Council of Ministers; the accountability of the European Central Bank (Eurofed) would involve obligations to consult the Ecofin (Council of Finance Ministers), rather than subordination to Ecofin guidelines; the governments (notably Germany) will determine exchange rate guidelines, in conjunction with a central advisory role of the Eurofed; the ecu would be hardened in line with the appreciation of the strongest EMS currency, but will not operate as a parallel, 13th currency as proposed by Britain; the final phase of EMU will be entered by mutual agreement, not in accordance with predetermined criteria; entry would depend on 'convergence' of inflation rates. Thus the stage is set for a two-tier EMU, with an inner group of low-inflation countries, with exchange rates relative to each other that are virtually fixed (France, Germany, Belgium, Luxembourg, the Netherlands and possibly Denmark) pressing ahead, with the door left open for others (e.g. Britain). Other countries, such as Sweden, will manage their exchange rates as if they are in the inner core of EMU.

The two-tier or multi-tier solution is a compromise which reflects the hierarchy of discipline which an EMU would impose: the high-inflation and poorer countries will have to adjust much more than their wealthier, low inflation counterparts. This is why the Spanish government threatened to refuse to sign the EMU Treaty at Maastricht without some guaranteed transfers from rich to poor areas. The Spanish position also reflects the problems for political union, and for the design of EEC institutions, which stem from the disparities in economic conditions across Europe, disparities which are intensified by higher capital mobility.

Single market restructuring: labour, capital and the 'new protectionism'
The move towards capital liberalization in Europe necessarily implies a shift in the structure of taxation, towards a larger revenue burden falling on indirect, regressive forms of taxation, such as VAT, although full convergence of VAT rates will not be in place until at least 1996. This is because direct taxes on incomes (personal and corporate, on wages and interest) will necessarily tend to fall to a lowest common denominator in a situation of mobility of capital and labour. In practice, labour is relatively immobile, although skilled labour is generally more mobile than unskilled labour. This means that it will tend to the upper level of income taxes which fall by the largest proportion, since less skilled workers tend to earn less and are less able to move around between different countries than higher income, highly educated, skilled and linguistically proficient workers.

The European situation seems likely to gravitate towards that in the USA, where post-tax income differentials for workers have been widening since the late 1960s, and where income inequality has intensified since the deregulatory push of the Reagan administration in the early 1980s. It is in this light that we might also note that in most of the EC states laws governing the level of minimum wages have been amended downwards, and wage indexation regulations are being undermined, in line with the Italian *scala mobile* discussed above. Differences in the structure of collective bargaining, levels of unionization and the segmentation of labour market regulation along national lines have served to divide labour and thus contribute politically to an (uneven) weakening of regulations concerning working conditions and relative income share of labour.

Attempts at reform of labour conditions by the European Commission in 1981 and 1982 were blocked by a number of member states in the Council of Ministers, with Britain at the vanguard of opposition. The macroeconomic debates and developments discussed above were thus paralleled by attempts to water down the counterpart to the 1992 single market programme, the Social Charter, to provide minimum guarantees concerning social welfare provision and health care, and to protect workers from the worst abuses of market and employer power. The neo-liberal thrust of the 1992 programme, in practice, is thus to avoid any propensity to intervene substantially in the free working of labour markets. This is because the changes are premised on the need to extend market discipline at both the micro- and macro-economic levels, and a strong Social Charter would mean less 'flexibility' in labour markets.

As has been noted, crucial to all this has been the role of the British government under Mrs Thatcher, which consistently made alliances with business and the peripheral nations of the EC to oppose the transnational-ization of welfare and employment rights according to a new European standard. What is already an unbalanced relationship between (trans-national) capital and certain forms of labour is thus likely to be exacer-bated by not only the transition to EMU, but also by the push of capital for more flexible and deregulated labour markets, in some cases supported by national governments, again, partly for reasons of political ideology, but more importantly, for reasons of international competitiveness.

Thus these developments need to be placed in the context of the restructuring of global production and the re-organization of production relations along post-Fordist lines. They also need to be understood in the context of the debates concerning social policy harmonization or coordina-tion. As Elizabeth Meehan has indicated, the former implies uniformity of provision, whereas the latter allows for national variations, and thus corresponds to the transnational/national dialectic with regard to produc-tion structures and macro-economic co-ordination both within and outside the EEC.[14] Thus while the EEC 1992 programme appears to be designed to promote the transnationalization of European production, social and labour market policy appear to be national in nature, allowing for labour movements to be fragmented rather than integrated on a pan-European basis.

Another way to look at some of these issues is to deconstruct the concept of 'protection'. Most of the language of G7, IMF and EEC communiques is built, axiomatically, on neo-liberal discourse concerning the desirability of free movement of factors of production and efficiency of markets. Protec-tion is thus seen as politically undesirable and economically inefficient intervention in the economy. Thus we need to ask, 'protection for whom and for what purposes?'

The type of 'protectionism' which really seems to characterize 1992 and other recent initiatives in the world economy (such as the North American Free Trade Area negotiations) is that accorded to the interests of trans-national capital from domestic interference. For example, the liberaliza-tion of services in the GATT (which can be highly intrusive, since they often involve movement of people to supply such services) and new GATT regulations to liberalize public procurement are meant not only to guaran-tee access to TNCs and financial firms, but also further to erode the conditions of existence of the welfare-nationalist state (*viz* welfarism and national allocation of government contracts to preferred local firms, or national champions).

In this context, a consistent policy of the European Commission since the 1970s has been to shift the terms of debate, and the focus of action, away from the promotion and protection of national champions, towards the promotion of European transnationals. Thus the ESPRIT (informatics research and collaboration among 12 European TNCs) and EUREKA programmes, along with the ERASMUS programme in higher education, are part of a general initiative to make European high-technology, knowledge-intensive transnationals more competitive *vis à vis* their overseas rivals. Thus internal market liberalization and policy co-ordination is a form of macro-regionalism in a more competitive and knowledge-intensive global political economy, and is offset by the need of European firms to gain access to markets and knowledge world-wide. For similar reasons, the 1992 initiatives have been accompanied by large numbers of mergers and link-ups between European and US firms, as well as those from other countries.

As has been noted, the Single Market Act was enthusiastically supported by many major European TNCs (such as Phillips, Fiat) and the 1988 Ceccini Report promised substantial gains for business in terms of one-off savings and new business opportunities. Faced with the realities of rationalization in an era of harsher competitive pressures, it now appears that there is a counter-tendency among some members of the European business fraternity (especially in France and Italy), to sustain subsidies at either the national and European level. A report by David Ernst of McKinsey and Co, suggests that many European sectors face a similar future to that experienced by the US airline industry following deregulation in the 1970s. There the number of companies initially expanded, with over 200 new carriers entering the industry. By the late 1980s, half of them were bankrupt or taken over by the bigger carriers, with profits down substantially across the industry.

Thus a period of intense competition, mergers, and a recomposition of capital seems to be ahead in Europe, with European companies dividing on the question of market liberalization, with the European Commission pushing hard for the elimination of subsidies, state preferential treatment and reduction of the public sector:

> . . . the Commission does have powerful allies. European businessmen who are fed up with competing against – or having to operate alongside – a bloated public sector wish it well. Carlo de Benedetti, an Italian industrialist, complains that Italy 'is in the second tier of Europe' thanks to its heavy handed state . . . International pressures will also force the EC government to be more stingy with aid . . . The anti-state brigade will also be helped by economics. Heavy social security payments and the cost of the Gulf War have made it hard for governments to balance their budgets . . . Some countries are already selling a raft of state businesses.[15]

On the other hand, little progress has been made on the harmonization of standards, VAT levels, and the opening of public procurement, which is worth perhaps 15 per cent of European combined GDP. Only about 2 per cent of public sector contracts flow across EEC frontiers. In addition, the electronics industry in Europe, and its interface with the European high-technology programmes noted above suggests that, in consumer electronics at least, the EEC seems to be attempting to promote European champions; this is also the case in semiconductors. There are also substantial frictions with Japan, over the propensity to subsidize the European car manufacturers, where European firms lag far behind the Japanese in terms of productivity.

Thus the clash between national (or European) and transnational capital looks set to intensify in coming years.[16] Uncompetitive firms will be forced out of business, and some management consultants predict a rapid rise in unemployment when 1992 really takes hold. Nevertheless, as the fears of many European businesses suggest, the general trend is for greater market liberalization, along both internal and external dimensions.

Immigration and 'widening' the EEC: economic, political and security aspects

Perhaps the key political issue in the EEC today concerns immigration. By early 1992 it appeared possible to discern some of the broader terms of the political debate over this volatile question. These seem to involve the reconstruction of a discourse of 'Europeanness' rooted in the mythical origins of Europe (i.e. in Græco-Roman and Judao-Christian myth) and related to the historical idea of 'Christendom'. This concept implicity constructs the political and social boundaries for the expanding EC, and provides a criterion of inclusion/exclusion which can be used to keep out 'unwelcome' immigrants (e.g. from the Mahgreb, the Levant, and the Orthodox and Islamic regions of the former USSR). In the rest of this section, I examine the immigration issue from a narrower political economy perspective.

Internal market liberalization may not go with the free movement of people, which are treated in neo-classical economics as a factor of production. As has been noted, whilst, for example, the EEC Single Market initiative, or '1992' involves the freer movement of capital, goods, services and labour (labour mobility is very low within the EEC when contrasted with the USA), a key political issue for the 1990s will be immigration policy. This is a politically explosive issue already in a number of countries, especially in Italy, France (where the Prime Minister, Edith Cresson, suggested in June 1991 that she was prepared to fly illegal immigrants back to their place of origin) and to a lesser extent Germany and Britain, and needs to be considered in the light of current negotiations to 'widen' the EEC to incorporate Scandinavian countries, and other EFTA countries such as Austria and Switzerland, to say nothing of the three 'vanguard states' of central Europe: Czechoslovakia, Hungary and Poland, and of course Turkey with its NATO pedigree.

(Illegal) immigration is already a key issue in the EEC, the USA and increasingly in Canada. What is driving the latest phase of migration is the disparities in economic conditions across countries and the restructuring of production more generally. The problem of labour migration within Europe is linked to the decline of older, Fordist-style heavy industries such as coal, steel, shipbuilding, textiles and relatively economically-backward regions dependent on agriculture (e.g. in the Mediterranean countries, Ireland). Declining heavy industries are found mainly in Northern Europe, in regions of high unemployment. The wider context is the restructuring of global production, widening disparities in economic conditions, including environmental decay (e.g. the 'lost decade' of the 1980s for most of Africa and Latin America), and the political chaos and collapse in many parts of the world, with the attendant threats of political violence and persecution.

In this context, the erosion of some types of 'protectionism' rather than others has both a political and a security dimension. This is first because of the ways in which influxes of immigrants may cause political problems and divisions in the labour force within a particular state (the more established workers may see guest-workers and other migrants as a threat to their jobs and living standards, or contributing to the growth of the black economy and thus the erosion of the state's tax base, or at worst as welfare scroungers: the rise of neofascist parties in France and Benelux are symptoms of this). Second, the internal policing of populations is an aspect of national security, and intrusive forms of policing may be legitimated on grounds of the suspect allegiance of newcomers to a given country. Applications for membership of the EC from central European countries, as well as more specifically from Turkey (and possibly Morocco) will be affected by these issues. Thus the European Commission's attempts to create a consensus on the need for a transnational social policy are blocked not only by neo-liberal parties and governments and TNCs, but also by coalitions including the security apparatus, some elements in organized labour, and occasionally right-wing parties.

From a more traditional political economy perspective it is worth remembering that many protected national capitalist firms are in the military-industrial sectors, and to a large extent, US military producers have cost advantages over their foreign counterparts (as is also the case for US media and mass communications, and also to a lesser extent informatics firms) and with the Cold War in eclipse, they can be expected to push for further liberalization of overseas markets. This issue can also be related to the traditional concern of governments to secure and to sustain a set of 'strategic industries' within the territories, for purposes of economic and national security. Traditionally this has involved control over communications grids, newspapers, television and other elements of the information society. All of these elements of protection are under attack in the 1992 programme, and so far a considerable degree of progress has been made on many of these questions, both in the EEC under the rubric of 'national procurement', and in the GATT negotiations. In the case of the EEC, agriculture has always been accorded a special 'strategic status', in the sense that it provided a means to stabilize the rural populations and to provide a redistributive social policy (although now its major beneficiaries are large-scale agribusiness and the mafia, and of course, the relatively economically-backward regions of the EC dependent on agricultural production).

Disciplinary neo-liberalism: efficiency, rationality and the 'new constitutionalism'

In other words, the new 'protectionism', albeit in sometimes contradictory ways, is designed to sustain economic openness and the forces of international economic competition, a competition in which the largest and fittest are likely to survive, and this applies as much to the position of states as it does to firms. Thus the arguments about the further institutionalization of GATT rules, and the widening of its ambit to cover services, including financial services, can be seen, to a significant extent in terms congruent with neo-liberalism, and in some important respects, attempts to reconstitute US national power. A key rationale for strengthening GATT in the ways proposed is so that mobile (productive) capital will be able to plan for long-term investment with more of a sense of security concerning the future, and underpinning the 'exit' option for mobile capital more generally (freedom of movement implies exit as well as entry).

All this is designed to create a macro- and micro-economic environment which is geared to the maximization of market or X-efficiency, with competition the key driving force in generating dynamism. This competition is seen as occurring between states (i.e. a new, outward-looking mercantilism, involving, amongst other things, a competition to provide an attractive investment climate for capital) as well as other economic agents.

There is, of course, contestation over the concepts espoused in the disciplinary neo-liberal discourse (which is not by any means homogenous). For example, some freedoms are prioritized at the expense of others (the freedom of capital in transparent markets seen as maximizing individual choice). Some concepts of efficiency (i.e. X-efficiency and micro-efficiency) and discipline are prioritized relative to others (e.g. macro-efficiency, and social efficiency). Thus in a book on EMS only one of the contributors (out of about 40 economists) pointed out the deflationary bias and welfare losses associated with the operation of the EMS, thus implying that the EMS and EMU could be viewed as flawed from the viewpoint of macro- and social-efficiency. The same economist noted that there had been no net job creation in Europe to speak of during the 1980s.[17] Nevertheless, the thrust of the Ceccini Report, as well as some independent analyses made by the Centre for Economic Policy Research in London, argue that 1992 and EMU will serve to generate considerable gains in dynamic efficiency (permanently adding as much as 0.25 to 1 percent to annual European GDP), albeit through a Schumpeterian process of 'creative destruction'.[18] The latter epithet certainly seems to apply to the process unleashed in east Germany after unification, and Poland since the application of IMF-style shock therapy since late 1989.

More generally, these issues relate to different concepts of rationality in the social sciences, such as those discussed in Jon Elster's *Ulysses and the Sirens*.[19] Neo-liberals are pressing for a set of binding constraints on state power and democracy, either indirectly through market forces as in pure liberalism (e.g. Hayek and the Austrian school, who call for the full privatization of monetary creation and regulation through market forces), or through some constitutionalist device which is more typical of the liberals of the Freiberg school (which characterizes Bundesbank thinking, and more generally, the conceptualization of the social market economy), arguing for autonomous central banks, or some combination of the two. For the new constitutionalists, market rationality is seen as preferable to the vagaries of political discretion and/or the collective will of the polis.

A key problem for constitutionalist arrangements in so far as they might be applied globally is the United States, since it is simultaneously the most economically central as well as the most inward-looking of all the major capitalist countries, reflecting a contradiction between 'subjective' and 'objective' aspects of the US political economy. The USA, especially given the record of its unilateralism over the last 20 years, needs, according to this discourse, to be like Ulysses eschewing the temptations of the sirens, 'bound to the mast', like other nations.

However, the domestic constitution of the USA itself would be vitiated by any subordination of the Congress in key areas of economic policy, reflecting that what is at stake is a question of sovereignty in two senses: the sovereignty of a nation in the conduct of its policy relative to other nations; and the sovereignty of the people expressed either directly or indirectly through voting into power elected representatives who are expected to fight for the interests of their constituents.

However, the problem goes much deeper, since the very structure of the US political economy, and the attitudes of the mass of the politically active population mean that the US popular consciousness is ethnocentric and inward-looking, and the economy partly reflects this in the way that a country of about 252 million people devours about 60% of the world's annual consumable resources. In this sense, a key problem for neo-liberal constitutionalist strategy (as well as for a solution to global environmental and ecological problems) is the lack of internationalization of the USA in a broad sense: the issue is not just the need for the USA to forego its unilateralism.

As David Law has pointed out, the relative decline of the US economy will probably have to go further before the USA is forced to accept the constraints on policy autonomy that other countries have to cope with.[20] This lies at the heart of the limits of the G7 as an institutionalized directorate for the world economy, and also sets limits to the transformation of its role in a more politically focused set of collective strategies *vis à vis* Soviet reconstruction, Third World issues and environmental questions.

Thus, even within the context of the terms of the debate as defined by Eurocrats and the forces of the right (who have made most of the running in the debates), there are substantial disagreements about the pace and phasing of, for example, the implementation of the Delors proposals and the internal and external impact of EMU and greater European integration. In consequence, although German unification appears to have injected political momentum in the process of West European unification, the problem of the legitimacy and in some sense the logic of the process is still not being addressed fundamentally. Political overload (i.e. a vast and complicated agenda for political leaders) merely compounds this problem. Thus it is a savage irony that whilst democratic institutions are being painfully (re-)constructed in the east, partly inspired by Western traditions of liberal democracy, attempts to establish more democratic foundations for supra-national West European institutions are notable by their absence.

Germany and the new Europe

Notwithstanding the new importance of the socio-economic laboratory experiment in Poland, and the political skirmishes over the Oder-Niesse line and the border with Poland, the most important changes in Europe outside of the former Soviet Union concern Germany. The collapse of the German Democratic Republic occurred when East German people simply voted with their feet and then at the ballot box to terminate the old communist order and to accept the economic and political *de facto* annexation of their nation by West Germany.

Now there is a new social and political landscape in Europe. The long-term consequence of unification is likely to be a more economically central and more powerful Germany. As a footnote to this probability, when compared with Poland, unification is a case of the extreme application of (IMF style) conditionality: the Economic, Social and Monetary Union of the two Germanies was premised on the acceptance by East Germany of not only the currency, but the entire gamut of socio-economic principles and institutions of the West, and, of course, the social market economy of the Federal Republic.

So far the costs of this process have been massive and have continued to rise, such that they are creating great fiscal strains with little evidence of positive results in terms of new investment and economic growth in the east of the new Germany. Indeed, OECD economists have observed privately that the macro-economic stance of the united Germanies during 1989–91 was very 'un-German'. The macroeconomic profile of the new Germany resembled that of Reaganomics in the first half of the 1980s: high budget deficits and a regime of tight monetary policy, thus confounding the claims of the Bundesbank President Karl-Otto Poehl made in early 1989 that monetary unification was a 'fantastical and phantasmagorical idea' that he would never see in his own lifetime, and when he saw it, he called it a 'disaster'. This reflects the subjugiation of the supposedly independent German central bank to the dictates of the political masters in Bonn. What we can expect in economic terms from all this, in the short- and medium-term is that the union will act as a drag on the very impressive economic performance of the German economy which characterized the 1985-90 period. German economic planners will have to work very hard to ensure that eastern German does not become another Mezzagiorno.

Recent evidence suggests that this will be very difficult indeed.[21] There was a 43 per cent fall in east German industrial production between July 1990 and February 1991 (west German output rose by 8 per cent between July 1990 and April 1991); a rise in east German unemployment (up from 2.8 to 8.6 per cent between late 1989 and May 1991) and short-time (up from 6.7 to 20.1 per cent in the same period) work in east Germany has risen very rapidly; the east German GNP fell by 15 per cent between 1989 and 1990, and OECD economists predict a similar decline between 1990 and 1991. The Truhandanstalt (the German privatization agency) has only privatized 12 per cent of the most viable *kombinate*; there is confusion over property rights and a backlog of claims. East Germany is now dependent on fiscal transfers for half of its total income. Only in the level of wages have the two Germanies come together: the ratio of wages per employees in east to west rose from 32 per cent in the second half of 1989, to 73 per cent at the end of 1990. The results of unification thus far indicate the size of the problem involved in transforming a communist planned economy into a capitalist and competitive one. If the process fails in Germany, where, one might ask, can it succeed?

In line with the development of the US external balance under Reagan, the fiscal costs of the unification/reconstruction process means that the vast balance of payments surpluses of the former Federal Republic have now disappeared and Germany has moved into deficit and will probably become a substantial net borrower on international capital markets for some time. One consequence will be to divert scarce supplies of capital (in 1991 there was a substantial global shortage of capital, partly because of the re-orientation of Japanese economic expansion in the direction of domestic growth). This will hit hardest the poorer countries, and in Europe these are on the European periphery, particularly those countries border-ing the Mediterranean, such as Greece, Portugal and especially Spain, which was the beneficiary of substantial investments of German capital during the 1980s.

Thus whilst unification might give a long-term boost to the (west) German, and perhaps European economy, its effects, like Reaganomics, will be globally contradictory. For example, Spain may have to raise its interest rates (or cut costs, including labour costs) to sustain capital inflows. Similar effects are likely to be felt in other members of the EC, and financial conditions may tighten in Europe (As well as world-wide, notwithstanding monetary easing in the US since 1991, following the end of the Gulf War, for counter-cyclical reasons, and because of the liquidity problems in the US financial system). In Britain this has made it more difficult (especially since EMS entry) to cut substantially interest rates during the recession which started in early 1990, worsening its general effects (unemployment has risen rapidly). This threatens the post-Thatcher Conservative Party with defeat in the forthcoming UK General Election.

Again, the conditions which explain these effects relate in part to the mobility of capital in the integrated financial markets, many of which are now offshore markets outside of formal governmental control. The second and more specific condition is of course the economic centrality of Germany in Europe. Here then, global as well as regional and German conditions interact to create the macroeconomic environment for German unification, and its wider economic effects. Long-term interest rates rose by 2 per cent following unification, so that real rates of interest in Germany in mid 1991 were at about 5–6 per cent, with short-term interest rates high. The German current account surplus which peaked at 5 per cent of GNP in 1989, became a deficit of 1.5 per cent of GNP in mid-1991. Martin Wolf summarizes the changes well:

> A year after [unification] a new Germany is coming into view: a fiscally expansionary Germany, a Germany whose monetary policy is under pressure and a Germany with a current account deficit. But most importantly, it is a Germany with a deep and perhaps enduring division [with the prospect of] an embittered eastern population.[22]

At a deeper level, German development is crucial for the future of Europe, not least because of the power of the German economy, the centrality of the deutschmark in the EMS, and the likely centrality of German models of macro- and micro-economic management in the new political and economic configurations of post-1992 Europe. Here the dimensions of past, present and future, integration and disintegration are particularly apposite as ways to examine the dialectics of the 'Europeanization of Germany' and the 'Germanization of Europe'. The latter refers to the way that both the German model, as an idea and a social practice, and the actual effects of Bundesbank monetary discipline have configured the socio-economic conditions in neighbouring countries. This includes not just those in the deutschmark-zone (which includes Austria), but also France since 1983, which has been 'more German than the Bundesbank' in pursuing monetary and fiscal discipline and a hard-franc policy. As the above discussion indicates, the macroeconomic aspects of this are in danger of being undermined because of the costs of German unification.

This was further underlined in early 1992 when German interest rates rose to their highest post-war levels as the Bundesbank attempted to control domestic inflation and to face off union demands for substantial pay increases. This meant, of course, further deflationary pressure on high unemployment countries in the EEC, such as France and Britain.

At the level of ideology, enthusiasts for *modell Deutschland* have characterized West Germany as a dynamic society which combines Japanese growth dynamics, North American-style innovation and ingenuity, Swiss currency stability, Scandinavian living standards and social welfare provision, as well as time-honoured German efficiency. They also claim a new quality, at least as far as German modern history is concerned: political stability, a value which its politicians hold obsessively, and which is underpinned by, and embedded in, the 'social-market' economy.

The historical evaluation of the (west) German model has involved a shift of its political centre of gravity from social-liberal to conservative-liberal since the early 1980s. This has gone with a crisis in the old-style Fordist strategies of accumulation, a diminution of the level and extensiveness of social welfare provision (at least until unification meant substantial transfers to the new east German *länder*). In Ralf Dahrendorf's phrase, this may herald the 'end of the Social-Democratic Century' in German political life, and with it, perhaps, the end of the social democratic Keynesian state, a process which may be slowed by the short-term costs of unification.[23] Thus in the German case, the crisis of post-war hegemony has not gone as far as in Britain, Holland, France and Belgium, but has, nonetheless, still occurred.

However, the ideology and practice of *modell Deutschland*, stands in substantial contrast to the neo-liberal model of Thatcherism, although there are points of agreement concerning the importance of financial discipline, market transparency and liberalization, and the emphasis on global competitiveness. The advocates of this new vision for Germany, which span the conventional political spectrum, see Germany as the politico-economic gyroscope for future socio-economic development in a unified Europe. Germany would form not only the crossroads between East and West (its traditional economic role) but also, and more fundamentally, the political and economic, and perhaps the ideological centre, from the Atlantic to the Urals.

The possibility that this dream might become a reality (or a nightmare) provoked considerable, if sometimes politically stifled reaction in other major European countries, as when Mrs Thatcher's longstanding *confidant* in the cabinet and ardent Thatcherite, Nicolas Ridley, was forced to resign in July 1990 after stating that the Germans were trying to 'take over' Europe. Widespread distrust of German intentions is still a feature of the European landscape, on both sides of what was the Iron Curtain.

Nevertheless, and partly in response to this, the indications are that the mainstream political forces, and perhaps more fundamentally, key elements in German industry and banking, see benefits in the Europeanization and globalization of the German economic position, the latter reflected, for example in the trilateral link-up between Deutsche Bank, Daimler-Benz, Mitsubishi and United Technologies. Similar types of strategy practised by other German companies suggest that, in a similar way to other giant transnationals headquartered in the US and Japan, only a global strategy and stance is feasible for long-term growth and survival, and the power of these interests will prevent any substantially inward-looking mercantilism, or economic nationalism, on the part of the new German state.

German leaders have seemed much less concerned with direct political hegemony or indeed, international political visibility, particularly in the wake of gaining acceptance from the allies for unification (the German government has generally allowed the French to make the running on economic and political union in the EC –in the form of Jacques Delors – and its reaction was muted to the Gulf War and to the putting down of rebellions in the Baltic Republics by Gorbachev). Germany extended huge credits to the USSR, despite the fact that the Soviet Government had not ratified the 4 + 2 agreement and as of April 1991 still had over 300,000 troops in east Germany (many of whom wish to stay there because they could not hope to have a comparable standard of living when they returned home).

At the pan-European level, major German electronics firms such as Siemens have led the way in helping to forge pan-European strategies of restructuring and co-operation in research and development (as with the EC's EUREKA programme). Germany is of course the key player in the negotiations over economic and political union and is making most of the running in sketching the details for the proposed European System of Central Banks.

Both of these types of evidence suggest a Europeanization of Germany, as well as the spread of German methods and policies throughout Europe. Germany's state-supported key economic power bloc (based in machine production, electro- and production technology and other basic industries, along with its large banks) is pursuing international strategies which are geared towards improving the competitive position of German producers in high-technology strategic industries, in the context of a macro-economic regime of monetary discipline and fiscal expansion; and a micro-economic policy which fuses supply-side policies with corporatism at the firm, industry and national levels. In this context, the Kohl leadership has sustained many elements of continuity in the German political economy, and has harnessed them to the widely-based support for qualitative modernization and organizational innovation. This has occurred in the context of an economy which is host to a small number of large, efficient, profitable and innovative transnational corporations, and a galaxy of

smaller satellite producers. This generates an impressive level of productive power: it is something that the so-called 'vanguard' states of central
Europe, to say nothing of some of the members of the EC, can only dream
about.

Post-Fordist modernization and the social market economy are being
increasingly characterized by both the centralization and the transnationalization of German capital. This is, of course, also true of French,
Italian and British capital, the latter of which has a long history of this type
of strategy. German strategy is being extended into eastern Germany, and
some of the former regime's *kombinate* are being absorbed into the
process, albeit with limited success so far. In business terminology this is a
synthesis between economic synergy and political strategy: transnational
alliances are designed to help guarantee access to economic opportunities
overseas, particularly North American and East Asian markets (and
capital), and the global posture means that Germany cannot be constrained within the confines of the EC nor shackled too directly in a
Franco-German *entente*. German strategy is, in other words, a new path
towards advancing German corporate, and national interests, in a global
context. If it chooses to forge an alliance with the globalist perspective of
the interests of the City of London and the largest UK transnationals, and
indeed the UK government, Germany can obviate any Euro-mercantilist
tendencies (coming from within the European Commission bureaucrats
and possibly the French government), and prevent the emergence of a
fortress Europe. This idea perhaps lies partly behind the emerging *rapprochement* between Germany and the UK in the EEC, with several key
members of Prime Minister Major's cabinet singing the praises of aspects
of the German model (this move also has the virtue of outflanking the
Labour Party before the 1992 General Election: Labour has moved in the
direction of praising the social market economy and the virtues of monetary discipline and central bank independence).

*The EEC, the West and the Eastern Question: economic strategy and
foreign policy*
Whatever the pace of the attempted reforms in eastern and Central
Europe, and now in Russia and the Commonwealth of Independent
States, under a programme of what can only be called 'disciplinary neo-
liberalism' (i.e. a modified version of the medicine applied during the
1980s in some Latin American countries under IMF conditionality), the
social transformations involved are such that, following Braudel, we
should expect their efforts to be contradictory, and to transform only
slowly the embedded social structures to create the conditions for a truly
market capitalist society. German unification and the costs of the Gulf
War, plus changes in the rules governing the allocation of international
finance under the auspices of the Bank for International Settlements (in

effect downgrading the credit ratings of developing and east European countries) all suggest that the process will be slow and tortuous, if indeed it succeeds at all.[24] The Russian reform programme was beginning to meet fierce internal resistance by February 1992, and the hungry are increasingly in a state of bewildered revolt at the massive price increases and elimination of subsidies which had once provided some degree of economic security.

Moreover, whereas Poland's Solidarity government appeared at one point to have had the degree of legitimacy to provide the political preconditions to absorb the necessary social dislocations and restructuring involved in preparing the economy for its subjugation to the power of capital, this has always appeared much less the case for both the increasingly authoritarian leadership of the USSR, and the Russian government under Boris Yeltsin. Moreover, both the Soviet and now Russian governments have been internally divided on the direction of change and its purpose.

In January of 1991, Gorbachev was suspected by many in the West of being on the verge of mental breakdown, and himself proposed the suspension of *glasnost* and press censorship was renewed. However, the Union was racked by centrifugal tendencies which the iron fist cannot contain. In this sense, from a longer-term world order viewpoint, the collapse of the USSR poses substantial problems, given the fact that the Republics seem determined to go their own way politically (e.g. the struggle between Ukraine and Russia over the control of the Black Sea fleet). Only under stable political conditions will the former USSR (or indeed any of its Republics) attract the levels of investment and technology they need from the rest of the world, or repay its debts to the rest of the world: these are large, especially to Germany. The Soviet leadership were, until their removal, attempting to cope with three major problems, on a scale probably never faced by any previous empire in history: substantially transforming and reconstructing the economy, re-ordering the political and constitutional structure, and retreating from dominance and control over a vast territory.

As I argued in an earlier version of this essay, a controlled break up of the USSR into its constituent republics and territories (either through formal sovereignty or else through substantial decentralization of power in a loose confederation) would open it up to the deeper penetration of the power of capital, since it would create new boundaries and thus territories/ populations competing to attract supplies of international capital. That is, of course, always assuming that this occurred under stable political conditions. By mid-1991 there were already many indications that this was already happening, that is well in advance of the failed coup. For example, the Ukraine government was actively discussing the introduction of a separate Ukrainian currency, and discussions were taking place concerning the division of powers between the centre and the republics concerning powers of taxation and other economic questions. The speed of these discussions accelerated in the first half of 1991, partly because of the collapse in Soviet economic activity (with massive food shortages, plunging oil production and vanishing foreign exchange reserves) and partly because of the need to appear to have solved the internal political and constitutional questions of the USSR before Gorbachev's attendance at the G7 summit in London in July 15–17, 1991.[25]

However, capitalists are unlikely to plan long-term investments in any substantial measure whilst there are continued fears of civil war throughout the CIS, and if the climate for investment is too politically or economically uncertain. One might tentatively conclude, therefore, that at best the post-Soviet future looks bleak, with substantial adjustment falling on the weakest members of society if the IMF/World Bank/Yavlitsky formulae are implemented in one form or another, with no guarantee of success. At worst, the post-Soviet political future seems to be one of growing contradictions and deepening crisis, especially since the West, particularly the USA, seems reluctant to provide the quantity and quality of assistance required to manage the transition to capitalism in an effective way, 'from Ottoman-style superpower to functioning market economy'. The USA, for example, was consistent in its opposition to a swift entry of the USSR into the IMF and World Bank, whereas the EEC was in favour of this. Now that the USSR has collapsed, the USA has agreed to process Russia's application quickly in 1992. Both the US and EEC are aware, however, that it will be very difficult to eradicate 70 years of Soviet Communism without substantial internal political struggle: a continuation of the present *impasse* is thus far from being an unlikely possibility.

The consensus view which crystallized in the West in 1990–91 concerning Soviet economic and political reform was that the best help that could be offered was in the form of expertise and knowledge. In the words of David Mulford the US Under-Secretary of Treasury for International Monetary Affairs, the USSR would have access to 'thousands of man-hours' of western, especially US expertise. These experts, we can be sure, will seek to develop institutions and initiatives which will involve the application and extension of what I have earlier termed 'disciplinary neo-liberalism', along the lines involved in the social restructuring of Poland. This is strategy at its highest level, in ways which are reminiscent of the post-war reconstruction of Western Europe and Japan in the Marshall Plan days. What we have at work here is the coming together of a range of institutions and what Gramsci calls 'organic intellectuals' concerned not just with minor economic reforms or adjustments, but with the political management of a socio-economic transformation, not just of a minor central European country, but with a major country, a post-war superpower. As the situation in the CIS has become increasingly tense in the winter of 1991–92, there has been much more effort at compensatory and humanitarian supplies of capital and goods, especially food, although on overall terms the combined initiatives seem to fall very short of anything which could be compared to the Marshall Plan, and appear to have been coordinated badly. Indeed, despite the fact that Yeltsin's Russian government has been over-supplied with economic gurus from not only Bonn and London, but also Harvard and Santiago, the execution of the first stage in Russia's efforts to create a functioning market capitalism has been politically and economically inept (the IMF now has an office in Moscow).

Again the blueprints for both Poland and the Soviet Union have elements of the 'new constitutionalism' stamped upon them, with some compensatory liberal elements in the form of transitional financing to help ensure the political survival of the Russian state, which is of course necessary for the strategy to have any change of working, since the costs of adjustment will continue to be tremendous and will generate further political unrest.

Assuming that the post-Soviet CIS is able to sustain itself politically in this transition we can expect to see, perhaps in 20 years the emergence of a more confederal political structure, and the rise in inter-republic competition to attract overseas supplies of capital. Thus the changes in the former Soviet Union will further extend and deepen the power of capital on a world scale, in so far as one aspect of this power involves the division of the globe into rival political sovereignties, and another is the spread of market relations and the monetization and commodification of everyday life. Finally, what the plans for the Soviet Union appear to illustrate is that the USA is crucial to any major international initiative, especially since both the IMF and EEC were charged with developing plans after the 1990 Houston Summit, and Germany had by far the biggest stake in political and economic stability in the USSR: the Soviets were massively in debt to the Germans. The US plans, developed with the agreement of Gorbachev, were designed initially to preempt the IMF and EEC initiatives.

This argument is reinforced by other developments relating to strategic realignments and military planning in the wake of the Gulf War. At a moment of deep internal crisis for the Soviet Union, we saw the use of US and allied military power in Third World contexts and the development of new concepts to reconstruct and to redevelop NATO. A key recent example is the creation of a smaller, harder and more mobile European flank of NATO and a Euro-counterpart to the US Rapid Deployment capacity seen at work in the 1991 Gulf War (which might be used not just in Yugoslavia, but perhaps in North and West Africa and the Middle East: it is no surprise that the UK, given its experience in the war against Iraq and earlier in the Falklands/Malvinas War, was put in charge of the EDRF).[26] In addition, the Gulf War retarded the momentum towards a more unified foreign and security policy for the EEC, and with it slowed down the impetus towards Economic and Political Union. The USA and the UK are closely aligned on the necessity of making security policy in a transatlantic frame of reference. The Gulf War once again dramatized the political and military limits to Japanese leadership in global politics. All this meant that Germany and Japan appeared to have little choice (along with the Saudis and the Kuwaitis) but to finance the US (and coalition) war effort.

Since the primary public rationale for US globalism since 1945, i.e. the containment of and struggle against (Soviet) communism is now being eroded, then we must conclude that the other key (and historically more frequent deployed) purpose of US military power, policing the Third World, is now more important than ever before. This aspect of US globalism is crucial to reviewing the implications of recent developments: a renewed capacity for intervention seems to be central to containing the 'adverse' political repercussions of the deepening of marketization and monetization and associated trends of capitalism (as well as problems attendant on the transition towards capitalism in former-communist states). More specifically, it is an added means to negotiate the contradictions in Third World countries' development which the debt decade has brought into profile during the 1980s and early 1990s (and is supplemented by plans advocating the prohibition of certain arms exports to Third World countries). In the Third World this seems to offer a parallel mechanism to the efforts of the IMF/World Bank to encourage state-building and marketization. In eastern and central Europe it can be seen as reinforcing demands that the political transitions involve political pluralism along liberal-democratic lines, as well as marketization *à la* Polanyi's arguments on the creation of a market society in nineteenth century Britain (where of course, the democratic element was notable by its absence, and political revolution had not occurred).[27]

Thus the new politico-military configurations and initiatives might be seen as central to the reproduction of a (disciplinary) neo-liberal order. The neo-liberal state is concerned to police not only markets but also populations more generally. Here it is worth noting the tremendous rally which took place in the global stock markets when it became clear that the USA was prevailing in the Gulf War: a US victory was widely interpreted as boosting confidence since it was performing its role as a global enforcer and guarantor of private property rights, as well as stabilizing the oil markets through the use of the Strategic Petroleum Reserve.

Seen from a more national viewpoint, the US government is keen to sustain its primacy *vis à vis* its allies. The military advantages it has partly enable the US government to offset US relative economic decline and sustain US political primacy. G7 proposals to strengthen the military capacities of the United Nations, the introduction of economic issues into the remit of the UN Security Council and military-security issues into both the G7 Heads and G7 Deputies (central bankers and Ministers of Finance) forums might be a means for the USA both to internationalize and institutionalize the 'tributary' arrangements of payments from other countries which paid for US expenditure in the Gulf War (the latter organized by G7 deputies). This could involve a more permanent system of global tax collection to pay for the 'international public good' of collective security. Much more thinking on this and related security questions needs to be done by International Relations scholars, and in this light the financial and broader macroeconomic constraints surrounding the financing of US military expenditures and expansion are crucial.

To conclude, European debates on future security arrangements and a possible shared foreign policy are likely to be sharpened then, because as yet there is very little to suggest that the US leadership is fully conscious of the need to reconstruct a more co-operative, consensual and co-ordinated form of international leadership, at least with its key allies in Western Europe and Japan. The US seems determined to use its vast military power to sustain its global primacy, and shows a willingness to attempt to extract resources in the form of tribute from its allies and clients to pay for it. Given the domestic inhibitions in Japan, limiting the scope and extension of the Self Defence Forces, Japan is perhaps the most vulnerable target for this type of 'tributary' strategy.

III. Conclusion: Limits To, and Prospects For, European Hegemony

All these considerations suggest that the possibilities of European hegemony, as something which could supplant US dominance in the global political economy, are limited. This would perhaps even be more the case if the European Community were enlarged in the next century (with the addition of Austria, Sweden, Switzerland, and possibly Hungary and Czechoslovakia). Part of the reason for this is the narrow, economistic vision on which the initiatives are generally based, the lack of congruence between political and economic aspects of the integration process, and the distinct lack of any clearly mobilized popular support for anything approximating this type of vision on the part of European peoples. In this sense, the EC initiatives are being forged against the grain of history, if we take this to involve democratization and the control of market forces by the state and society in post-war western Europe.

At the regional level, what this will mean for the contours of the emerging Europe is, of course, far from certain, although we are currently witnessing substantial momentum in the process of European unification. Nevertheless, integration, even in its current form, has a long way to go in a number of areas, particularly in the formation of a common defence identity and policy, and more generally a common foreign policy (the Gulf War has revealed substantial divisions here, for example between German reluctance, British pro-Americanism and traditional French independence).

Progress in economic and monetary union is continuing, and is proceeding more rapidly than most commentators could have imagined even two years ago, initially accelerated by German unification (and perhaps now being slowed as the costs of unification come into focus), developments in eastern and central Europe, by growing American protectionism, and the acute sensitivity to the Japanese challenge. However, because of the forces of transnationalization and globalization, and because of the heavy dependence of nearly all the European economies on international trade and increasingly, international production, it seems unlikely that we will see fortress Europe in the future, although the EC's growing economic integration will allow it to develop more countervailing bargaining power relative to the US and Japan (e.g. the recent deadlock in GATT negotiations between the EC and the US, which in part reflected the budgetary and social *impasse* in the EC caused by the Common Agricultural Policy, as well as competitive differences over services, intellectual property and government procurement regulations).[28]

More fundamentally, and this perhaps is the crux of the problem in terms of further integration in the EC, we are much further away from the development of both a common European identity and a set of political institutions which can gain democratic legitimacy and the capacity to mobilize substantially the European peoples. This constraint operates more powerfully than the pull of the German model, the push of French political initiatives, or the shall-we, shall-we-not hesitations and misgivings of the British (reflected, for example in the lament of the Prince of Wales that the coming of the Channel Tunnel would hasten the destruction of the 'island identity' and cultural separateness of Britain). In other words, the level of pan-European political development, along with an integrated and independent military-strategic apparatus is still far from complete. Indeed, it might be said that Europe is still, to use the title of the anthology edited by the Swiss philosopher Denis de Rougemont, in many respects simply the 'idea of Europe'.[29] It is still far from being a completed economic and political reality.

What Hegel once called the 'ruined fortress' and the 'dialectical crossroads of mankind', modern Europe as an integrated entity is perhaps still more an entity of the mind, of the ideal realm: a set of ideas, proposals and arguments perhaps rooted in Judeo-Christian and Græco Roman myth, at least when compared with its major economic and perhaps political rivals, the US (200 years of political development) and Japan (at least 1200 years). In this sense, Europe, in the form of the EC, has the potential to become a rival to the US, if it could be understood as something more coherent and integral. Inverting Hegel, and applying Marx, we might suggest that material pressures, and especially competitive struggles involving transnational capital, and those embodied in the European security problematic, are likely to be the motor forces which will create the conditions for the dream one day to become a reality. In this sense, perhaps the next catalyst for a deepening of this process of integration will be the political dynamics and conflicts caused by the disintegration of the USSR.

This does not mean, then, that the twenty-first century will be the 'European century'. There are simply no clear rivals to supplant US primacy, which involves integral capabilities in the economic, military, political, and in some senses cultural fields. Yet this is to think of global hegemony in terms of the primacy of one state, or collection of federated states, relative to others. What is a more fundamental issue is whether the global order has a hegemonic quality, in the sense used by Gramsci. This means that we need to think through the implications of a system which is gravitating towards something akin to one in which the pure logic of capital, operating on an increasingly global basis, is atomizing pre-existing social and political arrangements, and commoditizing and reifying ever wider spheres of social life, from health care to public service broadcasting to amateur sports.

One implication is to make the 'game' of socio-economic life, to use Susan Strange's metaphors, resemble either snakes and ladders or roulette, where effort bears little relationship to reward, and where the time horizons of the system become shorter and shorter. At the heart of the problem is the way in which the social basis of political participation in the emerging world order system appears to be narrowing, largely because of the tendency for the pure logic of capitalist market relations to intensify social inequality and to empower the strong at the expense of the weak, vulnerable or disorganized. This problem takes on added importance because of the pace of organizational and technological change driven by the intensification of competitive pressures. Such pressures force companies and governments to cut costs (including the costs to business stemming from health and safety, environmental and other forms of regulation and taxation). Governments, firms and workers now increasingly compete to attract scarce supplies of capital from their rivals in other localities, regions, and countries. A harsher, perhaps less democratic and legitimate order seems to be emerging, with a reconcentration of power in favour of large-scale capital.

At the popular level, failing substantial counter-hegemonic mobilization involving local, national and transnational efforts, we can expect an acceleration towards the re-institution of the self-regulating market, and the further restriction of the historical tendency towards greater democratization. If the 1992 programme is an indicator, any European super-state which might emerge, will probably in practice be more like a larger version of the nineteenth-century liberal states, with their limited franchise and dominance by the aristocracy and the bourgeoisie. This is to say that the form of state, and its relationship to civil society, according to the Eurointegrationist path, will be less based upon a politics of inclusion, welfare and corporatism, and increasingly on the logic of the self-regulating market. Instead of socialism, the workers of the future Europe are to be persuaded to aspire to the German social market model, as their Panglossian best of all possible in the best of all possible worlds. This, as noted, goes against the grain of history, and stands in contradiction to the re-birth of democracy in eastern and central Europe. In this sense the new 'Europe 1992' will probably be less 'hegemonic' than the more politically divided Europe of the 1950s and 1960s. The embedded liberalism and social hegemony of the transatlantic economic system which flourished after 1945 has, it would seem, begun to disappear, to be replaced by a form of disciplinary neo-liberalism, particularly dramatic in its effects in the poorer countries of the world.

The economic logic of neo-liberalism can be queried even in its own terms. Indeed, it is economically contradictory. This is especially so given the deflationary thrust of neo-liberalism now being applied in the context of the deepest global recession since the 1930s. Many commentators have noted that several parts of the world are enduring economic depression, e.g. Latin America (for about the last 10 years), most of Africa (for perhaps 15 years) and eastern and central Europe and the CIS (since about 1987). This points to what Keynesians call a massive drop in aggregate global demand, and what Marxists call a realization problem for the further accumulation of capital. Moreover, the international financial system, both as cause and effect of globalization, is fragile and is only as strong as its weakest link, as the recent panic over the collapse of Drexell Burnham Lambert revealed. Of course, there is greater internationalization of policy and corresponding support networks between central banks than was the case at the time of the Wall Street Crash of 1929 which precipitated the Great Depression of the 1930s.

Nevertheless, a global financial collapse in the 1990s is by no means an impossibility, and one would need to be a Candide to be optimistic about the global economic outlook for the next few years. Following Polanyi's analysis of the 1930s, global liberalization and recession/depression were the immediate conjecture for the remobilization of state and society against the logic of the self-regulating market. The repercussions in this period, it will be remembered, involved not only attempts to deal with the crisis through Keynesian policies (as in the New Deal), but also the imposition of neo-orthodoxies of sound money as well as Fascism and Nazism (phenomena which are beginning to resurface in a substantial manner in Germany and France). This problem would seem to be especially acute in east and central Europe and in parts of the CIS. Polanyi's 'double movement' may well recur in the very different conditions of the 1990s, that is when there is a partial, though undeveloped internationalization of authority, and a set of globalizing and homogenizing economic forces, which are much more deep seated and integral to contemporary capitalism than was the case in the previous era of widespread internationalization of capital in the late nineteenth and early twentieth century. The qualitative transformation this has brought will also mean changes in the terrain of political struggle to contain the worst excesses of these forces, and to democratize their power.

Reflecting outmoded concepts concerning the nature of the contemporary world order, it further seems that the leaders of United States have decided that the form of hegemony preferred is less Gramscian (i.e. consensual, legitimate) and more narrowly Realist (i.e. based upon dominance and supremacy, and US power relative to that of other states and socio-economic systems, e.g. Japan, Iraq, the challenge of Islam). Whether this can be the foundation for a stable, let alone more legitimate and authoritative world order is, in my view, rather doubtful. Given the collapse of the USSR, the EC may have no alternative but to develop its own military capabilities, independent foreign policy and economic defences to offset the dominance of the US in the security and economic structures by accelerating its unity, *faute de mieux*. Japan, in the absence of creative imagination on the part of its political leaders and the lack of substantial democratization, may be destined to remain very much a second-level political power, despite its formidable economic prowess, a prowess increasingly based upon working its population into the ground, as the working week gets longer, and the level of knowledge and labour intensification in the vanguard production facilities continues to rise. The failure to think globally on the part of the Japanese ruling classes means that the schizophrenia of Japan's relationship with the USA seems set to continue for the foreseeable future. Japan may, in due course, given some of the domestic changes just mentioned, try to offset the lop-sided dependence on the US through strategies of economic and political diversification.

The EC will also seek to undertake similar strategies of diversification, to hedge against the political risks of too great a dependence on the vagaries of Washington policy, especially given the hostility towards Japan and the growing tendency to scapegoat foreigners for the economic ills of the US. These possibilities, however, do not suggest a renewal of inter-bloc or inter-imperial rivalries, since neither the EC nor Japan would seek to provoke the US. Rather, they open up new potential for counter-hegemonic and progressive forces to begin to make transnational links, and thereby to insert themselves in a more differentiated, multi-lateral world order. This would be a way to advance the process of the democratization of an emerging global civil society and system of international political authority, currently monopolized by the forces of transnational capital, the governments of the major states, and supervised by the Bretton Woods institutions and the military alliances of the West.

NOTES

1. I am grateful to David Law for making these and other points. I also thank Robert Cox, Craig Murphy and R.B.J. (Rob) Walker. Some of the following argument was published in *Alternatives*, 1991, Vol. 16 (3) pp. 275–314, 'Reflections on Global Order and Socio-historical Time'.

2. Charles Maier, 'The Politics of Productivity: Foundations of American International Economic Policy After World War II', in Peter Katzenstein, editor, *Between Power and Plenty* (Madison, University of Wisconsin Press, 1978).

3. For an account of the discussions in the Labour cabinet at the time, and the subsequent impact of the IMF loan, see the memoirs of the Prime Minister, James Callaghan, *Time and Change* (London, Collins, 1987), chapter 14.

4. For an amplification, see Stephen Gill, *American Hegemony and the Trilateral Commission* op cit. especially chapters 4, 5, 9. For a more detailed conceptualization of the growing power of internationally-mobile capital see Stephen Gill and David Law, 'Global hegemony and the structural power of capital', *International Studies Quarterly* (1989), Vol. 33, No. 4 (1989), pp. 475–99.

5. Susan Strange, *Casino Capitalism* (Oxford, Basil Blackwell 1986). On the problem of speculative capital flows and the Bretton Woods system see, Marcello de Cecco, 'Origins of the post-war payments system', *Cambridge Journal of Economics*, no. 3, (1979), pp. 49–61. For a view advocating the abolition of central banks and the privatization of the creation of money so as to maximize market constraints on governments and other economic agents, see F. A. von Hayek, *The Denationalization of Money* (1990); on the varieties of monetarism see Robert A. Nobay and Harry G. Johnson, 'Monetarism A Historic-Theoretic Perspective', *Journal of Economic Literature*, vol. 15, no. 2, (1977), pp. 470–85. On recent issues relating to state policy autonomy and capital mobility, see John B. Goodman and Louis W. Pauly, 'The New Politics of International Capital Mobility', Annual Meeting of the *American Political Science Association*, 1990. [published by the Ontario Centre for International Business, York University, Toronto].

6. See, Yoichi Funabashi, *Managing the Dollar: From Plaza to the Louvre*, second edition. (Washington DC, Institute for International Economics, 1989); David Hale, G-7 Foreign and Economic Policy Coordination in 1991, Joint Conference of Ditchley Park Foundation and Chicago Council on Foreign Relations and Johnson Foundation, May 1991; David Law, 'Transatlantic Economic Cooperation: The Baker Initiatives and Beyond', in Stephen Gill (ed.), *Atlantic Relations: Beyond the Reagan Era*, (New York: St, Martin's/ Harvester Wheatsheaf), pp. 139–155; David P. Calleo, *The Imperious Economy*, (Cambridge: Harvard University Press, 1982); I. M. Destler and C. Randall Henning, *Dollar Politics: Exchange Rate Policy Making in the United States*, (Washington DC, Institute for International Economics, 1989); Ellen Kennedy, *The Bundesbank: Germany's Central Bank in the International Monetary System*, (London: Pinter, 1991), especially pp. 56–111; Claus Köhler, 'Economic Policy in a Framework of Internationalized Economic Relations,' in Philip Arestis (ed.) *Contemporary Issues in Money and Banking*. (London, Macmillan 1988), pp. 85–101.

7. Wayne Sandholz and John Zysman, '1992: Recasting the European Bargain', *World Politics* (1989), Vol. 42, No. 1.

8. On currency areas, see R. A. Ogrodnick, 'Optimum currency areas and the international monetary system' *Journal of International Affairs*, 1990, Vol. 15, No. 2, pp. 470–85. On Japan, see Eric Helleiner, 'Money and Influence: Japanese Power in the International Monetary and Financial System', *Millennium*, Vol. 18, no. 3, (1989), pp. 343–358; Susan Strange, 'Finance, information and power', *Review of International Studies*, Vol. 16, (1990), pp. 259–274.

9. For a useful review of the rational choice political economy literature dealing with these concepts and their applicability, see John T. Wooley, '1992, Capital and the EMS: Policy Credibility and Political Institutions'. Prepared for the Brookings Project on European Political Institutions Beyond 1992. Also presented at the American Political Science Association, San Francisco, 30 August–2 September, 1990.

10. For details see Susan Strange, *Casino Capitalism*, (Oxford, Blackwell, 1986); Jeffrey Frieden, *Banking on the World* (New York, Harper and Row, 1987).

11. My italics. Cited in Woolley, quotations from the Delors Report, paragraphs 4, 53, 32, 30.
12. See F. Giavazzi, S. Micossi, and M. Miller (eds.) *The European Monetary System* (Cambridge, Cambridge University Press, 1988); M. de Cecco and A. Giovanni (eds) *A European Central Bank?* (Cambridge, Cambridge University Press, 1989); especially Allan Drazen, 'Monetary policy, capital controls and seigniorage in an open economy', pp. 13–52; and Vittorio Grilli, 'Seigniorage in Europe', pp. 53–94, both in de Cecco and Giovanni eds.
13. See F. Giavazzi and L. Spaventa (eds) *High Public Debt: the Italian Experience* (Cambridge, Cambridge University Press, 1989). Significant here is that the case of Italy shows many of the problems involved with a swift liberalization of capital controls. The Italian government failed to pre-empt massive speculation against the lira after May 1987 and had to temporarily suspend liberalization and to introduce administrative credit controls. See Giavazzi et al (eds), *The European Monetary System*, p. 409.
14. Elizabeth Meehan, 'Sex Equality Policies in the European Community', *Journal of European Integration*, (1990), Vol. 13., p. 187. See also Martin Rhodes, 'The Social Dimension of the Single European Market: National vs. Transnational Regulation', *European Journal of Political Research* (March, 1991); Paul Teague, *The European Community: the Social Dimension and Labour Market Policy for 1992*, (London, Kogan Page, 1989); John Grahl and Paul Teague, 'The Cost of Neo-Liberal Europe', *New Left Review*, (1989), No. 174.
15. The *Economist* adds: 'Project 1992 will make this [i.e. the US airlines] shakeout look like a pyjama party. After decades of cossetting, many European companies have grown fat and lazy. That will make them vulnerable to new firms whose costs and prices are a fraction of their own. Moreover, whereas American deregulation was largely a domestic affair, the European version promises to be an international free-for-all. Powerful American and Japanese firms like Philip Morris, IBM, Fujitsu and NEC are already limbering up to do battle'. ('Survey: Business in Europe', 8 June 1991.)
16. 'Survey: Business in Europe', *Economist*, 8 June, 1991.
17. Giavazzi et al, *The European Monetary System*, op cit.
18. Richard Baldwin, 'The Growth Effects of 1992', *CEPR*, November, 1989.
19. Cambridge, Cambridge University Press, 1979.
20. David Law, 'Transatlantic Economic Co-operation', in Stephen Gill, ed., *Atlantic Relations: beyond the Reagan Era* (Hemel Hempstead, Harvester-Wheatsheaf, 1989), pp. 139–155.
21. The following are taken from Martin Wolf, 'A nation unified, and yet apart', *Financial Times*, 1 July 1991. Wolf's data are drawn from the OECD, and Kiel Institute and Brookings Institution Working Papers.
22. Martin Wolf, 'A nation unified, and yet apart'.
23. See also Ralf Dahrendorf, *Reflections on the Revolution in Europe* (Toronto, Random House, 1990).
24. Louis W. Pauly, 'Institutionizing a Stalemate: National Financial Policies and the International Debt Crisis', *Journal of Public Policy*, 1990, vol. 10, no. 1, pp. 23–43.
25. As I noted in July 1991, the much feted (Professor Grigory) Yavlinsky Plan for integrating the USSR into the world economy, jointly developed by Professor Graham Allison and Jeffrey Sachs of Harvard University, seemed unlikely to be fully implemented, mainly due to opposition to its scope from within the US Administration.
26. See David White, 'Smaller, faster, cheaper', *Financial Times*, 1/2 June, 1991. In the context of overall cuts in by the mid-1990s, mixed-nationality formations (with attendant problems of language, different codes of discipline, methods etc.) will, at some future point, form the nucleus of NATO defences, with an elite 'rapid-reaction corps under UK command, but still involving some US forces'. This had been discussed over the past 12 months in both NATO and the West European Union (WEU).
27. Karl Polanyi, *The Great Transformation: the political and economic origins of our times*, (Boston, Beacon Press, 1964, orig. 1944).
28. This is similar to the argument concerning the external impact and importance of EMU made by the EC and is the EC's international political rationale for the monetary integration of Europe. See Commission of the European Communities, Directorate-

General for Economic and Financial Affairs, 'External Dimensions', *European Economy*, No. 44 (October, 1990), pp. 178–200.

29. Denis de Rougemont, editor, *The Idea of Europe* (New York, Galaxy Books, 1966).

JAPAN IN A NEW WORLD ORDER

Makoto Itoh

1 Restrengthened Capitalism for a New World Order

History now runs quite fast. A definition of a new world order seems often outdated already a few months later. Transformation of the global politico-economic framework is proceeding so rapidly and in such an unexpected way as we approach the conclusion of this century. Through the transformation, however, four correlated dimensions of a new world order are clearly emerging; the end of the cold war, the restructuring of capitalism, US hegemony after the Gulf War, and attempts at international regional reunification like the EC.

In retrospect, global capitalism seemed to have been in a defensive position since the Russian Revolution. Its territory was actually much narrowed after the Second World War. East European countries, China, North Korea, Cuba, Ethiopia, Vietnam, Kampuchea and Nicaragua, for instance, opted for a socialist regime. Within capitalist countries, welfare policies, concessions to the demands of trade unions, as well as the burden of defence expenditures were regarded to be necessary costs to guard a free capitalist economic system against revolutionary socialism. The US hegemony which reconstructed a concerted politico-economic capitalist order in the post-World War II period was coupled with such a defensive position of capitalism until 1960s.

The seeming success of Keynesianism in this period was maintained essentially by the US politico-military dollar spending in order to defend a 'free' world, and was not achieved by mere economic policies to curb business cycles in individual countries. The same international and historical context must be stressed against the French Regulationist pure model of a Fordist regime of accumulation, which simply underlines domestic expansion of effective demand by increases in real wages in parallel with productivity under certain institutional arrangements.[1]

The decline of US industrial hegemony, her defeat in the Vietnam War, the successive great depressions since 1973, and the growing burden of the cold war extending to outer space appeared to work together in weakening further both the US international leadership and the global order of capitalism which were maintained through the cold war system. When the cold war was terminated in 1980s, however, a victory was sung unexpectedly by capitalism, not socialism.

East European countries and the USSR turned out to be in a much deeper crisis than global capitalism, a crisis more difficult to solve within their old 'socialist' regimes. Connected with the solid oppressive party and state bureaucracy, there was a basic difficulty introducing new technologies to overcome economic stagnation and a widening gap in consumption goods compared with the Western capitalist countries. The collapse of the old regimes in East Europe and the Soviet Union has thus a character of self-defeat, and it cannot be identical with a failure of sounder possible types of socialism. Despite this, a sense of victory presently gives global capitalism an easier and broader scope for restructuring.

The restructuring of a capitalist economy has shown its viability much more than had previously been expected. Since the great depression of 1973, micro-electronics (ME) technologies were developed and applied more and more widely so as to revitalise the capitalist market system. ME information technologies facilitated the promotion of factory automation (FA) and office automation (OA) which increased flexibility of labour management thus reducing costs of operation. Investment to raise productivity was directed towards more flexible and mobile units. Multi-models of cars or electric appliances were produced on the same conveyor belt lines so as to satisfy various consumers' needs in a market. Information about goods sold is automatically and instantly transmitted to suppliers to adjust production and distribution of commodities by a point of sales (POS) system. Development of information technologies also enabled capitalist firms to re-allocate their sites of operation in order to economise costs or to facilitate easier access to different local markets. Multi-national borderless types of activity were thus much increased by capitalist firms. Multi-national cooperation or merger among business and industrial firms also became widespread.

As a whole, the impact of ME information technologies has increased flexibility of capitalist firms, intensified their competition in supplying new types of goods and service and revitalised the competitive working of the market through deep changes in the organisation of labour. The rise of neo-liberalism in the 1980s was not a mere anachronistic reaction to the failure of Keynesianism, but reflected a revitalisation of a capitalist market economy (as I have analysed elsewhere).[2] Global capitalism is in this sense undergoing a historical reversal not merely in its dominant ideological and political superstructure but also in its economic substructure. This situation powerfully influences also former 'socialist' countries to adapt a radical package of marketisation as a panacea in the process of social change regardless of its actual effectiveness and feasibility.

Neo-liberalism's requirement for less government seems to contradict the US restoration of her politico-military leadership through the Gulf

War. The United Nations became more easily utilisable for this purpose, as a result of the end of the cold war and the dissolution of the USSR. The US has been able to strengthen its position as the guardian of the status quo for capitalist countries. However, the US cannot now afford to pay the necessary costs to maintain her politico-military hegemony. She actually had to depend on international support and collected about 54 billion dollars from Saudi Arabia, Kuwait, Japan, Germany and some others for the Gulf War. The collected amount is estimated at 5 billion more than the actual costs of the War.[3] It was a strange war in this aspect among others. It is dubious if the US can continuously depend on foreign countries to support the costs of her politico-military operations in the world. As a result the US will be deeply split between the intention to keep its restored hegemonic position in the world and its weakening economy. This must bring about a lot of strains and distortions throughout the world. For instance, the US will require that host countries share more of the costs of her military bases. The US is trying hard to sell more of its agricultural products through the Uruguay round of GATT negotiations without much consideration of the effects on the agricultural environment and peasants' life in other countries. Under the name of Pax-Universalis, the United Nations, IMF, and other international organisations may be utilised more to collect contributions as a sort of international taxation system to be controlled substantially by the US.

This second phase of US hegemony may well turn out to be an illusion based on the victory of the Gulf War, but actually based upon foreign money. Indeed, the regional structure of global capitalism is radically changing. EC unification can strengthen European politico-economic power to countervail US hegemony. Can it further challenge and be a substitute for US hegemony? What will be the position of a growing Japan and Asian countries in a new world order? From the perspective of the hegemony issue in a new world order, six scenarios are conceivable: (1) The second phase of Pax-Americana, (2) The age of Fortress Europe, (3) Pax-Nipponica, (4) Pax-Japamerica, (5) Trigemony led by the US, EC and Japan, (6) Pax-Consortis without any hegemonic country.[4]

Within the limits of the next decade or two, the scenarios (2), (3) and (6) must be difficult to realise. Although the Fortress Europe will be constructed, it will still be much concerned about internal issues and improvement, and will not pursue a monopolistic hegemony, being prevented by the bitter historical memory of colonialism and wars as well as for economic reasons. As for 'Pax-Niponica' Japan is not prepared to take leadership by herself. So long as Japanese capitalism can continuously strengthen its economic activity in a world market, it does not need a costly hegemonic position in a world politico-military order. The pacifist attitude among the Japanese people which supports Article 9 in the constitutional law will prevent Japan from becoming a military-hegemonic power. It would be desirable for a future more democratic international order if Pax-Consortis were realised. The precondition is the dissolving of the US intention to keep political hegemony and overwhelming military power, and this condition seems unlikely even after the dissolution of the Soviet Union.

The phase I type of Pax-Americana will not be restored, so long as the hollowing of US industry is so difficult to reverse. Therefore, the second phase of Pax-Americana must require international cooperation often through the United Nations and other international organisations. In this sense the remaining scenarios outlined above – 'Japamerica', and 'Trigemony' are not visibly far apart in their essence; they are complementary in one way or the other to form a new world order. The uneasy political, economic and military balance among the US, EC, and Japan will continue to be central to the motion of a new world order. Although the unification of EC will foster various conceptions of regional reunifications centring on the US and Japan in the Pan-Pacific area, those conceptions will be mutually overlapping rather than take the form of exclusive economic blocks, as we shall analyse later. Anyway, it is unimaginable to see a substantial reduction in multi-nationals' investment network, or in a wide stream of trade and finance between the US, EC and Japan. Therefore, unstable cooperation and rivalry among the US, Japan, and EC will go on in a new world order, where capitalism will actually work more flexibly and globally than before, involving more or less of East Europe, Russia, China as also the third world countries.

In such a global scene, what roles will Japan play?

2. An Ideal Model in a New World Order?

It is ironic to see that the US, a victorious single superpower, cannot serve as a model to be followed in a new world order.

Instead of the decaying US model, Japan is often regarded as an ideal new model in many aspects. Although the Italian model with reactivated small firms and the Swedish model of welfare corporatism also invite attention as possible alternatives to the American type of Fordist regime of accumulation which led global capitalism until 1960s, Toyotism or the Japanese model is more influential and actually powerful in the current world market. A high rate of economic growth in comparison with other advanced capitalist countries, a low rate of unemployment, increasing industrial efficiency with spreading ME technologies, restrengthened international competitive power, improved financial positions of most of big capitalist firms[5] – all of these seem to suggest that Japan is exceptionally crisis-free and is a very good post-Fordist model for the restructuring of a capitalist economy.

At the heart of Japan's economic success, it is generally believed, is the strength of the Japanese style of labour management. This is characterised in the main by life-long employment, trade union organisations based on the company, and a seniority order of wage and job escalation for regular workers in the big corporations. Loyalty and a disciplined attitude of workers is generated from such a core system of labour management, and is commonly found even among irregular workers both in big and in smaller corporations. Japanese workers and their trade unions usually are not opposed to, and often are even cooperative with, the introduction of new technologies in work-places so long as fellow workers are not dismissed as a result of technological change. Small group activities such as QC (quality circle) and ZD (zero defect) movements have been organised on the initiative of managers and often have been successful in encouraging positive contributions of individual workers to technological progress and refinement in the spirit of group behaviour at work-places.

Toyotism with its more flexible line of production, which is, in the image of the French Regulationist School, replacing the previous leading model of American Fordism with its hard division of labour on inflexible lines of production,[6] is obviously grounded upon such a corporative and loyal attitude of Japanese workers. The Japanese model of management is seen as ideal not just by capitalists and their managers in other countries. It is also praised by some Western leftists. From the Western workers' point of view, they say, the management system which stably maintains employment and enables workers to extend their intellectual ability to undertake multiple-jobs is desirable and they advocate learning the Japanese style of workers' team system, job rotation, learning by doing, and the custom of tenured employment.[7]

The famous Toyota *kanban* (small notice board to pass precise indications through a production process) system or its just-in-time system, which minimises stock of parts and semi-products in a main assembly plant, is realised not just by the internal labour management of the factory but also by utilising many disciplined medium and small firms as subcontractors where wages are lower and employment is more flexible and irregular. A parent big company takes good care of those subcontractors, once chosen and organised under its umbrella by supplying technological know-how and financial back-up. As high-tech products like cars, electric appliances and general machines incorporate more and more small ME parts, reliability of these numerous parts as well as that of handling them in assembly become decisive in determining the international competitive power of final products. Thus, ironically, along with spreading ME automation systems, reliability of remaining human elements in work processes beginning from production of small parts to final assembly become decisively more important than in the age of Fordism. The Japanese model of labour management and the long-term subcontracting system have particular strength in this aspect, as well as in both flexibility in introducing new methods of production and use of lower wage costs of younger regular and various irregular workers.

It is then interesting to consider how a capitalist market economy works according to the different intra- and inter-firm social organisation among human beings. This must overlap with one of the focal messages by the recent French Regulationist school and American Social Structure of Accumulation (SSA) school.[8] A capitalist market economy is actually quite different from a neo-classical model of a free market where atomistic individuals are always taken as basic units of analysis. In contrast, the importance of social organisation or human relations inside and among firms is crucial for the working of a capitalist market economy in the case of Japan. This can be used in opposition to simple neo-liberalism that recommends a competitive market as a panacea to cure all economic diseases (even in East Europe and the former Soviet Union).

It is methodologically important not to exaggerate Japanese traditional cultural characteristics in assessing the economic working of Japanese managerial organisations. Instead we should try to recognise in them more general factors as far as possible, and clarify what is sacrificed in forming them. For instance, it is not easy to explain why Japanese workers work so hard and for such long hours. Individualistic competition for higher wages does not count much here, since workers are in a seniority wage escalation system, or are paid more egalitarian wage rates as irregular part-timers. Motivation for hard working is given rather by ideological consciousness among general workers identifying themselves with the company or a team in a work-place where they belong. Even simple line-workers in Japan say 'our company' or 'my company' just like directors. This psychological attitude comes from trade union organisations based on individual companies, as well as from the escalation system which enables workers to be promoted to managerial positions at various levels. Poor prospects for older ages by the state pension scheme, extremely expensive houses or flats in urban areas, and rapidly increased educational costs also tend to force workers to work for the company, especially when combined with the difficulty of getting other comparable jobs once they have fallen out of the middle of the seniority escalation system. In addition, a prospect of a better future with a growing company surely inspires Japanese workers.

Thus, both pressure and encouragement by the market are certainly important for the motivation of Japanese workers, but these are not at all directly based on individualistic competition. Combined with these, social and ideological identity with the company and a team in the work-place should be underlined. From this observation, we can infer that a mere capitalist market in the abstract may not be a sufficient condition to mobilise workers' motivation, and also that workers' motivation may be mobilised even without a competitive market mechanism. At the root of the 'British disease' and of American difficulties in industrial restructuring is their failure to secure strong motivation of general workers in work-places, despite the presence of a typical capitalist market economy. While even under the centrally planned economy, Soviet workers were probably well-motivated and worked hard in the initial period of five year plans or in the World War II period to defend the motherland. People work for some social purposes or for ideals, not just for individualistic pecuniary income. This aspect of the Japanese model has to be noticed for both capitalist managerial tasks and left alternative strategies to reorganise firms and work-places so as to re-activate workers' motivation.

Are Japanese workers then obtaining the proper share of the result of their cooperative and hard work? Until 1974, they obtained an increase in real wages (if not directly proportional to productivity) through Shunto (annual spring labour offensives) in the post-War process of high economic growth. The gap between the annual increase of labour productivity and that of real wages tended to narrow in the 1960s, and then reversed in favour of real wages at the beginning of 1970s in Japanese manufacturing. Combined with a parallel increase in peasants' family income in rural areas, the increase in real wages extended a domestic market for consumer durables in this period, and formed a type of Fordist regime of accumula-tion. However, the picture drastically changed after 1975. Shunto continu-ously failed to raise real wages despite an increase in productivity. In Japanese manufacturing labour productivity more than doubled (its index increased by 117.3% in 1975–85) while the index of real wages increased only by 5.9% in the same ten year period. A similar stagnation in real wages continued further until 1988. A weak recovery of annual increase in real wages to 4.0% in 1989 had faltered to 2.1% in 1990, even before the current new recession really began.

Therefore, if Japan is taken as an ideal model of post-Fordism for the recent restructuring of capitalist economies, it is clearly characterised by a wide gap between increasing productivity and stagnant real wages. This sort of gap is more or less common among advanced capitalist countries in this period, but most conspicuous and greatest in Japan. Spreading FA and OA by means of ME technologies enabled Japanese capitalist firms to mobilise more and more cheaper part-timers such as housewives, by reducing the proportion of regular male workers so as to economise wage costs. Their wage rates as part-timers are usually about 700–900 yen (a dollar is now about 125 yen) an hour without any fringe benefits. The social position of trade unions which traditionally organised only regular workers was much weakened in the same process. The rate of organisation thus declined from 35.4% in 1970 to 27.6% in 1987.

In order to fill the gap between increasing living costs and stagnant real wages, more and more women had to work away from home, often as cheap part-timers. This situation has caused what Marx called the de-preciation of the value of labour-power by spreading the necessary costs of maintaining the economic life of a family among its members.[9]

There are two measurement problems here. Firstly, as the yen appreciated almost three times against the dollar (a dollar was constantly 360 yen from 1949 to 1971), Japanese wage rates seemed greatly heightened on a dollar basis. The average nominal wage rate in 1990 was 1821 yen an hour for Japanese manufacturing production workers, and it was already higher than that for similar workers in the US (by about 19%) and other advanced capitalist countries on a dollar basis. However, expensive living costs in Japan discount its real purchasing power, and indeed the real wage has been quite stagnant as discussed above. Actually the average area of housing per capita in Japan of 25.2 square metres was still below one half of that in the US and 30% less than in the UK in 1989, while the number of passenger cars in use per 1000 persons in Japan (the top producer of cars in the world), was also below one half of that in the US and 22% less than in the UK. Therefore, international comparisons of wages on a dollar basis do not correctly describe the real purchasing power of Japanese wages.

Secondly, if the nominal wage index is deflated not by a consumer price index (so as to get the real wage index) but by a GDP deflator for manufacturing to get the products wage index (which states the average amount of manufacturing net products purchasable by nominal wages), then we see that this index rose rapidly even after 1975, almost matching the increase in labour productivity in Japanese manufacturing. As a result the profit share in the value added in manufacturing did not recover much and remained rather stagnant.[10] This means that the result of the increase in productivity was mainly utilised for *competitive reductions of prices of products, especially in the world market*, or for paying off previous debt principal and covering increased energy prices as necessary costs of operation. Consequently Japanese manufacturing corporations could well absorb the increased price of oil in two oil shocks despite the highest dependency rate of energy import among advanced countries, intensified international competitive power, and much improved their financial position from a position heavily in debt into that of earning a huge financial surplus through the period of depression since 1973.

In the meantime, the result of the increases in productivity was not distributed to Japanese workers either in the form of increased real wages, or in the reduction of the notorious length of working hours. In 1985 total yearly working hours of manufacturing production workers was 2168 hours in Japan, which was 11% longer than in the UK, 13% longer than in the US, and 31% longer than in West Germany. This official data certainly does not include 'service' or 'home task' over-time work often performed without record and payment. In addition, many Japanese workers suffer from tiring and long commuting. Total commuting time of three hours a day or more is not rare for work-places in wide metropolitan areas. Thus, the annual total of free time for workers was 1858 hours in Japan in the middle of 1980s, 426 hours (23%) less than in the US, 545 hours (29%) less than in the UK, and 838 hours (45%) less than in West Germany.[11]

Through such long working hours, the intensity and stress of labour were much increased in the process of rationalisation for FA and OA. Many workers have to face just a display, key-board or a certain portion of an automatic assembly line in an isolated way with continuous tension. Occasionally a shift-work system forces some workers to continue a whole night and day work due to shortage of hands. Thus, tragic cases of *karoshi* (death from overwork) much increased throughout almost all the Japanese industries, ironically, when Japan was viewed as the most wealthy advanced country full of automation systems. The national defence council for victims of *karoshi* received about 2000 telephone consultations in two years from the middle of 1989.[12] In Februrary 1992, a group in Los Angeles appealed to the UN human rights committee that there are annually 10 thousands *karoshi* deaths in Japan. Cases of chronic fatigue syndrome, which makes workers really unable to work became openly diagnosed and also increased in number. As Japanese trade unions were traditionally concerned mainly about the Shunto type of wage negotiation, they could not effectively protect workers from such heavy overwork.

The Japanese model of post-Fordism cannot be taken to be an ideal harmonious social order particularly in view of the actual socio-economic conditions of workers. Its desirable flexibility in improving technologies and competitive power from a standpoint of capitalist managers is based largely upon workers' cooperation and sacrifice as we have seen. Cooperative attitudes among workers and group behaviour are in themselves not at all wrong. They are, however, far too narrowly mobilised for the interest of capitalist firms, and not for the workers' own class interest. This aspect of the Japanese style of management is being transplanted into many overseas factories often with a non-strike code; especially when factories are constructed by Japanese companies or their joint-ventures. The left in the Western countries should not ignore the undesirable conditions for workers in the actual Japanese socio-economic order, although they can utilise some desirable elements in it such as a more stable employment, learning by doing to extend workers' ability, or cooperative spirit for the sake of workers' class interest.

3 Japan's Position in a New World Order

What position then will Japan take in a new world order?

As the EC is being consolidated into a Fortress Europe, despite many internal disputes within the region, several conceptions of regional economic unification or cooperation have been floated in the Pan-Pacific area. The main examples are as follows: (1) A North American Free Trade Zone; (2) An Asia-Pacific Economic Cooperation Council (APEC), which organises the US, Canada, Australia, New Zealand, Japan, South Korea, and ASEAN countries (Malaysia, Thailand, Indonesia, Brunei, Singapore, and Philippines); (3) A Greater ASEAN, which adds Vietnam, Kampuchea, and Laos to ASEAN; (4) A South China Economic Sphere, containing Taiwan, Hong Kong, and southern part of mainland China; (5) An East Asia Economic caucus (EAEC), which intends to combine groups of countries in (3) and (4) together with Japan and Korea; and (6) The Sea of Japan Rim Economic Cooperation Sphere, which will possibly include Siberia and North Korea.[13]

The conception (6) is relatively new and Japan has not yet much developed actual international economic relations with Siberia and North Korea. In the context of recent dissolution of the USSR; however, this idea will gain attraction for both Japan and Russia. Especially prefectures such as Niigata or Hokkaido, which tend to be left behind the continuous economic growth in the sunny industrial long belt area of Japan's main island Honshu on the side of the Pacific Ocean, are eager to promote this conception. But the idea is still more or less in the air, since Russia may prefer to request international investment in natural resources in Siberia more open also to the US and EC, not limited to Japan as a sort of deal for economic support. Political issues on the northern four islands may delay Japan's positive cooperation with Russia for a while. If the conception (6) is realised to some extent (even without Russia), then it can easily be a subgroup within EAEC in (5), from Japan's standpoint. The same must be true for (3) Greater ASEAN, and (4) South China Economic Sphere.

It is important to note that (5) EAEC contains all the Asian high growth-rate countries, in Asian NIEs, ASEAN and others around Japan, forming the most sunny economic zone in the world. Indeed the real growth rates of those Asian countries in 1970s and 80s are much higher than that (about 4.5%) of Japan, sometimes more than twice as high, as in Taiwan, Hong Kong, for these two decades, and China for 1980s. Relatively good Japanese economic performance has been largely correlated with these prosperous Asian economies. Almost 70% of Japan's total official development aids (ODA) in the 1980s was concentrated into Asian countries, while the share given to African countries was about 15%, and that given to Latin American countries was about 10%. A large portion of Japanese exports, around 30%, go to Asian countries. A number of Japanese manufacturing companies have extended direct investment into Asian countries, and organised an international subcontract system in order to reduce production costs by utilising information technologies.

The whole picture reminds us of an old Japanese dream of the Great East Asia Co-Prosperity Sphere in the very year of the 50th anniversary of Pearl Harbor. Indeed, in addition to common religious and cultural traditions, ambivalent memories of the period of Japanese occupation and education, combined with a feeling against Western imperialism, makes Japanese business somewhat easier to do in Asian countries, though Japan's real attraction for those countries does lie in her actual good economic performance. Anyway, a characteristic of the conception (5) EAEC, which can include (3), (4), and (6) as sub-groups, is that it does not contain the US as a member country. If the EC and the North American Free Trade Zone become exclusive like real fortresses, Japan will be in a sense forced to consolidate this type of regional economic unification in order to escape isolation.

Having this latent possibility in mind, Japanese political and business leaders will not move directly in this direction. Japan has taken an international political position following the American lead since the end of World War II, and has enjoyed economic growth under the umbrella of US hegemony. She is not prepared to abandon the position as a junior partner in relation with the US, and to become an independent leader country, as we have mentioned in Section 1. This corresponds to a strong economic relation with the US. The share of the US in total Japanese exports is 31.7% in 1990, by far the biggest, though it has been reduced somewhat from its peak 38.9% in 1986. In the total outstanding amount of Japanese direct overseas investment of about 240 billion dollars at the end of 1989, more than 100 billion dollars is in the US, which is more than twice as much as the amount invested in EC or in Asia. In 1986–89 Japanese net overseas security investment increased continually at a rate of about 100 billion dollars per year, reaching 390 billion dollars in total, and a large portion of it went to the US. Japanese business circles would not like to give up these important business opportunities, which are linked with the current international political position of Japan.

As the US international trade across the Pacific Ocean has surpassed that over the Atlantic Ocean since the beginning of 1980s, and as the rate of US dependence on foreign trade has continuously increased to reach 7.2% on exports and 9.4% on imports in 1990, the US also cannot easily abandon business opportunities with prosperous Asian countries so as to withdraw into a North American Free Trade Zone. Actually one of the main purposes of President Bush's visit to Japan and other Asian countries at the beginning of 1992 was to widen Asian markets for American commodities and services. It is also important for the US to extract Japanese money in various forms, especially as the capital inflow into US securities is much reduced due to the lowered US rate of interest. Following Japan's approximately 13 billion dollar contribution to the Gulf War in 1990–91, further requests are being proposed, such as a substantial contribution (about a billion and a half dollars) to a US project to construct a super-sized superconductive accelerator for elementary particles (SSC), as well as an increase of Japan's economic share to support the US military bases.

The US and EC would not like to see the formation of a strong economic bloc in Asia around Japan and to be excluded from this most prosperous area. Actually, international networks of multi-national corporations in various forms as well as international trade are widening between Japan (and other Asian countries) and the US, and the EC. Therefore, attempts for regional economic reunification in the Asian area centring around Japan are much more complex than in the case of EC. Japanese political and business leaders continuously feel that their home ground is in Asia, especially when facing repeated Japan-bashing. However, on the grounds of its strongest international competitive power, the real economic interest of Japanese big businesses is also in maintaining the world market as broadly free as possible, in either form of phase II of Pax-Americana, or of Japamerica, or of trigemony as we have seen in Section 1. Japan may even become the strongest promoter for free trade in a new world order like the UK in the middle of the 19th century or the US in the post-World War II period.

Thus, Japan has not so far reacted strongly to any one of the conceptions of regional economic reunification or cooperation in the Asia-Pacific rim area. Those conceptions are not always harmonious but contain many conflicts. The trade frictions between the US and Japan, for instance, are likely to become more serious and to feed dangerous chauvinism on both sides. Political tension between the US and China may continue and deepen, as the legacy of cold-war in the US politico-military order will need a great ideological enemy country as a substitute for the former USSR. In addition to these, all the differences in the levels of economic development and in the political and social systems among Asian countries do not make a broad and comprehensive regional economic reunification in the Asia-Pacific rim area easy in comparison with the case of the EC. Therefore, this prosperous area in a new world order will remain not closely reunified and experience various overlapping ideas and attempts at regional cooperation and reunification. In such a situation, Japan will probably still continue politically to maintain plural conceptions of regional cooperation in order to keep the broadest business opportunities and politically a free hand as far as possible.

4 What is Japan's Real International Contribution?

As Japanese economic power, expressed by GDP per capita in terms of the dollar, for example, caught up and then surpassed that of the US by the middle of 1980s, it began to gather various arguments about how Japan should make a proper international contribution. Accusations were intensified, especially from the US, that Japan was enjoying a position as a free-rider to the Pax-Americana politico-military world order without paying the necessary costs. Moved by pressure from Washington, Japanese national defence expenditure and official development aid (ODA) were continuously increased as exceptional 'sacred' budget items even under the neo-liberalist tightening policies through 1980s. Since the middle of the 1980s, Japanese ODA has become bigger than that of the US, and so the largest in the world. Under Article 9 of Japanese constitutional law, which prohibits the use and preservation of military force as a means of solving international conflicts, Japan's defence expenditure was traditionally lower than 1% of GNP, an historically promised upper ceiling. The ceiling became rapidly fully filled and occasionally surpassed in the 1980s. Although the military industry in Japan is prohibited from exporting weapons and is relatively small, Japanese business circles tend to see that the US demand to increase defence expenditure so as to purchase more expensive high-tech weapons from the US is a necessary cost to mitigate trade frictions and to maintain the American market for Japanese cars, electric appliances and general machines.

In the course of the Gulf War, a new type of international contribution was demanded to give about 13 billion dollars of direct financial support in total to the US-led military operation in 1990–91. Since such a demand was internationally accepted not only by Japan, the case may possibly be used in the future again and again to let the US military forces act and operate in any size and at any time freely without caring much about the costs, or rather regarding it as a sort of rewarding war business whenever an opportunity is available. It was reported, however, that acceptance of this pecuniary demand was not seen as sufficient by US public opinion, and that a more direct military contribution was further expected.

In order to answer this, or remaining accusations as a free-rider, the Japanese government attempted to set up a Bill to Cooperate Peace Keeping Operation (PKO Bill), which would enable it to send Japanese Self-Defence Forces abroad under the control of the United Nations. This Bill was the biggest issue in Japan in the Autumn of 1991, since it seriously contradicts Article 9 of the constitutional law and popular pacifist feelings among Japanese people. Meetings and demonstrations among citizens and workers were organised against the Bill. Not only this, the government party (LDP) could not be unified due to its internal turmoil in the process of changing the party leader from T. Kaifu to K. Miyazawa. Furthermore, graft scandals involving Miyazawa himself and other important LDP members also weakened the position of the LDP. As a result the Bill failed to pass the Diet.

Then suddenly a new Bill for International Contribution Taxes, which would raise about 1400 billion yen of taxes on certain industries and consumption goods for the purpose of various international contributions not exactly defined in advance, was proposed. This Tax Bill also could not gather unified support even from LDP and business circles, and failed in the process of preparation. The idea will, however, be reformulated and proposed again in 1992, as international contributions will indeed be continuously demanded from abroad, while the Japanese government is suffering from a wide budget deficit particularly under the heavy pressure of 174 trillion yen of cumulative outstanding state debt.

International contributions and cooperation are, in the abstract, fair and acceptable. A danger in Japan, however, is that with projects such as ODA or even the solution of global ecological issues, state expenditures are always apt to be too much linked with the business interest of Japanese companies, and not spent totally for crucial real needs of the world peoples. This tendency is closely related to the character of the Japanese socio-economic order to give priority to the interests of capitalist firms, not caring much about the heavy work and sacrifice of labouring people, or caring little about the widening unevenness in regional economic conditions within Japan. Therefore, we have to note that various attempts of the Japanese people to reconstruct a sound socio-economic order such as the spreading of co-op movements, citizens' actions for rural elections or ecological issues often against the construction of a nuclear power station or a golf-course, workers' demands to reduce working hours, or some of their endeavours to reorganise more militant unions, have now important meaning not merely domestically. Most of them would necessarily imply more or less the revision of Japanese social priorities, which have been too much controlled by capitalist firms. and therefore might result in the reduction of the competitive earning power of firms as in the case of the reduction of working hours. These results must be desirable both for preparing a fairer and sounder standpoint in offering Japanese international contributions, being more independent from Japanese business interest, and also for mitigating trade frictions with the US and the EC.

At the same time, the left has to catch up with the international networking of multi-nationals, and try to communicate on how to arrange international cooperation of states more in the spirit of the real interest of people. The Japanese left needs to hear, for instance, the Western left's view on what is the real and desirable Japanese international contribution, how to set up an official institution to inspect the use of ODA for the people in the third world countries, as well as the promising domestic left alternative strategies in the West. It is also imperative for us to continue exchanging views on the future of socialism on the basis of critical analyses of a new world order. I hope that this essay may be of some use to encourage such international networking between the Western and Japanese left.

NOTES

1. The French Regulationist school was revitalised by M. Aglietta's works, *A Theory of Capitalist Regulation: The US Experience*, translated by D. Fernbach (London: NLB, 1979), and its contribution is extended by a series of theorists such as R. Boyer, A. Lipietz, and B. Coriat.

2. See M. Itoh, *The World Economic Crisis and Japanese Capitalism*, (London: Macmillan, 1990), Part I.

3. Concerned Members in the Academic Association for Economic Theories, [*The Gulf War to be Inquired*], (Tokyo: Concerned Members in the Academic Association for Economic Theories, 1991), p. 105. (Titles of books in square brackets throughout notes here are my translation from Japanese).

4. T. Inoguchi, 'Four Japanese Scenarios for the Future', in *International Affairs*, vol. 65, no. 1, Winter 1988–89, presents and argues on (1), (3), (4) or Bigemony, and (6) among these as possible scenarios for a quarter- or a half-century from now.

5. For more concrete data on these and other features of Japanese capitalism, see M. Itoh, *op.cit.*, Part II.

6. R. Boyer, [*A Guide to Regulation*], edited and translated by T. Yamada and Y. Inoue, (Tokyo: Fujiwara-shoten, 1990), makes such characterisation of the Japanese model in its introductory chapter.

7. For example, M. Kenney and R. Florida, 'Beyond Mass Production: Production and the Labor Process in Japan', in *Politics and Society*, vol. 16, no. 1, 1988, underlined these positive aspects for workers in Japanese 'Fujitsuism' as an advanced model of Post-Fordism. A series of international debates followed this on a Japanese quarterly journal *Mado*, promoted mainly by T. Kato.

8. A typical work in this SSA school is seen in D.M. Gordon, R. Edwards and M. Reich, *Segmented Work, Divided Workers*, (Cambridge: Cambridge University Press, 1982). Although the work analyses different historical periods in the US, the authors' viewpoints are suggestive also for understanding spacial differences among current capitalist countries.

9. K. Marx, *Capital*, translated by B. Fowkes and D. Fernbach, vol. 1, (Harmondsworth: Penguin Books, 1976), p. 518.

10. cf. M. Itoh, *op.cit.*, pp. 181–84.

11. Institute of Basic Economic Science ed., [*Creation of a Comfortable Society*], (Kyoto: Showado, 1989), pp. 45–47.

12. National Defense Council for Victims of Karoshi ed., *Karoshi: When the 'Corporate Warrior' Dies*, (Tokyo: Mado-sha, 1990), p. 7.

13. A map on *Nihon Keizai Shinbun (Nikkei)*, May 27, 1991, reprinted in S. Sugimoto, M. Sekisita, S. Fujiwara, F. Matsumura ed., [*Grasping Contemporary World Economy*], (Tokyo: Toyokeizai-shinpo-sha, 1991), p. 192, gives a picture of these overlapping conceptions of economic spheres in the Pan-Pacific area excepting (6).

AFRICA: THE POLITICS OF FAILURE

Basil Davidson

The bald fact is that in Africa we have squandered almost 30 years with ineffective nation-building efforts. Our policies were far removed from social needs and developmental relevance.

Olusegun Obasanjo, former Head of State of Nigeria: 17 April 1990: OECD conference, Paris.

No one now disputes the centrality of popular participation and the human factor as the only viable developmental paradigm for Africa.

Adebayo Adedeji, former Executive Secretary of the Economic Commission for Africa of the United Nations, quoted here from weekly West Africa, *11 November 1991.*

And to the above quotations let us add a third, a good deal older but still with plenty of pith and point, saying that 'in this country, social warfare is under full headway, everyone stands for himself and fights for himself against all comers, and whether or not he shall injure all the others who are his declared foes, depends upon a cynical calculation as to what is most advantageous to himself.'[1] If Engels had been writing about the arena of economic and political decision in Africa during the 1980s, instead of about England in the 1840s, he could have let his words completely stand. Moreover, 'this war grows from year to year, as the criminal tables show, more violent, passionate, and irreconcilable', and this, too, can be left to apply. Over these past years no few state powers – to call them governments would do them too much credit – became murderous tyrannies or else outrageous banditries whose chieftains, licensed still by 'world opinion' and its obedient press as being presidents or prime ministers, had ceased to care even for the verbal trappings of legitimacy. *Whatever happens, we have got the Maxim Gun, and they have not,* was a thought that is said to have reassured the colonial invaders of a hundred years ago. Nowadays, with the AK47, their local legatees can be safer still.

Yet Engels, writing about England during the 1840s, was able to conclude that the war in question was a class war in which the *fact* of the bourgeoisie and the *fact* of the proletariat were realities which must dominate the scene. This being so, other conclusions followed, including the end of the war and a future of widening peace; and the future would belong to these conclusions: about which, in this year of grace of 1992 rather little, from an Engels point of view, can be comfortably said. Now, we are told, everything is different: socialism has failed and history has ended, so that what we have now is what remains and what will remain, fiddled with or tarted up a little here and there but always surviving, more well or less well according to the ineffable mysteries of the Business Cycle but otherwise above the power of thought to see or move beyond it. For there is nothing beyond it. The presently scabrous horrors of most of Africa are not, as we had supposed, to be understood as the abrasions of a social process, as a wrestling of huge potentials whereby, soon or late, the conflicts of today may be overcome and left behind, meanwhile the science of serious analysis can be usefully applied. Not at all, for such ideas are exploded teleological myths and empty nonsense. These conflicts are part of an eternal landscape. Regime X may be on the skids, and President Y juggling with his foreign bank balances against imminent departure for Biarritz or wherever. But these are merely *faits divers* to be judged by the value of their TV footage. They have no other useful meaning and, as facts, can be left to rot until the advent of Regime Y and President Z: naturally and indeed inevitably, the mixture as before.

It may be so. But for those who find this prospect unacceptably begrovelling, or at any rate improbable, or at least open to doubt, there is bound to be something more to be said. The current scene in Africa, with which this essay is concerned, cannot be agreed to encourage even modest hope, let along millenial hope; but at the same time it gives clear indications that there is a great deal more to be said. Socialism in any of its statist forms in Africa has certainly failed wherever one or other of such forms has been applied beyond the mere verbiage of propaganda, and there may be a true sense in which history, in this dimension, has indeed ended. Yet this is saying rather little. The applications of socialism, whether of one sort or another, whether 'scientific' or simply well-intended, were small or short-winded, or in any case destroyed by the handy AK47 of this or that gang of bandits (sometimes home-grown, sometimes not). They will not be tried again; it is far from certain that they will even be remembered. But then there is this other failure to be considered. Along with the failure of socialism there is the still larger and much more wounding failure of whatever, in Africa, has been introduced as capitalism: the failure, that is to say, to solve by the methods or systems of capitalism any great social or economic problem of indigenous African development. But isn't failure, in this context, perhaps too strong and final a word? Won't capitalism in Africa, just as in Europe and North America and Japan (yes, and the 'four little dragons' of Asia) work itself through to the stabilities of success? And if there are still sceptics to say no, it won't, then what prospect may one see for Africa while the future opens this ideological void in which the one system, like the other, is frustrated? These questions call at any rate for argument.

* * *

If we accept the currently most probable statistical measures, which are those of the World Bank and various agencies of the United Nations Organisation, Africa's prospect over the next thirty or forty years or so is one of gathering catastrophe in terms of deepening impoverishment, social dislocation, and inability to secure a better balance of profit and loss with the world of achieved industrialism. This is what the standard measures indicate. Even when allowing for a possible or even, as some say, probable pandemic of AIDS, the overall population will at least double over the next couple of decades, while the average continental capacity to produce more food – not to speak of other useful or essential things – will barely rise by more than the odd percentage point. Meanwhile the number of persons obliged to depend on purchased food will rise still more steeply and, it appears, irreversibly. Though still slower than in Latin America, the rate of 'urbanisation' – in plain language, the rate of increase in the number of refugees from rural impoverishment who survive in the squalor of service-less cities (cities which do not deserve the name but are nonetheless given it) – has continued to climb over the past thirty years and will go on doing so. 'By 2025', according to some prudent conclusions, 'Southern Africa is projected to reach the level of urbanisation that presently exists in the developed world and Latin America. About half of the population of eastern and western Africa will live in urban areas at that time. In absolute terms' – applicable just as well to northern Africa – this means that the urban populations of Africa 'will increase from four to twelve times above their 1940 levels by 2025.'[2] Africa, in short, will be a continental slum.

Worse: for if these huge new 'urban' populations cannot make food grow out of city streets, while rural producers do not improve on their statistically deplorable performance of past decades, the necessary food will have to be imported: but there will be no money available to pay for such imports. Said the G7 leaders in July 1991, when asked about this: 'We agree on the need for additional debt relief measures, on a case by case basis (applied to the most indebted countries), going well beyond the relief already granted.' Nice words: but will it happen? Financially regarded, most of Africa is now in hopeless bankruptcy. External debt (in whatever way it is measured, short-term or long-term) has risen annually for many years now, and in 1992 is pretty well double what it was ten years earlier. Most of this debt is now well understood to be irrecoverable, and all that stays in question is the manner in which 're-scheduling' takes place, this being the verb for non-payment that is currently in fashion. There are various ways in which this actual and prospective burden of external debt can be calculated. 'Debt-service' is one of them. This means, crudely put, the proportion of the proceeds of exports which must be used to meet the demands of interest payment to external lenders before such proceeds can be used for anything else. This proportion is thought to have stood at around fifteen percent in 1985, and is certainly higher today, perhaps a lot higher. Even if no higher, this export of African wealth by way of debt-service is such that little or no capital remains behind for the purposes of productive investment. So Africa is not only poor: in relation to the industrialised countries, but also in relation to its own past history, Africa is getting poorer at a speed that ought to be found alarming by others than the victims (who certainly find it alarming). There is no current perspective, whether in the statistical measures or any interpretation of those measures, that this rate of impoverishment can be decelerated.

Now it is possible to question this prospect even when accepting the general veracity of the logic in the statistics. Doomsday scenarios, we are reasonably told, don't come true: the fruitfulness of life, as well as the fragility of statistical measurement, stands always gallantly in the way. This may be so in this African case, and we will come back to the possibility that it is so. In any case it needs to be said that many official statistical measures in this Africa are no more than propagandist artifacts. No one knows how much Africa-produced food, for example, comes to market through illegal or 'parallel' channels and never gets into anyone's statistics. We do not know who eats it, or how it is paid for. The case is general. As long ago as 1982-84 the United States Department of Commerce came to the conclusion, after wrestling in vain with the artifactual statistics of the West African republic of Benin (formerly the French colony of Dahomey), that some ninety percent of that republic's internal trade passed through unrecordable channels[3]: and it is a fair estimate that this conclusion, if somewhat higher than the probable average for other republics, was not excessively so. The statistics of most African nation-states, in other words, reflect an overall situation where the organs and agents of the nation-statist system no longer possess any significant measure of accountability. They are not to be believed because they are not seriously intended to convey belief.

Even when allowing for this deficiency – that the state no longer commands the respect of the citizens, and is more often seen, in practice, as being itself illegitimate – it still appears that Africa grows quite rapidly poorer in its capacity to satisfy the reasonable daily and even minimal demands of large populations for the basic needs of life. Measurement, once again, is more than difficult. There being no official welfare system in most African situations, it would seem on the face of things that rapidly increasing rates of non-employment in African 'urban areas' must indicate a widespread condition of, or imminence of, sheer starvation. But somehow or other, this is seldom what is seen. Corpses are not being carted off the streets of large African 'cities' in anything like the numbers that the statistics would lead you to assume: in this way or in that, the 'urban' masses manage to stay alive far more often than the official figures must lead you to think that they should. Petty crime, gang warfare, lineage solidarity among those not yet severely divorced from their rural origins, and a host of ingenious escape routes from starvation appear, so far at least, to suffice. Civil society in terms of a rule of law, of a reasonable hope of amelioration, of social obligation and mutual respect, may go to the wall and in many cases has already reached the wall; but the surface appearances of life can still mislead. Another sheaf of statistics claims that a majority of Africans have a life expectancy at birth that has increased by some twelve years in recent times: from an estimated 37.8 years in 1950-55 to 49.4 years in 1980-85.[4]

All too clearly, the statistical evidence is at least unsatisfactory. Nonetheless the bulk of this evidence has to be accepted for want of any more reliable measurement. Even when allowing for the escape-routes provided by smuggling, illegality of other kinds, and all the rest, a large fraction of Africa's peoples remains in dire and even hopeless poverty, and the fraction is in all probability becoming annually higher rather than lower. By all the official evidence, in any case, the politics of capitalism, in any practical and *applied* sense, have entirely and even clamorously failed to promote any general and often any particular development in and of Africa's socio-economic structures. It may be useful to insist on this, if only because our Higher Journalism likes to tell us that the policies of capitalism, if only sufficiently applied, must always prevail in the end. On that view, Africa's current crisis of severe impoverishment is only another *fait divers,* another unlucky pile-up on the freeways of free enterprise such as good policing and sensible behaviour will soon sort out. Only patience is required. The workings of free enterprise may be hard to understand; they infallibly succeed in the end. Now this note of cheerful optimism sounds more or less clearly, if sometimes *sous entendu,* from all the great programmes and planifications of these recent years; and it has, no doubt, its own historicist legitimacy. Britain did succeed in emerging from the mass impoverishment of the 1840s by a process of holding on and plunging ahead, and British capitalism, at any rate till the 1900s, became a wonder of the world. If this could happen to Britain in the 19th century, surely it can happen to Africa in the 21st? What does the prospect have to say about that?

* * *

The answer could be argued theoretically, of course, but here in this brief essay, which will avoid prophecy, I will consider it only in the case of one or two actual examples. They can offer no more than provisional or indicative answers but these, standing on facts rather than fantasies of the statistical sort, may still be useful. There is the case, to begin with, of the republic of Zaire, a country (or supposedly a country) which occupies a very big chunk of the tropical zones, is rich in natural resources, contains a population perhaps annually increasing at a rate of three percent, and has a destiny for all these reasons which cannot sensibly be separated from the destiny of the rest of Africa, tropical or not. It will not be unreasonable to say that whatever happens in Zaire is going to happen, or is already happening, in much of the rest of the continent.

Zaire has been rather little noticed by the Higher Journalism, though the record in this respect is less deficient in the USA than in Britain. This British indifference to Zaire may be from mere bewilderment at complexities that seem all too exotic and peculiar, or else, as I have argued in another place, because the nation-state of Zaire, of what used to be the Belgian Congo until 1960, is really not there at all but is in truth a myth, a mere verbal usage, an idea without an existential content.[5] Since the late 1960s, the country called Zaire has been run not by a state power in any sense national by vocation or in origin, but by a presidential extended-family network of self-appointed 'authorities' and bureaucratic potentates, small in their number but great in their capacity for greed. 'The virtually unlimited power of those at the top', on a recent and well qualified judgment, 'has allowed them to plunder the natural riches of their country and to amass great fortunes.'[6] As early as 1976 in this degradation, which still continues in 1992 – a degradation reported by a wide variety of competent observers – the archbishop of Kinshasa, the country's capital, could affirm without denial that 'agonising situations' were now to hand: situations in which 'the thirst for money transforms men into assassins . . . and whoever holds a morsel of authority or means of pressure, profits from this to impose on people and exploit them.' Meanwhile, although not in a sense intended or foreseen by Marx and Engels, even this notional state in Zaire has been withering away. For in 1960 this enormous country possessed 88,000 miles of motorable roads, enough to stretch a meagre though valuable essential network over wide regions. But in 1985 the total mileage of motorable roadway had dwindled to 12,000; and of these no more than 1,400 were said, reliably, to be paved.

Looked at with attention, this state in Zaire is little more than its capital of Kinshasa, half a dozen biggish provincial towns together with zones of mineral extraction and crop plantation in the hands of foreigners, plus an army large but of dubious loyalty and an airline to carry the fortunate few between these points of 'state power'. Beyond this 'structure', out there in the bush, there is the limitless forest with its dissidents or rebels or, whenever the army gets down to work, its victims. In these circumstances, capital accumulation on behalf of any properly national project has been impossible outside the realm of propaganda. Accumulation has meant the building of private balances in banks abroad, as well as various means of nourishing these deposits; and while foreign entrepreneurs, perhaps needless to say, can and do operate within this 'structure', they do it with an ever more prudent hand. As for the statistics of this state in Zaire, these reach an artifactual nature of a positively dreamlike quality.

So it would seem, on the face of it, that capitalism's cheerful optimism can have no place here. Again, though, there is more to be said. Human ingenuity being what it is, Zaire begins to possess what some recent observers suggest must be the beginnings of a potentially and perhaps eventually dominant bourgeoisie by means of a 'second' or illicit economy of trade, and even of production, which has arisen from the futility and venality of the official, legal and 'first' economy. Necessity here, it would seem, has been operating as the mother of what is clearly a great deal of shrewd invention. Faced with the piracy of those who command state power, 'rural and urban dwellers devise strategies to survive Zaire's stringent conditions: urbanites who cannot live on their wages organise supplies of foodstuffs from rural areas, sending kerosene, salt, soap, cooking oil and other items that are unobtainable or unaffordable in rural areas to kin who send them manioc, rice, plantains, beans and other staples in exchange.'[8] Janet McGaffey, to whom principally we owe these enlightenments, calls this manifold withdrawal from any attempt to live and behave as the state officially supposes that people must and do a 'disengagement from the state'; but also, since this disengagement permits some escape from statist piracies – at a price in various bribes and conjurings – she sees it as a trend 'significant of class formation, because some of its activities allow considerable accumulation'. At the same time, 'for some rural and urban workers the activities of this ("second") economy provide a favourable alternative to wage labour and thus the means to avoid proletarianisation.' A 'new class' thus arises; and 'this new class is the beginning of a true economic bourgeoisie, as yet small and with an undetermined future.' Only abolish the worst coercions and perversions of the Zairist dictatorship, operative now over nearly thirty years, and the potential for growth of this 'new class' should become multiple and dynamic.

Comparable bourgeois 'emergences' could be easily displayed in a number of African countries, Nigeria and Kenya being the obvious examples south of the Sahara Desert. I do not know how many sterling millionaires there may be in those two countries – or other millionaires in other countries north of the Desert – but they are not few and they are becoming more, while a post-*apartheid* capitalism in South Africa will surely enlarge the same contrasts between private fortunes and public squalors. Yet it barely needs arguing, I imagine, that these phenomena are by no means necessarily those that confirm the development of a class system able to produce and guarantee a respectable bourgeois future. If it could so guarantee, then one must have expected the economies of Latin America, long since, to have advanced from political tyrannies of the Zairian sort to the sunny uplands of Westminsterial tolerance and virtue. *Pace* McGaffey, whose optimism I admire but cannot share, the pincers of the actual and existing economic order seem all too certain to nip any such useful development in the bud. A New Economic Order, very true, might quickly change this perspective by reforming international terms of trade and other such mechanisms. But as matters stand now the subordinate nature of these ex-colonial (or 'neo-colonial' in a much used term) systems of exchange has ensured that the transfer of real wealth to ex-imperial (or 'neo-imperial') economies in North America and Europe has continued, and still continues, no matter what depths of impoverishment thereby ensue.

It would therefore seem more likely that these ex-colonial economies have come too late to the feast: in one or other degree of failure, they will not be able to climb the stages of growth to the blessed level of high mass consumption, or anything like it. This seems to be where we 'are at' today. And even if a prolonged study were to expose this conclusion as an unjustified pessimism, it would still be the case that this is almost surely how a vast majority of these impoverished populations see and understand their situation and their future. If this is true, as the bulk of the available evidence undoubtedly agrees, then the grim paradox of our times is that the legacy of capitalist success in developed economies is what has become fatal to any such success in those that are not developed. It is a paradox, moreover, from which there is so far no known means of escape.

* * *

Socialism promised to provide an escape. Under whatever gloss or label, this promise of a means of escape from capitalist failure is what has typified the operative meaning of socialism to its African adherents, devotees or militants. Push aside quantities of verbiage, and you will invariably find that the dynamic attractions of the idea of socialism – of this or of that socialism, whether utopian or scientific or whatever, whether intellectually coherent or merely the waffle of demagogues – have consisted in their demonstration of standing for the reverse of whatever has been understood by the consequences of capitalism; and on this, of course, the world is nowhere near the point at which the last relevant word has been said. Nor do I think for a moment, all recent history notwithstanding, that the achievements of revolutionary movements of anti-colonial insurrection – I am thinking here of Africa, although the same may be true elsewhere – can be written down as failures. In the Portuguese African colonies, so often cited, these movements reached their objectives, more often than not and against huge obstructions, with a remarkable degree of moral solidity and intellectual coherence. Only then – and especially after 1977 – were they denied, turned back and eventually ruined. Partly by their Marxism-Leninism imported from a Stalinist Moscow, reinforcing bureaucratic centralism against the participatory politics of the liberation war. And partly, after 1978, by the armed banditries invented and inserted and

fuelled by the *apartheid* regime in South Africa with more or less enthusiastic American support and finance.

Could it have been otherwise without these 'East-West' interventions?
There is much to suggest that it could have been otherwise: but in other
international circumstances. That discussion would be out of place here.
What we have is that none of the socialist routes of escape has proved
viable: the capitalist failure is accompanied by a socialist failure. It may be
said that this failure of the 'capitalist model' has been far greater and more
clamorous than the failure of the 'socialist model', for the 'capitalist model'
has been far more often and persistently tried and has had the benefit of an
enormously greater quantity of external finance and advice. But this is
meagre comfort. The socialist project has failed at almost all levels. Yet I
should like to insist upon the failure of the 'capitalist model' – thinking still
about Africa – because the policies of capitalism are still put forward as
though they at any rate have not failed. There seems little danger that the
Soviet model, or anything like it, will ever be tried again. But the standard
Western model is still in high fashion, and is paraded now as though its
credentials and credits were really beyond sensible criticism. And I point
this out here not as some kind of last-ditch socialist alibi but because those
credentials and credits are so very few and feeble.

Consider only the remedies advised for the salvation of countries
subjected to one-party rule or to the no-party dictatorship for which one-
party rule has generally prepared the way. Africa can show a dismal string
of such countries. For them the advised remedies consist of organising a
system of many parties. And no doubt there is everything to be said for
political competition in the matter of ideas, objectives, persons and
methods. But what will prove effective in class-structured countries of
'actually existing capitalism' may still prove nothing of the kind in countries without crystallised class structures and a corresponding economic
system.

The African examples are many and various, if now conveniently
forgotten. In 1960 – but the example could be easily repeated – the
Somalian colonies became independent (and largely united) under a
parliamentary dispensation of admirable ingenuity. Several political parties were in attendance at this birth, and the most influential of them had an
undeniably representative quality. But few years passed before it became
abundantly clear that this multi-party system was deep in trouble. And the
reason for trouble was only in small degree a question of human frailty.
Corruption and perversion came in because the multi-party system could
not be in practice what it claimed to be in theory. The reason for this was
not a weakness in constitutional drafting. The reason was that the Somalis,
as a people and political culture, were not structured on class-divisive lines
but on clan-divisive lines. This led straight into clan and sub-clan clientelism. By 1968, with clientelism run riot, Somalis had achieved no fewer than

62 parliamentary parties (*read:* groups for dividing up the spoils of power) for an electorate far smaller than Somalia's 3 million people; and such was the uproar and corruption that a military *coup d'état* was carried out in 1969 without a shot being fired. And today, in the wake of fresh disasters essentially of the same clan-structured origin, Somalia has ceased to be a state in any practical sense.

This is the clientelist bankruptcy that receives its complete confirmation, if one were still needed, in the Zaire whose miseries we have already briefly inspected. With the ferocious but inept Mobutist dictatorship near collapse in 1990, a return to multi-party democracy was proclaimed; and by 1991 Zaire enjoyed the blessings of . . . yes, no fewer than 230 political parties[9]. So it has come about that the nation-statist frameworks of the capitalist model – the model installed at decolonisation, but in this respect no differently from the socialist model – have produced a pair of harsh alternatives; and it is with these alternatives that Africa's political fate is now challenged. What has happened is this: either there has been a strong centralised state, buttressed by an overweening army and an abundant police force, and this strong state, having no roots in any broad public participation, falls under bureaucratic and then personal dictatorship: at which point the Zairian misery is reached. Or there has been a weak centralised state and this, for essentially the same reasons in lack of public legitimacy, becomes the victim of 'multi-party' clientelism – Europeans have liked to call it 'African tribalism' – at which point another dictatorship duly awaits. It can be said that this degradation was encouraged in the Soviet-style cases – Ethiopia's under the Mengistu dictatorship is probably the most obvious among them – because this was what dominant actors in Moscow thought would best suit them. But is there anyone to imagine that the Mobutist dictatorship in Zaire could have been installed, and could then have survived for more than a quarter of a century, unless this had suited the interests of dominant actors in the West?

In terms of current perspectives all this belongs to the failure of post-colonial politics. Much more could be said to the same effect: in today's ideological void, when one or other grim alternative still awaits, the failure becomes ever more flagrant. Of course we hear it said that this failure comes from African incompetence, irresponsibility, or sheer ignorance. There have been plenty of all three. But I suspect that history will award the greatest and most damaging incompetence to a little mentioned source: to the readiness of African intellectuals, whether in public life or not, to listen obediently to whatever advice or guidance that arrives from outside Africa. One can't but notice that every great plan of revival or 'restructuring' evolved by this or that portentous agency in the developed world, time after time for year after year, has been greeted with respect by African authorities, and not seldom with subservience, before being applied with attitudes of rigid discipline. The West has known best; for

some, even the East has known best. In any case Africa itself has not
known best. And so we arrive at continental immiseration on a scale never
known before.

Lately, the connection has been noted. If the think-tanks and aid
industries have so regularly got it wrong – that they have so repeatedly had
to contradict each other – perhaps Africans in Africa may after all be able
to get it right, or at least less wrong? The question has been asked: The
answers thus far remain partial and tentative. But they still strike notes that
are new.

* * *

The problem is at any rate clear. It is to mark out and begin to follow a
pathway round the two alternatives, each of which depends in one sense or
another upon a non-representative centralism: so as to reach a condition in
which the state regains its historical accountability. Regains: this needs
emphasis. For the pre-colonial state in Africa, whenever successful in its
stability and capacity for self-development, possessed accountability, enjoyed legitimacy, deployed a representative quality. These achievements
were reached by a multiplicity of structures, compensatory mechanisms,
and practical compromises of a style and nature no longer possible or
desirable in the world of today.[10] But the principle of that success hasn't
therefore changed. To find a pathway round the twin alternatives of failure,
the politics of success has to be a politics arising from the arenas of mass
debate. Which means, in practice and result, arising from local decision.

Thirty years ago and less, this was what thinkers in the mould of Amílcar
Cabral and the few others like him argued in their time and place. They
argued for 'people's participation' in the process of politics, for *particip-
ação popular,* as the high road to state legitimacy. But few listened, few
took them seriously: the guiding voice from outside, then, was either
Marxism-Leninism-Stalinism, or else it sang the charms of bountiful Free
Enterprise; and one or other form of *non*-participation followed. But
today it begins to be different. In one way or another and a variety of
languages, the case for 'people's participation' (however defined) is what
today's really interesting African thinkers argue among themselves and to
whomever else will listen.

'No one now disputes the centrality of popular participation and the
human factor as the only viable developmental paradigm for Africa'[11] is a
statement that carries a very solid weight in its context, for its maker,
Adebayo Adedeji, has a staunchly deserved reputation for penetrating
insight and integrity of judgment. For several years when he was recently
secretary-general of the UN Economic Commission for Africa, he has
used his considerable reputation to reinforce the politics of representative
democracy; and in this respect, among African intellectuals, he has been

by no means alone. I could fill this essay with comparable quotes, and anyone who closely follows the African political scene could do the same. The 'centrality of popular participation' – the need for it, the means of achieving it – is what, these many voices say, can save the state from clientalism on one side and dictatorship on the other.

That 'no one now disputes' this centrality is of course a huge exaggeration. All sorts of interested persons dispute it: the clientelist politicians and their bureaucratic hangers-on, the 'strong men' and their subordinate killers, many hopeful members of extended families down to the third and fourth generation, all these and many more dispute the centrality of participation as a means of government. Any number of elected committees bent on making participation work will find themselves packed with energetic persons bent on preventing any such thing. No doubt; the known cases are many and will certainly be more. It remains that displacing centralised force and fraud by decentralised structures of discussion and decision is the only programme now available that wins widening respect and commands serious purpose.

Considered broadly, this trend of thought – already to some extent a trend of action, too – is still at an early stage of its development. A listing of relevant 'cases' would mention initiatives in perhaps a dozen countries: in Uganda since the advent of Musaveni, in Ghana since the recent years under Rawlings, in Nigeria at various moments over the past dozen years but especially over the last four or five with Babangida presiding, now and then elsewhere. The heritage of Cabral and his kind has also found impressive legatees, moreover, in what may now perhaps be reckoned as the most successful of all the anti-colonial movements of armed struggle: the Eritrean People's Liberation Front which fought its way to power in Eritrea against truly overwhelming military odds in 1990 and then, though still unnoticed by the world at large, presented the world with a consummately skilful political *dénouement*. For instead of simply declaring a state and taking possession of it, there being no longer any force anywhere to prevent them from doing this, Isseyas Afeworki and his colleagues did not do this. They remained loyal to their wartime politics of participation. They would declare the independence of Eritrea and the foundation of an Eritrean state in two years' time when things had settled down, when representative parties could be formed, when elections by universal suffrage could be held under a constitutional rule of law: elections in advance of which the EPLF, the victorious front of liberation, would have declared itself dissolved. When, in short, participatory politics freed from the many constraints of the war could begin to enjoy a free run.

More widely in the vast region of the Horn of Africa, the case of post-Mengistu Ethiopia provides another scene of relevant evidence. The winners here, chiefly but not solely the Tigray People's Liberation Front, passed at once to declarations of a similar intent. The very difficult and complex 'nationalities question' in Ethiopia, bitter fruit of the old imperial dictatorship and its many years of gross discrimination in favour of the ruling Amhara, would be solved by policies of decentralisation to auto-nomous assemblies and executives; and by the end of 1991, with the process still underway, it could at least be said with confidence that these policies were beginning to work. 'Submerged' or 'forbidden' nationalities, to use the language of the old Austro-Hungarian Empire, have already found themselves welcomed to the light of legality and recognition, and, while blinking somewhat in half-disbelieving surprise, have begun to make their voices heard. And all this has been done, let it be added, in the absence of any mandatory advice or guidance from the outside world, including, crucially, the USA and the USSR. It is a combination of circumstances that merits thought.

We shall see. I have heard it argued, for example, that policies of consistent devolution of powers 'to the periphery' – to the 'grass roots', in another familiar usage – will mean endless fission and secession into unworkable groups, tribes, nationalities, nations, even nation-states. Cer-tainly, consistent devolution may threaten administrative efficiency. But against this there may be two things to be said. The first is 2that some loss of statist efficiency is probably part of the price, at the position we have reached now, that Africa will have to pay for the revival of civil society, although this price may well be a lot less in practice than may be feared. The second, more important, is that nationalism in Africa – as distinct from clientelism masquerading as nationalism, which is what we so often have today – is not in itself a potent force. Its roots are often shallow, its rhetoric weak, its attraction powerful only when a people's welfare is felt to be denied or repressed. In a large sense African nationalism has been the child of colonialism: remove the hand of repression and the evidence suggests, more often than not, that trans-ethnic co-operation, even trans-ethnic fusion, ceases to be difficult.

A simple historical comparison can make the point. Forty years ago, early in the process of formal decolonisation, widespread movements of anti-colonial nationalism in East and West Africa declared for pro-grammes of federalising unification: so that, for example, fourteen colo-nies of France should become two federalised unions and not, as Paris then insisted and as what befell, fourteen nation-states; and something of the same kind came under discussion among the nationalists of (then) British East Africa. None of these initiatives won any tolerance in London or Paris. But in 1975, wrestling with the early years of the nation-state disaster and again pressing ideas of their own, the leading nationalists of sixteen West African states declared themselves in favour of forming a unified 'economic community', since when they have proceeded somewhat fur-ther. If little has so far been achieved, the objective is still there and has been lately reaffirmed in a formal treaty.

It may go without saying that all such efforts to break out of stagnation or regression take place in a world more surely dominated than ever before by powerful systems of trans-national capitalism in the developed world; and no one in Africa today, so far as I know, questions their continued mastery of the international scene. But what is beginning to be widely questioned, I think, is the automatic assumption that what is good for the developed world can necessarily be good for – in this case – the African world. No doubt policies of political devolution – participatory policies – will be applied within market economies, within capitalist economies of some kind or other. But the actual nature and functioning of those economies, and who commands them and how they are to be commanded and promoted, remain questions to which there are as yet no clear and obvious answers. An impressive essay in last year's *Socialist Register* posed the question, for Hungary but also more widely for Eastern Europe, of what kind of capitalist economies can be built without capitalist classes; and the question remains open for Africa as well.[12] In much of Africa the basic policy of the past thirty years has been to use surplus extracted from rural economies in order to industrialise urban economies, and the policies of devolution are now aimed precisely at rectifying the excessive and even reckless ways in which this policy has been applied. If this means 'slowing down development', so much the better, for 'rapid development', more often than not, has meant no development. What African thinkers seem now to be working towards is a system within which market economies work for those who serve and use them, locally and now, having regard to their own capacities and needs. How far the developed world of multinational concentrations of power will bring itself to tolerate this devolutionary politics of participation, and its democratic implications, is another question to which, at present, we do not have an answer.

NOTES

1. Frederick Engels, *The Condition of the Working Class in England,* Leipzig 1845, here from Marx and Engels *On Britain,* Moscow 1953 English edition, p. 165 and *passim.*
2. Chinua Achebe and three others (eds), *Beyond Hunger in Africa,* London 1990, James Currey, pp. 44.
3. Chris Allen, *Benin,* note 5 to ch. 4, p. 134: London 1989, Pinter Publishers.
4. Achebe, p. 43.
5. Basil Davidson, *The Black Man's Burden: Africa and the Curse of the Nation-State,* New York 1992, Times Books; London 1992, James Currey: at various points in an analysis of nation-statist failures in Africa with comparisons to Eastern Europe.
6. Janet MacGaffey, 'Economic Disengagement and Class Formation in Zaire', in Donald Rothchild and Naomi Chazan, *The Precarious Balance:* Boulder and London 1988, Westview Press; p. 175. Dr MacGaffey has argued this case at length in her new book, *The Real Economy of Zaire,* University of Pennsylvania Press and James Currey London, 1988, but I have not yet been able to read it.
7. J.A.A. Ayode, 'States without Citizens', in Rothchild and Chazan, p. 106.
8. MacGaffey, p. 183.
9. Mark Huband, *The Guardian* London, 29 July 1991.

10. cf. Davidson, *passim*.
11. Adedeji as reported in the weekly *West Africa,* 11 November 1991.
12. Peter Bihari, 'From Where to Where? Reflections on Hungary's Social Revolution', *Socialist Register,* London 1991, pp. 279.

THE GULF WAR AND THE NEW WORLD ORDER

Avishai Ehrlich

More than a year ago I was involved in a campaign in Israel against the impending war in the Gulf. Considering the mood of Israelis it was an impossible task. One of our difficulties was to convince people that the war might really happen. We felt that behind the pervasive dismissive attitude lay a great fear. The media played a double game: it reported repeatedly about the availability of various weapons of mass destruction in Saddam's arsenal, but it always allayed people's fears by playing down the danger, creating a nerve racking see-saw between alarming and calming. There was also the fear of Israeli retaliation, fuelled by some carefully placed nuclear remarks by government members. Some of us felt that below the serenity lay deep terror.

Some of my friends thought that we ought to amplify the fears and bring them to the surface by detailing the worst scenarios. Others were adamant against building on fear, arguing that this could backfire by pushing people to demand a pre-emptive strike. Indeed, upon the first Scuds most of our support disappeared. Some, usually liberal, literary figures unexpectedly joined with the racist Kahane followers in a demand to use Israeli nukes in a retaliatory strike on Baghdad. Later on, some colleagues, experts on strategic studies, speculated and lamented that Israel lost its deterrence stance due to its inaction. The gas masks distributed during the war are now permanently in our homes and are currently being replaced by a better model.

For some, the Cold War is over. Exterminism seems, for Europeans and North Americans, a nightmare from the past. Thompson and Halliday can set aside, at last, their fine arguments about the structure of the Cold War, the symmetrical or asymmetrical responsibility of the, now deceased, Soviet Union. They can ponder now about the future of CND and END. Western intellectuals will, no doubt, delve into Globalism, will construct and deconstruct New Social Movements, and argue about multinational-ism and democracy. For others, less fortunate, who live in the semi-periphery, in the Middle East in particular, the waning of the core's Cold War has not changed much yet. For us the danger of exterminism has increased in this interim of the new world order. Actually the term 'Cold War' has always been a misnomer, an incorrect designation, as far as non-core countries were concerned. At the turn of the decade, between 1989 and 1990, there was war in 39 states.[1] For safety's sake, at least for the super powers, lest it becomes all consuming, war was conducted outside – in our sphere, where we were the proxies.

In their introduction to *The New State Of War And Peace*, Michael Kidron and Dan Smith speculate that the new world order '. . . may, like the old, be well armed and prone to war or, at least, military risk-taking. But there would be two differences. New enemies would draw different lines of conflict and confrontation. And, unlike the Cold War, the new order will not – at least for a time, if ever – threaten total annihilation in total war.'[2] Kidron and Smith obviously think about Soviets and Americans confronting and threatening each other – but these powers never fought each other directly. They interjected themselves into third party conflicts and subsumed these conflicts within their contest. From the bi-polar system mentality of the Cold War almost every conflict, intra-national and international, was viewed strategically – not in itself or regionally, but in its imagined implications on the bi-polar global balance of power. What is being 'discovered' after the collapse of bi-polarity is that Communism and the Soviet Union are not, nor ever were, behind, or the cause of, many conflicts. As nationalist or fundamentalist regimes clash with the interests of the industrialised world, and as there is no more danger of escalation between the super powers, there is more likelihood of direct western involvement in local conflicts. The fact that these conflicts no longer threaten total global annihilation only increases their likelihood.

How did the Gulf War end? Did it end? Why did it start? What was it about? It had to do with oil, that much is clear. It had to do not so much with production sale or price, for Iraq too, had it stayed in Kuwait, would have also produced and sold, since Saddam needed the money even more than Sheik Jabar. It had to do with control. It had to do with safeguarding oil regimes for the West. But to safeguard from whom? Not from the collapsing Soviet Union or from a Soviet allied state, but from fundamentalist Islam and Iraqi nationalism. The Ba'ath regime exterminated the Iraqi Communist Party. By 1984 it renewed its diplomatic relations with the United States which it severed in 1967 as a result of the Israeli-Arab conflict. Iraq acted for itself, but also in Western interests against a previous threat to oil regimes by Iran's Ayatollahs. In the 1980–1988 Iraq-Iran war, the same Saddam, cruel and dictatorial as he ever was, was supported and supplied by Kuwait, Saudi Arabia, by other Islamic and Arab states as well as by all major Western countries.

The story of Iran's Islamic revolution of 1979 is in a similar vein. The revolution was not pro-Soviet. The Ayatollahs' objection to Communism was expressed both by their support of the Afghani rebels against the

Communist regime backed by the Soviet army, and by their suppression of the *Tudeh* (Iranian Communist Party) and other Marxist movements. The Islamic revolution toppled an oil regime, the autocratic Shah, who had himself been reinstated in a CIA-instigated coup in 1953 against an elected nationalist government which tried to nationalise the oil industry.

The Iran-Iraq Gulf war was not directly related to the bi-polar world order; it was a regional war, its origins preceded the Islamic revolution in Iran and had to do with the way in which the borders of modern Iran and Iraq were drawn by Britain. Charles Tilly is correct in observing that '. . . colonial boundaries that Europeans had imposed almost without regard to the distribution of people became defended frontiers of post colonial states . . '.[3] Iran and Iraq have related ethnic-religious or linguistic minorities across each other's border. They also have a dispute over Iraq's narrow access to the sea in the Gulf, similar to the dispute that Iraq has had, since its independence in 1932, with Kuwait over the way the British-drawn borders strategically parcelled out the previous Ottoman province of Basra, and left Iraq without a coastline.

The Gulf War 1991 cannot be understood without its predecessor – the Gulf War 1980–1988. It was the consequence of the consequence of the fundamentalist revolution of 1979 in Iran. That revolution destroyed the central oil regime in the Gulf, on which the West relied to secure its interests in this economically essential zone. Since the withdrawal of Britain from the Gulf in the 1960s, the West assigned the task of chief local guardian to the Shah. Unlike the other oil regimes (Saudi Arabia, Kuwait, Bahrain, Qatar, the United Arab Emirates and Oman), Iran was tempted to build a strong and modern army, and the Shah started the White Revolution which was supposed to secularise and modernise Iran. The Iran experiment, a test case to conservative autocratic modernisation theory, in which many Western social scientists were involved, was an attempt to move away from the traditionalist model which prevails in the other oil regimes.

In those states the regime relies on the traditional semi-tribal power structure and tries to preserve it against social change. Oil revenues redistributed through the traditional ruling clans maintain a clientalist consent. This traditional structure – called 'the rentier state'[4] – is in essence a politically and economically dependent and weak structure. To prevent the possibility of a military coup most of these countries have a minimal army, and the military forces are organised in different segregated institutions to provide countervailing forces in case of revolt. Oil revenues provide the highest standard of living to part of the population. It is a 'post-modern' consumer society without any productive base – consumption is entirely based on import. There is no indigenous working class, nor a substantial peasantry. The service sector is maintained by foreign workers, temporarily resident, with no citizenship or any political rights, living in segregation from the relatively small citizenry. This weak state structure means that in a security crisis the regime must depend on external forces.

The religious revolution in Iran created such a danger. The spectre of the export of the revolution threatened the rulers in the area and the Western oil regime. The new Iranian state was not a danger to the West because of its Islamic laws and imposed life style – in that sense it was more of a threat to the large secular section of Iranian society. The danger posed by the Islamic state was that it was a strong state that announced that it did not intend to abide by the existing world order and that it represented a new world order unto itself. The threat by Iran to the West was not a pro-Soviet challenge. Neither was it an economic challenge: no-one knows exactly what is, after all, an Islamic economic system. The threat was of a different sort. The Islamic principle represents the subordination of the market to ideological and political principles. This, plus the fear of the expansion of the sphere of influence of these ideas, was the real threat. Ayatollah Khomeini decreed both the USA and the USSR 'devils'; his involvement in Afghanistan, and Soviet fears of the spillover of fundamentalist Islam into the Soviet Union's large Islamic population, made him no less a threat to the East than to the West. The Iranian revolution was a threat to the bi-polar world order by the introduction of another world order, neither Washington's nor Moscow's but International Islam.

1979 was a remarkable year: Khomeini returned to Iran in January. Saddam Hussein became president of Iraq in July. Carter ordered the formation of the Rapid Deployment Force to respond to threats especially in the Gulf in October. The Soviet Union invaded Afghanistan in December. In January 1980 the Carter 'Doctrine' stated that the United States would use military force to protect its interests in the Gulf.[5] It is in these events that the roots of the two wars in the Gulf are to be found – and perhaps also the roots of the coming of the second Cold War, as Iranian affairs dominated the election campaign which brought Reagan to power.[6]

With the collapse of the Shah there was no other power in the Gulf except Iraq that could stop Iran. Iraq, however, was not among the trusted oil regimes. The Iraqi regime is another species which did not fit the neat bi-polar classification of the world. Initially a state created by the British, it, like Egypt, deposed its King in a military coup in 1958. It became, a decade later, a one-party, the Ba'ath, militarily-ruled dictatorship. The Ba'ath, in Iraq (and in Syria), has borrowed organisational principles from Stalinism and Fascism; it stands for pan-Arabism, but in fact, is strongly Iraqi nationalist. Ruling in a personality-cult style, the regime built a strong state. As Iraq too is a large producer of oil, it benefited, like other rentier states in the area, from huge oil revenues which were used to bolster the army and the state-party apparatus; but it also created a clientalist welfare state, a fairly good secular education system, agricultural moderni-sation, as well as state-owned strategic industries.

Saddam did not start the war with Iran on behalf of the US. He did it in order to take advantage of what, he thought, was a weakening and disintegrating Iranian army due to the revolution and to the stoppage of supplies by the US. Iraq's aims were nationalist: to reverse concessions wrenched from Iraq by Iran during the Kurdish revolt over the Shatt-al-Arab, Iraq's only outlet to the sea; and to regain control over Khuzistan – an area inside the Iranian border of Arabic speaking population. Iraq was also afraid that the Islamic revolution might spread among its large Shi'ite population in the south.

The war which was started from Iraqi nationalist considerations served, however, the interests of the pro-Western oil regimes and the two super powers. As long as the two major military forces in the area were occupied in sapping each other's strength, they could not afford to foment other major troubles. The two regimes, which did not fit into the bi-polar structure but were independent because of oil, were therefore 'helped' by both super powers and their allies to destroy themselves. The helpers, meanwhile, pocketed hefty profits from arms' sales. The Soviet Union first supplied Iran and then supplied Iraq, the West supplied both all along. We know now that US intelligence helped to avert an Iranian victory against Iraq and allowed private sales of US arms from as early as spring 1982.[7] The US support for Iran was also started earlier than had been thought, only a few months after Reagan took office in 1981. The help was covert and illegal, without the knowledge of the legislative branch (the Iran-Contra affair), via a third party, Israel, which had its own axe to grind against Iraq and seized the opportunity to destroy Iraqi nuclear installations in June 1981. The result of this help was to prolong the war and thus make it more expensive and more costly in human lives. Another effect was a build up of armies and weaponry on a scale and sophistication never before seen in semi-peripheral armies.

Iraq, however, was not a dependable ally, and this worried the US and Saudi Arabia. It was Iraq which, after being pushed back by Iran in 1982, started the attacks on oil tankers in the Gulf, threatening the international flow of oil. There was little the US could do about this at the time. The Rapid Deployment Force was in its embryonic stage. The US now needed an alternative infrastructure other than Iran to be able to move large forces quickly and to prepare for battle: ports, airfields, electronic surveillance, control and command posts and stored equipment. It was not until 1982 that the Saudis were willing to pay and host the Americans. What started as the sale of five AWACS planes developed secretly under Reagan and the new king, Fahd, into the most sophisticated battle infrastructure anywhere outside the USA. Construction was not completed until 1990 at an estimated total staggering cost of $200 billion.[7]

Three points follow from this analysis: 1) With the collapse of the Shah there was no proxy powerful enough to defend the Gulf oil regimes – and the USA had to get involved directly. The Iraq-Iran war provided the interval necessary to get organised. 2) US performance in the Gulf war in 1991 depended on the preexistence of a mammoth infrastructure and could not be replicated instantly in many other areas. 3) The size and cost of the Gulf infrastructure, described as 'the single greatest investment in [military] infrastructure in the history of man',[8] coupled with the continuity of turmoil in the area, means a long term future US presence in the Gulf and commitment to the Saudi regime – since its collapse, and the takeover of these installations by an 'unruly' regime, would threaten the stability of the whole area.

The end of the Iran-Iraq war was long overdue. It had run its course by June 1982, when the Iraqi invasion of Iran was repulsed. Iraq proposed a ceasefire, but Iran, now backed by arms from the US, declined. A stratagem was devised at this point, first by Iraq (September 1982) and then by Iran (May 1984), to involve 'Oil' in the war. Hitting ships, loading facilities, refineries, was to hit the enemy's economic ability to carry on with the war – but also to cause worry to the powers 'out there', and to make them also want to end the war. Instead, Kuwait and Saudi Arabia increased their pumping of oil, insulating the world economy from the effects of the war. Attacks on shipping were not confined to Western interests. The first superpower vessel to be hit was Soviet – by Iranian speed boats, followed shortly, in May 1987, by a missile (French) attack by Iraq, on the *USS Stark*, killing 32 American sailors. Another front opened by Iran was to attack clandestinely Kuwait and Saudi Arabia – Iraq's backers. The most famous was the attack on the Grand Mosque in Mecca in July 1987, but there were many others before. Bombardment of cities was started by Iraq: ironically, the Scuds were provided by the Soviets but the mobile launchers, the same as those used later against Riyadh and Tel-Aviv, were purchased from the USA. Gas, missile and nuclear technologies were sold to Iraq (and Iran) mainly by the West.

The last phase of the war, 1987–1988, was characterised by the US being drawn, more and more, into direct hostilities and military action against Iran: the US starts escorting Kuwaiti ships, Iran mines the Gulf, US forces attack Iranian vessels, Iran attacks a US tanker; in retaliation the US destroys Iranian offshore oil rigs, Iranian mining continues, the US attacks more oil rigs and Iranian military vessels and expands escort to other nationalities' ships in the Gulf. In a rebuke to Reagan's statement on the limits of sovereign actions of governments, Khomeini declares, on January 7th 1988, that the government has the power unilaterally to revoke any lawful agreements that are 'in contravention of the interests of Islam and the country'.[9] Saudi Arabia severs diplomatic relations with Iran in April. On July 3rd the *USS Vincennes* shoots down Iranian Air flight 655 over the Straits of Hormuz; 290 civilian passengers are killed. On the 18th of July Iran accepts UN resolution 598 calling for a ceasefire and the war stops on the 20th of August 1988. By the end of the war it seemed as if the US, Iraq, Saudi Arabia and Kuwait were on the same side – against Iran – and that the USA was on a war path with Iran. The Soviet Union was not on any side in the dispute: it too stood for the right for free navigation in the Gulf, but was already deep in internal trouble.

The war which could have taken place between Iran and the US did not happen; instead it was waged against Iraq. Maybe it was because the Iranians knew when to back down. Perhaps, and this is just a speculation, they had more sense than Saddam, two years later, to understand that the US was 'after them' and was looking for an excuse to deliver a mortal blow to a regime which caused the US much trouble and embarrassment. After all, Saddam had reason to believe that the oil regimes and the US owed him gratitude for 'sacrificing himself' for the sake of the world oil order. He too knew that there was nobody else who could have engaged the Iranians at that point. Perhaps this explains his anger with Kuwait's arrogance – demanding back the debt which he owed them! Egypt performed much lesser services for the US during the 1991 war yet half of its debt to the US, the World Bank and the Gulf states was erased. Saddam could reasonably have hoped that the Saudis and Kuwait would return to their OPEC quotas and stop lowering oil prices by over-production, so that Iraq could recoup some lost revenues from the war years. He had reason, perhaps, to believe that his dispute with Kuwait over the ownership of the Rummeilla oil field, an old dispute, could now be settled on better terms. There was something strange about the Kuwaiti arrogant, self confident, stance to their negotiations with Iraq prior to the invasion. All this does not exonerate Saddam. The way he let himself be manipulated into this situation is extraordinary.

In 1992 Iran is now the stronger power, and rearming. Can it, after the Iraqi experience, feel safe that another adventure will not be schemed against its Islamic regime in due course? Maybe Saddam still has a role to play in the next act in this drama? Of late there have been rumours about a second strike against Iraq, rumours about a possible action against Libya. Sudan is in the grip of a fundamentalist group and the media claims that it has now become the latest haven for international terrorism. What about Algeria, where democracy has been prevented from taking its fundamentalist course? Tunis is straining to halt fundamentalism as is Jordan and the PLO. Egypt recently had to forbid a publication as blasphemous in order to placate its fundamentalist movement and so even does Saudi Arabia. Lebanon is not quiet yet, there too Shi'ite pro-Iran movements are still very active. On the secular nationalist pole Syria's Assad, more careful than Saddam, has not yet become a reliable ally of the United States.

In other words, even after the Gulf War, the Middle East remains the most dangerous region in the world, not least, of course, because of the continuing ramifications of the Arab-Israeli conflict. The strategic importance of the Middle East to the West made it the major recipient and purchaser of arms in the world. The oil revenues and the Israeli-Arab conflict were – and remain – the major causes for this arms build up. The result is the existence of some of the largest armies and the most technologically advanced arsenals outside the major powers. Nor did the end of the Cold War put an end to nationalist strife in the area. Although the modes and scale of the Israeli-Arab conflict were greatly enhanced by the rivalry between the superpowers it does not have its roots in the Cold War but precedes it.

A major shift towards the West among the Arab states confronting Israel started long before the collapse of the Soviet Union. The Israeli-Egyptian peace accord of 1979 was part of the US containment policy towards the Soviet Union as it removed the most important Arab military force from the conflict's power equation. By doing this, the US neutralised the ability of the Soviet-backed Arab countries to conduct war against Israel. Israel, now under the ever more militantly nationalist government of Begin, utilised this peace for intensified absorption and settlement of the 1967 occupied territories. The resistance of the Palestinians was dealt with by the Israeli invasion of Lebanon in 1982. This was meant to destroy the power base of the PLO and was colluded in by the Reagan regime which perceived the PLO as a 'terrorist' danger to the New World Order. The Israelis also offered the US their services to restore the old order in civil war-torn Lebanon. Israel failed to restore the Maronites to power, but it managed to deal the PLO a major blow. Ironically, instead of Palestinian influence in the south of Lebanon, there arose the Iranian backed fundamentalist 'Hezbollah' organisation which extended its influence in this mainly Shi'ite populated territory. American marines who landed in Lebanon in 1983 failed where the Israelis failed. But Syria came to an agreement with the US about quelling the civil war in return for control over most of Lebanon (the south remains under Israeli control). The continuation of the improvement in relations between Syria and the US was seen in Syria's participation in the allied forces against Saddam and in its taking part in the peace process with Israel.

The PLO, weakened after its withdrawal from Lebanon and at a political dead end with the Intifada, had made its bid towards the US in 1988 by renouncing the armed struggle and by its willingness to recognise Israel in return for a formula which would eventually lead to a Palestinian state in the West Bank and Gaza. But while Syria has managed to reap some tangible results from its rapprochement with the US, the PLO has not. Palestinian frustration was expressed in an anti-American position during the Gulf War. Israel has gained most, in the short run, from the collapse of the Soviet Union. First and foremost, the huge wave of 450,000 Soviet Jewish immigrants was the first demographically significant addition to the ratio of Jews to Arabs in more than two decades. This wave has sowed panic among Palestinians and has increased Israeli resistance to a compromise. Second, the collapse of the Soviet bloc and Soviet influence in the world has brought the renewal and establishment of diplomatic relations between Israel and many countries which either never had relations with Israel, or severed their relations with it after 1967. Israel is no longer the pariah among nations that it was, and this without any changes in its policies. The new situation was best demonstrated in the rescinding of the UN resolution which equated Zionism with racism. As a result, Israel feels confident it may persist in its settlement policy and reject any withdrawal from the occupied territories. In line with American requirements for the New World Order, it participates in 'peace talks' but has hitherto man-oeuvred successfully to forestall and delay any progress. Both the elections in Israel and the elections in the US will effectively postpone any signifi-cant pressure on Israel until 1993.

While Israel appears to go along with the US, it has its own nationalist agenda which in the longer run is not consistent with the stabilisation of the Middle East. Moreover, the persistence of the Israeli-Arab conflict is a major factor in the continuation and escalation of an arms race in the area. Any agenda which is ostensibly part of the new world order's orientation towards disarmament cannot ignore Israel's nuclear project – which is far more advanced than any in the area. While Israel is quick to blame others for selling technologies for arms production to Iraq and other countries in the area, it is itself the main beneficiary of such sales, as well as the major arms producer in the area. Israel is now building a second nuclear strike capability, including anti-ballistic missiles (financed by the Star War project), its own military satellite, and submarines capable of carrying nuclear missiles (built and financed by Germany). Israel's chemical and bacteriological capabilities are also second to none in the Middle East. Any pressure by the US on Arab and Islamic countries in the area to disarm, which does not include Israel, is merely hypocritical. Arabs have rightly complained that while the US discourse on the New World Order is couched in universalistic terms it is not applied universally.

The Soviet Union or Communism have never been at the heart of the Gulf disputes. These only obfuscated another issue which, with the disappearance of the Cold War, is becoming very clear. At issue is the state and its position in the international capitalist order. To put it differently: the problem is 'the taming of the state', the lesser states, that is, and their subordination to the needs and rules of the World Market. The era of the bi-polar world order coincided with the period of establishment of the majority of the states of the world. The dismantling of the colonial order and the epoch of National Liberation started between the two world wars; however, since World War II it has gained momentum to produce, for the first time in history, a world of states, or, the state on a world scale. The concomitance of the process of National Liberation with the Cold War influenced both: National Liberation became part of the content and meaning of the Cold War, and vice versa, the Cold War influenced the forms of the new states and their behaviour internally and externally.

The existence of the two political systems in global competition – with an ability for Mutually Assured Destruction – gave many new states a certain leeway and freedom of behaviour. They could find shelter, or at least support – political, economic and military – in the fold of the other bloc. At the same time, the ability of each superpower to impose uniformity on those within its sphere was limited by the competition between the superpowers and the possibility of switching sides. Within each bloc there evolved a cluster of 'core' states and 'peripheral' states. The core states were the ones that could become a *casus belli* between the superpowers; on the other hand, 'core' states were expected to resemble more uniformly the political and economic blueprint of the hegemonic power within their bloc. They had less freedom of internal change and mutation – lest the change be suppressed. States on the rim of the blocs varied quite a lot. Internal and regional conflicts and the need for credit, or all three, were the main dynamic forces which pushed new states towards one super power or another. In all, bi-polarity made possible a world zoo of states with a wide variety of species. This plethora, itself an outcome of the Cold War, has been perceived, however, as an outcome of 'Independence' and created fierce expectations in many new states of norms of freedom of the state, internally towards its own people, and externally towards other states, as an unrestricted sovereign.

This belief in the 'rights of states', was pursued by some regimes more vigorously than by others. These regimes, despite their often self pro-claimed 'socialisms' were first and foremost Statist and Nationalist. Many internal policies, such as nationalisation of natural resources, state mono-polies, a large state economic sector, agrarian reforms, health, housing and education projects, state regulated markets, mass mobilisation and one party systems were expedient 'Strong State' building strategems. These 'rights of states' often clashed with 'rights of the markets' and produced tensions or confrontations between these regimes and the main capitalist countries. Within a bi-polar conception of the world this was taken by many western socialists as a vindication of the 'progressive' nature of these regimes and of the need to defend them. This attitude which had its heyday in the 1960s in Western Maoism and Third Worldism still exists but it has become much weaker in the absence of a 'socialist bloc'. 'Markets' express disagreements with states through investment, loans and mercantile choices. After the Second World War, through the Bretton Woods regime, more powerful tools of international monetary control over states were created. These mechanisms, however, necessitated the participation and involvement of states. Since the 1970s, because of the growing debt-crisis, the IMF and the World Bank, controlled by the industrialised capitalist states, became powerful tools of controlling states and their international socio-economic policies. The GATT and Free Trade agreements further restricted the rights of states as free economic actors. The UN and its various organisations also serve the function of limiting intra- and inter- state actions. The UN, however, depends on states and its weakness since 1945 to the end of the 1980s was itself a reflection of the divided bi-polar world order. The self-neutralising effects of the Cold War on the ability of the UN to reach decisions and to implement them left states much leeway and freedom of action.[10]

All these tools were not sufficient to safeguard 'rights of markets' against states as they lacked sharp teeth – the compulsory aspect associated with coercive ability. That is one of the reasons why capital remains, in the last instance, dependent even in the epoch of supranational and multinational corporations, on states. When it comes to enforcement there is still no substitute. Supra-national interests lack an autonomous political apparatus; they must rely on the might of states to work on their behalf. Although the state, historically, precedes capitalism, capitalism works through states and, hitherto, has not been able to dispense with their services.[11]

Despite the emphasis on economic measures to bring maverick states back in line, the major capitalist states never flinched from showing their muscle. As a matter of fact, after a lull in the 1970s, as a result of Vietnam, they escalated their overt military activities against other states in the 1980s: the US in Lebanon, Grenada, Bolivia, Libya, Iran and Panama; France in Lebanon, against Libya in Chad, in New Caledonia; Britain against Argentina. All these operations were against semi-peripheral or peripheral countries and were not directly related to bi-polar disputes. Moreover, they were taken against states within the rim of their own sphere or against regimes not associated with the other superpower. Operations against states within the other superpower's sphere tended to be covert.

With the collapse of the Soviet bloc the conditions which made possible a certain pluralism of forms of states have changed. The capitalist countries do not need any more to contain themselves and the pressure for disciplining and reforming the behaviour of third world states has increased. The direction of the demands being raised is to curtail the legitimacy, the ability and the effects of the use of force by small and medium states in international relations. These refer to economic or territorial gains by force, to the ability to purchase or produce arms, in particular arms of mass destruction and to the use of covert military operations against other states (state terrorism). Another direction allegedly sought for the New World Order is to pressure states to respect the human rights of their populations and to push towards democratic regimes.

These directions, if pursued, will erode two aspects of the idea of sovereignty: the ability of the state to wage war and the limitation of the legitimacy of the use of coercion by the state internally. These, coupled with economically enforced policies of self-regulating markets via the IMF and the World Bank, and further extensions of free trade agreements, forecast a world of territorial states but of states devoid of most of the powers attached to the idea of nationalism and national self determination.

Furthermore, these ideas, noble as they may appear to be, do not pertain equally to all states. They will amount to taking away powers fiercely coveted and hard-won by many new states. These policies will be viewed by many states as the further concentration and centralisation of force, along with wealth, in the hands of a few rich capitalist states, increasing inequality and diminishing the chances of others to improve their standing in this hierarchy of states. Of all the states who will resist these measures, the most effective ones will be regimes which have the economic means to invest heavily in amassing power to build strong states. Some of them are in the Middle East; and Iraq is likely to be one of them.

NOTES

1. M. Kidron, D. Smith: *The New State of War and Peace*, N.Y. 1991, p. 23.
2. Ibid., p. 7.
3. C. Tilly: 'War and State Power' *In Middle East Report* July–August 1991, p. 38.
4. H. Beblawi, G. Luciani (eds.): *The Rentier State*, London, 1987; G. Salame (ed.): *The Foundation of the Arab State*, London, 1987; B. Berberoglu (ed.): *Power and Stability in the Middle East*, London, 1989.
5. C. F. Doran, S. W. Buck: *The Gulf, Energy and Global Security*, Boulder, 1991; C. A. Kupchan: *The Persian Gulf and the West – The Dilemmas of Security*, London, 1987.
6. Doran and Buck, *op.cit.*
7. *The New York Times*, Jan. 26th, 1992, p1 + 4.
8. S. Armstrong: 'Eye of the Storm' In *Mother Jones*, Nov–Dec 1991, pp. 31–35.
9. Doran and Buck, *op.cit.* p. 217.
10. See, for instance, R. Vernon and D. L. Spar, *Beyond Globalism*, N.Y. 1989; C. Chase-Dunn: *Global Formation*, Camb, 1989.
11. See debate on N. Harris's *National Liberation*, London, 1990; in *International Socialism* No. 50, 51, 53, 1991.

RUPTURED FRONTIERS:
THE TRANSFORMATION OF THE US-LATIN AMERICAN SYSTEM

Roger Burbach*

The United States is intent on consolidating a new order in the Western Hemisphere, an order that is embodied in the emergence of the North American Free Trade Association and the Enterprise for the Americas. George Bush made the Enterprise and free trade the cornerstone of US-Latin American policy when he toured Venezuela, Brazil and other countries in South America in December 1990, calling for an end to trade barriers and the free movement of capital from Alaska to the Straits of Magellan.

This new order marks a shift in the terms of economic exploitation and intervention by the United States. Under the banner of neo-liberalism and free trade, US governmental and corporate leaders, in conjunction with other hemispheric elites, are not only intensifying their exploitation of the continent's human and material resources, but are spreading immiseration and poverty more widely than ever. Indeed, this condition now severely affects the societies of the north as well as those of the south.

Little attention is devoted to this transformation of the US-Latin American system because, unlike the US counter-revolutionary wars in Central America in the 1980s, today's interventionism does not pit US-backed armies against guerrillas or national liberation movements. This is a 'quiet interventionism' that aims at controlling societies from within and at altering their economies in fundamental ways. The US-sponsored drug wars, the repression and deportation of migrants, the IMF and US-backed slashing of social budgets, and the efforts to impose a continental economic union that benefits big capital while confining labour to its geographic boundaries and paying the lowest possible wages – these are forms of intervention that are just as debilitating and devastating for the Latin peoples as the more formal counter-insurgency interventions of the past.

The drug wars illustrate how social, economic and political intervention are increasingly intermeshed. Some critics of US policy argue that the United States is now particularly concerned with the flow of drugs, that it is actually using the drug issue as a guise for intervening militarily.' In

Colombia and Peru the United States is opposed to the guerrilla movements, and in fact some of the US drug war funds have gone for military training to combat armed guerrillas in Colombia and Sendero Luminoso in Peru.

But it can also be argued that the United States is just as determined to eliminate the drug lords of Latin America because they are autonomous economic actors, capable of accumulating substantial amounts of capital independently of the transnational corporations. Colombia is a case in point. Although US investment in Colombia declined in the 1980s, the country had one of the highest economic growth rates in Latin America.[2] Much of the internal investment for this growth came from the drug trade, as the cartels invested in industry, agriculture and commerce in order to launder and legitimise their drug fortunes.

The US military intervention in Panama can also be viewed from this perspective. There the United States intervened not under the old anti-communist banner, but to remove a US trained military ruler and his entourage because they had dared to set up their own system of profiteering and enrichment that was not endorsed by the US government.[3] In sum, under the guise of an anti-drug campaign, the United States is intervening in a variety of ways. The drug issue enables the United States to beat down economic and political challengers, to step into rural areas where peasants and guerrillas are engaging in 'illegal activities' and more generally, it gives the US a new rationale for confronting hemispheric adversaries now that the 'communist menace' has collapsed.

An even more basic change in the Americas is that a common form of exploitation is now taking place on a hemispheric-wide basis, affecting US society as well as the southern countries. There is no longer one totally different pattern of investment and exploitation for Latin America and another for the United States. International boundaries have been broken down in the quest for markets and cheap labour resources. 'Capital flight' now affects the United States as industries are moved southward, social services gutted, and society stratified into two tiers, one rich and opulent, the other increasingly marginalised and poor. In the last 15 years, the income of the top 5% of the US population has increased by over 50% when adjusted for inflation, while that of the lower 60% of the population has declined. Today, one in five children in the United States live in poverty.[4]

Moreover parts of US society are becoming subject to kinds of repression and control not dissimilar from what more typically occurs in Latin America. Civil liberties are increasingly restricted, repression is intensified at the community level in the name of stopping drugs and crime, and there are increasing moral crusades over issues such as abortion and sexual behaviour. In California for example, the state supreme court is ordering that prisoners on death row be executed more quickly, and as the videotaped beating of Rodney King reveals, the Los Angeles police today are as racist and repressive as the stereotyped sheriffs of the south were a generation ago. Be it in the United States, Panama, or Mexico, a system of law and order is being espoused that attempts to contain social unrest, monitors and controls the movement of peoples, and seeks to impose a system of social values and beliefs that serves the needs and interests of those in power.

The Drive for NAFTA and the Enterprise

The intensified exploitation and the new interventionism in the hemisphere are rooted in fundamental challenges that the US ruling class is facing. As is now commonly recognised, the United States may have won the cold war, but it is losing the war as the world's leading economic power. The rise of Japan, Germany and a unified Western Europe as dynamic power houses means that the United States is no longer the world's hegemonic economic power.

Simultaneously, US business is encountering difficulties in accumulating capital at home. The drop in domestic savings destined for investment, the crisis of the savings and loan and banking sectors, the decline of the US economic infrastructure, the enormous indebtedness of all sectors of the economy, and the gyrations of the stock market – these are critical signs that all is not well for the US bourgeoisie.

The push for a North American continental common market is an effort to keep Japanese and European capital at bay during this difficult period while the United States builds up its economic clout. As a columnist in *Business Week* pointed out, there are similarities between NAFTA (North American Free Trade Association) and earlier efforts by the British to maintain their empire through preferential trade agreements.[5] The United States, by locking other countries on the continent into its economic system, hopes to be in a better position to exclude and compete with Japanese and European capital. And even if full scale trade wars do not break out and the latest round of GATT negotiations on lowering international tariff barriers are successful, NAFTA will enable US corporate capital to take advantage of the cheap labour resources to the south and to better compete for markets on a global level.[6]

The drive for NAFTA and the Enterprise for the Americas is also a response to basic changes occurring within the Western hemisphere itself. Across the Americas, the boundaries of the nation-state are being ruptured. Migrants, commodities and capital now flow across the northern and southern continents and the Caribbean with an intensity never experienced before. Virtually all social classes are contributing to this process: the business classes, led by US capital, which seek better markets and investments; the popular masses that ignore national boundaries in their quest for economic opportunities and for an escape from the social and political turmoil gripping many of their homelands, and the middle and professional classes, which for better or worse, are purveyors of cultural and social attitudes that cross national boundaries, either through professional and job activities, or simply through tourism and travel.

The governments of the individual states in this hemispheric system do exercise a semblance of control over these hemispheric processes. But their historic dominance is eroding. NAFTA and the Enterprise for the Americas are explicit attempts by the US ruling class, in conjunction with other leaders in the Americas, to exert and maintain their control over these internationalised social and economic dynamics. It is no secret that NAFTA's objectives are to slow the flow of migration to the United States and to enable transnational capital to expand its control over the region's markets and labour power.

From the perspective of the United States, Canada will play a largely dependent role in this process. With an economy and a population smaller than that of California, Canada is to be intermeshed economically with the greater US system. Canadian raw materials, particularly petroleum and lumber, are to be placed at the disposal of this system, and in return for their cooperation, Canadian capitalists are at least in principle to be granted 'equal rights' to participate in joint ventures, to invest in the United States and to help pillage the rest of the continent.

As for the current negotiations to extend the Canada-US agreement into a continental wide system, President Bush during a state visit by Mexican President Salinas de Gortari in December, 1991, declared that he was determined to push ahead with an accord in 1992 in spite of earlier qualms about forcing such an agreement through Congress during a presidential election year. A few Democrats are raising questions about the impact of NAFTA on US labour, but by and large both Republican and Democratic politicians are supportive of NAFTA, as evidenced in Congressional support for the 'fast track' negotiations between the United States and Mexico. Certainly there is little opposition among the region's governments, as nationalistic policies – once the ideological life-blood of regimes, such as the one in Mexico – are tossed out of the window with little political opposition.

The reality, however, is that both NAFTA and the Enterprise for the Americas project may do little to stabilize the hemisphere. In fact they may contribute to even greater social and economic dislocation. Because NAFTA and the Enterprise are built on a foundation of intensified economic exploitation, they offer no real social or political vision for dealing with the growing social and economic problems that are afflicting the bulk of the hemisphere's populace.

Canada, the first country to begin continental integration with the United States in 1989, has already lost manufacturing jobs as big capital works both sides of the countries' common border. Environmentalists, some labour leaders, and even a few local business groups in the United States are concerned about the impact of economic integration with Mexico. Opposition to NAFTA and the Enterprise at the grass roots level will only grow as the adverse impact of corporate-led economic integration is felt throughout the hemisphere.

Neo-Liberalism and the Origins of Crisis

The origins of NAFTA and the Enterprise are to be found in a decade-long economic crisis that has afflicted the Americas, both north and south. In Latin America, the 1980s are commonly referred to as the 'lost decade'. Per capita growth rates during the 1980s were stagnant or even negative some years. By 1990 the per capita GDP of Latin America and the Caribbean had regressed to 1977 levels.[7]

During the Reagan years, neo-liberal theorists and monetarists were fairly successful in putting forth the view that the lost decade was the fault of the Latin American countries. They argued that for years the Latin American governments engaged in irresponsible economic policies by erecting protectionist barriers, subsidising state enterprises, and engaging in wasteful social spending.[8] This interpretation is a flagrant distortion of reality to obscure the real origins of the economic crisis that hit Latin America in the 1980s. It conveniently ignores the fact that from 1960 to 1980 Latin America's economic policies stimulated both internal growth and exports. The increase in the gross domestic product averaged 5.6% per annum, and over all the region's economy grew by 200% during those two decades.[9] This growth rate was more than double that of the United States, and only a few countries in east Asia matched Latin America's economic performance.[10]

The truth of the matter is that the economic crisis of the 1980s is the responsibility of transnational capital, the US state, and the military regimes that held power in most of Latin America in the 1970s. It is true, as the neo-liberals argue, that the huge international debt burden and the inability of the Latin American nations to repay that debt led to the liquidity crisis of the 1980s and the inability to attract capital and foment economic growth. But why did the Latin American nations become insolvent? Was it due to their protectionism? To their attempts to develop domestic industries? Or to their wasteful spending on social programmes?

Any serious student of economic and political developments in the 1970s is forced to recognise that if any particular actors bear responsibility for the crisis of the 1980s, it is the international bankers and the military rulers. (One major exception to this is the Mexican regime, which will be discussed later.) From 1970 to 1982, a period when military regimes either controlled or took control of over three-fourths of Latin America's population, the debt of the region jumped from $25 billion to $318 billion.[11] Wasteful state spending did occur during this period. But much of it was due to increased military budgets, corruption within the military itself, or subsidies for pet industries that were run by the military or by favoured sectors of the local bourgeoisie. The Argentine military leaders, who controlled the country from 1976 to 1983, demonstrated a particular ability to run their country into the ground with wasteful military spending capped by an inept war in the Malvinas islands.

The transnational bankers were more than willing to look the other way, or in many cases to lend funds for dubious economic projects. The 1970s was a period in which the international banks were flush with capital due to the surge of petrodollars in the world's financial system, and the willingness of the central banks of the developed world to pump funds into the banking system. There was an abundance of banking capital, and Latin America, which was rich in resources and had demonstrated a capacity for sustained economic growth, became a major target for the banks to invest their funds.

In spite of the irresponsible policies of the bankers and the generals, the Latin American countries (and other third world borrowers) might have avoided a liquidity crisis if the international markets had not dealt the third world a major economic blow in the early 1980s. The prices of raw materials and agricultural products – coffee, cotton, bauxite, copper, tin, bananas and sugar – the mainstays of the Latin export markets, dropped precipitously. Furthermore, the price of manufactured and industrial products, the major exports of the developed world, continued to rise, leading to a decline in the terms of trade for commodity producing nations. In 1982, the non-oil exporting countries were buying two thirds as much with their goods as in 1970.[12]

One factor leading to the decline in the terms of trade was that a significant portion of the international capital lent in the 1970s went to expand agricultural and mineral production. The Latin Americans were simply following the rules and logic of the capitalist market place in that they sought to expand their exports in order to repay the loans and to accumulate profits and capital for their own economic growth and development. But virtually all third world nations were following the same economic logic. As a result, by the 1980s there was a glut on the world market of most primary commodities and this of course led to falling prices. Moreover, the industrialised capitalist countries were developing manufactured or synthetic substitutes that curtailed the need for some third world products. The classic example is the use of artificial sweeteners and corn syrups which significantly curtailed the need for sugar cane.

In the early 1980s, reports by the World Bank, the IMF, private banks, and even government agencies acknowledged that the basic problems confronted by Latin America and other third world countries were due to factors in the international market place that were beyond the control of third world governments. But the rise of neo-liberal doctrine during the

Reagan and Thatcher years quickly shifted the blame for the crisis to the third world nations. Standing logic on its head, neo-liberalism argued that what was needed to resolve the crisis was not coordinated international efforts to regulate overproduction, or a moratorium on debt payments, but an end to any and all types of regulation. Only more of the same – the free market – they argued could turn the economies of the third world around.

As the 1980s wore on, most of the countries in Latin America bowed to the dictates of neo-liberal doctrine and the pressures of institutions like the IMF and the World Bank. They dropped their tariff barriers, sold off state industries, and basically threw their economies open to foreign capital. Initially banking and transnational capital did not respond to the prostration of the Latin American countries. It recognised that due to the so-called 'debt overhang' and the conditions of the international market there was little or no profit to be made by financing or investing in Latin America.

Indeed, throughout the mid and late 1980s capital was sucked out of Latin America by the transnationals – particularly the banks – and capital flight rather than capital investment was the overriding characteristic of the decade. Resources flowed from the south to the north in ever larger quantities while domestic investment and consumption shrank. In 1989, Latin America and the Caribbean transferred current net resources abroad equal to 10% of their gross domestic product. As the UN Economic Commission on Latin America proclaimed, during the 1980s 'the countries of Latin America were net exporters of vast amounts of financial resources to the developed countries, a phenomenon that thwarts the aspirations of its peoples and confutes the principles of development and international co-operation.'[13]

The results were devastating for the peoples of Latin America. The region as a whole could not import the capital equipment it needed to undertake new development projects, all social services were curtailed, infant mortality rates increased, street crime and delinquency jumped in virtually every country, education at all levels declined, and most importantly, hunger and malnutrition increased.[14] Latin America experienced not simply a lost decade but a lost generation. Millions of people who grew up or came of age in the 80s lacked the basic health, nutritional and educational necessities needed to effectively participate in the region's development.

US Capital as Economic Scavenger
What is little noted is how capital, and particularly US capital, began to pillage the continent during the 1980s as never before. It is not merely that the bankers extracted vitally needed financial resources out of the continent. US industrial capital also stepped up its exploitation in certain selected areas of the hemisphere, especially in the latter part of the 1980s.

The devaluation of most Latin currencies – under the aegis of IMF austerity programmes – meant that the cost of labour power in the south dropped from the perspective of the transnationals.

As a result investment jumped in labour intensive industries, especially the *maquiladora* factories which utilise cheap labour in border areas or free trade zones to export to US markets. Overall, US direct investments in all of Latin America and the Caribbean expanded by 37% from 1986–1990.[15] This is a modest increase compared to US direct investments in the developed countries of the world (Western Europe, Australia, etc.) where US investment rose by almost 70% during the same period. However, when the investments are broken down by country, one finds that a chosen few in Latin America and the Caribbean were receiving the bulk of US investments. The most notable expansion occurred in Mexico, where US direct investments doubled from 1986 to 1990, from $4.6 billion to $9.3 billion. The Dominican Republic and Chile had relatively higher increases in US investment (although the absolute amounts were significantly less), while Argentina, Peru, Columbia, Paraguay, Ecuador and other countries actually experienced net declines in US investment.[16]

What accounts for this pattern of US investment? *Business Week* in 1988 already detected the thrust of the new wave of US capital expansion. In Mexico it noted: 'After the debt crisis and peso collapse in 1982, cheap Mexican wages triggered a *maquiladora* explosion.'[17] Other sources reveal that the expansion continued unabated throughout the entire decade. In 1982 there were 600 maquiladora plants, in 1986, 850, and in 1990, 1,500. The number of workers employed in the maquiladores leapt from 125,000 in 1982 to 450,000 in 1990, over one tenth of Mexico's industrial work force.[18] Even *Business Week* was struck by what this meant for the Mexican workers: 'US employers turned to the most vulnerable – and cheapest – workers: young women and girls. Women represent two-thirds of the maquiladora labour force, and many are teenagers. The result is a labour force that's miserably underpaid – even for Mexico.'[19]

Another periodical, *South*, notes that countries in the Caribbean and Central America were trying to follow Mexico's example by setting up industrial tax free zones to attract foreign capital. The Dominican Republic has been particularly determined, setting up eight such zones for foreign investors.[20] These Dominican zones even preyed upon their weaker neighbours on the same island – Haiti – drawing away some US investors who did not like the political and economic conditions there after the fall of the Duvalier regime.

The other major country, Chile, had a slightly different attraction for US capital. There, the reign of General Augusto Pinochet had smashed the labour unions and driven down the cost of labour. However, it was not the *maquiladores* that flourished in Chile but the fresh fruit industry. Low wages, combined with Chile's capacity to produce fruits for the US winter market, made agriculture a particularly attractive area for investment. Pinochet also trumped most other Latin American countries in offering easy access to Chile's natural resources. The country's virgin hardwood forests, some of the last on the continent, attracted significant foreign investment.

It is these types of investment that both NAFTA and the Enterprise will foment in the Americas. The extraction of resources and the brutal exploitation of labour is certainly nothing new for foreign capital, but what differentiates these hemispheric projects from previous ones is that they do not even make a pretence of creating a more just society. Capital simply wants to go in and suck out whatever profit it can as quickly as possible. One Mexican specialist on the *maquiladora* industry observing that 'capital is being subsidised' in so far as the *maquiladores* pay no taxes, and make no investments in urban infrastructure (the workers live in abominable conditions) concludes: 'It is an open question as to whether this (*maquiladora*) process brings any real benefits for Mexico.'[21]

Until recently capital and the capitalist state often recognised that if they were successfully to exploit the third world they had to build a certain infrastructure. This was the logic behind the Alliance for Progress of the 1960s. Then it was believed that the population had to be educated to be an effective workforce, roads had to be built to move the resources to market, major water and irrigation projects were needed for the cities and agriculture, and the working population needed minimal health care and certain urban amenities to survive and reproduce. It is true that these projects and programmes did not eliminate poverty or marginality. But they did provide a limited infrastructure that helped ameliorate some of the backwardness, and at least provided a few public benefits, such as electricity, basic education, and some minimal health care.

But neo-liberal capitalism has broken with this trend in capitalist development and expansionism. It has no interest in developing the social infrastructure. Indeed its most obvious tendency is to slash all social programmes, to force societies to be 'efficient' – in other words to invest their capital exclusively in projects that have an immediate return for the capitalist class.

The Latin Americanisation of the North

Although the US led by George Bush denies it, NAFTA and the Enterprise will also intensify the exploitation of US society. US capital over the past decade has driven down the standard of living of working people in the United States as part of its global effort to maintain its own profits and wealth. The term 'Latin Americanisation' can be used to describe many regions and cities of the United States, not simply because of the increased importance of Latin immigrants, but because of the growth of poverty, homelessness, petty street merchants and beggars. US urban centres today look more and more like their Latin counterparts.

US capitalism has returned to a phase akin to that of robber baron capitalism of the late 19th century. Entire social strata in the United States are being cast aside and economically marginalised as demonstrated by the demise of the US farming class, the elimination of millions of jobs through the deindustrialisation of parts of the United States, the abject impoverishment of the ghettoes, and the growth in the ranks of poor whites and blacks stripped of the dignity they once held as members of the middle or working classes.

This brutalising phase of US capitalism has one salient characteristic that distinguishes it from the earlier era of the robber barons – it is rooted in the decline rather than the ascent of the US economic system. In the late 19th century, the new US bourgeoisie was building an industrial and economic machine that would soon surpass that of the European powers. The capital accumulated through ruthless exploitation of the US working class was by and large reinvested in steel mills, railroads, oil wells, factories and large grain exporting firms.

In the late 20th century, the US working class once again feels the tightening of exploitation by US capital, but this time the new surplus is as likely to go to support the opulent and ostentatious life styles of the rich as it is to be reinvested in productive enterprises. Supply side economics, the pro-business policy of the Reagan years, did not stimulate investment – it merely enabled the rich to get richer by cutting their taxes. In the corporate world, merger mania, financial speculation, and greenmail became the buzz words of the 1980s as young business executives became intent on making quick fortunes at the expense of the rest of society.

US capital, while stepping up the exploitation of its own peoples, is willing to work with the ruling classes of other countries in the Western hemisphere that accept the US rules of the game. In the early 1980s, there was significant opposition among Latin business leaders to US-imposed economic policies, particularly the austerity policies, because they often led to the collapse or depression of entire industries. But today, we are witnessing the emergence of new 'lean and mean' bourgeoisies that are willing to abide by the terms of the neo-liberal game.

Mexican entrepreneurs who once saw US capital as a threat are now willing to engage in a multiplicity of joint ventures with US transnationals. In Argentina, where the bourgeoisie has historically looked towards the British and Europe, the country's business leaders are dropping their barriers to foreign investment hoping that US capital and the Enterprise for the Americas will help resuscitate their economy. Carlos Salinas de Gortari of Mexico and Carlos Menem of Argentina, both of whom come from political parties that once stood up to US hegemony in the hemisphere, are today opening up their countries to the United States and leading their bourgeoisies and political organisations into supporting and participating in close knit working alliances with US capital.

What accounts for the abandonment of any pretence at nationalistic policies by the Latin American elites? Fundamentally, international capital boxed them in, leaving them no alternative but openly to play the neo-liberal game. In the case of Mexico, the country's economy experienced many of the problems mentioned above that led to the debt crisis. The country had borrowed heavily in the 1970s to finance many new investment projects, but then the prices of its exported commodities, including petroleum, fell significantly in the early 1980s while the interest payments on the country's debt rose.

It is true, as the monetarists assert, that the Mexican state accumulated the bulk of the debt. But as James M. Cypher points out in his *State and Capital in Mexico,* much of this debt directly benefitted the private sector. Many state investments provided a basic infrastructure needed for private investors; the funds borrowed by the state were often placed in private banks where they were available for use by anyone, including businesses that needed to buy foreign exchange for imports; even more importantly, the state often directly lent foreign exchange to private firms for investment purposes, which they then repaid to the state in devalued national currency; and finally, in some cases the more inefficient private enterprises were taken over by the state, thereby adding to the state debt since the government assumed the enterprises' loans.[22]

When Mexico found itself unable to repay this debt, the international monetary institutions and the Reagan administration insisted that they would not provide refinancing or new capital unless the government slashed social spending and sold off state enterprises. The result was a bonanza for private capital, particularly transnational capital, which bought up many of the enterprises at bargain prices.

As Cypher notes for Mexico, and as the UN Economic Commission on Latin America and the Caribbean has pointed out for Latin America in general, the capitalist classes actually deepened the liquidity crisis by sending their capital abroad to the developed world.[23] Capital flight rather than capital investment was the general rule of the Latin American business classes in the 1980s. With their own economies in severe depressions, thanks in large part to the IMF imposed austerity programmes, profits at home were meagre and they simply saw better opportunities abroad. Much of the capital sent abroad was invested in the international stock markets or deposited in interest bearing banking accounts in international banking centres like Miami. The US real estate market also drew sizeable Latin investments, particularly in California and the southwest where many 'second homes' were purchased so the upper classes could vacation or send their children for education and assimilation into the American 'way of life'. These investments dovetailed with the increased flow of Latins to the commercial and shopping centres of Miami, Houston, San Diego, and other cities, where they purchased the luxury and consumer goods that they wanted to maintain their life styles at home while the masses experienced the worst economic conditions since the 1930s.

The Potential for Rebellion

At the present moment, there are no systemic challenges to the new US order for the hemisphere. The national liberation movements have been dealt serious blows in recent years, the drug cartels have been put on notice that the United States will wage war against them, and the few remaining nationalistic political figures, like Cuauhtemoc Cardenas in Mexico, are finding it difficult to maintain a popular base as pro-US politicians consolidate their hold.[24] In the medium term it is possible that Brazil, which has not totally dismantled its protectionist barriers against transnational capital, could pose an alternative to the Enterprise for the Americas. It is attempting to form a trade bloc with Uruguay, Paraguay and Argentina. But it is unclear if this bloc will really consolidate, or merely become another regional economic formation that succumbs to foreign capital. As noted earlier, Argentina under Carlos Menem appears more intent on grovelling before US capital than in mounting a regional challenge with Brazil.

If a challenge is to appear, it is most likely to come about through a social explosion in the Latin country closest to the United States – Mexico. On the surface this would seem to be highly unlikely at present. In 1991, Mexico's economic growth was a stunning 5%, the highest after a decade of many negative growth years. This was the first time in modern history that Mexico was in the midst of an economic boom while the US was in a recession. The old saw 'when the US catches a cold, Mexico gets pneumonia' did not hold true. Moreover the boom was fed by a major influx of foreign capital – approximately $10 billion according to one estimate.[25]

However, this boom is fraught with dangers for the ruling classes of Mexico and the United States. While they were busy cutting deals and enriching themselves, the basic wages of workers actually shrank when adjusted for inflation.[26] Moreover, Salinas de Gortari has announced that the *ejidos* – the large communal tracts of land that are the backbone of subsistence for much of Mexico's peasant population – are to be abolished. The *ejidos* will be parcelled up in hopes that commercial agriculture, particularly that geared to the US market, will come to predominate.

This is an explosive social mix. A general rule in many third world upheavals is that an economic boom has laid the basis for revolution. Development is often very destabilising as it leads to increased popular demands. When these demands are frustrated or repressed, they can lead to violent upheavals. The Sandinista movement in Nicaragua for example took hold while the Somoza regime was sustaining annual average growth rates in excess of 5% per year. And in Mexico itself the revolution of 1910 occurred after a long period of economic growth and foreign investment under the regime of Porfirio Diaz. In Mexico and Nicaragua, peasants were being expelled from their land as the demand for labour power increased in the urban areas. Peasants and workers were driven in revolutionary directions by both hope and despair – despair over being forced off their lands and into an exploitative labour market, and hope because of the fact that new opportunities and possibilities were appearing before their eyes as the new middle classes and the rich flaunted their wealth.

There are very real dangers for the United States in its efforts to set up a free trade association with such a large third world country as Mexico. The very attempt to consolidate an economic union with Mexico may actually exacerbate certain tendencies that US rulers want to control. For one, it is not at all clear that stepped up US investment in Mexico will lessen the flow of immigrants to the United States. *Maquiladora* industries have now been growing along the border for almost three decades, and these have done nothing to stem the flow of immigrants. If anything they may actually accelerate immigration as Mexicans become more aware of wage differentials and economic opportunities north of the border.

Finally, the consolidation of a formal economic alliance between US and Mexican rulers does provoke its own direct contradiction – growing collaboration between those north and south of the border who are the victims of the union. One cannot make too much of this potential in the short term, for cooperation among workers and the exploited has almost always lagged far behind the growth of collaboration among the bourgeoisies and state rulers. But one cannot ignore the fact that important coalitions and groupings began to emerge for the first time in early and mid-1991 when legislation for NAFTA was being pushed through the US Congress. Environmentalists, labour unions, human rights groups and non-governmental organisations – both north and south of the border – began to hold meetings and discussions together. Canadian churches and labour unions have been particularly active in leading a continental charge against transnational capital and the NAFTA trade agreement. And Mexican national leaders, like Cuauhtemoc Cardenas, are touring the United States and Canada, hoping to find political allies his party could cooperate with in opposing US intervention in Mexico's affairs.

Growing economic integration is a fact of hemispheric life. The integration itself probably cannot be stopped but the conditions and terms of that integration provide ample grounds for carrying out political struggle. NAFTA does in fact mean an intensification of the exploitation of workers, particularly women; it means a deteriorating environment, as residents on both sides of the border already know; and it also means a crack-down by US and Mexican border police and troops as they try to control the destabilising aspects of a commercial union.

Objectively, these conditions would seem to offer new political space for those who participated in the solidarity and progressive movements of the 1980s to redirect their efforts towards the issues raised along the US-Mexican border. Only the future will tell whether a new generation of continental activists have the political will and vision to take advantage of the imperial weaknesses that are emerging with the rupturing of hemispheric frontiers.

The author wishes to thank Nora Hamilton and Devra Weber for their assistance and comments on this article.

NOTES

1. The NACLA, *Report on the Americas*, 'Coca: The Real Green Revolution,' March, 1989. See also Washington Office on Latin America (WOLA), *Clear and Present Dangers: The US Military and the War on Drugs in the Andes*, WOLA, Washington, D.C., 1991.
2. Colombia was one of only three countries in Latin America and the Caribbean with a positive per capita growth rate – Chile and the Dominican Republic were the other two. See Jorge G. Castenada, 'Latin America and the End of the Cold War,' *World Policy Journal*, Summer, 1990, p. 485.
3. John Weeks and Phil Gunson, *Panama: Made in the USA*, Latin American Bureau, London, 1991, pp. 47–55.
4. See for example, *Business Week*, 'The Rich are Richer – and America May be the Poorer,' November 18, 1991, pp. 85–88.
5. Robert Kuttner, 'A Vote for Free Trade with Mexico is a Vote Against Free Trade,' *Business Week*, May 6, 1991, p. 18.
6. *Fortune* magazine took this approach in 1989 when it argued that the three main trade blocks, led by Western Europe, Japan and the United States, could each benefit without necessarily engaging in a trade war. See *Fortune*, 'North America's New Trade Punch,' May 22, 1989, p. 127.
7. *The Economist*, 'Latin America's Economic Reforms,' October 19, 1991.
8. See A.E. Brett, *International Money and Capitalist Crisis*, Westview Press, Boulder, Colorado, 1983. See also John Toye, *Dilemmas of Development*, Basil Blackwell, Oxford, 1987.
9. G.T. Global Financial Services, G.T. Global Special Report: Latin America, The New Investment Frontier, 1991, p. 2.
10. Abraham F. Lowenthal, Partners in Conflict: *Latin American and the United States in the 1990s*, Johns Hopkins Press, Baltimore, p. 147.
11. *Statistical Abstract of Latin America*, Vol. 28, Editors: James W. Wilkie, Enrique C. Ochoa and David E. Lorey, UCLA Latin American Center Publications, University of California, Los Angeles, 1990, p. 847. See also United Nations Economic Commission on Latin America and the Caribbean, (ECLAC) *Economic Survey of Latin America and the Caribbean*, 1984, Santiago, Chile, 1986, pp. 53.
12. Op. cit. *Economic Survey of Latin America and the Caribbean*, 1983, UN Santiago, Chile, 1985, p. 39.
13. United Nations Economic Commission on Latin America and the Caribbean, *Economic Survey of Latin America and the Caribbean*, 1989, Santiago, Chile, 1991, pp. 39, 129.
14. Lowenthal, *Ibid*, p. 216.
15. Department of Commerce, *Survey of Current Business*, August, 1991, p. 104. The Netherland Antilles are excluded from these calculations because they are simply banking platforms where the flow of capital gyrates wildly.
16. *Ibid*. US investment in Chile rose from 265 million in 1986 to 1.34 billion in 1990. In the Dominican Republic, it went from 199 million to 478 million in 1990.

17. *International Business Week,* November 14, 1988 'Will the New Maquiladoras Build a Better Manana?' p. 62.

18. Roberto A. Sanchez, 'Condiciones de Vida de los Trabajadores de la Maquiladora en Tijuana y Nogales,' *Frontera Norte:* Publicacion Semestral de el Colegio de la Frontera Norte, Tijuana, Julio-Diciembre, 1990, p. 154.

19. *Op. cit., International Business Week,* p. 62.

20. *South:* Business Technology, Politics and Leisure, 'Enclave of Entente,' May, 1988, p. 44.

21. *Op. cit.,* Roberto A. Sanchez, 177–78.

22. James M. Cypher, *State and Capital in Mexico: Development Policy Since 1940,* Westview Press, Boulder, Colorado, 1990, pp. 137–43.

23. *Op. cit. Economic Survey of Latin America and the Caribbean,* 1989, Santiago, Chile, 1991, pp. 127–39.

24. For a perspective on the current state of the national liberation movements, see Roger Burbach, *The Soviet Collapse, Socialism and the National Liberation Movements,* Cross Roads, March, 1992.

25. *Los Angeles Times,* 'Despite Weak US Economy, Mexico Leaps Ahead,' by Juanita Darling, November 30, 1991, p. D1.

26. *Ibid.*

POST-COMMUNIST ANTICOMMUNISM: AMERICA'S NEW IDEOLOGICAL FRONTIERS

Joel Kovel

In the eight years since *Socialist Register* devoted an entire issue to the phenomenon of anticommunism,[1] the scarcely thinkable has happened. Anticommunism has won. No longer the ideology of one side in a global struggle, it now stands uncontested astride its fallen adversary. What are the implications of this turn of events? What happens when there is no longer a Communism to hate?

The Cold War would be better called the 'Forty Years War,' since it was anything but cold for all the Caucasian fraction of its command structure,[2] and also because its intensely ideological character suggests comparison with the Thirty Years War, last of the overtly religious bloodbaths to have wracked the Western world. The ideological fervour with which the Cold War was waged was a throwback to pre-Enlightenment days, even though the Western side, spearheaded by the United States, professed to be fighting for Enlightenment virtue against Eastern barbarism. This claim was very successfully advanced, to the extent that the terms 'democracy' and 'freedom' came to be automatically associated with 'capitalism' in the dichotomous thinking which characterised Cold War discourse.

Anticommunism manifests an ideology, which is to say, a nexus of ideas configured by power.[3] But ideologies are not spontaneous concoctions of the brain. They are produced and consumed, and have their own enduring institutional structure. The national security state which formed itself after the second World War in order to manage the fortunes of the American empire employed a rigid, Manichean logic of anticommunism in which all darkness lay on the Soviet side and all light on the side of the West. It reproduced this logic in the minds of its elites, and, combining itself with existing instruments of repression such as the FBI and new ones such as the CIA, disseminated it throughout society. For this task, the state apparatus used techniques of terror and co-optation to draw into its orbit dominant sectors of the media and academy, the artistic community and the churches. Thus much if not all of civil society became anticommunist.[4] But if anticommunism has such a structure and is more than a simple reaction to Communism, then we must expect it to remain active after the collapse of the enemy. In fact, given the deep-rootedness of the ideology and its spread throughout civil society, we would argue that it must persist beyond the expected flailings about of cold warriors and militarists seeking gainful employment in a post-Communist world.

The American Model

Anticommunism is not the reaction of capitalism to communism in the abstract but the ideological formation of a particular capitalism as it undergoes class conflict in its national setting. Each nation of the capitalist world therefore has its own anticommunism, though the anticommunisms are coordinated in a transnational campaign reflective of empire and the transnational character of capital itself.[5] In this pattern, the United States has a special standing, because of the scale of its anticommunism, suggested above, but also because of certain peculiar qualities acquired by the ideology as it has been shaped in America. It is not that anticommunism in the United States is more fervid than other varieties, or more bloodthirsty. The anticommunist slaughter of 1965 in Indonesia, for example, wiped out perhaps a million lives in a few weeks, and though crucially abetted by the CIA, did not have the hallmarks of an American operation.[6] In 1933, General Maximiliano Hernández Martínez set into motion a comparable degree of carnage in response to a Communist-inspired insurrection in El Salvador, with heartfelt encouragement but only minimal material help from the United States.[7] Many other examples could be cited, such as in Guatemala, where the regime, though installed and supported by the American security apparatus, carries on anticommunist repression with a naked ferocity which exceeds Yankee standards.[8] No doubt the United States has directly killed more in its anticommunist crusading than other capitalist states – witness Korea and Vietnam.[9] But it has done so differently, in a way which gives America special status in the annals of anticommunism.

Of the two characteristics which define this status, one is suggested by the use of the term, 'crusade,' to describe American anticommunist ventures. American anticommunism is characteristically done for a higher purpose. This is no mere embellishment disguising brutal conduct but an active component of the ideological complex itself. One might spell it out further: anticommunism, American style, cannot be separated from the redemptive quality which has marked national character since the Puritans of Massachusetts Bay set out to build a 'City Upon a Hill,' a New Jerusalem that all the nations might admire. This peculiar and very potent spiritual project of Puritanism was carried forward into the pursuit of empire as the ideology of Manifest Destiny, and internally as the Gospel of Wealth with its ethos of salvation through individualistic capitalism. When the time came to take up the challenge posed by 'Communism' in all its many manifestations, Puritan spirituality, diabolism and all, was swiftly retooled for the challenge.

A second specifically American feature is the degree to which anticommunism defines a politics of identity. In other countries, to be a communist is to be a certain kind of member of that society. Thus Chinese communists were Chinese people who happened to be Communists. One could be imprisoned or massacred for this belief, or be forced to live clandestinely, yet still retain one's national identity. Indeed, in a number of important instances such as Vietnam, Communists could claim to be the true nationalists and patriots. It has been just the opposite for the United States. Here, to be a Communist was to be *ipso facto* disloyal, a traitor pushed off the edge of society into an abyss of non-being. More significantly, since the actual role of the Communist Party in American history is, though not negligible, a minor one, any association, however remote, with the label of Communism becomes a mark of Cain. Jews, blacks, homosexuals, feminists, non-communist or even anti-communist leftists such as anarchists – whoever is out of line or 'alien' has been made to feel the sting. This mechanism became a powerful engine of conformism and the stifling of independent, critical thinking. The bizarre House Committee on Un-American Activities combined the signifier of Communism with that of 'Un-Americanism' during its thirty-year life span (from 1938 to 1968) and used the anxiety of the association to fuel a gigantic repressive apparatus. Anticommunism is therefore integral to the overall weakness and fragmentation of left politics in the United States. It is a much more effective, because internalised, means of repression, which succeeds mainly by severing the bonds between its victim and the body of society, rather than through the overt sanctions which define other varieties of anticommunism – though needless to add, these are plentiful in America as well. At the height of the inquisition, figures such as J. Edgar Hoover succeeded in instilling a positive connotation to anticommunism: one proved one's 'Americanism' not simply by avoiding Communism but by being anticommunist. It became an article of faith affirming one's membership in the body of society.[10]

In sum, anticommunism in America is no mere set of ideas. It has been, rather, the ideological aspect of a comprehensive structure of belief and inclusion, sharing certain features of religion. As would a religion, anticommunism bound the nation and its elites together and gave them a higher purpose through the evocation of an enemy called Communism. Rallying against Communism gave a boost to an uncompleted process of nation-building; while the repressive energy released through 'Americanism' made the struggle against the left all the more successful.

From an instrumental standpoint, anticommunism has succeeded wildly. Externally, the enemy has been vanquished; while internally, a nation welded together against Communism sees itself as identical with its state and ruling class. In the process, the contribution of the working class to national identity has been sacrificed, and labour becomes a near-negligible political force.[11] Anticommunism became therefore more than a mobilisation against the enemy; it has been the signifier of a whole society organised about its terms – the anticommunist society. A splendid triumph for business, no doubt. But at what cost? And what lies before this anticommunist society after its designated enemy has ceased to exist?

New Ideological Frontiers

We must qualify at the outset: the designated enemy has not entirely ceased to exist. The United States security apparatus still finds him here and there, and most of all where he has been for the past thirty two years, stuck in their throat in Havana. The dynamics of Castro-hating in the United States are still active, embedded in a nucleus of rabidly anticommunist exiles and the right wing of the Republican Party. They have never once stopped trying to strangle or decapitate the Cuban revolution, and even today, when Cuba is suffering severe miseries and is no longer a regional revolutionary influence, they still demand Fidel's scalp as tribute. Hence the well-known implacability of United States policy towards Cuba, joined wholeheartedly by the Free Press. Given the salubrious effect of a military escapade on Bush's flagging domestic political fortunes (a definite if minor cause of the Gulf War), one can never rule out an invasion, especially as the Soviets are no longer a regional factor. This remains unlikely, however, given the risks posed by fierce resistance; and in all likelihood, Castro and Cuba will be left dangling in the wind, a cautionary tale for those who contemplate stepping outside the order of things.

However, even where the triumph of capitalism seems unequivocal, the logic of anticommunism remains. That the Soviet Union has disintegrated undoubtedly diminishes some of the ideological pressures at the upper levels of the state apparatus and portends some cutting back of the Pentagon and the CIA. But anyone who counts on a major 'peace dividend' following the end of the Cold War had just as well believe in the tooth fairy. The structures remain in place, as do the basic contradictions that drive them and the prevailing mentality of the men in charge. Though the Communist as such no longer exists as a threat, the overall project to which communism was an antagonist and which anticommunism was designed to secure remains in crisis and in need of ideological buttressing. From another angle, there remain many very influential people whose living has depended on playing the various cards of anticommunism and who are not at all inclined to give up these habits of thought and expression. From the weapons industries, to Congress, to the command structures of the media and the academy, America is staffed by men and women schooled in anticommunist ways of thinking.

One zone where this remains important comprises the nations once under the aegis of the Soviet Union. So long as these remain less securely capitalist than Switzerland, anticommunism will have its work cut out. The experience of Stalinism, along with exposure to Western media and technocrats, understandably led to an infatuation with capitalist markets in societies emerging from Soviet control. For a while, then, all the Western propaganda system had to do was to congratulate itself and show images of ecstatic crowds pulling down statues of Lenin. As the bitter realisation began to sink in, however, that the future of the ex-Soviet bloc within the capitalist world system would be more akin to that of Mexico than West Germany, the tone had to shift. How to justify the fact that those released from the bondage of Communism would have to give up guaranteed rights to housing, employment and education, and their factories with recreation clubs and day care centres, for structural unemployment, inflation, gross differences in wealth and widespread banditry?[12] Only by continually drilling into the mass mind hosannas for deliverance from the devil Communism. As disillusion and despair set in across the former Soviet bloc, then, the post-Communist agenda for anticommunism develops. The beating of a dead horse replaces the call to crusade.

One can always count on *The New York Times* to lead in matters of this kind, and it is hard to find a week in which a post-Communist anticommunism does not figure prominently in its coverage. Here, to cite but one example, is a front-page article by Stephen Engelberg, dateline Warsaw, of October 24, 1991, and headlined 'Poland's Cure is Taking, but Side Effects Hurt.' Under a photo of a glittering department store which suggests Harrods or Bloomingdale's, Engelberg informs us that 'after 22 months of economic shock therapy, Poland's stores are bursting with goods, the once gray cities are splashed with brightly painted new shops and the private sector is growing at a dizzying rate.' The cities 'bustle with signs of economic rebirth, and local newspapers bulge with help-wanted ads.' But – oh, the tragedy of it all – this 'tough medicine . . . has caused some severe side effects that will sorely test the resolve of the new Government. . . .' Engelberg goes on to mention the 10 per cent unemployment (odd, in view of all the help-wanted ads) and the recession which could drive the Polish GNP 'down as much as 10 per cent below the already anaemic 1990 levels.' These he blames, remarkably, not on structural capitalist tendencies but on a 'crucial Communist legacy: a shortage of apartments is keeping workers who lose their jobs in the dismal one-factory towns from moving into the newly prosperous urban areas.' In sum, there is still all-good and all-bad in the world. Whatever is praiseworthy in Polish society comes from the almighty market; whatever is condemnable comes from the Communist past. Notably, this thesis is secured through the discourse of health and illness. Communism was a disease; capitalism is the cure, and anything which goes wrong through its agency is only a side-effect. Sometimes cures hurt, but take your medicine, and you'll be all right in the morning.

Such thinking – and the policies compatible with it – is certain to be reproduced endlessly insofar as it remains necessary to justify the ways of God to Man. In this respect, anticommunism in some form will remain an ideological fixture so long as capitalism is crisis-ridden and even a glimmer of class struggle remains on the horizon. Not, that is, until the last worker wholeheartedly and once and for all accepts the rule of capital can the ideological apparatus rest its case. The mere passage of the aberration known as Communism, Soviet-style, is by no means, then, a sufficient condition for the withering away of anticommunism. The actuality of Communism, after all, was never the main issue for anticommunism. What counted ideologically was the symbolic fodder which could be made of it, and for this purpose, the ghost of a dead Communism is not much worse than Communism's living presence.

We have seen, however, that for the United States, one cannot simply talk about anticommunism as something foisted by elites upon a passive population. The ideology is both an instrumentality and something else – and this something has had certain spiritual qualities as well as being in some way part of the glue which holds the nation together. What happens in a post-Communist era depends, therefore, on what anticommunism in all its ramifications has done to America.

At the end of the cold war, the United States stands as the reigning military force and the world's sole superpower, indeed, strategically stronger than ever thanks to control over oil resources won through the Gulf war. Yet America is also unmistakeably a society in decline. The giant economy stagnates, government is held in contempt, corruption and cynicism dominate public life, and public confidence in the future is the lowest since the depths of the great depression of the 1930s. Class differences are widening as real wages of workers steadily decline while millions of people who once thought themselves middle-class[13] move downward into inferior, deskilled jobs. With increasing numbers of the poor being written off, major sectors of the country approach Third World status. An example: when I trained as a physician we took pride in the fact that tuberculosis, the leading cause of death in the nineteenth century, was about to be eradicated, thanks to powerful antibiotics and, principally, advances in public health. Today, lethal, antibiotic-resistant tuberculosis is reaching epidemic proportions in the rapidly-growing and AIDS-infested prison population,[14] from whom it is soon to spread to the ghettoes. Even before this happened, the life expectancy of black males in New York's Harlem had drifted below that of men in Bangladesh. Soon – who knows? – it will reach the level of Zaire. But this is forgotten by a white majority despairing about its own downward mobility, and increasingly subject to the logic of racism. As the American Dream – that vision of the self-made man winning success in a land of infinite opportunity – evaporates, American society seems to be slowly disintegrating before our eyes.

What has been the role of anticommunism in this; and what are its implications for the post-Communist era? We may take up these questions at the level of means as well as ends.

Corruption of Empire

> You were our heroes after the War. We read American books and saw American films, and a common phrase in those days was 'to be as rich and wise as an American.' What happened?
>
> Vietnamese Communist officer to his American prisoner.[15]

The Means

New Deal social democracy and the war against fascism were necessities and not preferred options for the American elites. Nevertheless, they were also vehicles for a tremendous amount of good will which came America's way in the 1940s and helped resurrect the rather tarnished ideal of the United States as the land of the free. Indeed, so taken was Ho Chi Minh with the democratic potentials of America that he actually approached United States officials to enlist their aid in his struggle against French colonialism.

Scarcely if ever in human history has a reservoir of affection been emptied so rapidly. For the American elites lost no time in their efforts to reverse these unwanted adversaries and alliances. Fascists were recruited into what was for them the real, anticommunist, war, and labour was crushed.[16] The friend of self-determination became once more, and more strongly than ever, the gendarme of the status quo. The shocks of the McCarthy era and the formation of the national security state with its permanent garrison were manifestations of a violent about-face, which restored traditional bourgeois hegemony in the course of an expanded imperial role. We need not detail these events. What I want to highlight here is their essential moral contradiction, deriving from the fact that this bastion of reaction continued to see itself an as emancipator, and tried to foist this notion upon the world.

There is a background. The aggravated high-mindedness of American anticommunism continues the moral dynamic which has marked America since its Puritan origins, manifest as the need to feel virtuous and an inability to admit wrongdoing.[17] To this day, for example, the American government has never admitted fault for any of its escapades, from Hiroshima to Baghdad – in remarkable contrast to the willingness of Germany to admit guilt for the crimes of Nazism or the Soviet Union for those of Stalinism. Even Japan inches closer to an admission of national guilt than the United States.

But it is not simply a case of denial; a moral reversal is also involved. Characteristically, the American responds to wrongdoing by seeking some high, even transcendent ground upon which his aggression turns into a means of redemption. Here is a recent specimen, the response of pundit George Will to the invasion of Panama. Will, a confidant of Presidents and top Washington insider, wrote in his nationally syndicated column of December 25, 1989, three days after the Americans landed: 'This intervention [in Panama] is a good-neighbor policy . . . It punctuates a decade of recovery of national purposefulness . . . and a year of militant democracy. . . .' Dismissing Bush's rationale that the United States invaded to save American lives, Will continues: 'There is a richer, an unapologetically nationalistic case to be made . . . a constant of America's national character . . . has been a messianic impulse . . . It rises from the belief that national identity is bound up with acceptance of a responsibility to further democracy. Not the aggressive universalisation but the civilised advancement of the proposition [democracy] to which we, unique among the nations, are dedicated.'

The cold war represented an expansion of both ends of the moral dialectic. Heightened aggressiveness was conferred by super-weaponry and the exigencies of policing the empire against global insurrection; while at the same time a heightened demand to feel virtuous was conferred by the legacy of antifascism noted above and, critically, the logic of anticommunism itself. Once committed to the ideology, they also became its instruments. Anticommunism, with its absolute apportionment of good to the West and evil to the Soviets, trapped the security elites in an expanding vortex of violence and denial, each side of which implied the other as a response. Compelled to feel virtuous, they could only justify their aggression by worst-case analysis of the Communist adversary – which in turn only stimulated more aggression on their part. Lawlessness was built into this dynamic, since everything done in the name of anticommunism would by definition be removed from moral self-reflection.

Institutionally, the vortex gave birth to the CIA and the era of covert operations: relentless mayhem carried out with a democratic, smiling, nice-guy facade. From its very beginning, the security apparatus became a state within the state, utterly undemocratic in its purported defence of democracy and regulated finally by the logic of anticommunism. It was only a matter of time before elements of gangsterism appeared in the workings of the national security state. The result of this has been a growing split of schizophrenic proportions in the American state. While an increasingly captive press continues to bleat about the 'fundamental decency' and devotion to democratic rights of the United States, an increasingly lawless security apparatus works its will, bombing, invading, subverting international agreements, sneering at the World Court (which condemned the United States in 1986 for its war against Nicaragua), and so forth, confident that it can get away with just about anything.[18]

But all the media manipulation in the world cannot stimulate authentic patriotic conviction after four decades of sustained criminality. There is simply no way to generate a sustained crusade out of such material. Note the qualifiers: 'authentic,' and 'sustained.' There seems to be little difficulty, given the strength of the propaganda system and the weakness of alternative views, to get people believing in America again, as George Bush so skilfully did during the Persian Gulf war. Bush then explicitly stated that Operation Desert Storm was going to overcome the 'Vietnam Syndrome' (as if objections to imperialist war were a disease). And the popular frenzy as the yellow ribbons were hauled out across America while the free world defended civilisation against Saddam, 'worse than Hitler,' Hussein seemed to prove Bush right. Even allowing for the unprecedented degree of cheerleading coming from the media and intellectual elites, the response was remarkable, especially given the high degree of doubt evinced almost up to the outbreak of war. In this respect, Desert Storm amply revealed the reserves of jingoism latent in the American heartland as well as the capacity to mount a crusade resembling the most ardent escapades of the wars against Communism.

But there was a catch: only the quick fix of a swift, overwhelming military victory could succeed in mobilising the American people. Bush knew well that the popular will could not be counted upon to support anything less. Had war lasted another month, and more significantly, had any kind of casualty level been suffered by American forces, the frenzy would have faded as quickly as it arose. The Gulf war had to be fought as a high-tech media extravaganza precisely because the rationale of sacrifice is gone, without which its actual motivation of naked imperial greed ('our oil under their soil') could no longer be rationalised. As no coherent framework of explanation could be sustained, Bush's glorious escapade was written on water. Now, nine months later, as this is being written, the great victory over the Saracens seems to have gone down memory hole. 'Can anyone recall,' writes Tom Wicker, official liberal of *The New York Times*, 'a disappearance more precipitous than that of the national celebration of Desert Storm, last winter's great victory in the Persian Gulf – the war whose fighting men and women, unlike those of Vietnam, were to be honoured and remembered?'[19] No doubt Bush will do what he can to revive the chauvinism of Desert Storm as his re-election bid approaches, and he will get all the help he wants. But the empire has destroyed its own spirit.

The 'Vietnam Syndrome' is therefore still alive. Vietnam, like every aspect of the Cold War, involved a swindle. But there are swindles and swindles; some proceed by exploiting heartfelt belief, while others have to conjure that belief, then exploit it. The Vietnam war, at least in its beginnings, may have been the last occasion for the mobilisation of the crusading mentality, grounded in fears of Communism as a mortal enemy, and also in a residue of authentic pride in America. Soviet Communism was never the enemy it was made out to be, but it was a real and powerful antagonist; and the United States was never the beacon of liberty it made itself out to be, but it had retained some legitimate self-respect as the defender of freedom against fascism. Vietnam squandered the remnants of that legitimacy. It was the war in which the true nature of the security apparatus surfaced, to stain, forever, its image as the benevolent protector of freedom.[20] This was a major reason the United States lost the war; and it was this actual loss and humiliation, so utterly foreign to a seemingly charmed country which had thought itself immune from the sufferings of history, which seared the lesson into the national consciousness as the 'Vietnam syndrome.' A mere victory over Saddam Hussein or his next surrogate is not going to undo the structural underpinnings of a declining imperial spirit.

The Ends

Exposed to the largest educational and informational apparatus in the history of civilisation, the average American remains astoundingly ill-informed and apathetic about the condition of the world.[21] Of course this has a lot to do with the fact that information is processed by a propaganda system which is more likely to befuddle rather than enlighten the citizen. But there is a deeper aspect to the problem which is both cause and effect of the low level of political intelligence, and relates directly to the power of anticommunism in America.

The great waves of anticommunist repression were, we have observed, astonishingly successful, and most successful of all was that which took place during the Cold War. In reversing antifascism and social democracy, the elites set loose a peculiarly American reign of terror. Relatively few lives were lost, relatively few prison terms were handed out, and only a few thousand people lost their jobs. Yet the title of David Caute's book remains apt: a 'Great Fear' stalked America, an archaic, diabolising fear of internal pollution and betrayal. When the waves of repression subsided, left opposition politics had been crushed in the United States. Combined with 'post-industrial' changes in the nature of production, the triumph of anticommunism left America as the nonpareil specimen of capitalism. The dream of the bourgeoisie had come true: the proletariat had withered away; anticommunism had helped secure class struggle on the most favourable possible terms to business, leaving in its wake a largely opposi-tionless society characterised by the accommodation of labour to capital, the functional identity of the Democratic and Republican Parties, and the most threadbare left-wing politics of any nation in modern history. Rea-gan's triumph was made possible by this clearing away of opposition, which led the way to rampant militarism, deregulation, a further assault on labour, transfers of wealth from poor to rich, and unbridled corruption and looting. And the collapse of Communism has seemingly sealed the process, confirming capital in its American heaven.

The results of this marked degree of hegemony are now becoming obvious as a series of disasters: industrially, where a get-rich-quick economy destroys its own base; environmentally, where the United States leads the world in the production of waste and the opposition to the regulation of pollutants; in health policy, where the legacy of the crushing of 'socialised medicine,' i.e., some degree of humanity and distributive justice in taking care of people, leads to a fabulously cruel and irrational health system;[22] and of course, militarily, thanks to the famous military-industrial complex. But there is also a kind of intellectual climate resulting from the loss of tension which conditions all the other aspects and needs emphasis.

We have noted already that anticommunism produces an identity of the nation with its business elites. Repression of the contribution of labour to society leads to that homage to capital which has become so axiomatic in America that any serious criticism of society, much less, advocacy of social transformation, is seen as quixotic. Another kind of repression emerges at this point, not simply of Marxism, but of that which Marxism stands for: the notion that history is the story of class struggle, which gives human events a dynamic and a structure. In anticommunist America one is not to think thoughts such as these. One arrives instead at the flaccid sense that history is over, and that it never meant very much anyhow. A profound weariness and cynicism occupies the place where critical/dialectical thinking used to occur. Since the underlying structure which makes society intelligible is erased, society becomes a mystery, its various phenomena merely strung together like the words of a game of Scrabble, and as easily forgotten. Thus even factual understanding of the world is lost.

The security apparatus in the era of Reagan/Bush may be said to have undergone something of a 'postmodern' mutation. The effect was obvious in Reagan, whose peculiar relation to truth was conditioned by his career as actor and huckster for General Electric. However, Bush's rather similar, albeit more unconvincing, behaviour indicates that we are dealing with structural changes having to do with the convergence of politics and mass culture rather than individual variations.

Reagan's peculiar psychology helped make true whatever the image-makers decreed as suitable to the needs of the apparatus. As Michael Rogin has written, two seemingly antithetical elements – amnesia and spectacle – are conjoined in the postmodern politics of empire.[23] Each fluidly transgresses the truth and becomes necessary for the other. Forgetting makes spectacle possible and spectacle makes forgetting possible. And both operate to carry anticommunism forward into a postmodern mode where the actual presence of the Communist enemy becomes a minor incidental. History is drained of meaning, including the history of anticommunism, in this age of photo opportunity and special effects, of terrorism industry[24] and loyalty industry. In the informational economy history becomes just another raw material for commodification. As in a Disney theme park, it becomes excavated, extracted, processed, cycled and recycled ceaselessly until it turns into a kind of symbolic plasma. With wars fought as video games and enemies manufactured like hit tunes, Bush and his successors will have a free hand to synthesise as many incarnations of Communism as they please.

But none of it can take hold, not because Communism was the 'real thing' so far as demons go, but because anticommunism has debilitated the collective mentality of America. Anticommunism defined a feasible, if grotesque, state religion during the heyday of the American empire; but it also destroyed the basis of social reason, thus exemplifying Gramsci's aphorism that when the old order is dying while the new one cannot be born, society itself becomes irrational. If people can recover neither memory of the past nor imagine a future, they remain imprisoned by a present defined by sensation and spectacle. Increasingly unhappy with this state of affairs yet forbidden to think in terms of real alternatives, they vote out the incumbents in office in a kind of generalised disgust, or sink bitterly into a new isolationism, a sentiment exploited by the ultra-right Patrick Buchanan in his bid for President.

Something must be set forth to replace the ideological focus on Communism, in order to organise the inchoate frustration of a society which offers no hope beyond the fantasies conjured by Hollywood and Madison Avenue. For all the liberal facade, America has always needed the devil, and never more so than now. It is by far the most punitive society of the Western world, with the highest rates of incarcerations, long sentences, and, of course, executions; yet politicians never cease inveighing against 'being soft on crime,' or pressing for harsher penalties. A rational, humane policy towards drug abuse is unthinkable in this climate – how could it be, when dope fiends and narco-terrorists are demanded by the apparatus?

Because anticommunism also defined a politics of identity (think only how it facilitated the integration of Eastern European nationalities into American society, or aided the integration of the armed forces), it served as a kind of social glue as well as a spiritual ideal. The loss of its rationale serves to catalyse the disintegration of America, much as the loss of the Communist ideal fosters tribalism in what used to be the Soviet bloc. In each case, fascist potentials are raised as the usual scapegoats are paraded forth. Leading the way in America are attacks on blacks (as beneficiaries of affirmative action), women (who face reversal of abortion rights), gay people (who are suffering increasing numbers of violent assaults), and, remarkably, Jews. I say remarkably, because it seems that American Jewry had so embourgeoisified and ingratiated itself, through Israel, with the national security state, as to have finally achieved its dream of safety. But it seems also as if there is never to be full immunity against the anti-semitic plague. As financial institutions collapse, talk of Jewish bankers and their conspiracy is heard once more, and the foul David Duke has been able to do what had been thought unthinkable – actually recreate Nazi ethos as a viable political option in America, gaining no less than 55% of the white vote in his losing race for the Louisiana governorship, despite an unprecedented campaign against him which broadcast his fascist record into every home in the state. But Duke is only exploiting a path laid down by George Bush, who made viciously racist smears respectable in his campaign against Dukakis.

Along with this has come a new wave of attacks on the defenders of the scapegoats. Artists attempting to voice the forbidden find themselves facing the Yahoo mentality as at no time since the 1920s. And at the universities, where the few remnants of an emancipatory consciousness can be transmitted to the younger generation, a new McCarthyism arises, its object no longer the Communist as subversive, but the grotesquely named 'politically correct,' that is, those who insist on anti-racism, anti-sexism, and anti-homophobia as political principles. 'Are you now, or have you ever been, politically correct?,' becomes a new watchcry. As with Communism, the presumption is that the Politically Correct are, if not dominant in universities, strong enough to make a real bid for power, and moreover, that their intolerance constitutes an actual threat to liberal society. Remarkably, the Politically Correct are considered the McCarthyites, out to intimidate and repress decent conservative Americans. Thus ex-Marxist historian Eugene Genovese wrote in the *New Republic*, 'As one who saw his professors fired during the McCarthy era, and who had to fight, as a pro-Communist Marxist, for his own right to teach, I fear that our conservative colleagues are today facing a new McCarthyism in some ways more effective and vicious than the old.'[25]

One does not know whether to laugh or cry when faced with such reasoning, which by seeking to defend liberal society only succeeds in putting another nail in its coffin. Marx's judgment that when history repeats itself, it returns as farce, seems particularly apt here – except that there is nothing funny about this farce. The facts of the matter are that American universities remain largely in bed with the state and corporations, and that the assault on political correctness is transparently a reactionary thrust against the growing multiculturalism of America.

Whether this multiculturalism will succeed in forging a revolutionary subject is quite dubious given the erasure of the vision of the whole by anticommunism. Even so, it will be fiercely attacked, not for the actual threat, but because the dominant Right is unappeasable. No matter how hegemonic its domain, no matter how burnt-out and pathetic its opposition, the Right cannot rest, must find enemies and subversives. This is not because the right is paranoid in any psychological sense. It is due, rather, to the very nature of its success. The monstrous swindles of anticommunism have made it impossible to *name* what was ailing the system and what could rise against it. As fundamental inequities in wealth and power grow, and as, therefore, the potential for resistance continues to mount, so, too, must a shadow-play of life-and-death struggle between the defenders and disturbers of the order be perpetually enacted.[26]

Marx and Engels long ago described a Communism in its infancy as the 'spectre' haunting Europe. Now the spectre outlives Communism itself, attached to all sorts of peculiar phenomena. As ever, these phantoms will be used to organise consent to capitalist rule. Yet as a declining America flounders about to impose its New World Order, an opening is still available through which potential resistance can be turned into actual resistance. What ultimately determines the persistence of anticommunist dynamics in a post-Communist era is the fact that what came to be called Communism after 1917 was an aborted socialist alternative and not true socialism. So long as capitalism organises society, no effort will be spared to keep this truth down. That is not in question. The question, as ever, is whether truth can awaken in the hearts and minds of the people, that they may rebuild a viable socialism and begin making history again.

NOTES

1. Ralph Miliband, John Saville and Marcel Liebman, eds., *Socialist Register 1984: The Uses of Anti-Communism.*
2. According to testimony of former Defense Secretary Robert McNamara before the Senate Armed Services Committee on December 3, 1990, as many as 22,000,000 people died in over 150 armed struggles since the Second World War.
3. Terry Eagleton, *Ideology* (London, 1991), has a thorough discussion of the ramifications of the term.
4. For general studies of the heyday of anticommunist repression in America, see Cedric Belfrage, *The American Inquisition 1945–1960* (New York, 1989 [1973]); David Caute, *The Great Fear* (New York, 1978); for the press, see James Aronson, *The Press and The Cold War* (New York, 1990 [1970]); for a survey of cultural repression, see Stephen Whitfield, *The Culture of the Cold War* (Baltimore, 1991).
5. See, for example, Reg Whitaker, 'Fighting the Cold War on the Home Front: America, Britain, Australia and Canada,' *Socialist Register 1984*, 23–67.
6. See William Blum, *The CIA – A Forgotten History* (London, 1986) p. 217–222, for further references. For recent revelations see Kathy Kadane, 'Ex-agents say CIA compiled death lists for Indonesians,' *San Francisco Examiner*, May 20, 1990; Ralph McGehee, 'The Indonesian Massacres and the CIA,' *Covert Action Information Bulletin*, 35 (Fall 1990), 56–58 (also reporting the latest efforts at cover-up). The *New York Times* called the coup 'one of the most savage mass slaughters of modern political history;' while *Life* wrote that the violence was 'tinged not only with fanaticism but with blood-lust and something like witchcraft.'
7. For an eyewitness account, see Roque Dalton, *Miguel Mármol*, trans. Kathleen Ross and Richard Schaaf (Willimantic, CT, 1987).
8. The memoirs of Rigoberta Menchú, for example, detail an astounding degree of sadism by the Guatemalan army as it has repressed Indian uprisings, *I, Rigoberta Menchú: An Indian Woman in Guatemala*, ed., Elisabeth Burgos-Debray, trans., Ann Wright (London, 1984). The current Serrano regime, like every other, came into office pledging to end political violence. Yet according to the Guatemalan Human Rights Commission, 700 political killings have taken place during his first ten months in office. Allison Martin, 'Guatemalan bishop: No justice, no peace,' *Guardian*, December 11, 1991, 13.

9. According to Joyce and Gabriel Kolko, *The Limits of Power* (New York, 1972), 614–6, the United States killed more than 3,000,000 people in Korea. A similar number were killed in Indochina.

10. During the HUAC inquisition of Hollywood, Chairman J. Parnell Thomas responded to Ring Lardner Jr's refusal to testify as follows: 'It is not a question of our wanting you to answer that. It is a very simple question. Anybody would be proud to answer it – any real American would be proud to answer it – any real American would be proud to answer the question, "Are you or have you ever been a member of the Communist Party?" Any real American,' Eric Bentley, ed. *Thirty Years of Treason* (New York, 1971), 187.

11. See Mike Davis, *Prisoners of the American Dream* (London, 1986).

12. Both economically and criminally – thus, street crime has increased five-fold in Prague since the capitalist accession.

13. It is an article of faith for vast numbers of Americans to identify themselves as 'middle class,' a term pertaining to status and income rather than Marx's notion of class as a form of praxis related to ownership and control of the means of production. Thus the bulk of American proletarians, reasonably well-off and without real class-consciousness, think of themselves as middle class. The effect may be considered an outcome of anticommunism's stifling effect on class conflict. See also Benjamin DeMott, *The Imperial Middle* (New York, 1990).

14. I have been told recently that Governor George Deukmejian presided over a quadrupling of the prison population of California during his three terms of office. In the country as a whole there are currently more African–American men in prison than in college.

15. Stanley Karnow, *Washington Post*, October 24, 1965.

16. See Christopher Simpson, *Blowback* (New York, Weidenfeld and Nicolson, 1988), for documentation of the extent and unseemly haste of United States recruitment of Nazis into its war against Communism.

17. To be sure, Puritans had a heightened awareness of sinfulness. However, this was directed away from the practical reality such as expropriation of Indian lands, and couched in the discourse of diabolism and original sin. Thus Puritans would flagellate themselves endlessly about how they had fallen away from God, while insouciantly justifying their extermination of the subhuman and diabolical Indians. See Richard Slotkin, *Regeneration Through Violence* (Middletown, CT, 1973).

18. And indeed it can. An apotheosis of sorts came recently with the dropping of all charges (by a Reagan-appointed Federal court) against Oliver North and John Poindexter, architects of the Iran-Contra scandals, along with the merest slap on the wrist for Elliott Abrams, (suspended sentence plus 100 hours of Community Service[!]) self-confessed perjurer before Congress for his role in the same.

19. December 19, 1991, A31.

20. The Korean War was no less genocidal but it was much more successfully kept out of view – in part due to the better-defined character of the lines of battle, and in part due to the relatively open expansion of television coverage in Vietnam (a lesson the state was to take to heart in Grenada, Panama and Iraq, in all of which coverage was tightly controlled). See Jon Halliday, 'Anti-Communism and the Korean War,' *Socialist Register 1984*, 130–163.

21. One instance among the numberless, which I chanced to hear over the radio: asked on the eve of the fiftieth anniversary of Pearl Harbor what it was they thought of first when the name, Japan, was mentioned, a group of High School seniors responded, 'Tienamin Square.'

22. It is not often realised how directly anticommunism played a role in the health care crisis. However, as Paul Starr describes it, 'compulsory health insurance became entangled in the cold war, and its opponents were able to make 'socialized medicine' an issue in the growing crusade against communist influence in America.' For example, 'a House subcommittee investigating government propaganda for health insurance concluded that "known Communists and fellow travelers within Federal agencies are at work diligently with Federal funds in furtherance of the Moscow party line."' Then there were incidents in the Senate such as the following: 'In his introductory remarks the first day, Senator Murray, the committee chairman, asked that the health bill [put forward by President Truman] not be described as socialist or communistic. Interrupting, Senator Robert Taft of Ohio, the

senior Republican, declared, "I consider it socialism. It is to my mind the most socialist measure this Congress has ever had before it." Taft suggested that compulsory health insurance, like the full employment act, came right out of the Soviet constitution. When Murray refused to allow him continue, Taft walked out, announcing that Republicans would boycott the hearings.' And that was all for national health insurance. Paul Starr, *The Social Transformation of American Medicine*, (New York, 1982), p. 284, 283.

23. Michael Rogin, '"Make My Day!": Spectacle as Amnesia in Imperial Politics,' *Representations* 29 (Winter 1990), 99–123.

24. See Edward Herman and Gerry O'Sullivan, *The 'Terrorism Industry'*, (New York: Pantheon, 1989), for a discussion of how discourse on terrorism is produced according to these principles.

25. Quoted in Christopher Phelps, 'The Second Time as Farce: The Right's "New McCarthyism,"' *Monthly Review*, 43 # 5, October, 1991, 39–57.

26. This tendency will be reinforced by the immanently anticapitalist logic of the ecological crisis, which remains intractable so long as a profit-driven system reigns. As a result, the tide of red-baiting already laps at the green and environmental movements.

HOLLYWOOD'S WAR ON THE WORLD:
THE NEW WORLD ORDER AS MOVIE

Scott Forsyth

Introduction

'Time itself has got to wait on the greatest country in the whole of God's universe. We shall be giving the word for everything: industry, trade, law, journalism, art, politics and religion, from Cape Horn clear over to Smith's Sound and beyond too, if anything worth taking hold of turns up at the North Pole. And then we shall have the leisure to take in the outlying islands and continents of the earth. We shall run the world's business whether the world likes it or not. The world can't help it – and neither can we, I guess.'
Holroyd, the American industrialist in Joseph Conrad, *Nostromo,* 1904.

'Talk to me, General Schwartzkopf, tell me all about it.' Madonna, singing 'Diamonds are a Girl's Best Friend,'
Academy Awards Show, 1991.

There is chilling continuity in the culture of imperialism, just as there is in the lists of its massacres, its gross exploitations. It is there in the rhetoric of its apologists – from Manifest Destiny to Pax Britannica to the American Century and now the New World Order: global conquest and homogenisation, epochal teleologies of the most 'inevitable' and determinist nature imaginable, the increasingly explicit authoritarianism of political discourse, the tension between 'ultra-imperialism' and nationalism, both of the conquerors and the conquered.

In this discussion, I would like to consider recent American films of the Reagan-Bush period which take imperialism as their narrative material – that is, America's place in the global system, its relations with diverse peoples and political forces, the kind of America and the kind of world which are at stake. I will query to what extent the New World Order, the latest moment in imperialism's grisly proclamations of global hegemony, is pictured, prepared or contested in certain popular films of our time. Readers will see that this is an updating of analysis of what has been called Reaganite cinema from the 70s and 80s. Left critics have argued that Hollywood over the last twenty years had responded to social and political conflict and change with particular intensity. By integrating and aestheticising some of the politics of the movements of the 60s and 70s – civil rights, anti-war, counter-culture, feminism – films challenged much of the iconography and generic myths of old Hollywood and retained youthful audiences alienated by popular anger over Vietnam, Watergate, racism, etc. But Hollywood has enthusiastically joined the Reagan 'counter-revolution'. Not only with the children's serials dressed up as blockbusters, like *Star Wars, Rocky, Superman, Indiana Jones,* or *ET,* which amused and reassured, but memorably with the string of war thrillers – *Rambo, Missing in Action, Top Gun* – which specifically relayed strategic and tactical Reaganite themes of anti-communism, 'freedom-fighting', vengeance and military masculinity.[1]

The films of the later 80s and early 90s both continue these trajectories and revamp them. How has Hollywood responded to the waning of the Second Cold War and then the collapse of the Communist adversaries, ultimate Reaganite wish fulfilment? To the continued conflict and turmoil throughout the third world? To continued economic crisis and social decay at home? To the waning of Reaganism itself?

The Gulf War as Movie: 'Globocop'

'No one in the world doubts the decency, courage and integrity of America.'
George Bush, February, 1991

'I can't find the words to express how the leadership of this government sicken me . . . (they) are a bunch of corrupt thieves, rapists and robbers.'
Anti-war activist Ron Kovics in *Born on the Fourth of July* (1990)

American culture has always stretched across this ideological traversal; the brutal realities of the American enterprise as settler-state, as imperial power, produce both the confident, blood-dropping simplicity of Bush and the inarticulate anguish over what America really does. Squaring these contradictory perspectives is often the project of American literature and film, even as an authoritarian chill creeps over political and cultural discourse in the West. The case study for this fear remains the overwhelming role the media played in the successful promulgation of the Gulf War. The Gulf War as media spectacle is crucial to understanding the ideology and aesthetics of the dominant culture. How imperialism represented and continues to represent itself was on display at the most politically controlled and conscious level. The success and strength of this obscene celebration of massacre and racism depended on the convergence of aesthetic and ideological developments of venerable standing in American and Western imperial culture. But it also witnessed their transformation and intensification in the media of the 80s.

It will not give solace to the many thousands of dead and dying in the West's brutal 'liberation of Kuwait' that to millions in the West it was really just another movie. But of course this was a movie on a grand scale, its promotion, pre-production and execution and exhibition the most costly block-buster of all. The authoritarian narrative propulsion of that build-up was immense; as Ted Koppel helpfully explained, it would have been a real 'letdown' if war had not broken out. At a superficial level, the attraction of the spectacle was that of *vérité* documentary, the excitement of 'real' events relayed live. But that representation was obviously managed and controlled in the most rigid manner by teams of anchormen and 'experts'; the model was not only World War II propaganda, both Allied and Nazi, but the lessons learned in producing the smaller spectacles of Grenada, the Libyan raid, the invasion of Panama.[2]

For most of the audience, the media's war drew wildly on diverse fiction and entertainment forms. We couldn't help notice that Bush and his generals talked with the staccato grim humour of movie tough guys: they would kick ass, beat the Vietnam Syndrome, not fight with one arm tied behind their back, here's the luckiest man in Iraq tonight . . . In the manner of generals, they were re-fighting the last war, but it was Rambo's cinematic version, not the real one.

Similarly, we sometimes felt we were watching an exciting Western; a Toronto tabloid headlined the day of the land invasion *High Noon.* Or we switched to turgid talk shows with only retired generals as guests. More upbeat, many American commentators were obviously inspired by the Super Bowl. Much war footage was literally Nintendo-style, but also, in the extreme sanitation of the censorship, like horror or pornography; what we couldn't be shown provided a ghoulish frisson. Or we watched fragments of war flicks: jets took off repeatedly, just as in *Top Gun,* poignant vignettes of the boys or – ersatz feminism served – women at the front. Even generic details like an enemy who is both awesomely powerful and finally inept cannon fodder, a 'turkey shoot', were reproduced. Melodrama proved useful with weeping families at home or gas masks on, we were inside brave Israelis' homes. But the millions of Palestinians, maskless, under murderous curfew only miles away, were invisible. 'Our' side were constantly humanised. 'They' were faceless masses or demonised, calling on explicitly racist imagery of the Islamic Other deep in the West's Christian heart. The personalisation of the war as a crusade against Saddam as a particularly brutal dictator was audaciously successful, given his status as a typical pliant puppet, 'our son of a bitch', for years before the war.

The war marched on in homecoming parades, variety shows, highlight videos, on the Academy awards, with cards and dolls. Although it may be difficult to dramatise a war of such a character, we can expect new *Top Guns.* One wonders how the central strategies of firebombing civilians or destroying water supplies or napalming surrendering, retreating convoys or burying conscripts alive will play on the silver screen.

The essence of the New World Order's proclamation at the completion of the war was that America asserted an absolute right to extreme military intervention in the majority of the world we call the third world, that

Western economic interests are sacrosanct, that the most iniquitous relations in the world's economy must be absolutely enforced and maintained.
The same old imperialism announced itself as re-invigorated. In the
service of this order, the war was really a demonstration massacre, its story
pre-determined; its numbing display as spectacle ensured everyone would
get the message.

The War on the Third World

'All over the world, rock and roll is all they play.'

Theme from *Red Scorpion* (1989)

The essence of the New World Order, culturally, economically and
militarily, is the threat to the third world – and the third world is
everywhere in the popular media of the 80s. Even the ubiquity of the
phrase indicates a naturalisation of grotesque hierarchies of unequal
development. It provides exotic peoples and geography for countless rock
videos and commercials and it fills the headlines with lurid and repetitive
news of economic and natural catastrophes, famine, civil war, massacre
and ecological devastation.

Seen through the prism of recent Hollywood war and cop thrillers, the
third world is a frightening place for America. It is a world where America,
as nation, state and myth, is constantly menaced and Americans fear a
litany of villains – drug lords, crazed Arab terrorists and dictators,
revolutionaries or Communists, especially if they're Vietnamese and,
decreasingly, if they're Russians. In image and atmosphere, the menace is
as much the hordes of the dark jungles or teeming cities of that world, and
their swarthy colours and unfathomable exoticism: racial spectres haunt
the screens with extraordinary intensity. Thankfully, those hordes are
exorcised in gorgeously bloody climaxes. But as terrifying, *they* are
increasingly invading the metropolitan shores, or worse, they are already
here! For America itself can often be pictured only as a class-polarised
social world reduced to the nightmares of fearful whites menaced by
Reaganism-scarred ghettoes, saved only by the military power of the state
or its vigilantes. Of course, America and its feisty individualist heroes fight
back, usually with the technological bombast and super-masculine mus-
cularity which Stallone, and Schwarzenneger and Norris and, now, Van
Damme and Seagal have taken from the comic books to the wide screen.
(Not to mention those instances where the heroism required is *more* than
human – *Robocop, The Terminator.*) Generically, these films have taken
the precise location the Western occupied on the silver screen, moving
from continental conquest and genocide to encompass the global dimensions of American imperialism. In particular, they dramatise strategic
Reagan-Bush campaigns – the militarisation of the War on Drugs and the
continuing War on Terrorism, that is *their* terrorism, not *ours*. The

aesthetics of this cinema is literally visceral, centred upon elaborate illusions of grisly violence, first as evidence of the brutality of America's enemies, then as celebratory vindication of 'our' heroes' sadistic righteousness, as punctuation in cyclical and repetitive narratives of outrage and vengeance. But that bloody victory, satisfactory as it is, is usually provisional and precarious. America in the movies is both weak and strong, never safe for long.

This movie plays over and over, in countless television cop or spy shows or in the mercenary/commando thrillers, like *A-Team, Mission Impossible, Lightning Force, Counterstrike,* in racks of direct-to-video action flicks, and in many sequels to key Reaganite films. I will discuss a thematically representative number here. To begin with an egregious case, *Flight of the Intruder,* released during the Gulf War, refights the Vietnam War once more and concludes with an ecstatic celebration of the barbaric Christmas bombing of Hanoi in 1972, neatly eliding defeat. John Milius *(Apocalypse Now, Red Dawn)* is the sub-Kipling laureate of Reaganism, the most consciously reactionary of important Hollywood directors and writers. Here we see the generic simplification of central truths of the Right: the war could have been won; politicians and bureaucrats tied our hands; the purpose of the war is irrelevant compared to the successful use of power. Milius even has the audacity to begin the film with Johnson's announcement of the escalation of the war in response to the faked Tonkin Gulf incident, without comment. In the familiar master narrative, the heroes organise a renegade raid, in this case on downtown Hanoi, against the bureaucratic constraints, which force them to kill only 'farmers'. (With disturbing similarity to what we were watching on TV, the plot goes to absurd lengths to claim their bombs will hit nothing but 'concrete and steel'). The macho warrior culture of the Navy is just cute; that the heroes are bloodthirsty becomes humorous: 'I do love the work'. In an interesting variation, the heroes are saved from courtmartial when Nixon orders the Christmas raid. Kissinger's Madman Theory is the climax, with napalm bursting to the strains of both rock and roll and the Lord's Prayer.

This generic reduction of Vietnam to being a site for retro imperial fantasy played all decade. But the most impressive films about Vietnam continued to be anti-war. *Platoon, Casualties of War, Full Metal Jacket,* and *Born on the Fourth of July* have powerfully retained the repugnance and disgust a generation felt for that horrific war. They have been particularly acute in dissecting the sick, but absolutely 'normal' masculinity the military and a militarised society requires for the maintenance of everyday rule. This is the inverse of Milius' cute psychopaths. Similarly, they attempt to use the 'realism' of current representation of violence to provoke the moral outrage the war and its 'normal' atrocities demanded. *Born on the Fourth of July* even begins to take on the authoritarian nationalism of America in a painful and intimate fashion: 'There is no

God, there is no country!' the crippled hero screams. It is worth noting, however, that even these serious films can address the war only in the vaguest of political terms – it is a tragedy, certainly, but as much one of the American spirit, at war with itself. The Vietnamese can hardly be given any voice whatsoever, the war as imperialist against revolutionary struggle has no purchase in the truncated discourse of American liberalism. For example, Oliver Stone, the most radical and manifestly political of Hollywood directors, specifically folds the anger and militancy of his film into Democratic rhetoric, literally into the Party's 1976 convention.

While the strength of these films' anger should prevent Vietnam's total reduction to generic playground, this is the direction of the cop thriller *Off Limits* or the anti-war comedies *Air America* and *Good Morning, Vietnam*. The hilarious satire of the CIA's airline in Cambodia does provide a clear view of the machinations of American interests in Indochina, the drug-dealing, mass-murdering, dictator-loving realities behind those perpetual good American intentions. Unfortunately, the lovable comic heroes, like Robin Williams' manic disc jockey never disavow those intentions: they just become cynical or 'wise' about human tragedy.

Elsewhere, our heroes roam the third world, searching for new enemies, often literally as sequels to earlier rampages, always offering their adventures as 'good, small wars' that can be fought and won. Fresh from refighting Vietnam, *Rambo III* wipes up the Russians in Afghanistan. The film's chief interest, aside from the aesthetics of 'blowing things up good', lies in its determination to prettify Reagan's 'freedom fighters', here that most loathed enemy, Islamic fanatics. The iconic purchase is easily provided by that venerable trait of American and imperial heroism, the desire to 'go native', to dive into violent primitivism. Similarly, in *Red Scorpion,* a KGB Rambo, sent to destroy tribal rebels, joins them and the CIA, to the sound of rock and roll, as noted above, against Russians, Cubans and their African puppets. This undisguised celebration of UNITA or RENAMO seems to have been scripted by the South African secret service. *Delta Force 2,* having wiped out Palestinian terrorism in the opening film, sets its target on a favoured contemporary villain, a psychotic drug lord, who must be kidnapped to justice from his lair in a suitably corrupt and pliant Latin American country. The plot is one of numerous homages to the invasion of Panama and capture of General Noriega. As always, it is insubordinate commandos who must do the job, there are hostages to be saved and bureaucrats to be battled. The film goes to great lengths and extreme racist humour to justify 'morally' America's intervention militarily in sovereign nations: only America has the 'integrity and courage' to act resolutely; the weakness and corruption of the third world justifies the ferocity of the treatment meted out.

Notably, the military leaders, as in *Flight of the Intruder,* come on-side, with a wink and a nod, so the mission can be accomplished: the Right is confident that the vigilantes and renegades are now in charge. For example, Clint Eastwood welcomes and reprises the Grenadan invasion in *Heartbreak Ridge;* it's a good chance to test that masculinity all these warriors spend so much time training to acquire. In *Toy Soldiers,* the 'rebel' sons of officers – at a training school, of course – prove their mettle to their dads in a battle with Columbian drug terrorists. Likewise in *Delta Force III,* state and tough guys are of one mind. The enemy is again Arab fundamentalist terrorism: this time with the Bomb. As in numerous films, the most visceral racism pictures Arabs as either exotic background or 'Indians' to be massacred. Not only is there no question the military fully supports our daring commando raid into some tinpot third world dictatorship; interventionism is not even at issue. In fact, the Americans are joined by Soviet commandos in what is surely the New World Order's favoured generic variation so far, the superpowers in alliance against crazed Arabs. A similar alliance of macho Yanks and Soviets propels *Iron Eagle II's* attack on yet another crazed Arab dictator.

This cooperation between the old enemies appears in a few films and, along with the replacement of Soviet villains with drug lords and Arabs, it is undoubtedly a reference to the collapse of Stalinism as an enabling condition of the ferocious interventionism the New World Order promises. As in the real world, the presence of the Soviets was a restraint and a challenge for unbridled American power, throughout the Cold War's hot wars in the third world over the last decades. But in general, Hollywood has not responded to the 'end of the Cold War' with anything like the topical opportunism of third world thrillers. The spy thrillers which dramatised the central, bipolar confrontations of the Cold War seem to be temporarily marginalised. There are a few exceptions. Soviets can still be villains who wish to destroy America, as in *The Hunt for Red October,* a noxious Red-baiting fantasy, but the film announces itself as dated, 'Before Gorbachev came to power'. In *Spies Like Us* and *The Russia House,* brutal espionage games are mocked and both CIA and KGB are defeated by romance. In *No Way Out,* the hero in the midst of insane CIA/State Department intrigue is a KGB agent. But the basis of these films is a banal convergence theory, a liberal version of the Cold War, and both sides can be equally culpable or venal.

Hollywood thrillers are much more involved with terrorism than the manifest ideological battle with Communism. *Die Hard* and *Die Hard II: Die Harder* are particularly clear updates of this central Reaganite melodrama. (Of course, it was usually placed within the Communist conspiracy, but these films illustrate its useful portability). The films play, almost parodically, tales of a lovable rebel cop battling bumbling bureaucrats to save 'America'. Secondary animus is directed against contemporary careerist feminism in a feeble resuscitation of a male-dominated couple and against 'the media', in a hysterical Spiro Agnewish denunciation of its complicity with 'our' enemies. But the real interest is the portrayal of terrorism itself. Like key earlier films, *(Red Dawn, Invasion USA)*, that ultimate fear, the invasion of America is at stake. Advanced capitalism is attacked in its most exemplary edifices, bank towers and airports. The America saved is weak and vulnerable to a terrorism it has created. This conundrum and plot reversal speaks to both the enormous popular cynicism about politics in America since the Iran-Contra scandals and its unsatisfactory cover-up by media and Congress, and to the pervasive fear of America's decline.

Of course, in most films such decline and weakness are blamed on others or cleansed by purgative violence. In *Delta Force II* the drug lord taunts that America is morally corrupt and needs his drugs . . . just before his spectacular death. *Marked for Death* presents the drug trade and the threatening relationship between America and the third world as a literal invasion of Jamaican gangs. Here the defender of America from this scourge must, in a particularly extreme version of vigilante justice, personally invade Jamaica to defeat the drug lords. The film stands out, even among the films discussed here, for its visceral racism and the blatant political coding given its villains. The gangs are the most loathsome combination imaginable – Rastafarianism, voodoo, quasi-revolutionary cult and conspiracy against the children of America.

In many important Reaganite narratives, hostages provide the plot and vengeance motives. This anxious lineage harks back to the captivity narratives of early settler America and on through the foundations of the Western in literature and film. The sagas of innocents held by savages speak to deep fears and desires about miscegenation, civilised identity and the nature of the American project in general. They can explore the delights of 'going native' – either to begin to oppose the 'civilising mission' altogether or for taking on the savagery necessary to its achievement. Hostages figure schematically in many of the thrillers mentioned above, but nowhere so emotionally effective as in *Not Without My Daughter*. This women's melodrama goes to the source of the great hostage trauma of recent years, Iran, for a 'true story' recreation. An American is brutally held with her daughter in Teheran by her born-again Islamic fanatic husband. We are forced to respond to the fanatical faces of the Islamic Other with fear and total incomprehension. While American racism seems to provide some of the motives for the husband's conversion, its extremism overwhelms and invalidates any liberalism. The feisty heroine escapes finally: an American flag fills the screen as she whispers 'Baby, we're home'. It is a useful example of how vague liberal ideas can be subordinated to the vigour of reaction.

In contrast to the emotional power of this film, feminism is either ignored or appropriated with casual opportunism in many of the films discussed. Women are occasionally allowed to be tough guys.[3] Mostly they figure as objects of the outrages of America's enemies or as sexual entertainment for heroes and audience. In these melodramas, masculinity is the overwhelming concern. The extreme masculinity the films construct and celebrate is a fantastic, comical solution to America's weakness. Women, and sexual escapades, punctuate the films, as protection against the homoeroticism of the military camaraderie of all these male groups – the buddies, the platoons, the army itself. These are films of functional male hysteria.

In a few films, the third world can be sensuously attractive as well as dangerous. In *Revenge,* a basic military hero crosses the border to Mexico for an adventurous discovery of real masculinity and erotic bliss with the wife of a drug lord. Despite that lover's brutal death, the film ends in mystical male communion; this is one drug lord who gets to live. *Wild Orchids* also uses the third world, in particular Rio and its carnival, as a site of wild abandon where Westerners can overcome their repressions and discover their sexual desires. It is also, rather lamely, one of the few films to attempt to represent the working of transnational capital. In most of the films, the only transnational economies are those of the drug trade and the military.

Overall, most of these films about the third world offer several important political allegories. First, the narrative trope of rebel heroes against spineless, amoral bureaucracy maintains a vicarious and vacuous individualism which social reality allows little room for: an ersatz rebelliousness is enlisted for the status quo. This also negotiates central confusions in conservative ideologies about the state itself. On the one hand, the Right detests its laxness, liberalism and bureaucracy and set out through the 80s to destroy the social, welfare and regulatory functions built up over decades of social compromise in advanced capitalism. On the other, Reaganism bloated that state even more with unprecedented military Keynsianism, vast subsidies of all kinds in its 'socialism for the rich' and the reinforcement of the repressive apparatus to police the class relations of a leaner, meaner capitalism. This double movement is fictionally negotiated; the heroes fulfil the needs of the *nation* for, and despite or even against, the state. These *para-state* warriors do what the state should do, glorifying its repressive might at second hand, privatising and deregulating state violence itself. Of course, this narrative also literally played in newspaper headlines all decade, in Reagan's dirty secret wars, in the secret armies of Oliver North or Adolph Coors, in the death squads of every American client state. The importance of the cinematic version is to make these horrors and violations entertaining and 'natural'. While this narrative still propels countless films and TV thrillers, increasingly our rebels and commando squads become legitimate agents of the state, their illegality or immorality is much less of an ideological problem in fiction just as it is not a problem for the US news media in Panama or Iraq or Nicaragua.

A central contradiction for dominant ideology in art is always that even the most reactionary resolutions require the exciting dramatisation of fears, dilemmas and disruptions of the normal social order. The third world in general – its unavoidable place in the world – causes fear and anxiety in all these films. That fear is materially rooted since the social turmoil and economic devastation the West brings is hurled back in collective struggles of revolution, nationalism and communism. Perhaps the fear is a translation and rejection of the liberal or Christian guilt many Westerners experience contemplating the widening gulf between rich and poor, the evident pillaging of the 'developing' world by the developed. This fear and guilt is obviously part of American political discourse and strategy, however liberal or reactionary. But in the revenge flicks, such struggles are folded into the narratives, depoliticised, criminalised; any action against America is likely criminal or insane. The masses appear as passive background or target practice for super-heroes. The third world is something like a vast ghetto, whose relationship to America is only threat or military target. This drastic circumscription fits the exigencies of a New World Order and its string of 'low intensity conflicts' with alarming simplicity. But still those threatening masses linger as image.

As noted earlier, America in the movies is both mighty and weak, never safe for long. On the one hand, smug triumphs, banal rhetoric and globalising hubris conclude most of these films. But the fears which begin the films are of American weakness in the face of global hostility. America is rarely represented with interests to secure in the third world; this is much less explicit celebration of the benefits of imperialism than, for example, British imperial culture of the late 19th century. The only transnational economies seem to be drugs and guns; America brings rock and roll . . . and death. Often America is represented only by the 'democratic' military group or the super-heroes. Like the ambivalence about the state, the simultaneous reduction of American presence and celebration of its global reach addresses a contradiction in ideology: it tries to square isolationism with the demands of super-power imperialism. It dramatises the extremism of contemporary international inequality, but also shows some hesitation or confusion about its appropriately benign or democratic costume. This American weakness also surely refers to bourgeois anxieties about America's decline in the world economically in relation to European and Japanese capital or other foreigners. The future of American national capitalism, let alone its leadership, in an emerging and uncertain transnational economy is not sure. The combination of weakness and might speaks to the contradiction between ultra-imperialism and nationalism for *America* itself.

Wars on the Ghettoes

'. . . in the conservative tradition, crime is a figure for class struggle.'

Fredric Jameson

Of course, America does not need to invade ghettoes around the world, it has plenty right at home. That is where the War on Drugs really started to say No! If we switch our view briefly to the related and complementary films which play out their violent dramas domestically, in America itself, this weakness of America is even more glaring. Cinematically, the nation's social landscape is very often a ghetto nightmare of violence, drug-addicted despair and gang war, with a few crusading cops to stave off anarchy. The central political contradiction the films reveal, in their intense overlapping of bombast and anxiety, is that the America heroes defend and fight for all over the world is a hollowed-out shell at home. This is not an exact political economy, of course, but a dramatisation and fearful extrapolation of real social and political processes and conflicts.

In dozens of TV cop thrillers, in the crudely sensational police *vérité* shows like *Cops,* in film after film, the social decay of urban America is literally the narrative pre-text and structure. To cite some recent films, from hundreds of examples: the *Death Wish* and *Dirty Harry* series and their many imitators over 20 years, the *Beverly Hills Cop, 48 Hours, Lethal Weapon* series, the teen gang 'tragedies' like *Colors* or *Boyz n' the Hood,* all the films of Stepen Seagal, the authoritarian educational morality tales like *Stand Tall,* the striking revival of the gangster film, *The Untouchables, Goodfellas, The Godfather III, King of New York, New Jack City,* or to cross genres, in the nightmare ghettoes of *Jungle Fever* or *Bonfire of the Vanities.*

These films dramatise American capitalism, often more expressedly than the third world allegories discussed above. Again, this social decay filled the headlines of news media all decade: the homeless, de-industrialisation, racial conflict, gang wars, drug epidemics, declining living standards and the institutionalisation of the so-called under-class, to note the obvious. But the ghetto predates Reagan, it is the structural form of the constitutively racist nature of American capitalism. The films' use of the ghetto variously contains this history – of slavery, of civil war, of the Great Society reforms, of the civil rights movement and its derailment, of the Black Panthers – even while they dramatically address conjunctural exacerbation. The Hollywood ghettoes are filled with echoes of the past and victims of Reaganism; either as objects of sentimental sympathy or as villains to fear and vanquish.

In more reactionary films, that is all they are and this fear is specifically racial; it is the black and increasingly hispanic masses who are demonised and criminalised and targeted in film after film. They are the exact equivalent to the exotic masses of the third world; repeatedly, the ghetto is labelled a jungle. Normal America appears, as in the third world films, largely to be outraged and invaded by this always-there third world inside the first. Similarly, this circumscribed world becomes part of the justification for military action as solution to these socially and politically produced dilemmas. Here the repetitive tale of rebel against bureaucrat and against evil criminal is an argument for increased militarised policing, for reduced rights for everyone to defeat the menace, for harassment and destruction of dissidence, always coded as criminal. It is the same argument that played in the Reaganite media, judiciary and Congress all decade.

There is a class dimension in this narrative and imagery, as well, most obviously, with the rich in their towers and the poor in their jungles below. But, importantly, and more submerged, this is also a fear of the working class, in America historically multi-racial. The working class is practically invisible in American cinema, but the destruction of America's industrial infrastructure, the punitive assaults on working class jobs, wages, rights and unions are part of and pre-condition of this devastated American cityscape, coded into racial and criminal antagonism.

But this view of urban America decayed and declining should also be seen as anxious from a bourgeois perspective. The destruction of urban infrastructure, of whole regions and industries, of that 'normal' social life called a bourgeois civil society is also a source of ruling class worry. (Even if the films, and much of that ruling class, favour the most violent and authoritarian responses.) Capital may well hurtle with elastic mobility around the globe but the creative destruction of productive capacity is still destruction. American capitalism is still left with its declining profits, its financial speculation bubble bursting, its questionable ability to compete in a competition it has organised. This destroyed America speaks to the anxieties of a national capitalism declining in a rapidly transforming world. To take one generic detail: a striking number of the ghetto thrillers climax in empty, gutted factories of the Northeast Rustbelt. The fierce ideological resolutions play against and are surrounded by the literal evidence of America's glory days and its present decay. As will be noted, the critique of capitalism becomes increasingly explicit in recent American film.

In a number of films, a progressive slant on Jameson's remark begins to take shape. In the long tradition of social bandits, several films place criminality as a justified social response to intolerable conditions, gang warfare as the only collective struggle available. The gang in *New Jack City* and *King of New York* justify their crimes as responses to the Reaganite devastation, the class struggle directed against their communities. These good/evil drug lords are partially valorised against the usual renegade cops. Christopher Walken's over the top *King* is especially notable: he leads the black youth in a crime crusade for socialised medicine! (This is testimony to both the insistence of the social in contemporary criminality and the extreme circumscription of 'normal' political discourse.)

Elsewhere, in Hollywood genres, social banditry has enjoyed tremendous popularity in the last few years: the film and TV *Robin Hood,* the anti-corporate outlaws of *Young Guns I* and *II,* the brilliant overlayering of gender and class in the feminist outlaw saga of *Thelma and Louise.*

This class and ethnic struggle is part of the gangster film's history in Hollywood: the gangsters rise in revenge against a white and WASP class structure. Of course, the social rebellion has an expressly capitalist trajectory. The social structure violates the class mobility the American Dream offers; the gangster's organisation is specifically a shadow version of capitalist enterprise. But it always foregrounds the criminality of legitimate business. When Don Corleone wants to go legit, he tries to buy a transnational corporation; the subsequent intrigue and double-dealing leads him to conclude sadly: 'the higher up you go, the crookeder it gets'. This is an easy translation from American capitalism of the 80s, popularly understood as criminal, in its wheeling, dealing boondoggles, the conviction of key financial figures, the indicting of most of the Reagan cabinet, the S&L scandals, and on and on. Several liberal or comic 'exposés' cover the same territory – *Wall Street, Working Girl, Bonfire of the Vanities:* even cartoon superheroes struggle in film noir nightmares of decaying capitalist cities – *Batman, Darkman, Who Framed Roger Rabbit?* A popular cinematic critique of American capitalism has clearly developed, with confused and vague political features.

Often, this social explanation of crime and capitalism specifically refuses politics. Young gangsters pointedly mock the failed reformism of their civil rights elders in several films. The derailing of that movement and the bankruptcy of the black Democrats in real social conflict is clear enough. The vague politics of black nationalism and pride, would-be capitalism, or return to moral rearmament and patriarchal certainty, circulate in these ghetto thrillers. But the climatic solutions offered are usually the same law and order vengeance across all the films.

This version of America may be considered apocalyptic, but Hollywood is prepared to go even further. A series of successful science fiction films through the 80s projects a capitalist, and particularly Reaganite, future, only a few years away. It is a future of collapse, of further catastrophic decay, of more extreme gang and racial warfare. The future is both technologically hyper-modern and socially barbaric. This is the dark, dystopian inverse of the triumphalism and utopianism of rhetoric and headline. Hollywood has seen the New World Order already – its a New Bad Future, as one critic puts it. With generic roots in both dystopian sci-fi and film noir and the particular influence of *Blade Runner* and the *Mad Max* series, recent films have become more explicitly anti-capitalist. *Robocop I* and *II* project a mad fantasy world of corporate megalomania, drug-dealing, ghetto-bashing and precisely condemn its capitalist basis. The cop avenger narrative fits unevenly with the anti-Reaganite satire, but even the robot-hero is a parody of the artificial masculinity these super-heroes require. *Gremlins II* unleashes its nasty monsters on the totalitarian techno-utopian tower of a Donald Trump clone. In *They Live,* it is finally revealed that yuppies, the ruling class and Reagan himself are alien lizards. (I always suspected this.) It is the homeless and the displaced working class who lead the assault on the TV towers. A victorious rebellion also concludes *Total Recall.* Here corporate maniacs have created a slave capitalism on Mars. Schwarzenegger must lead a mutant proletariat to wash away this intolerable world in an apocalyptic ecological and class explosion. Class struggle is usually absent or submerged in mainstream film; oppositional films like *Matewan* with its celebration of union courage, or the cleverly hilarious assault on Reaganism and call for a return to the days of militant resistance in *Roger and Me,* are rare exceptions on commercial screens. But these sci-fi entertainments call for and contain images of collective struggle against domestic and international capitalism; the movies are capable of imagining different futures.

The Sequel? Contradiction and Resistance

'It's never over, so we never lose!'

> CIA agent in *Havana*

As I have indicated, notwithstanding the simple and disturbing picture many films offer, the same Hollywood, in the waning of Reaganism since the Iran-Contra Scandals of the mid-80s, has also produced films which, more or less militantly, criticise capitalism's role in the world. These films carry the politics of anti-racism and black nationalism, protest at the imperial rampaging of America's armies and spies, and positively portray anti-imperialist struggle, particularly in Central America and South Africa.

Cry Freedom!, Biko, A Long White Season and *A World Apart* sympathetically dramatise the collective struggle against South African apartheid and have been part of the popular solidarity which has aided that fight. *The Mission* exposes the depravity of Christian and European invasion of Latin America hundreds of years ago. It shows those usually faceless and voiceless in militant and armed resistance. Liberation theology is also given an unusual, spiritual presence on screen. This is important, as well, to *Romero* in contemporary El Salvador. The portrayal of the atrocities which maintain the New World Order, as it has existed for decades, is moving and provocative. The sympathetic picture of leftist opposition is particularly important as a corrective to *Salvador,* which was even more corrosive in its condemnation of America's role, but derided or ignored the opposition altogether. The vicious satire of *Walker,* following American imperialism in Nicaragua back to its beginnings and forward to the contemporary world, was particularly militant. It was also, in solidarity, produced in Nicaragua, difficult for an American company in the late 80s. Somewhat more gently, *Ishtar* portrays the CIA as vicious maniacs and romanticises fanciful third world revolutionaries. Turning to domestic imperialism and racism, the hero of *Dances with Wolves* goes native in service of native struggles; *Glory,* in the American civil war, movingly celebrates armed black self-liberation in that second unfinished American revolution; *Do the Right Thing!* updates that militancy expressly to racial antagonism now; and *The Milagro Beanfield War* champions Hispanic resistance to racism and ongoing economic attack.[4]

It would be appropriate and conventional to offer Marxist qualifications to this praise. Indeed, several of these films direct their anger into liberal sentimentality, fudge issues of class, hinge their identification on Western or white characters, slip into the portrayal of third world people as exotic or passive. But, nonetheless, they contribute, and are evidence of, an increasingly coherent critique of imperialism, America's role in it and the direction of struggle against it. They will be an invaluable beginning in cultural politics of solidarity and resistance over the years to the crimes the New World Order is likely to perpetrate. (This discussion obviously leaves aside the essential and admirable work in oppositional documentary film and video on many of these themes by militants throughout the third world and in solidarity work in the first.)

A concluding example is even more striking. *Havana,* in 1990, is a specific romanticisation of the Cuban revolution. In homage to *Casablanca,* its hero must be transformed from desultory gambler to commitment. While Bogey had to learn to defend Democracy, Redford must come to the side of the revolution: in this case, the continent's most obsessively detested target of American imperialism for 30 years. It is an important sign of cultural contradiction that Hollywood can produce such a glamorous ode to a revolution, and a revolution likely to be the next target of the New World Order.

Hollywood's belligerence, its war on the third world and much of the domestic population, is a translation of the military and economic targets of the restructuring of American and global capitalism and its particular present-day variants. But the America which must carry out the task is a disastrously weakened shell of its former glory, all puffed up ideology and armed bullying, constantly preyed upon by internal and external enemies, at war often with itself as well as the world. In 'triumph', American culture also pictures itself in something of a death agony. The resolution of such fears requires the utmost in delightful violence but constantly raises the very dilemmas and fears, in an exciting and disruptive way, which it claims to resolve. At both the utopian level of the New World Order, and the string of 'good small wars' it promises and Hollywood aestheticises, its targets are those produced, made miserable by and variously resisting the system which all the violence is required to maintain. Necessarily, the targets keep fighting back, even in the form of endless sequels. But Hollywood has also produced important images of resistance and critique, as well, where the logic of struggle against this system becomes popularly comprehensible. But even the worst triumphalism parades in debased or demonised form its own potential 'grave-diggers'.

'Did you win or lose?', Redford's newly committed gambler asks the CIA agent fleeing revolutionary Cuba in 1959 for a new assignment in, of course, Saigon: the foreboding answer is 'It's never over so we never lose.' It is crucial to see that this phrase is both triumphal boast *and* anxious prediction. The Left must surely, however the New World Order purports to rearrange the terrain and intensify the onslaught, begin to rebuild its own sense of intransigence. The New World Order promises the same misery throughout two thirds of the world and increased travails for the working classes and oppressed of the 'rich' first world; it will produce the same kinds of courageous opposition capitalism always has. This message is there in the shadows of Hollywood's, and capitalism's, 'glorious' wars.

NOTES

1. For a comprehensive survey, see Michael Ryan and Douglas Kellner, *Camera Politica: The Politics and Ideology of Contemporary Hollywood Film,* (Bloomington and Indianapolis: Indiana University Press, 1988); also, Robin Wood, *Hollywood from Vietnam to Reagan,* (New York: Columbia University Press, 1986), Scott Forsyth, 'Evil Empire: Spectacle and Imperialism in Hollywood', *Socialist Register 1987,* (London: Merlin Press, 1987).

2. It often seemed the military and the media were literally following the lessons of authoritarian propaganda; the categories of the Frankfurt School's analysis of cultural industries, built up in relation to war propaganda and military intelligence, never seemed more *emotionally* astute, albeit theoretically overstated. See Theodor Adorno, 'Freudian Theory and the Pattern of Fascist Propaganda' in Paul Roazen, (ed.), *Sigmund Freud* (New Jersey: Prentice-Hall, 1975).

3. In a complementary discussion of fear of the third world in science fiction, the heroine of *Aliens* is considered an example of opportunistic feminism enrolled in defence of the first world against a monstrous and metaphoric third world. See Charles Ramirez Berg, 'Immigrants, Aliens and Extraterrestials: Science Fiction's Alien "Other" as (Among Other Things) New Hispanic Imagery', *CineAction,* 18, 1989.

4. Other films, though aware of issues of imperialism and racism, are much more equivocal. *Mosquito Coast* and *Farewell to the King* are both consciously Conradian parables. In the former, a crazed patriarch flees a corrupt America to recreate the settler Utopia in the Caribbean. This cross between *Swiss Family Robinson* and *Heart of Darkness* specifically mocks America's sense of itself in the world, its claims to ultimate knowledge and technological hubris. But the hero's descent into madness exonerates America once more. In the latter, the ever-surprising John Milius condemns Japanese, British and American imperialism in the most extreme nativist fantasy of historical regression. Away from civilisation, a white king can rule over an arcadian jungle of patriarchal bliss.

SOCIALIST REGISTER 1989
REVOLUTION TODAY; ASPIRATIONS AND REALITIES

Contents of Socialist Register 1989

Capitalism, Socialism and Revolution by Leo Panitch, Revolution and Democracy in Latin America by Carlos M. Vilas, The Southern Africa Revolution by John S. Saul, One Revolution or Two? The Iranian Revolution and the Islamic Republic by Val Moghadam, 'Revolutionary Reform' in Soviet Factories by David Mandel, Obstacles to Reform in Britain by Tony Benn, Reflections on Revolution in an Age of Reaction by V.G. Kiernan, The Marxist Case for Revolution Today by Ernest Mandel, Our Morals: The Ethics of Revolution by Norman Geras, Fatherland or Mother Earth? Nationalism and Internationalism from a Socialist Perspective by Michael Löwy, Revolution Today: Three Reflections by Frieder Otto Wolf, Feminism's Revolutionary Promise: Finding Hope in Hard Times by Johanna Brenner, Religion and Revolution: A Brief for the Theology of Liberation by Lawrence Littwin and Notes on the Cuban Revolution by Saul Landau.

SOCIALIST REGISTER 1991
COMMUNIST REGIMES THE AFTERMATH

Contents of Socialist Register 1991

The Communist Experience: A Personal Appraisal by John Saville, Perestroika and the Proletariat by Leo Panitch and Sam Gindin, A Future for Socialism in the USSR? by Justin Schwartz, The Struggle for Power in the Soviet Economy by David Mandel, Perestroika and the Neo-Liberal Project by Patrick Flaherty, "Real Socialism" in Historical Perspective by Robert Cox, The Roots of the Present Crisis in the Soviet Economy by Ernest Mandel, Privilegentsia, Property and Power by Daniel Singer, For a Socialist Rebirth: A Soviet View by Alexander Buzgalin and Andrei Kalganov, Marketization and Privatization: the Polish Case by Tadeusz Kowalik, From Where to Where? Reflections on Hungary's Social Revolution by Peter Bihari, Nicaragua: a Revolution that Fell from Grace of the People by Carlos Vilas, Soviet Rehearsal in Yugoslavia? Contradictions of the Socialist Liberal Strategy by Susan Woodward, The Socialist Fetter: A Cautionary Tale by Michael Lebowitz, What Comes After Communist Regimes? by Ralph Miliband.

Earlier back issues also available

SOCIALIST REGISTER 1990
THE RETREAT OF THE INTELLECTUALS

Contents of Socialist Register 1990

Seven Types of Obloquy; Travesties of Marxism by Norman Geras, Marxism Today, An Anatomy by John Saville, The Uses and Abuses of 'Civil Society' by Ellen Meiksins Wood, Defending the Free World by Terry Eagleton, Postmodernism and the Market by Fredric Jameson, The Eclipse of Materialism: Marxism and the Writing of Social History in the 1980s by Bryan D. Palmer, Statism, New Institutionalism and Marxism by Paul Cammack, The Welfare State: Towards a Socialist-Feminist Perspective by Linda Gordon, Intellectuals Against the Left: The Case of France by George Ross, Derrida and the Politics of Interpretation by Eleanor MacDonald, Should a Marxist Believe in Marx on Rights? by Amy Bartholomew, Liberal Practicality and the US Left by John Bellamy Foster, Intellectuals and Transnational Capital by Stephen Gill, Why We Are Still Socialists and Marxists after all this by Arthur MacEwan, Eulogy Beside An Empty Grave : Reflection on the Future of Socialism by Richard Levins, Counter Hegemonic Struggles by Ralph Miliband.